# THE HISTORY
OF THE
## 36TH (ULSTER) DIVISION

O socii, neque enim ignari sumus ante malorum,
O passi graviora, dabit deus his quoque finem.
                    VIRGIL: *Æneid.*

---

And he hadde been somtyme in chyvachie,
In Flaundrés, in Artoys and Pycardie,
And born hym weel.
            CHAUCER: *Canterbury Tales.*

---

*Dawbeney*—            Wise princes, Oxford,
Fight not alone with forces. Providence
Directs and tutors strength; else elephants
And barbèd horses might as well prevail
As the most subtle stratagems of war.
                    FORD: *Perkin Warbeck.*

THE MEMORIAL TO THE 36TH (ULSTER) DIVISION AT THIEPVAL

# THE HISTORY
## OF THE
# 36TH (ULSTER) DIVISION

By

CYRIL FALLS

Late Lieutenant, Royal Inniskilling Fusiliers
and Captain, G.S., 36th Division

WITH AN INTRODUCTION BY
FIELD MARSHAL THE LORD PLUMER
G.C.B., G.C.M.G., G.C.V.O.

M'CAW, STEVENSON & ORR, LIMITED
THE LINENHALL PRESS, BELFAST
AND 329 HIGH HOLBORN, LONDON, W.C.
1922

*This History is dedicated to the men of the*
## ULSTER DIVISION,
*returned from the War, and to those who have not come back; of whom I name two friends:*

HARRY GALLAGHER, D.S.O.,
*Captain, Royal Inniskilling Fusiliers,
killed at the Battle of Messines, 1917;*
*and*
GEORGE BRUCE, D.S.O., M.C.,
*Brigade Major, 109th Brigade,
killed near Dadizeele, 1918;*

*Patterns to men-in-arms.*

# INTRODUCTION

THE History of the 36th (Ulster) Division is the record of a great effort and a great achievement. The effort which resulted in its inception was the outcome of the determination, on the part of a people brought up in great traditions and inspired with a fervent spirit of loyalty, that they should be worthily represented in the fierce and prolonged struggle which from the outset was clearly foreshadowed. The achievement was the response made to the call by their representatives, the gallant deeds accomplished, the courage and determination displayed, and the sacrifices made.

The narrative gives a very clear picture of what the campaign in France and Flanders involved for the troops engaged in it. There is no reference to any great strategical movements or brilliant tactical operations, because there were none such to describe. It brings out, however, quite plainly that the victory was gained in the only way in which it could have been gained, by sheer hard fighting, carried out continuously, now on a small, now on a large, scale, but always by troops who never admitted defeat.

This was the character of the struggle into which the Ulster Division was plunged from its entrance into the campaign until its close, and the book describes very fully the part it played in it. Each chapter is a little history of itself, which frequently has sufficient subject-matter for a volume, and which always contains a record of events or incidents of absorbing interest. It is not a narrative of a series of unbroken successes, and there is no pretence that all the efforts made by the Division were successful. Readers of the History will find stories of failures, but they were glorious failures, the account of which no-one need feel ashamed to describe or peruse.

A tribute, no more than is due, is paid to Major-General Sir Oliver Nugent, K.C.B., D.S.O., the General who was in command of the Division for the greater part of the campaign, and who led it throughout with a confidence in it only equalled by its confidence in him. All who served under him will always hold him in affectionate remembrance, and all Ulstermen should realize that they owe him a debt of gratitude.

# INTRODUCTION

I hope this History will be read, not only by those who served in the Division and their relatives and friends, but by all Irishmen.

Young men approaching manhood and young women approaching womanhood should read it, and ponder over the example their predecessors have set them. For all who read will realize that in the great struggle which convulsed Europe for more than four years the men of Ulster did not fail.

PLUMER, F.M.

MALTA,
    25th November, 1922.

# PREFACE

THE History of the 36th (Ulster) Division is published under the patronage of the Right Hon. the Lord Carson of Duncairn, the Prime Minister of Northern Ireland, and Major-General Sir O. S. W. Nugent, K.C.B., D.S.O.

Its publication once decided upon, the first step taken was the formation of an influential Committee; the second, that of a Guarantee Fund to cover the whole cost of its production, which was, within a few weeks, largely oversubscribed.

The materials upon which the History is chiefly based are the official War Diaries in the possession of the Historical Section (Military Branch) of the Committee of Imperial Defence. To the officials at 2, Cavendish Square I am indebted for courtesy and assistance in matters of difficulty. I have made use also of a very large number of contributions sent to me by those who served with the Division, from Sir James Craig and Sir Oliver Nugent to several private soldiers. So long is the list that I cannot acknowledge my debt to these contributors by name, but I desire to thank one and all for material without which the record would have been bald and dry, material which has, I hope, enabled me to give some tinge of humanity to the History. In several cases these personal contributions have been of greater value still than this. They have—and this is true especially of the Retreat of March, 1918—furnished me with a record of incidents upon which official Diaries throw no light. Two such incidents, in particular, the defence of a company of the 12th Royal Irish Rifles at Le Pontchu Quarry, near St. Quentin, on March the 21st, and the last stand of the 2nd Royal Irish Rifles at Cugny, three days later, have hitherto gone unrecorded, because the survivors of these heroic episodes fell into the hands of the enemy.

I have also to thank Sir Oliver Nugent, Colonel-Commandant W. M. Withycombe, C.B., C.M.G., D.S.O.; Brigadier-General C. J. Griffith, C.B., C.M.G., D.S.O.; Brigadier-General A. St. Q. Ricardo, C.M.G., C.B.E., D.S.O.; Major H. F. Grant Suttie, D.S.O., M.C., and Major J. C. Boyle for their trouble in reading the History in MS. and for their many helpful suggestions. The Honours List, a very big undertaking, is based almost entirely on the compilation of Mr. Andrew Jardin, M.S.M., formerly Chief Clerk in the Administrative Branch of Divisional Headquarters. In this and other matters connected with the History I have had much assistance from my wife.

The most important acknowledgment, on behalf of the Committee and all interested in the publication of the work as well as on my own, is due to Captain Kenneth M. Moore, M.C., who acted as Honorary Secretary. The whole of the business side of the undertaking has been conducted by him.

# PREFACE

Into it he has thrown all his organizing ability and his enthusiasm. No appeal has been made to him in vain.

I have only to add that it has been my endeavour to make this History not a mere record of battles, but, so far as space has permitted, a picture of life as it was lived in the days of war. Lacking the second, the first is like dry bones without flesh to cover them. If I have succeeded in combining the two, I have right to hope that I have made a contribution, however small, to history in a general sense, as apart from military history.

It is to-day a favourite pretension that the war was as uninteresting as it was terrible: a vast error, based upon a temporary reaction, when not upon a pose. I made recently the discovery that between 1906 and 1921 there were published over one hundred books on the Napoleonic Wars. The number would have been far greater but for the fall in the publication of all books between 1914 and 1919. So, a hundred years hence, men will be delving into our records of the late war. Soldiers will be studying the lessons of its battles. But a yet greater number of seekers will be demanding with curiosity how men lived in such circumstances, how they reacted to the strain of war, what compensations they found. It behoves those who were eye-witnesses to depict it in all its aspects, not to shrink from discovering its horror, indeed, but also not to pretend that it had not a better side. The picture now so often painted, representing the war as a single scene in a torture chamber, whence men emerged physical or mental wrecks, may be good anti-militarist propaganda, but it is false, because incomplete. From those experiences many men have emerged happy and strong. Many knew how to snatch some happiness even from their midst. A far greater number can see, in retrospect, that they played a part in one of the most dramatic, as well as one of the most terrible, tragedies in history. That stands for something of good, amid all its evil, in any man's life. The comradeship of war's days is a memory not less happy.

It is not alone because the story of the Ulster Division is a record of courage and fortitude, in which men who are my friends had part, but because it represents in a microcosm man in one of the greatest and most curious catastrophes the world has known, that I have had, however unworthy of the task, a pleasure so intense in writing this book.

C. F.

# CONTENTS

| CHAP. | | PAGE |
|---|---|---|
| I | THE RAISING AND TRAINING OF THE DIVISION: SEPTEMBER 1914 TO SEPTEMBER 1915 . | 1 |

Lord Kitchener and Sir Edward Carson — Sir Edward Carson's Appeal—Formation of the Division —A Commander appointed—Training begins—The Clan Spirit—Realities of War—The Move to England —Lord Kitchener's Tribute—His Majesty's Review.

| II | THE DIVISION IN FRANCE: OCTOBER 1915 TO JUNE 1916 . . . . . . . | 22 |

First Experiences—Picardy—107th Brigade in Line—The Division enters Line—Holding a Quiet Front—Rations—The Brighter Side—Preparation for Offensive—Reorganization of Artillery.

| III | THE BATTLE OF THE SOMME: JULY 1ST, 1916 | 41 |

New Aspect of Warfare—Plans for the Attack— Artillery Programme—A Successful Raid—Anniversary of the Boyne—Attack North of Ancre—Advance of 107th Brigade—A Desperate Situation—July 2nd —Causes of Failure—Move to Flanders.

| IV | FROM THE SOMME TO MESSINES: JULY 1916 TO JUNE 1917 . . . . . . | 64 |

In Line before Messines—Warfare Underground— Trench Mortar Battles — The Policy of Raids — Lieutenant Godson's Ambush—A Series of Raids —La Plus Douve Farm—A Growth of Activity— Shelling of Ulster Camp.

# CONTENTS

| CHAP. | | PAGE |
|---|---|---|
| V | MESSINES: JUNE 1917 . . . . . | 82 |

Preparation for the Offensive—Plans for the Attack—Second Army Methods—Medical Arrangements—Waiting for Zero—First Objective reached—Wytschaete captured—Artillery moves Forward—Pack Transport—Death of Captain Gallagher—German Commander's Problem—Von Richthofen.

VI THE BATTLE OF LANGEMARCK: AUGUST 1917    107

Plans of the Allies—107th Brigade enters Line—Wieltje Dug-outs—Barrage Plans—Failure of 108th Brigade—The Division's Losses—Causes of Failure—General Nugent's Suggestions.

VII YPRES TO CAMBRAI: SEPTEMBER TO NOVEMBER 1917 . . . . . . . . . .    125

The Hindenburg Line—Fighting at Yorkshire Bank—Raiding Activity—The Livens Projector—Life amidst Desolation — British Organization — Problem of Man-power—Work in the Mist.

VIII CAMBRAI AND AFTER (I): NOVEMBER 20TH TO 22ND, 1917 . . . . . . .    143

Plans for Cambrai—Task of 109th Brigade—Tanks move up—Capture of Spoil Heap—Defence of Flesquières—Results of November 20th—Gains of November 21st—Mœuvres: November 22nd—A New Phase.

IX CAMBRAI AND AFTER (II): NOVEMBER 23RD TO DECEMBER 31ST, 1917 . . . . .    162

Plans for Nov. 23rd—The Grapple at Bourlon—Relief of 36th Division — The German Counter-offensive—British Withdrawal—Defence of 9th Inniskillings—Attack of 11th Inniskillings—Relief in a Blizzard—Summary of the Battle.

X THE GERMAN OFFENSIVE ON THE SOMME (I): JANUARY TO MARCH 22ND, 1918 . . .    181

The New Line—Reorganization of Division—System of Defence—Dispositions—The Weeks of Waiting—Morning of March 21st—The German Assault launched—Defence of Le Pontchu—Breakthrough to the South — Defence of Racecourse Redoubt—Heroic Action of Lieutenant Knox—The Second Withdrawal—Open Warfare begins.

# CONTENTS

| CHAP. | | PAGE |
|---|---|---|
| XI | THE GERMAN OFFENSIVE ON THE SOMME (II): MARCH 23RD TO 30TH, 1918 | 208 |

Sights in Ham—Both Flanks turned—Dawn of March 24th—2nd Rifles at Cugny—Relief of 36th Division—Horrors of the Retreat—A Gap between the Allies—Colonel Place captured—Counter-attack at Erches—What the Division achieved—Action of the Artillery—Defence of XVIII. Corps.

| XII | FLANDERS: THE 108TH BRIGADE IN THE MESSINES-KEMMEL BATTLE: APRIL TO JUNE 1918 | 232 |

Back to Ypres—108th Brigade on Messines Ridge—Fighting at Wulverghem—A Black Day—Withdrawal from Poelcappelle — German Rebuff in Flanders—Changes in Command—Back after a Rest.

| XIII | BACK TO THE MESSINES RIDGE: JULY TO SEPTEMBER, 1918 | 248 |

Successful Raids — The Enemy withdraws—A Fighting Retreat—September 3rd and 4th—Attack of September 6th—Move to Ypres—The Hope of Victory.

| XIV | THE ADVANCE TO FINAL VICTORY (I): SEPTEMBER 28TH TO OCTOBER 17TH, 1918 | 262 |

Attack of September 28th—Advance of September 29th — Menin-Roulers Road reached — Review of Situation — Death of Captain Bruce — Attack of October 14th—A Great Day—Courtrai entered—Difficulties of Supply.

| XV | THE ADVANCE TO FINAL VICTORY (II): OCTOBER 18TH TO NOVEMBER 11TH, 1918 | 280 |

Plan for Forcing the Lys—Success of the Crossing—Attack of October 20th—The Advance continued—Kleineberg Ridge occupied—General Jacob's Tribute—Special Order of Marshal Foch.

| XVI | THE END: NOVEMBER 1918 TO JUNE 1919 | 294 |

Preparations for Christmas—The Divisional Fund—Characteristics of 36th Division—The End.

| APPENDIX I | ORDER OF BATTLE | 305 |
| ” II | LIST OF HONOURS AND AWARDS | 313 |
| INDEX | | 347 |

## MAPS

I   The Battle of Albert, 1916
II  The Battle of Messines, 1917
III The Battle of Langemarck, 1917
IV  The Battle of Cambrai, 1917
V   The Position before German Attack, March 21st, 1918
VI  The Retreat of March 1918
VII The Final Advances, 1918

Sketch in Text

## ILLUSTRATIONS

The Memorial to the 36th (Ulster) Division at Thiepval . . . . . . . Frontispiece
Major-General Sir C. H. Powell, K.C.B. facing page 14
Major-General Sir O. S. Nugent, K.C.B., D.S.O. . . . . . . . . „ „ 36
Winners of Victoria Cross, 1916 . . „ „ 76
„ „ „ „ 1917 & 1918 „ „ 184
Major-General C. C. Coffin, V.C., C.B., D.S.O. . . . . . . . . „ „ 244

# The Battle of Albert, 1916.

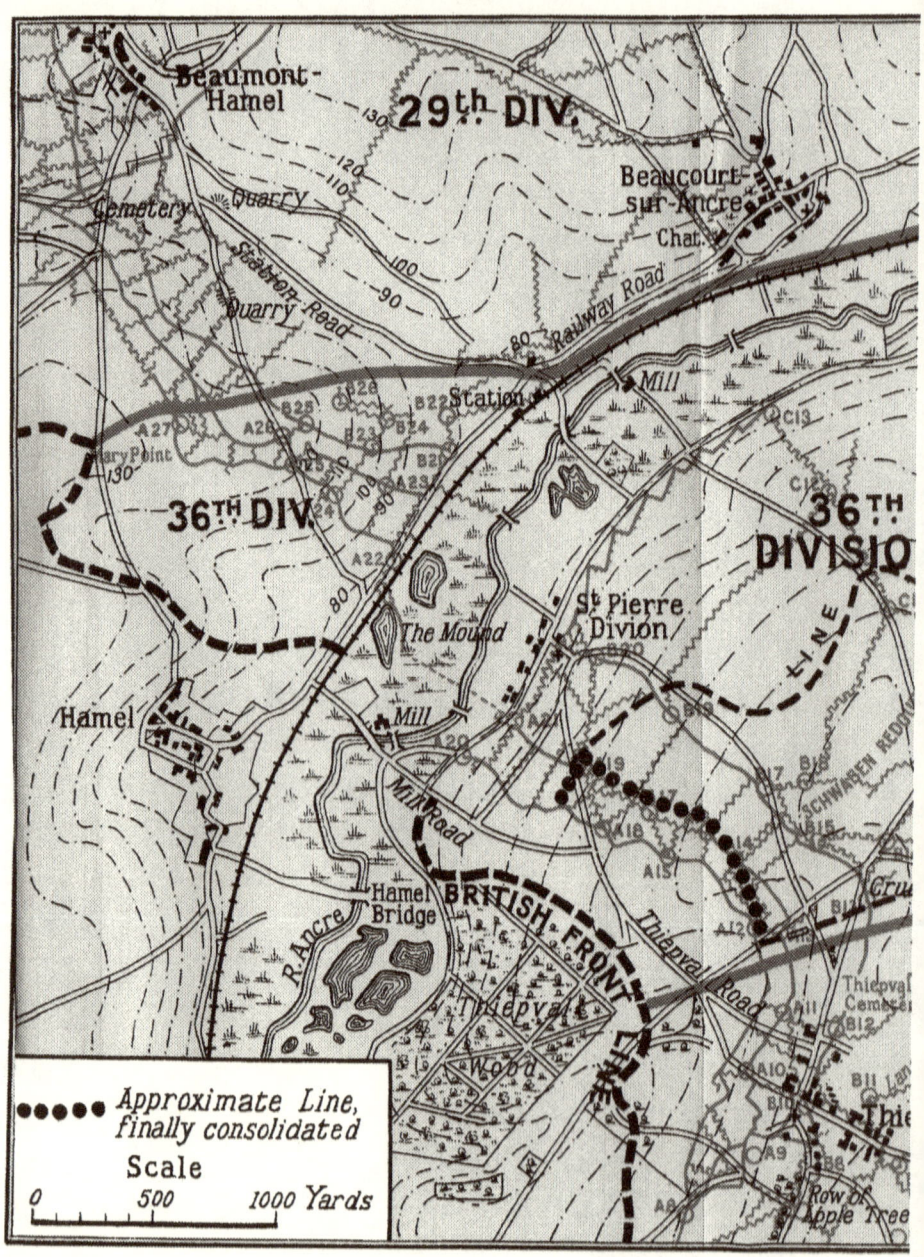

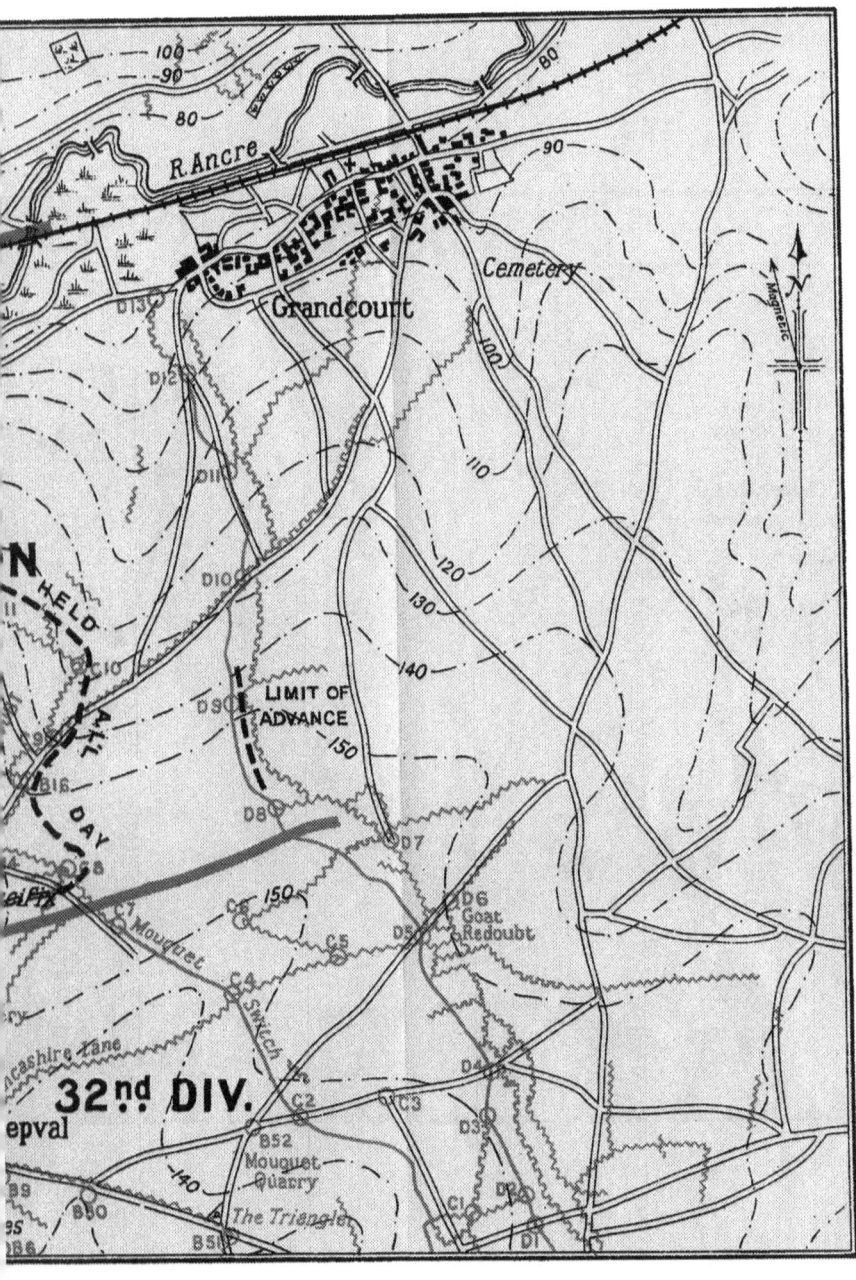

Map I.

# The Battle of Messines, 1917.

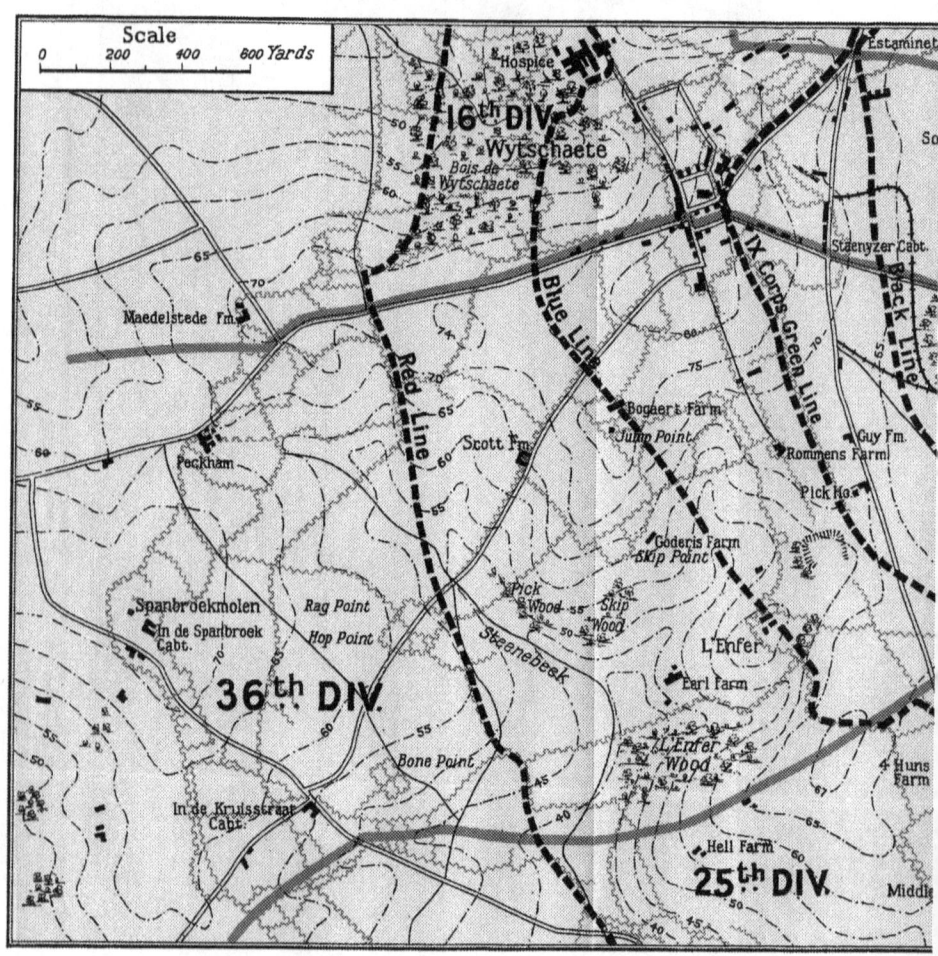

Map 11.

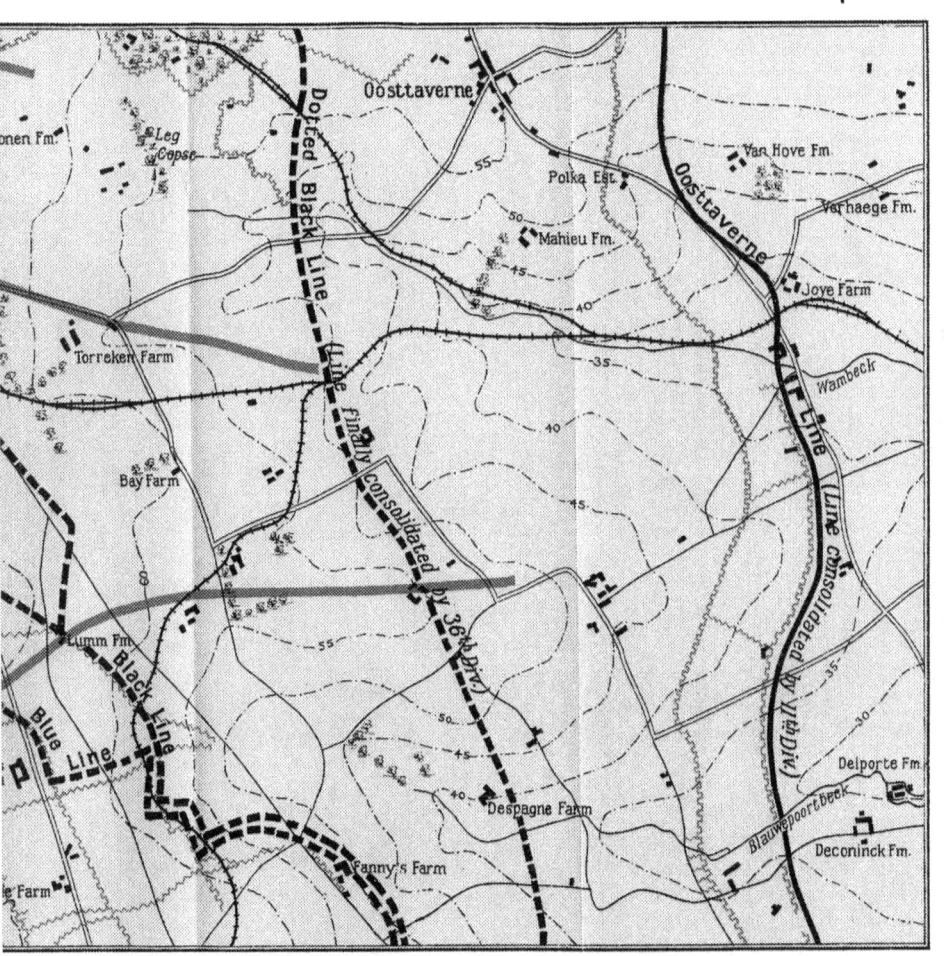

# The Battle of Langemarck, 1917.

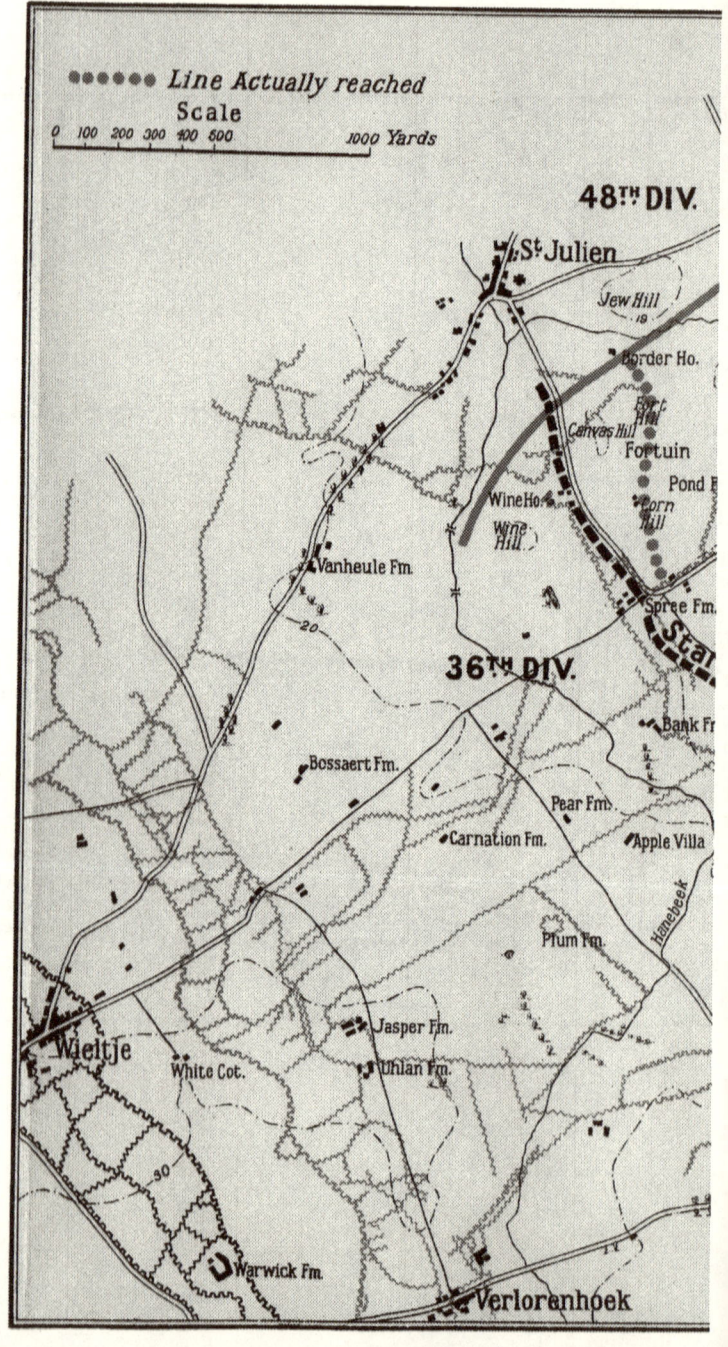

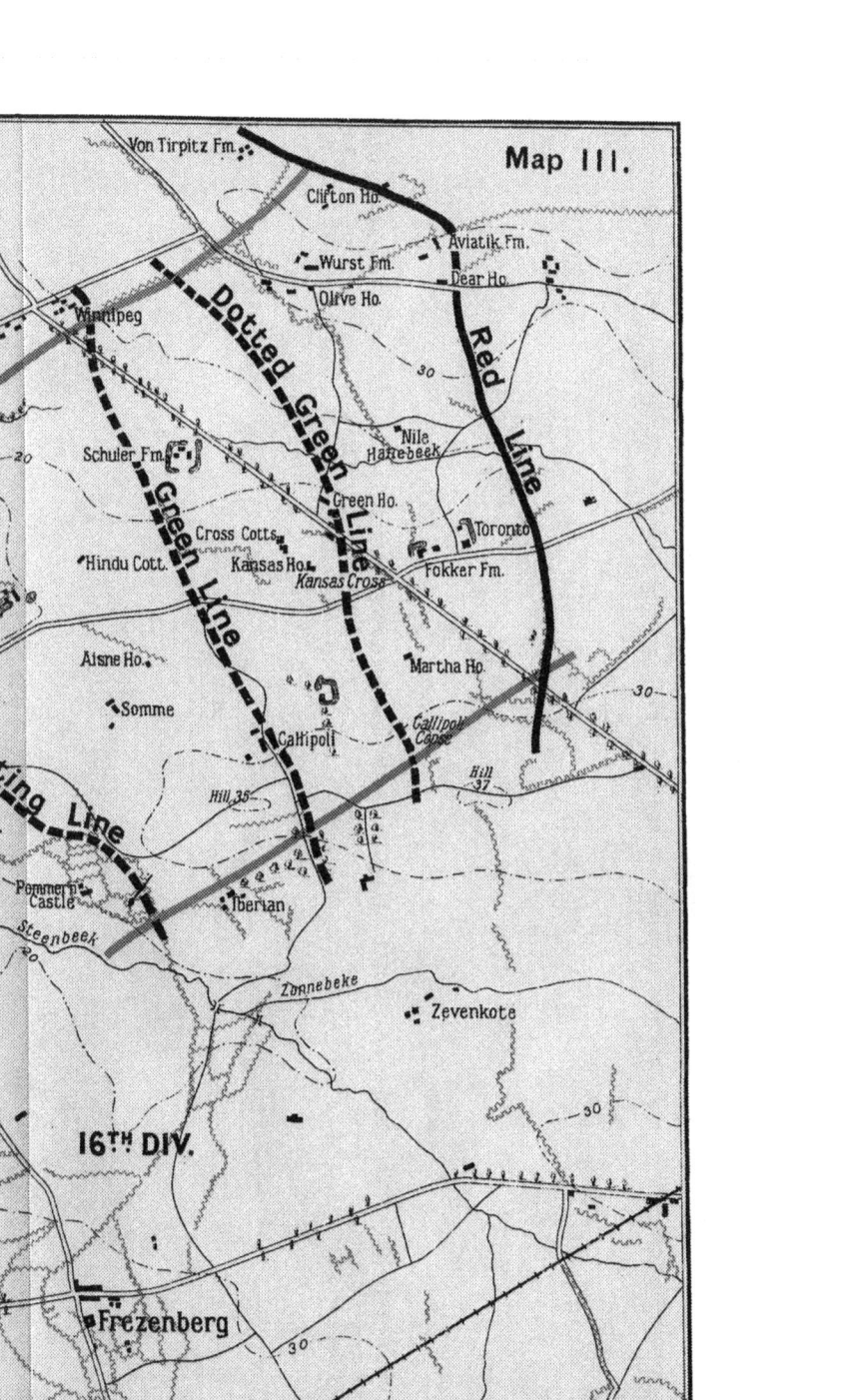

# The Battle of Cambrai, 1917.

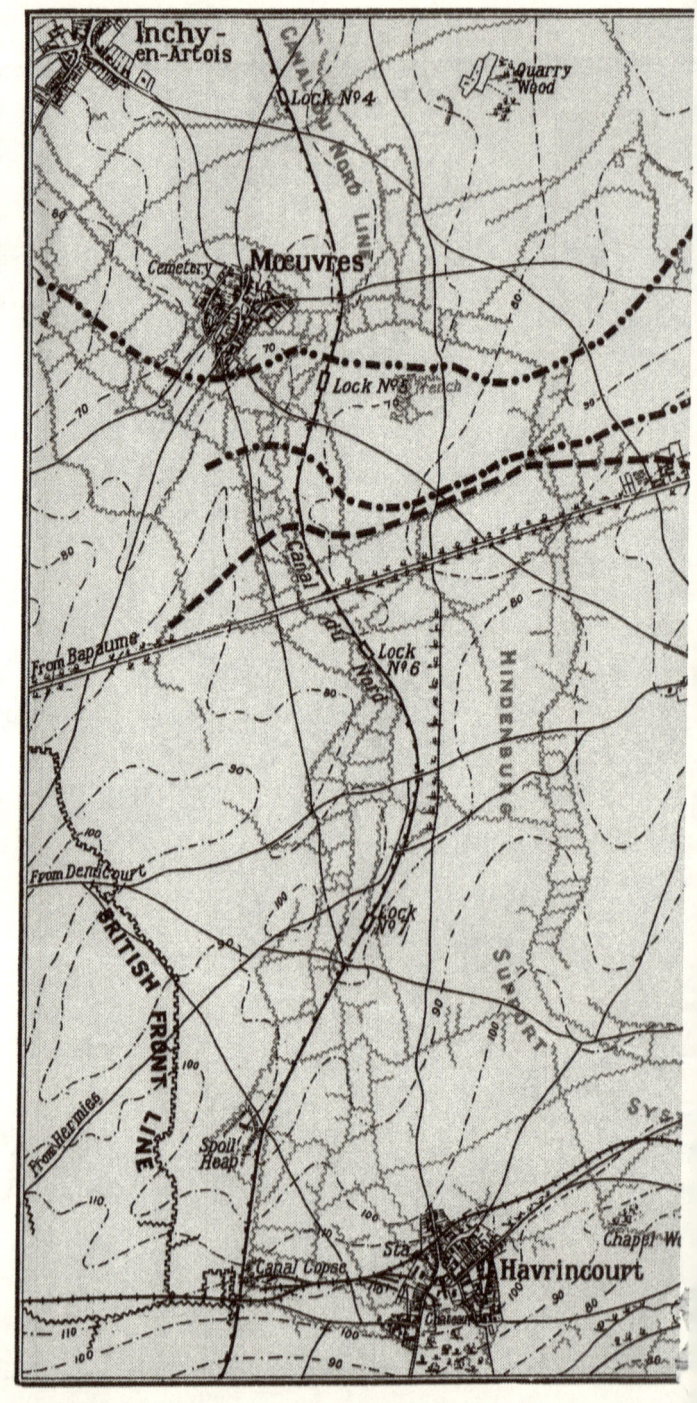

Map IV

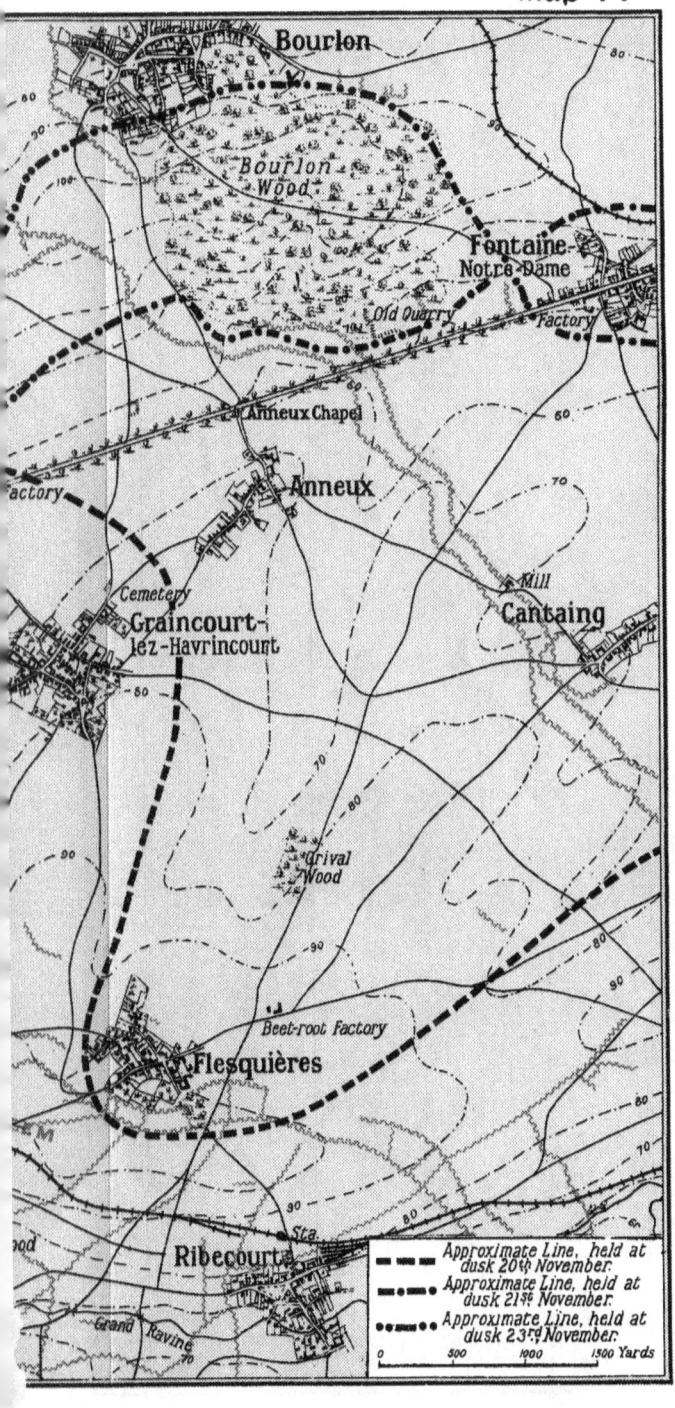

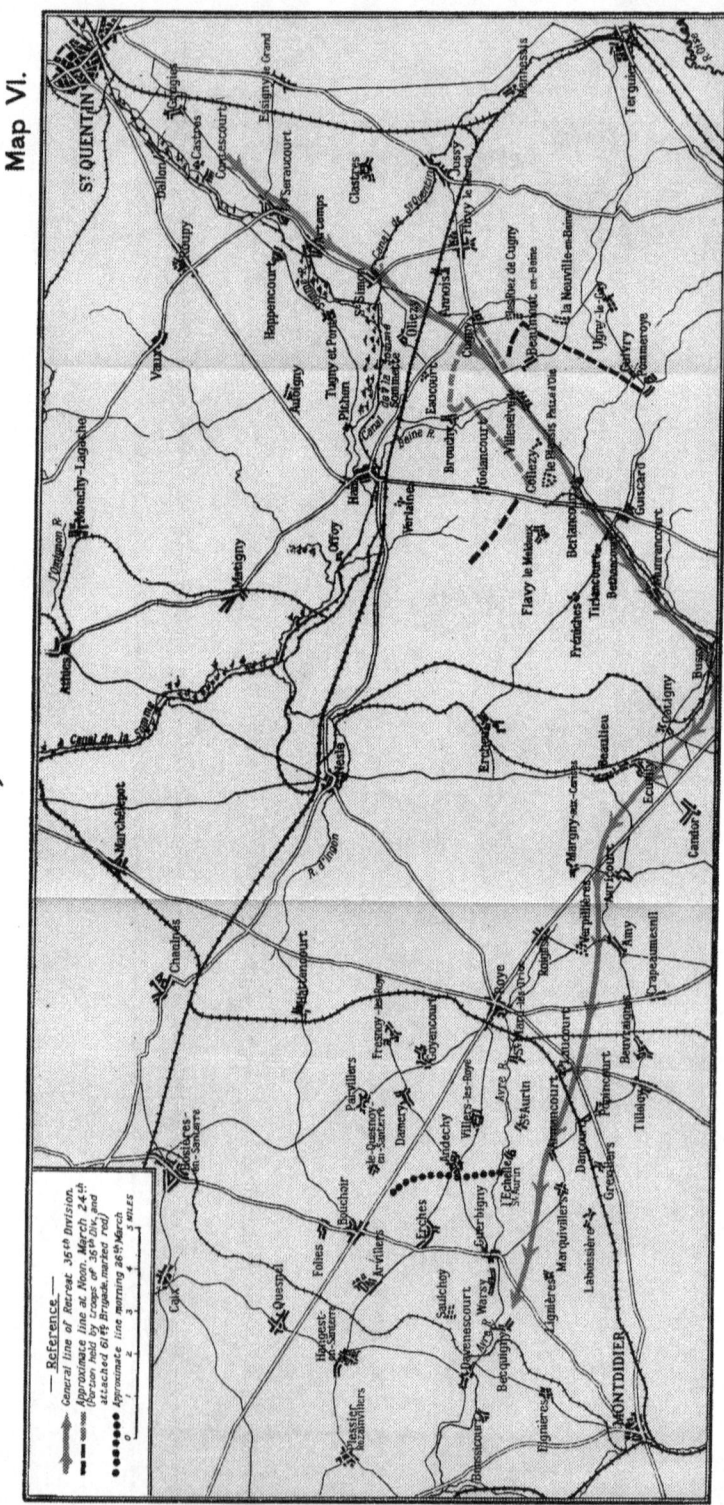

Map VI. The Retreat of March, 1918.

# The Position before the German Attack, March 21st, 1918.

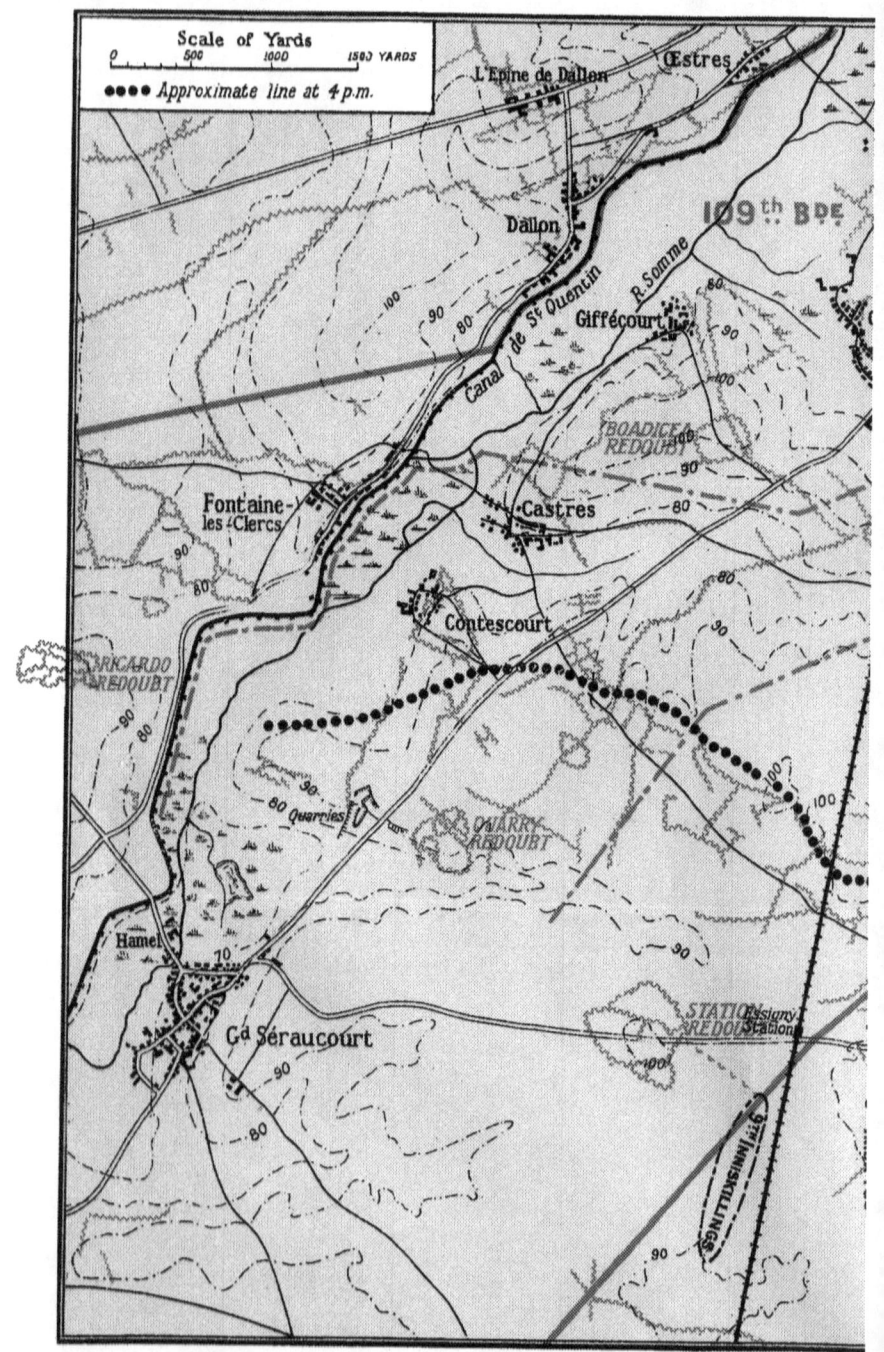

Map V.

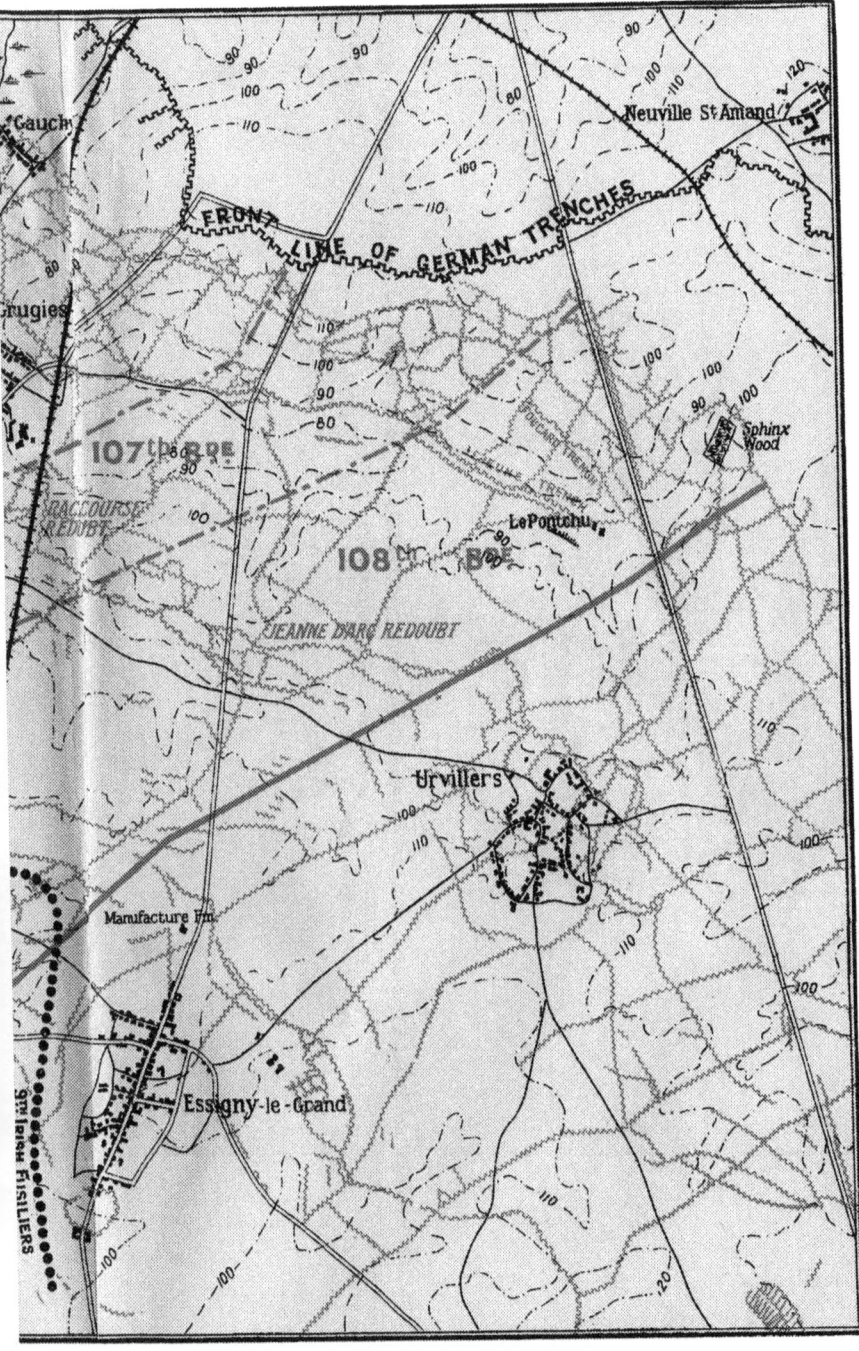

# The Final Advances, 1918.

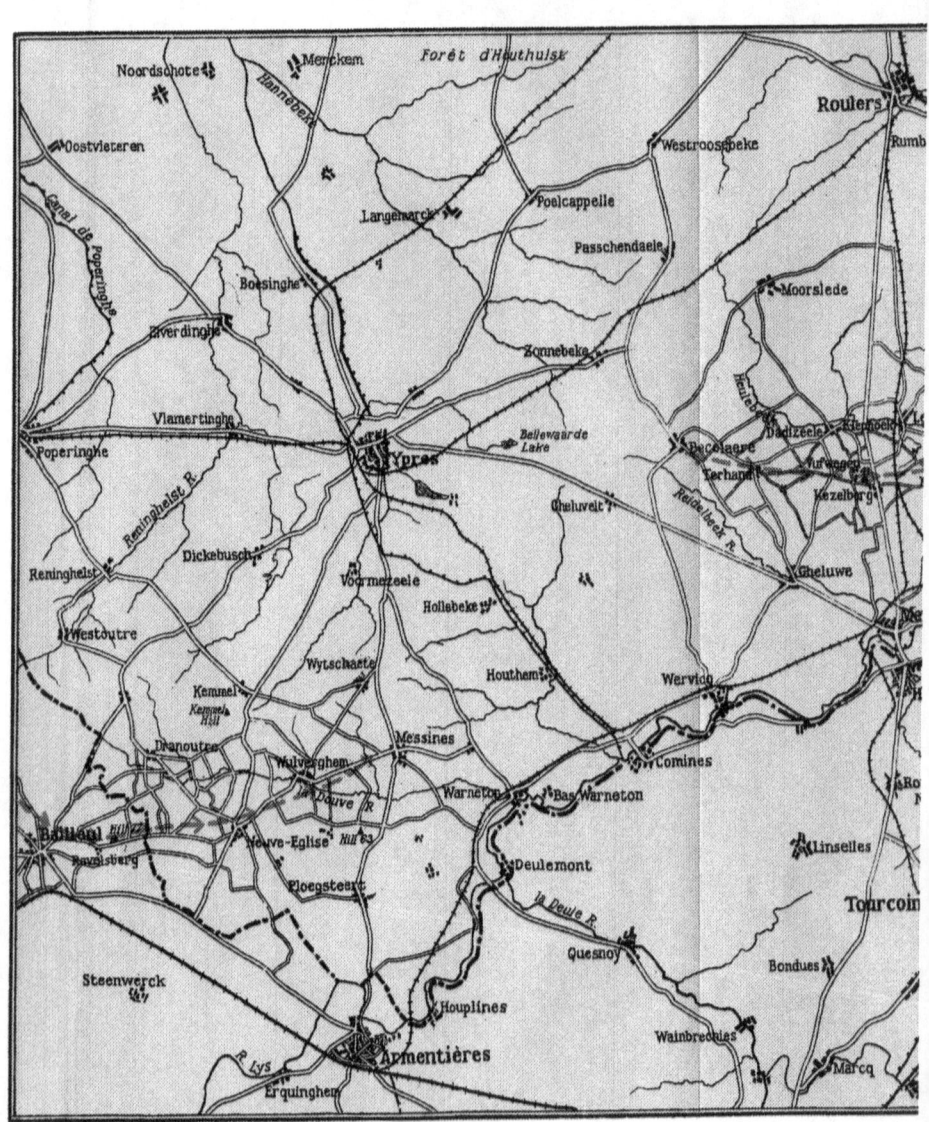

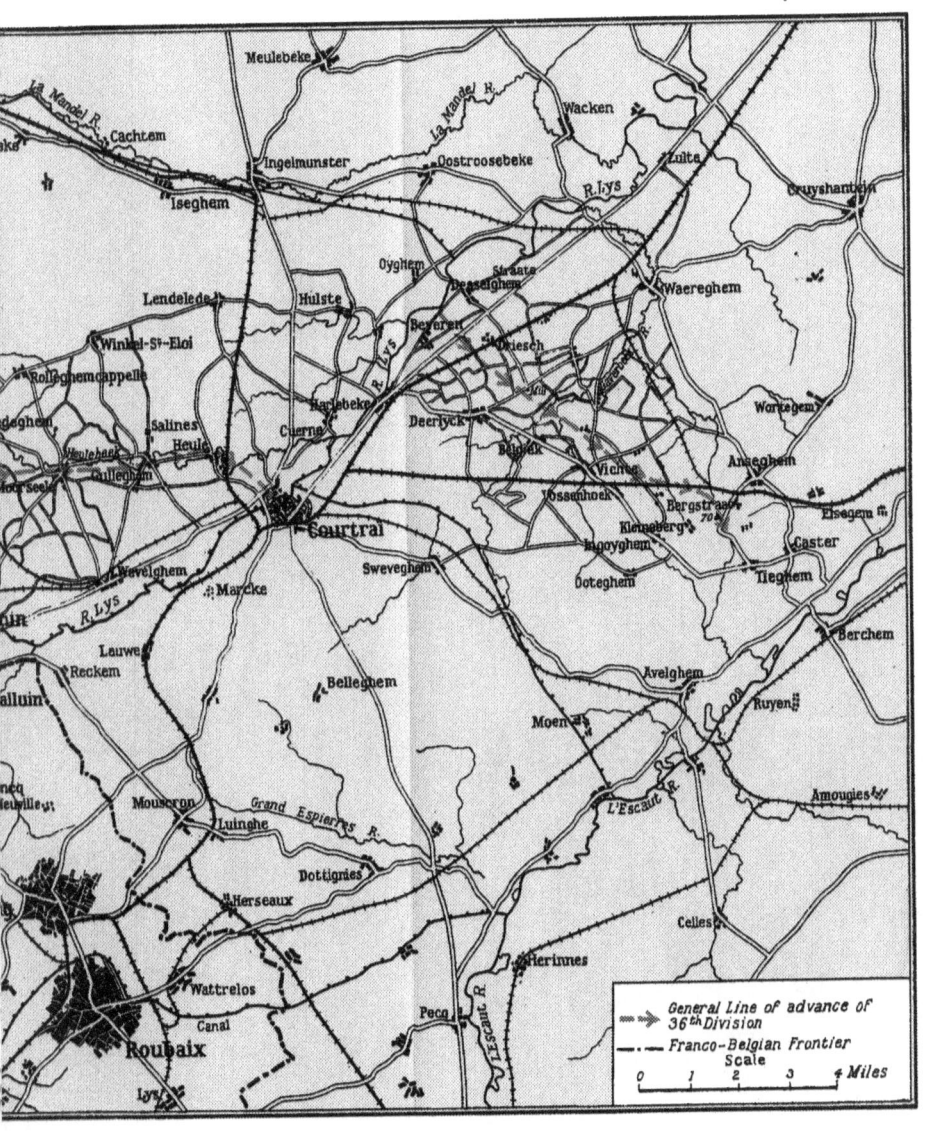

Map VII.

# THE HISTORY OF
# THE 36TH (ULSTER) DIVISION

## CHAPTER I

### The Raising and Training of the Division: September 1914 to September 1915

It is no rightful part of the historian of a Division in the Great War to embark upon preliminary sketches of the state of Europe or of the movements in international politics that preceded the catastrophe. If once he begin to seek for causes he must seek far. Three pistol shots fired in the narrow streets of Serajevo may be likened to an accidental spark that explodes a great charge. But the charge was long laid. War had been determined upon in Berlin. Without that accidental spark, there can be no doubt that it would shortly have been deliberately exploded by a detonator from that quarter. If the divisional historian cannot trace the laying of the charge, which had been accumulating, it may be a hundred, and certainly fifty, years, let him not begin by dealing with what were merely the final accretions. Let him begin with the beginning of the war. War was declared between this country and Germany on the 4th of August, 1914.

There are, however, certain local circumstances anterior to that declaration, which have an intimate connection with the particular Division that is the subject of this History, and so could not be omitted without robbing the latter of much of its significance. The Ulster Division was not created in a day. The roots from which it sprang went back into the troubled period before the war. Its life was a continuance of the life of an earlier legion, a legion of civilians banded together to protect themselves from the consequences of legislation which they believed would affect adversely their rights and privileges as citizens of the United Kingdom—the Ulster Volunteer Force.

The Ulster Volunteer Force, or U.V.F., as it soon came to be known the world around, was the creation of Sir Edward Carson.* He believed that if the Imperial Parliament were to persist in its declared intention of forcing the Protestant population of Ulster into an Irish Parliament, without its consent, the inevitable consequence would be civil war in Ireland. Unorganized resistance would be ineffective, and would beyond doubt lead to disorder and unnecessary bloodshed. That the attempt would be made appeared certain. The fate of the Government was bound up with its Home Rule Bill. A failure to carry it through would have involved instant defeat in the House of Commons, wherein the Irish Nationalist Party held the balance of power. All the signs pointed to a clash. It appeared to Sir Edward Carson that the surest defence of the political ideals of his followers lay in convincing the people of Great Britain that Protestant Ulster would fight for the preservation of liberties and traditions which it held dear, which, in its eyes, were now menaced. It was in this faith that he gave his approval to the formation of the U.V.F.

It was on the advice of Lord Roberts, a warm advocate of Ulster's cause, that Sir Edward Carson invited General Sir George Richardson to take command of the U.V.F. Under his leadership the force was organized on a territorial basis. At the outbreak of war it contained over 80,000 men between the ages of seventeen and sixty-five, and a number of women, enrolled not only as nurses but for many of those supplementary services which were not allotted to women in the European war until a comparatively late period. The people of Ulster entered into their adventure in the same spirit that they entered into that of the war when it came,

* Now Lord Carson of Duncairn.

a spirit of single-minded faith in their leaders and in themselves. Admirably did Mr. Kipling sum up their attitude in the lines:
> Believe we dare not boast,
> Believe we do not fear.

Probably their worst danger was over before the declaration of war. The incident at the Curragh, as well as conferences at the War Office, at Aldershot, and elsewhere, of which the general public never knew, had made it clear that the Army could not be used to enforce the legislation projected at the cost of civil war. General John Gough, V.C., then Sir Douglas Haig's Chief of Staff, visited Ulster in July, and stated that the idea of coercion was abandoned. He is known to have formed the opinion that the Ulster Volunteers could, with experienced leaders, be made a very formidable fighting force. He, as well as the Government, knew that those leaders would not have been lacking.

Lord Kitchener, once at the War Office, was not long in arriving at the same opinion as General Gough. He was appointed Secretary of State for War on Wednesday the 5th of August. On Friday the 7th he sent for Colonel T. E. Hickman,* a Member of the House of Commons, President of the British League for the Defence of Ulster, who had acted as Inspector-General of the U.V.F., and said to him: " I want the Ulster Volunteers."

Colonel Hickman replied: " You must see Carson and Craig."

Lord Kitchener saw them. Sir Edward Carson's position was not easy. He was most eager to help by every means in his power. But he had a heavy responsibility towards the people of Ulster. If the fighting men of the Province were to go to the war, and in their absence a Home Rule Act, such as they had banded themselves together to resist, were to be forced upon those they had left behind, they would have had cause to reproach him. The Prime Minister was asked for an assurance with regard to the Home Rule Bill.

* Now Brigadier-General T. E. Hickman, C.B.. D.S.O., M.P.

No definite assurance could be obtained from him. A political truce had come into operation at the beginning of hostilities, but it was ill-defined, and the Prime Minister evidently did not see his way clearly out of the difficulties of his situation.* Sir Edward raised some minor points, asking that the word " Ulster " might succeed the number of the Division which it was proposed to raise. To this Lord Kitchener at first demurred, but the appelation was subsequently granted.**

A short delay ensued. The news from France was bad. A meeting of the Ulster Unionist Members of Parliament, attended by Lord Roberts, was held at Sir Edward Carson's house in Eaton Place. The result of the meeting was that, then and there, Colonel Hickman took a letter to Lord Kitchener, offering the aid of Sir Edward and the Council in raising as large a force as possible from the Ulster Volunteers, without any conditions whatsoever. Later that day there was another meeting between the Secretary for War and the Ulster representatives at the War Office. At first Lord Kitchener was modest in his demands, thinking that a Brigade from the U.V.F. would be ample, at least as a start. Captain Craig*** assured him they could recruit a Division. Lord Kitchener at once appointed Colonel Hickman and Captain Craig as Chief Recruiting Officers for the Ulster area.

Captain Craig, on leaving the War Office, jumped into a taxicab in Whitehall and went straight to a firm of outfitters with which he had had dealings in equipment for the U.V.F., and gave an order for 10,000 complete outfits. Returning to the House he was somewhat exercised in his mind as to where the money was to come from to pay for

---

\* Sir Edward Carson's apprehensions were found to have been justified when, on September the 15th, Mr. Asquith's Government passed the Home Rule Act, the whole of the Unionist Party leaving the Chamber as a protest against what it regarded as a breach of the Truce.

\*\* As, of course, were the titles " Scottish," " Irish," " Welsh," " Northern," " Southern," etc., to other Divisions.

\*\*\* Now the Right Honble. Sir James Craig, Bt., Prime Minister of Northern Ireland.

all this. He spoke to Mr. Oliver Locker-Lampson,* one of Ulster's staunchest friends, who pulled out a cheque-book and said :

"Don't say another word! There's a thousand pounds to go on with, and nine more will follow in a day or two. This is out of a special fund just available for your purpose."

In the first days of September Colonel Hickman and Captain Craig crossed to Ireland to begin their work. On the 3rd of the month Sir Edward Carson made a great appeal, at a meeting of the Ulster Unionist Council in Belfast, to the men of the U.V.F., urging them to come forward for the defence of the Empire, the honour of Ulster and of Ireland.

In Ireland much had happened meanwhile. A large number of Ulstermen, the eager spirits who would not wait, had already enlisted. Of these the greater number had gone to the 10th Division, then being formed. Others had crossed the Channel and joined Manchester and Glasgow battalions. At Omagh Captain A. St. Q. Ricardo, D.S.O.,** Reserve of Officers, had been put in charge of the Depot, and in mid-August had, anticipating the formation of an Ulster Division, begun to recruit men from the Tyrone Volunteers for a battalion of Royal Inniskilling Fusiliers. In a very short time he had two companies, which were, as they had as yet no official status, attached to the 5th and 6th Battalions of the Royal Inniskilling Fusiliers. In these battalions some of the officers subsequently elected to remain, and went with the 10th Division to the Dardanelles. When the Ulster Division was formed these two companies became the nucleus of the senior battalion of the 109th Infantry Brigade, the 9th Royal Inniskilling Fusiliers.*** This was an exceptional incident, since Captain Ricardo, before taking up

* Now Commander Locker-Lampson, C.M.G., D.S.O.

** Now Brigadier-General Ricardo, C.M.G., C.B.E., D.S.O.

*** Captain Ricardo was asked officially to ascertain the views of the Nationalist Party, in his district, which had a military organization of its own. They replied that they would help on the following conditions: (a) they would guard the shores of Ulster only, and would not leave it; (b) they must be allowed to keep their arms at the end of the war.

his duties at the Omagh Depot, had been Adjutant of the Tyrone Regiment, U.V.F. Throughout Ulster, however, a preliminary recruiting campaign had been carried out, promises to enlist on the official formation of an Ulster Division being obtained from members of the U.V.F.

The short delay may have lost a few men to the Ulster Division, but it had created an atmosphere of expectation and excitement. When the recruiting officers arrived the men came forward with a rush, above all in Belfast. A building near the Old Town Hall had been taken over. As each man came out of the former after attestation, he entered the latter, was passed from department to department, emerging from another door a recruit in uniform, leaving his civilian clothing to be packed up and sent home. In this respect the Ulster Division was peculiarly fortunate. The men who enlisted in it had not to endure those weeks of drilling in wet weather in their civilian clothes, with inadequate boots, which were productive of moral as well as physical discomfort. For this advantage they were indebted to the foresight and powers of organization of Captain Craig and his assistants, the generosity of their friends, and the aid of the big business men of Belfast; the work being carried out without any cost to the State. Captain Craig made further visits to the War Office, on one of which he pointed out to Lord Kitchener that the camp accommodation in Ulster was insufficient. Lord Kitchener replied that such details must be arranged by others. Knowing him well from South African days, when he had learned to regard him with the highest admiration, Captain Craig answered that it was all very well to talk in that autocratic manner, but that at present he himself had not the weight behind him to carry the matter through. The response was characteristic. Lord Kitchener summoned in succession the Adjutant-General, the Director of Personal Services, the Quartermaster-General, and the Director of Fortifications, and said to them:

"Take Craig away and see that he gets what he requires."

Captain Craig was then able to return to Ireland, and set

## FORMATION OF THE DIVISION

about the building of hutted camps at Clandeboye, Ballykinlar, and Newtownards in the east, and Finner on the Donegal coast.

The organization of the Division proceeded swiftly. A large house, 29, Wellington Place, Belfast, was taken over and equipped as Headquarters. Three Infantry Brigades were formed: the 107th from the City of Belfast itself; the 108th from the counties of Antrim, Down, Armagh, Cavan, and Monaghan; the 109th from Tyrone, Londonderry, Donegal, and Fermanagh, with one Belfast Battalion. The Pioneer Battalion was also recruited in County Down, mainly from the Lurgan area. The Royal Engineers, of which two Field Companies only were raised at first, the 121st and 122nd, as well as the Divisional Signal Company, came mainly from Belfast, above all from the great shipyards. Royal Army Medical Corps personnel was recruited and sent to Clandeboye, where, on the appointment of an A.D.M.S., Colonel F. J. Greig, it was formed into three Field Ambulances, the 108th, 109th, and 110th, and moved to Newry. So successful was recruiting for the R.A.M.C. that Colonel Greig was instructed by the War Office to raise a Casualty Clearing Station, the 40th, which served both in France and at Salonika. The Royal Army Service Corps personnel was fine both in physique and intelligence. The horses were good, as was natural, seeing how large was the proportion of horses bought for the Army in Ireland, and among the officers were some excellent horsemen and horsemasters. Indeed the horsemastership in the Division was throughout the campaign of a very high order, the Infantry contriving to keep their mules sleek and fat and the Artillery their gun-horses fit and well-groomed amid conditions which none can realize who did not witness them. A Cavalry Squadron and a Cyclist Company were also formed, the former being unique in that it was a service Squadron of the Inniskilling Dragoons.

One question which received much attention and gave rise to much discussion was that of a Divisional Artillery. It was reluctantly decided not to raise one in Ulster, though this meant losing many an Ulsterman to other Divisions. The U.V.F. had no artillery and consequently no partially trained force upon which to draw. It was thought that the raising and training of artillery in Ulster would take so long that it might delay the departure to the front of the Division for several months. In those days, it will be remembered, the one feverish anxiety of the men of the New Armies was lest the war should be over ere they were able to play their part in it! In the event, as will later be explained, the Division went to France in advance of the Artillery that had been raised for it, with a Territorial Artillery attached.

The 36th Divisional Artillery was raised, six months after the rest of the Division, in the suburbs of London, though from quarters stranger to one another than towns fifty miles apart in Ireland. The 153rd and 154th Brigades R.F.A. were formed by the British Empire League, of which one of the moving spirits was General Sir Bindon Blood. They were recruited chiefly from Croydon, Norbury, and Sydenham. The 172nd and 173rd Brigades, on the other hand, came from North-east London. They were formed on the initiative of the Mayors of East and West Ham and recruited from those districts.

The first date recorded in the Artillery annals is that of May the 5th, 1915, when sixty recruits of the 153rd Brigade assembled at 60, Victoria Street, the headquarters of the British Empire League, and marched to Norbury, where they were billeted in private houses. Londoners from South and North did not meet until July, when the four Brigades and the 36th Divisional Ammunition Column were moved to Lewes. It was within a few days of the arrival of the rest of the Division, already at a high standard of efficiency, in England, that serious training of the Divisional Artillery really began.

To the great regret of all Ulster, it was ruled that Sir George Richardson, owing to the seniority of his rank, could not take command of the Division. He remained in Belfast, working for the good of the cause, and none can speak more

## A COMMANDER APPOINTED

highly of his efforts and his loyalty than Sir James Craig and General Hickman, the chief organizers of those early days. "Trusted by every class," writes an officer who had long worked on his staff, "he was able to induce employers to permit those of their workmen to enlist who were not indispensable, and to perform the much more difficult task of making the skilled craftsmen of the shipyards realize that their duty to their country called them to remain at work, helping the Navy and Merchant Service to hold command of the sea, on which our success depended equally with our victory on land." How they and others, notably the makers of linen for aircraft, who were, for the most part, women, played their part, cannot be discussed here, though it is a record worthy the pen of a eulogist. What is less generally known to the people of Great Britain is that in Ulster not a strike occurred throughout the course of the war.

Major-General C. H. Powell, C.B.,* an officer with a distinguished record in the Indian Army, was appointed to the command of the Division. Colonel Hickman, after remaining in Belfast till the three Brigades had been formed, went to Finner to take command of the 109th.

The following is the formation of the Division as finally constituted :—

### COMMANDER :
Major-General C. H. POWELL, C.B.

### ASSISTANT ADJUTANT AND QUARTER-MASTER GENERAL :
Lieut.-Colonel JAMES CRAIG.

### GENERAL STAFF OFFICER, 2ND GRADE :**
Captain W. B. SPENDER.***

---

\* Now Sir Herbert Powell, K.C.B.

\*\* A G.S.O., 1st Grade, was not appointed to Divisions in training at home.

\*\*\* Now Lieut.-Colonel Spender, C.B.E., D.S.O., M.C.

ROYAL ARTILLERY.*

(Brigadier-General H. J. BROCK.)

153rd Brigade, Royal Field Artillery.
154th Brigade, Royal Field Artillery.
172nd Brigade, Royal Field Artillery.
173rd Brigade, Royal Field Artillery.
Divisional Ammunition Column, Royal Field Artillery.

ROYAL ENGINEERS.

121st Field Company, Royal Engineers.
122nd Field Company, Royal Engineers.
150th Field Company, Royal Engineers.

107TH INFANTRY BRIGADE.

(Brigadier-General G. H. H. COUCHMAN, C.B.)

8th Battn. Royal Irish Rifles (East Belfast Volunteers).
9th Battn. Royal Irish Rifles (West Belfast Volunteers).
10th Battn. Royal Irish Rifles (South Belfast Volunteers).
15th Battn. Royal Irish Rifles (North Belfast Volunteers).

108TH INFANTRY BRIGADE.

(Brigadier-General G. HACKET PAIN, C.B.)**

11th Battn. Royal Irish Rifles (South Antrim Volunteers).
12th Battn. Royal Irish Rifles (Central Antrim Volunteers).
13th Battn. Royal Irish Rifles (1st Co. Down Volunteers).
9th Battn. Royal Irish Fusiliers (Armagh, Monaghan, and Cavan Volunteers).

109TH INFANTRY BRIGADE.

(Brigadier-General T. E. HICKMAN, C.B., D.S.O.)

9th Battn. Royal Inniskilling Fusiliers (Tyrone Volunteers).
10th Battn. Royal Inniskilling Fusiliers (Derry Volunteers).

* Formed May 1915.
** Now Sir G. Hacket Pain, K.B.E., C.B., M.P.

11th Battn. Royal Inniskilling Fusiliers (Donegal and Fermanagh Volunteers).

14th Battn. Royal Irish Rifles (Young Citizen Volunteers of Belfast).

PIONEER BATTALION.

16th Battn. Royal Irish Rifles (2nd Co. Down Volunteers).

DIVISIONAL TROOPS.

Service Squadron, Royal Inniskilling Dragoons.
36th Divisional Signal Company, Royal Engineers.
Divisional Cyclist Company.
Royal Army Medical Corps.
    108th Field Ambulance.
    109th Field Ambulance.
    110th Field Ambulance.
    76th Sanitary Section, R.A.M.C.
Divisional Train, R.A.S.C.
48th Mobile Veterinary Section.

The present is perhaps the most suitable moment for mention of the reserve battalions, of which six were formed in 1915 : the 17th, 18th, 19th, and 20th Royal Irish Rifles, 12th Royal Inniskilling Fusiliers, and 10th Royal Irish Fusiliers. The 36th was the sole Irish Division to have its own reserve formations. In addition to the provision of drafts, these battalions had important tasks in the disturbed period following the rebellion of Easter Week, 1916. A detachment from the 18th Royal Irish Rifles, which battalion was commanded by Colonel R. G. Sharman Crawford, C.B.E., took part in the capture of "Liberty Hall."

Training was in full swing by the end of September, 1914, the 107th Brigade being at Ballykinlar, the 108th at Clandeboye and Newtownards, and the 109th at Finner ; where the accommodation consisted at this early date almost entirely of tents. By good chance the weather of the first three weeks of October was fine and mild, but thereafter, and before the hutting was completed, a very wet and severe winter set in. The U.V.F. training was a great advantage. It was easy to handle bodies of men, the most ignorant of whom could at least number, form fours, march in step, and keep alignment from the first. And the old organization held till it could be replaced by the new. As one Commanding Officer writes : " The U.V.F. officers and N.C.O.'s kept the men in order till we straightened out into the regular army formation." The enthusiasm of the men of those days of 1914 is something that no officer who served with them can ever forget; something perhaps, also, that none but those officers who began their training in the first six months of the war ever witnessed. There is a slow-burning flame in the Ulster blood that keeps her sons, once raised to the passion of great endeavour, at a high and steady pitch of resolution. They took their work with extraordinary seriousness. They were all anxiety to learn. They made their platoon commanders, beginners for the most part like themselves, struggle to keep ahead of them in the art that both were acquiring. How many of the junior officers must remember those "conferences" of sergeants and section leaders after parade hours and the circle of keen heads bent inward toward them; how many the "parades" on the mess table, matches for sections, inked on one side so that after many manœuvres the front rank might remain the front!

The Infantry of the 36th Division was formed on perhaps the most strictly territorial basis of any Division of the New Armies; the general rule being that battalions were drawn from the larger regimental areas of the U.V.F., companies from the smaller, and platoons from battalion areas. This had the great advantage that it engendered a natural companionship and spirit of pride in the units. The company, the platoon, was a close community, an enlarged family. In after days, in the trenches and in billets behind the lines, the talk, not only of men from Belfast and the larger towns, but of those from the country villages, would be of streets and, in the latter case, of farms and lanes of which those present had known every detail

## THE CLAN SPIRIT

from childhood. The old clan-names of the Northumbrian and Scottish Borders were clustered thick together. A platoon would have five Armstrongs or Wilsons or Elliots, a company half a dozen Irvines or Johnstons, a battalion half a score of Morrows or Hannas. To be set against that great accretion of moral force which springs from such a survival of the clan was the minor disadvantage that the non-commissioned officers for the most part, and certainly all the juniors amongst them, were the brothers and cousins and close companions of the men they commanded. It was not that their orders were disobeyed; it was rather that there was at first a diffidence about the orders, which sometimes appeared to be rather in the nature of persuasive requests. In a few units the non-commissioned officers were changed about, so that they came in contact with men with whom they were less familiar. But the problem was never a serious one, and it finally disappeared. The only other disciplinary problem was that of week-end leave. The great bulk of the men of the 107th and 108th Brigades and most of the Divisional Troops were training near their homes. They could not understand why they should be kept in camp doing nothing on Sundays when they might have been visiting them. Though leave was given generously enough, this remained a sore point till the Division moved to England. Apart from "absence without leave" there was no crime to speak of. Such occasional blackguards as were found in the ranks were swiftly disposed of, a sentence of "discharged as incorrigible and worthless," which was, as a fact, quite illegal in time of war, being their fate.

The Divisional Commander was a firm believer in marching, not only as a preparation for that feature of military life, but as a creator of toughness and endurance to meet the varied strain of war. By the early months of 1915 one brigade route march of from twenty to twenty-five miles, and shorter battalion marches each week, had become the general rule. Equipment being slow in making its appearance, General Powell had rucksacks, of the Alpine pattern, made in Belfast, to be carried, fully loaded, on the march instead of the pack, and bolts from the shipyards to take the place of small-arm ammunition in the pouches. There was, as might be expected, some grumbling at what appeared to be a needless imposition, but the troops benefited by the experience, and Sir Archibald Murray, when they marched past him the following summer, remarked how easily they carried their packs. Numerous recruiting marches were also carried out, which provided further training in marching and march-discipline, and at the same time exhibited detachments of the units from the countryside to the remotest villages in their area. Everywhere they were received with the greatest pride and enthusiasm.

For the rest, the training was that of all the New Armies. The Infantry had " D.P." rifles, the R.E. for a long time no material save what was bought for them. Little musketry could be carried out, such as there was being done with a handful of short service rifles allotted to each battalion, and in some cases with rifles borrowed from the U.V.F.— upon which inspecting Generals turned a blind eye. By Infantry and Sappers alike trenches were dug, as an officer of the latter acidly remarks, about eighteen inches wide and with perpendicular sides. But that, of course, was a universal experience. Much discussion took place upon the relative merits of trenches sited upon the forward and reverse slopes of undulating ground. Not till 1918, and then to an extent but small, was any choice to be left by the enemy in the siting of positions. The R.A.M.C. was the first to be equipped. The people of Ulster showed its affection for its Division by the presentation of very fine motor ambulances, each of which bore inscribed upon the body the name of the town or association from which it came. In some of these cars the gangway was sufficiently wide to take two additional stretchers, which proved an inestimable boon in the Battle of the Somme.

The winter, it has already been remarked, was a very wet one. The health of the troops was generally good, a few cases of that dreadful disease cerebro-spinal menin-

Major-General Sir C. H. Powell, K.C.B.

gitis causing the medical staff its greatest anxiety. In order, however, to spare the men as far as possible from strain and discomfort, and to allow those that remained to be accommodated in the huts as they were completed, some units were moved out of the camps; the 9th Irish Fusiliers\* of the 108th Brigade, and the 11th Inniskillings\* of the 109th, for example, moving to barracks, the first to Holywood and Belfast, the second to the town that gives the regiment its name, Enniskillen. In January the 109th Brigade, less the 10th Inniskillings, moved to Randalstown. The 10th Inniskillings remained on the West coast till the first days of May, suffering the wildest weather in their exposed camp, but probably no worse than was suffered by the rest of the Brigade in the first days at Randalstown, which became such a quagmire that men who slipped from the "duck-boards" between the huts sometimes sank to their knees in the mud. As weather improved and the hutments were completed, the full Brigades reassembled in their camps, the 10th Inniskillings marching across Ireland, from west coast to east, to rejoin. With the spring there began a new era of intensive training.

Meanwhile had been fought the Marne, the Aisne, the two Battles of Ypres, Neuve Chapelle. The life in France was impossible to imagine for those who had not seen it. Not all the marching and countermarching, the attacks, the trench-digging, the bivouacks, and cooking of meals in the open could print for the mind's eye an adequate picture of that. But gradually, through letters, through the recitals of wounded friends, men began to form some conception of the realities of modern war, as fought against a race which, for courage, endurance, and resource, ranked with the most formidable warrior peoples of the world's history. The gas attack in the Salient was evidence, if any were still needed, of the temper of the new Germany. Men did not blanch, but it was inevitable that, to the more seriously minded

---

\* In future, battalions of the Royal Inniskilling Fusiliers, Royal Irish Rifles, and Royal Irish Fusiliers will be alluded to as "Inniskillings," "Rifles," and "Irish Fusiliers," respectively.

among them at least, another and a grimmer picture than that which had been present with them at the beginning should form itself. They had answered many calls, chief among them love of country in various aspects. Mingled with this had been, however, the spirit of adventure. The old rowel that had driven Ulstermen over the seas, making them colonists and administrators, was sharpened again by the war. It pricked on these young men, the flower of their country. Now, perhaps, the spirit of happy adventure faded a little, but it was replaced by that of hard resolution and duty. The training had had its physical results. The troops were strong and supple in their strength. But it had had a moral result also. The Division was no longer a mass of men, even of drilled and disciplined men. It had become, in the mysterious fashion that such things happen, welded into a whole, a spiritual unit. Little by little the group-spirit had grown, till before the troops quitted Ireland a sensitive observer might fancy he could detect it whenever he came in contact with them.

One factor in this group-spirit and in the whole life of the Division, which is here approached with diffidence, but which could not be omitted from a faithful record, was the element of religion. It is sometimes forgotten that the Covenant of the seventeenth century was taken almost as widely in Ulster as in Scotland. Undoubtedly something of the old covenanting spirit, the old sense of the alliance of " Bible and Sword," was reborn in these men. It was the easier recreated because of the strength of religious feeling which had existed in times of peace in Protestant Ulster, one of the few parts of the country wherein the reformed churches had not, by their own admission, lost ground in the last thirty years. Religious feeling inspired the men of Ulster in those days of training, and remained with them in the days of war. The General commanding the 4th Division, to which the 36th was attached for instruction after its arrival in France, spoke of his astonishment at finding so many Ulstermen reading their Bibles. The writer of this book can bear witness from personal observation that it was not uncommon to find a man sitting on the fire-step of a front-line trench, reading one of the small copies of the New Testament which were issued to the troops by the people at home. The explanation was that, on the one hand, religion was near and real to them; on the other, that they were simple men. They saw no reason to hide or disguise that which was a part of their daily lives.

The people of Ulster were given an opportunity to see their Division as a whole. On May the 8th it was inspected by Major-General Sir Hugh McCalmont at Malone, afterwards marching through Belfast, the salute being taken by the General at the City Hall. It was a fine day; the City was dressed in bunting, and the main streets rocked with a mass of enthusiastic spectators, who had crowded in by special train from all about the Province. The troops were to remain two months longer in Ireland, always on the tiptoe of expectation of a move, but that was the real farewell of Ulster to the Division she had given to the nation.

Early in July the Division moved to Seaford, on the Sussex coast, leaving the 9th Inniskillings to recruit at Ballycastle from the shameful disease of German measles! But a small proportion of those 15,000 men had ever previously crossed the Irish Sea. The English were new to them, as they were to the English. The impressions made on either side were favourable. The men were treated with the greatest kindliness, and, for their part, their behaviour was excellent; reassuring, indeed, to some of those residents who had been perturbed at the idea of this incursion of "wild Irishmen." Not a few of the people of Seaford, on seeing the announcement of this History in the press, wrote to the author and spoke of their pleasant memories of the Ulstermen's sojourn in the district. Seaford made a fine training area. It was a healthy place, and the splendid downs behind the town were ideal for tactical exercises. Soon they were scored with white chalk trenches. On one occasion, when the whole Division, with the exception of the Artillery—Infantry, Cavalry, Cyclists,

Engineers, R.A.S.C., and R.A.M.C.—had been engaged in night manœuvres, it was discovered when dawn broke that a deep trench had been cut across a very valuable gallop belonging to an Alfriston training stable. An apologetic letter was sent to the owner, who wrote back expressing his pleasure that his ground had been put to a purpose so useful, offered half his jumps to the mounted units and young officers for practice, and scarcely hinted that he hoped the occurrence would not be repeated.

In the last week of July, when the troops were carrying out their usual routine of training, a message was received that Lieutenant-General Sir Archibald Murray, Deputy Chief of the General Staff, would hold an immediate inspection. The result was of great importance. Sir Archibald Murray informed Lord Kitchener on his return that the Ulster Division was worthy of a higher place than it occupied on the latter's private list of troops for the front. It was not Lord Kitchener's fashion to ponder such questions.

" I'll go and see them to-morrow ! " was his reply.

At half-past four on the 26th of July came a telephone message that the Division was to parade for Lord Kitchener at 11 a.m. the following day.

July the 27th was a bright, sunny day. Lord Kitchener came, dashed at the waiting horses with such speed that before anyone could speak he was on the back of one with a doubtful reputation, by no means intended for his riding, and rode off. Colonel FitzGerald, his Military Secretary, said he had never seen him better pleased, and was quite unable to persuade him to leave the field for another engagement. To General Powell he remarked that he was relieved to find he had under his hand a Division ready for the front at a moment's notice.

One incident of this inspection, related by the A.D.M.S. of the Division, must be recorded, as it throws an interesting light on Lord Kitchener's quickness of eye for and memory of details. The personnel of the Field Ambulances was of fine physique, the mounted men including many farmers' sons. As the Field Ambulances passed the saluting point,

Lord Kitchener turned to the A.D.M.S. with the remark: "Those men are too fine for the R.A.M.C. You will have to give me two hundred for the Artillery." The A.D.M.S. replied that he hoped they would not be taken, as they had undergone a very thorough training; to which Lord Kitchener, raising his voice, simply repeated: "You will have to give me some of those men for the Artillery."

A few days later an officer from the Adjutant-General's department came down. He said that, at the moment, men were in fact not particularly wanted for the Artillery, but that as "K." had ordered it, they must be taken. The upshot was that, from a large number who volunteered and some reinforcements from Newry, one hundred and fifty were transferred to the Artillery, with the promise that they should be used to reinforce that of their own Division—a promise that, it is to be feared, was not in the majority of their cases fulfilled. The sequel came two months later, when Lord Kitchener was present at the King's Review. On reaching the 108th Field Ambulance, the A.D.M.S. rode out to take up his position behind Lord Kitchener, who turned to him and asked: "How many men did you send to the Artillery?" "A hundred and fifty, sir." Lord Kitchener, somewhat gruffly: "I thought I told you to send two hundred." The A.D.M.S. thought it best to leave it at that.

Returning from the Seaford review, Sir Archibald Murray pointed out to the Secretary for War that the 36th Division was not quite so ready for France as he had supposed, since, though it had had practice on the ranges at Seaford, as well as in Ireland, it had not completed its official musketry and machine-gun courses, and was not equipped for the front. Nor was the training of the Divisional Artillery, which Lord Kitchener had not seen, nearly sufficiently advanced. Lord Kitchener gave orders that musketry and equipment should at once be completed, and that a fully trained Divisional Artillery should be attached to the Division. Shortly afterwards he said to Sir Edward Carson, referring no doubt to the New Armies only: "Your Division of Ulstermen is the finest I have yet seen."

Owing to lack of accommodation it was a few weeks before the Division moved to an area where its musketry could be carried out. By the 2nd of September it was assembled at Bordon and Bramshott. Here the final equipment arrived, and there was feverish activity in fitting it. Here also the musketry course was fired, for the most part with American ammunition, which gave unsatisfactory results.* And here the rest of the Division came to closer quarters with its own Artillery, which had arrived at Bordon from Lewes on August the 31st. To be frank, there was some dismay when it was discovered how elementary was its training. A year was the estimate by some regular officers of the time needed to make it fit for service. The critics had yet to learn what could be accomplished by intensive training, directed from above with skill and energy, backed by hard work, loyalty, and the swift intelligence of the Cockney from below.

The senior officers were now sent to France for instructional purposes, being attached to the 5th and 18th Divisions. On their return, news met General Powell that during his absence Major-General O. S. W. Nugent, D.S.O.,** who had commanded a Brigade in France with distinction, had been appointed to succeed him. The grounds of the decision were unexceptionable: that Divisions should be taken to France by general officers with experience of the conditions of warfare in that country. There was, however, throughout the Division, much sympathy with General Powell, who had been allowed to make his tour in the line in ignorance of the fact, which the staff officers with whom he came in contact knew, that his successor had been appointed. He received the honour of the K.C.B. in recognition of his high services in the training of the Division. Sir Herbert Powell finally went to Vladivostok in charge of the British Red Cross. The new com-

---

\* The writer saw one man, at whose shoulder he had stood on a U.V.F. range while he put five huge bullets from an Italian Veterli into the bull's-eye, miss the target twice at 600 yards.

\*\* Now Sir Oliver Nugent, K.C.B., D.S.O.

mander was to remain with the Division for over two and a half years. To-day his name is universally associated with it.

On September the 30th, the 36th (Ulster) Division, with the 1st/1st London Territorial Artillery, was reviewed by His Majesty King George the Fifth. It was desired not to prolong unduly the march past, as His Majesty always insisted on waiting till the last man had gone by, and General Nugent decided that the Artillery should advance in column of batteries, and the Infantry in column of half-companies with reduced intervals. It was a high test, triumphantly accomplished. Lord Kitchener informed General Sir A. Hunter, G.O.C. Aldershot Command, that the inspection was the quickest the King had made since the beginning of the war: a triumph of staff work and of drill. None of those who saw them is likely to forget the physique or the bearing of that splendid body of men. It is hard to think without emotion of what the Division was that day and the fate that awaited it.

Lord Kitchener was there again, smiling and obviously well-pleased. His Majesty warmly congratulated General Nugent, and, turning to Sir George Richardson, who was present, told him what a fine Division had been given by his Ulster Volunteers. As the King's motor-car overtook some of the troops marching back to camp the men burst out into wild cheering, so that the car swept along a loud-roaring line—an unrehearsed and spontaneous exhibition of loyalty.

At the time of His Majesty's inspection the Advance Parties were already in France. In the first days of October the Division crossed the Channel, the mounted portion and transport to Havre, the dismounted to Boulogne.

The year of preparation for battle was over.

## CHAPTER II

### THE DIVISION IN FRANCE: OCTOBER 1915 TO JUNE 1916

GENERAL NUGENT and his Staff arrived at Boulogne at midnight on the 3rd of October. Between the 5th and the 9th of the month the Division concentrated in the area round Flesselles, where, some ten miles north of Amiens, Divisional Headquarters were established. Here the troops realized for the first time that France did not always mean the firing-line. The sound of guns was, strangely enough, heard less than it had been at Seaford, though the Vérey lights that could be seen by night against the sky were evidence of the proximity of the trenches. The countryside of the Somme was poor of soil, though the industry of the inhabitants extracted good crops from it, and curiously unlike that of the North of Ireland in its absence of pasture. It was, however, pleasant enough, high and rolling, the sites of the little villages in the uplands determined by the scanty water supply, but traversed by numerous streams in the valleys, full of beautiful panoramas wherever woodland interposed to break the monotony of its contours. The villages were not uncomfortable so long as troops could be widely spread. When, however, they were used as "staging areas" and billeting was at all close, their poverty was only too apparent.

Of this, some portions of the Division had early experience. On October the 9th the 107th Brigade and the

1st/1st London Brigade R.F.A. moved up for attachment to the 4th Division, and instruction in trench warfare. The 4th Division at this time held a wide and comparatively quiet front north of the River Ancre, which had been taken over from the French during the previous summer. The general method of instruction in vogue was the attachment of formations and units to those next larger; that is, a battalion to an infantry brigade, a company to a battalion, a battery to a brigade of artillery. The troops in this preliminary experience of trench warfare suffered less from the enemy than the elements. The weather was bad, roads and trenches were wet; the billeting accommodation *en route* was scanty, and while in rest behind the line, consisted almost entirely of war-worn tents without floor-boards. The men in those first days scarce seemed to notice these things, so intense was their eagerness and curiosity. The conventional and traditional grumble of the British private soldier, a *sotto voce* accompaniment to the most generous efforts and the most unselfish devotion, was forgotten here. One of the Brigadiers of the 4th Division said of them:

" The men are extraordinarily quiet, and I thought at first somewhat subdued, and put it down to the big marches they had had. But when I came to talk to them I found they were like new schoolboys, taking in everything, deadly keen, and only afraid of one thing—letting down their unit in any way. I have never seen any men with such quiet confidence in themselves, in spite of their efforts to hide it."

The attachments lasted five days, the 107th Brigade being the only one which was not divided between two divisions in the line. Its attachment being complete, the 108th was sent up, two battalions to the 4th Division and two to the 48th, further north. Then, towards the end of the month, the 109th Brigade had its turn with the same two Divisions. Meanwhile the R.E. Headquarters and the three Field Companies had moved to Arquèves, to work on the new Third Army Line, later to become important as the Amiens Defences. At this task they were soon joined by the 16th Rifles (Pioneers), while they also had as companions French Territorials. All worked hard and well, though in the light of subsequent experience their trenches were far too narrow, and their traverses too small by half. The troops not under instruction in the line were kept hard at work training, officers from the 4th Division having come to initiate them into the mysteries of bombing—mysteries to which they took in kindly fashion. One instructor declared that the national sport of the Ulsterman, the throwing of kidney-stones in street riots, was an admirable preparation for bombing. Another introduction was to gas helmets, the horrible bags of those days without even mouth-pieces. Passing through a gas-chamber in these bags was unpleasant, though accepted as a necessity, but "doubling" and marching in them, as ordered by some zealous instructors, was purgatory, and resulted in some of the men being violently sick. On October the 21st the Division, except for such infantry and artillery as were under instruction in the line, moved slightly further west, toward Abbeville, to a more comfortable and spacious area about Bernaville and Canaples, with Headquarters at Domart-en-Ponthieu.

The Higher Command had decided that the 36th Division was not to enter the line as a formation for the present. The Battle of Loos was not long past, when troops fresh from England had been pushed into the fight at its fiercest and after very long marches, with disastrous results. It was determined that in future divisions should be given a chance gradually to accustom themselves to the conditions. Another decision which had been arrived at was that New Army and Territorial Divisions should receive an admixture of thirty per cent. of regular infantry by the transfer of brigades. Orders were received for the transfer of one brigade to the 4th Division. The 107th, in the command of which General W. M. Withycombe, C.M.G., had succeeded General Couchman, was selected to go. The 12th Brigade of the 4th Division was transferred to the 36th Division in exchange.

By November the 4th the 107th Brigade, with its Light Trench Mortar Battery, which had just arrived from England, and the 110th Field Ambulance, were clear of the 36th Divisional area. On the 7th the 12th Brigade marched in to take its place. The 2nd Lancashire Fusiliers of this Brigade were transferred to the 108th Brigade in exchange for the 11th Rifles, and the 2nd Essex to the 109th in exchange for the 14th Rifles. These inter-divisional changes lasted a month only. Any advantages they may have had were found insufficient to counterbalance the dislike of the break-up of their old formations felt by battalions of both Divisions.

The Division as now constituted passed a winter very different from that of its expectations. Late in November it moved down to Abbeville, with Headquarters at Pont Remy, on the bank of the Somme just outside that city. For the time it was concerned more with sanitation than with war. Never was such cleaning of streets, such draining of middens, such wholesale carting away of manure-heaps, as when the Ulster Division marched into an area. The inhabitants wondered and gaped, and a humorist wrote home that the troops "were sweeping onward through village after village in the North of France."

Some writers—among them, it is to be regretted, a well-known dramatist and critic of Ulster birth—have spoken unfavourably of the French peasant and his attitude to the troops. There can be few men of the 36th Division who look back upon the peasant-farmer of the Somme with anything but affection and admiration. For their part, the villagers testified by their letters and expressions of regret, whenever a unit moved, how good had been the terms between troops and civilians. The Calvinistic Ulsterman was sometimes a little startled and pained at first on finding a countryside so liberally besprinkled with shrines and crucifixes, but, if he were a countryman, especially, he made the surprising discovery that these countrymen of the Somme were very like himself. They thought twice before speaking once; they had a certain dourness; they did not wear their hearts on their sleeves, though they were furnished with those organs in the proper places.

On November the 26th two of the Field Companies, the

121st and 150th, were returned by the Third Army, and began to assist and supervise the infantry at work in the villages. In view of the projected spring offensive, not actually launched till after midsummer, all these back areas were being prepared to accommodate large bodies of troops in some comfort. Bunks were put into barns, the holes which had appeared in the lath and mud walls, through shortage of male labour in the villages, were repaired, and excellent horse-lines, with standings of chalk and stone, were built. The timber was cut locally and sawn by the troops themselves, using their own saw-mill.

On November the 27th the Ulster Divisional Artillery, so called at that date to distinguish it from the London Territorial Artillery, which was known as the 36th Divisional Artillery, landed at Havre, and joined the Division in the area east of Abbeville. It had remained at Bordon since the departure of the Division. Its training was not yet complete, and it was to have a course of gunnery at Cayeux, on the coast, south of the mouth of the Somme, before entering the line. The only other important event, from the military point of view, to be recorded before February, was the formation of the 108th and 109th Machine-Gun Companies, from personnel and guns withdrawn from the battalions. To replace the guns each battalion was issued with four Lewis guns, which number was gradually increased till, a year later, it had been quadrupled.

Christmas 1915 was celebrated by the troops in their billets with sport and festivities. Many units had bought sucking pigs from the farmers, and fattened them in anticipation of the event; none had failed to provide some luxuries. The villagers took part in the merrymaking, and in most of the officers' messes the people of the house drank with their guests the toast of victory. For very many of the men in those Somme villages it was one of the happiest Christmases they had ever spent, and one on which they looked back in after years with delight. Within a few days the services of the Pioneers were lost for a long period to the Division. They were ordered to construct, under the

Chief Engineer of the Third Army, a broad-gauge railway line between Candas and Acheux. For the rest, there was little change in the daily life of the Division. On New Year's Day it moved back again to the area about Domart, roughly that in which it had been previously billeted. The same work—wood-cutting, repairing and "bunking" of barns, construction of horse-lines—continued, with the exception that it was done in different villages. When the work was well in hand some training was interspersed with it. Not till January the 30th was the Division ordered to hold itself in readiness to take over a portion of the line. It had passed the worst of the winter by no means disagreeably.

The 107th Brigade had existed in a fashion less idyllic. On arrival in the 4th Division area two of its battalions, the 8th and 15th Rifles, were transferred to the 10th and 11th Brigades respectively, while in exchange it received three battalions, the 1st Rifle Brigade, 1st Royal Irish Fusiliers, and 2nd Monmouths. Three days later it took over the left sector of the 4th Division front, astride the Mailly-Maillet—Serre Road, the Brigade Headquarters being in the former village. Here for upwards of two months it remained, alternating with the 10th Brigade in six-day tours in the line. In November the weather was indifferent; by December it became very bad indeed. Men sank in the mud so that they had to be dug out by their comrades with spades. The communication trenches were so deep in water that they were for the most part impassable. Movement from front to rear had to take place after dark, in the open. "Trench feet," a disease then generally known as "frost-bite," though caused by constant immersion of the feet in water far above freezing-point, became prevalent. Rubber thigh boots, most precious of boons to men in such sectors, were all too rare as yet, and had to be doled out with parsimony. Battle casualties were light in this sector, but the life in it was very far from pleasant. On New Year's Day the Brigade, now returned to its original formation, exchanged it for the right sector of the front held by 4th Division, south of the Mailly-Maillet—Serre Road. Of this sector the chief peculiarity was a tiny parallelogram of trenches jutting out from the British line on the high ground east of Beaumont Hamel, known as the Redan. It was a most unpleasant corner. In the first place, it was not more than fifty yards from the German lines, and the mine-craters which fringed its eastern edge, which were occupied at night by British posts—a doubtful policy, as it appears to-day—were in constant danger of surprise. During the 107th Brigade's tour one post was, indeed, bombed by the enemy and a man taken out of it. In the second place, the Redan was the scene of constant mining, and the bugbear of battalions in reserve, which had to send up large working-parties to carry sandbags filled with chalk for the miners. It was the one point in our trenches which received fairly constant attention from German gunners, and the average weekly casualties in this tiny lozenge were probably higher than on the whole of the rest of the 4th Division's front. One of the best pieces of work performed by the 107th Brigade during this period was the construction, by the 8th Rifles, in one night, of a trench a hundred yards in length and protected by a double "apron" of wire, which denied to the enemy ground which would have given him important observation. The digging and wiring were carried out without arousing the least suspicion among the German sentries.

The Brigade had during these three months established an excellent reputation, both for work and for demeanour under fire. General Nugent had suggested the reconstitution of the 36th Division on its old basis on the grounds that, with three Brigades of Ulstermen, it would be more homogeneous and of greater fighting value than as at present constituted. This suggestion was favourably received. The men had not been unhappy in the 4th Division, but feelings of local patriotism were still strong in them, and they were most anxious to return. It was announced that the reconstitution—the first of any division so dismembered, and the only one which occurred for some time—would

## THE DIVISION ENTERS LINE

take place simultaneously with the Division taking over a portion of the front.

The 1st/1st London Artillery had departed, two howitzer batteries to the East, and the remainder to the 38th Division in Flanders. The original Artillery, henceforth the 36th Divisional Artillery, was completing its training on the coast. With its exception the whole Division now marched linewards, between the 2nd and 6th of February. The 4th Division had meanwhile extended its right flank, and had the 11th Brigade on the right of the 107th, its outer flank on the River Ancre, just east of Hamel. As the new divisional boundaries were to be the Ancre and the Mailly-Maillet—Serre Road, all that was necessary to complete the relief and reconstitute the Division was for the 108th Brigade to relieve the 11th. The 36th Division then took over, at noon on February the 7th, its first line, with the 108th Brigade on the right, the 107th on the left, and the 109th in reserve. Headquarters were at the large village, or small town, of Acheux.

Of the next six weeks there is little of interest to report, save a heavy bombardment of the left flank of the 107th Brigade and of the 12th Brigade to the north of it. Shelling with 210, 105, and 77-mm. howitzers and field guns lasted for about half an hour, after which the artillery lifted range to rear lines and communication trenches. The 9th Rifles at once manned their battered trenches, some men getting out beyond the wire and opening rapid fire. There was no attack, though a party of the enemy succeeded in entering the trenches of the 12th Brigade, to be quickly ejected. It was curious that in this, its first bombardment, and a not inconsiderable one, the Division did not suffer a casualty.

A mine exploded in front of the Redan cost the lives of three men of an attached Tunnelling Company, who were buried in a blown-in passage. Otherwise, during this period the weather was probably an opponent more formidable than the Germans. The men in the trenches lived under conditions of the deepest discomfort. For weeks together the communication trenches were knee-deep in water. Previous troops had dug deep sumps in the bottoms of the trenches, covering them with boards, with the idea of draining off the water. But the water soon filled these and rose till it floated off the boards. Then would come some unfortunate fellow splashing his way along the trench, to plunge into the hole and be soused in icy water to the waist or higher. Some of the ills then endured were, it must be admitted, not unavoidable. There was a certain lack of revetting material, it is true. Few of those who were compelled to use it will forget one notorious communication trench, "Jacob's Ladder," which ran from the village of Mesnil to that of Hamel, down a forward slope completely exposed to the enemy. By night the road could be followed without worse risk than occasional bursts of machine-gun fire, so that large bodies of men had seldom to use this trench. By day, however, men clawing their way through its mud experienced the sensations of flies in treacle. When time and material had become available for the revetting of its sides, all this was changed, and "Jacob's Ladder" lost much of its evil reputation. But on the front line trenches more could have been done than was accomplished. The chief methods of drainage employed were the digging of large sumpholes in the parados of the trench to carry off the water, and the pumping of it out over the parapet with hand-pumps, whence, of course, it presently filtered back to the trench bottom. Scientific trench drainage, by means of trenches cut for the purpose, had as yet made little progress, though the undulating character of the country was suitable to it. It is scarcely an exaggeration to say that the Division suffered more from the wet at this time than during the following winter in Flanders, in flat country and on a water-logged soil, simply because in the latter case the R.E. and infantry had learnt by experience how to deal with it.

If the 36th Division had yet something to learn by way of prevention in these matters, it had little as regards cure. When rubber boots—"gum-boots, thigh," in the parlance of the Ordnance—became commoner, "trench feet" almost disappeared. The men laughed at the special grease with which they were provided to rub their feet, but they used it as they were ordered to do. Contrary to legend, but a small proportion was really used for the frying of food. They laughed also at the foot drill, each man rubbing the feet of his next number once a day, but to a great extent they carried it out. Excellent as these things were, the best remedy of all was found to be dry socks. Drying them in the trenches was difficult, but it was easy to send up dry ones by the ration parties at night, who took back the wet ones with them and dried them during the following day.

As this History is intended not alone for men who fought in the war, but also for their relatives and friends at home, a few remarks on the routine of holding a line of trenches, commonplace to the soldier as they may be, are perhaps permissible. Let us imagine a division with two brigades in line, and one in reserve. Each of the brigades in line would have two battalions in the trenches, relieved at regular intervals, though never on the same night, by the other two. These intervals were from four to eight days, according to the weather and state of the trenches. The distance of the rest billets from the front line, again, depended upon accommodation, the enemy's command of the country from his observation posts, and the activity of his artillery. They might be three or four miles back. At this time the battalion which held the line at Hamel, on the right bank of the Ancre, rested in Mesnil, little more than a mile from the German lines. The battalion in the trenches had probably two companies in the front line, one in support and one in reserve, and carried out interbattalion reliefs in the course of its tour. The front and support lines were held by posts consisting of sections, about ten or twelve men in these early days, half as many later on. These posts furnished each a single sentry by day, and double sentries by night. For half an hour before and half an hour after dawn, the hour of surprise attacks, the troops would "stand to" in their trenches. In winter months this was the hour of the rum-ration—very welcome after a cold or wet night. Each company had one officer permanently on duty in the trench, night and day. In the trenches these periods were practically reversed. Night was the time when most of the work, all the wiring, all the patrolling of " No Man's Land," was carried out. Roughly speaking, the battalion in the line was responsible for the work as far back as its headquarters, with the expert assistance of a few sappers. Behind that worked the resting battalion—though parties from this had frequently to assist the battalion in line also—under the direction of the R.E., of which one Field Company was in general attached to each brigade. It was important that the infantry should know the sappers, and look upon them as assistants rather than task-masters. The Pioneer battalion had generally some special task of importance allotted to it under the direction of the C.R.E.

A Machine-Gun Company at this time formed part of each brigade. The guns were distributed in depth in the trenches, but much further forward than was the case later on, when the number of Lewis guns with the infantry had been increased. Such subtleties as machine-gun barrages, indirect fire, the linking of guns by telephone to battalion headquarters, had as yet scarce been conceived. Machine gunners and infantry had their ammunition and bombs in boxes let into the parapet, these stores increasing in size from front to rear.

The artillery, in rear, was also distributed in depth. Covering two brigades, as we have imagined, it would probably be divided into two groups, the group commander living at or near the headquarters of his infantry brigade. For this purpose the present formation, four artillery brigades, of which one was a howitzer brigade, was clumsy and extravagant. The howitzer brigade, for example, was invariably split between the groups, and its commander " functioned " as an administrator, but not as a combatant. This system was to be modified later. The guns were in pits, hidden as well as possible among trees or houses, or if in the open covered with "camouflage" to match the surrounding fields. The dug-outs of their detachments were close at hand, and, close at hand also, were pits containing from two to four hundred rounds per gun. At dusk the guns were laid on the "night-lines"; that is to say, each was set so as to fire upon a certain zone, in accordance with a previously arranged plan. A sentry in an observation post watched the line. Within a few seconds of a telephone call or an "S.O.S." rocket going up, the guns could open fire. An artillery liaison officer lived with each battalion in the trenches.

The rations arrived each day for all these people in the following manner: The Divisional Supply Column went daily to railhead with its lorries to meet the "pack train," bringing up the supplies to the "refilling point," and dividing them into four groups, one for each infantry brigade and one for all the rest of the divisional units. Here, under the supervision of the Brigade Supply Officer, the supplies were parcelled out, loaded into the horsed supply wagons, and taken to the transport lines of the units, where they came into the keeping of the Quartermaster. In a very quiet part of the front, when the railhead was far advanced, the supply wagons could draw direct from the railhead, cutting out altogether the Supply Column and its lorries. Divisions were urged to do this when possible to save petrol. Let not the innocent, however, imagine that uses were not found for the lorries thus set at liberty!

The food we need follow no further, except in the case of a battalion in the trenches. For all other units its preparation was comparatively simple. But to supply the man on the fire-step with hot food at regular intervals was a problem of some difficulty. Rations were brought up to battalion headquarters after dusk by the transport. In a well-organized battalion—and battalions varied much in this respect—the maximum was done before the food left the transport lines, the minimum when it arrived. That minimum was the heating. In some sectors of the front it used to be said that cooking was impossible. As a fact, there never was a sector wherein, with resource and ingenuity, at least the *heating* of food already prepared was impracticable. For extras, the stock-pot was the soldier's best friend; and unhappy was he if his battalion did not possess it. Ration biscuit, soaked in stock and put through a mincing machine, made "dough" which produced cheese biscuits, sausage rolls, jam tarts. As for the dry rations, tobacco, etc., they were put into a sandbag for each section, labelled with the number of that section. So, at least, marched affairs in a battalion of which the internal economy was at a high stage of efficiency.

The evacuation of wounded may also be briefly described. On a casualty occurring the wounded man was brought by the regimental stretcher-bearers to the Regimental Aid Post, a dug-out or shelter near a communication trench, generally in the neighbourhood of battalion headquarters. A mile or two further back was the Advanced Dressing Station, to which the Field Ambulance stretcher-bearers carried "lying-down" cases and conducted "walking" cases. If possible, wheeled stretchers or a trench tramway were here employed. At the A.D.S. food in some form was always ready; wounds were re-dressed if necessary, morphia given if required, and the soothing cigarette added. Then the cars of the Field Ambulance conveyed the casualty to the Main Dressing Station; *i.e.*, the headquarters of the Field Ambulance. This was to all intents and purposes a temporary hospital, where the wounded man might obtain rest, and further surgical aid if required. It was the last stage in the divisional chain. From it the cars of the Motor Ambulance convoy took him to the Casualty Clearing Station, whence a hospital train bore him to the base hospital or, during an offensive, direct to the hospital ship.

The above is an attempt to sketch, without entering into its ten thousand complications, some of the main features of the life of a man in the trenches. War, at that time and in such a sector as this, had not acquired many of the horrors that were to come. Bombing by aeroplanes was in its infancy; so was the use of gas shell. Long-range shelling of villages with high-velocity guns was almost unheard of hereabouts. With regard to all shelling there would appear to have been conventions. Those who have seen German shells at Mailly-Maillet dropping at dusk, the hour when the transport started for the line, on to the Serre and Auchonvillers Roads, but never closer than one hundred yards to the first houses of the village, will agree with this opinion. The surroundings were far less grisly and depressing than they afterwards became. There was, it must be remembered, save that at Ypres and that which at the moment was being fashioned at Verdun, no devastated area wider than a narrow ribbon from the coast to Switzerland. From the Mesnil Ridge, where the observation posts of the Division were manned by the Cyclist Company, the country behind the enemy's lines showed green and smiling. Villages which the troops were not to see at close hand save as ruins, Irles, Pys, Grévillers, Bihucourt, were intact. The time could be read with the aid of a telescope by the church clock of Bapaume. On the British side, villages a couples of mile back were little disturbed. Martinsart was no farther from the enemy, and here it was possible to call on Brigade headquarters at their château as one returned from the trenches, and drink a cup of tea poured out by the daughter of the house, who rang for a British orderly to bring hot water. Mediæval idyll! With spring appearing, the trenches drying, and the grasses above them filled with field flowers; with the Valley of the Ancre taking on a new beauty as its trees were feathered green; with nature bursting into life, man's thoughts could not be ever fixed upon death. Warfare, to many of the men in the Division, must have seemed less than terrible in these days. But they were the last of the good days. The terrible was not far off.

In the first week of March the Division extended its front, the 109th Brigade taking over the sector south of the Ancre, known by the name of Thiepval Wood. At the same time the 36th Divisional Artillery, back from its final training at Cayeux, took over the defence of the long line.

By the last day of the month the latter had been shortened to the two-battalion front astride the Ancre, the 31st Division having come into line on the left. The two sub-sectors were known as Thiepval Wood and Hamel respectively. The Hamel sub-sector was comfortable and quiet, troubled by nothing worse than the aggressions of a new long-range medium trench mortar, which often smashed in its communication trenches, but seldom caused many casualties. The battalion which held it was responsible for the defence of the Ancre and its swampy valley, filled with miniature lakes. This was carried out by the reserve company in the village, which found a platoon for small and isolated posts, the most advanced being at the bridge on the Thiepval-Hamel Road. The men enjoyed this duty better than any other. They were never shelled, they had no work to do, and they could employ their leisure fishing in the stream, with the chance of an occasional shot at wild duck or widgeon. Thiepval Wood, on the other hand, with an appearance of quietude that deceived visitors and newcomers, was wont to be transformed by sudden and not infrequent bombardments into a very unpleasant spot indeed. It was here that on the 10th of March the 10th Inniskillings suffered their real baptism of fire. At three in the afternoon there had been ranging shots from all calibres of artillery upon the wood, strengthening the belief of the man in the line, which was accepted with some hesitation by the Staff, that the army opposite possessed a "travelling circus" of heavy artillery, moved from point to point for the covering of raids. Precisely at midnight came a roar of explosions, a whistle and screaming of shells, a crash of falling trees. All telephone lines were cut, and S.O.S. rockets failed to ignite, but the artillery soon opened fire on its own initiative. On the right of the battalion front the trenches were pounded beyond recognition, and soon littered with dead and wounded. The garrison of the trenches manned their fire-steps and opened rapid fire on the enemy's front line. Not till 2 a.m. did the shelling die down. Then it was found that the enemy had penetrated the trenches of the

Major-General Sir O. S. Nugent, K.C.B., D.S.O.

troops on the right of the Division, killing a number of officers and men, and taking several prisoners. In a Special Order of the Day, congratulating the 10th Inniskillings, the Divisional Commander stated that " there seemed no reason to doubt that the German bombardment was intended to cover a raid similar to the raid which actually took place elsewhere the same night." The battalion had the further honour of mention in the despatches of Sir Douglas Haig. Its losses amounted to some thirty killed and wounded.

From the moment when the Division first entered the line, preparations had been made for the long-planned offensive. By the month of May this work was intensified. It is difficult to give in a few lines an adequate idea of the scope of such preliminary labour. The mere plans and instructions issued by the Staffs of the Division, its formations and units, would fill the greater part of this volume. There were miles of tramway to be laid, gun-pits for the new artillery to be constructed, roads to be improved, new communication trenches cut, and innumerable dug-outs excavated. The heaviest task of all was the building of two causeways over the Ancre and its marshes; the only communications with our line on the left bank of the river being some crazy wooden foot-bridges put up by French troops. As a first step the drainage of the marshes was examined, and many obstructions in the small streams removed. The flooded area was thus decreased, but there were at first frantic protests from the Division on the right when the water rose behind its lines. This flooding was, however, but temporary. The construction of these causeways was entrusted to the 122nd Field Company R.E., which employed large infantry working parties in two shifts, from dusk to dawn. The causeways were built of sandbags filled with chalk. The river was constantly swept at night by machine-gun fire, and the casualties suffered were not inconsiderable, particularly on the northern causeway. The mainstay of the whole scheme of preparation was the Pioneer battalion, which had already made its name by the construction of the Candas-Acheux railway. It was for this battalion a proud day when railhead for supplies and personnel opened at Belle Eglise Farm on the line that was its handiwork. But the whole of the Division worked with a will also. Tasks were nearly always completed before the allotted time, for which the sole explanation lay not entirely in the good hearts of the men, but also in the splendid physique of the Division at this period.* The artillery dug on the Mesnil Ridge an observation trench known as "Brock's Benefit," in honour of their General, which contained a whole series of "O.P.s," and will be very well remembered by a long series of divisions subsequently inhabiting that sector.

The first raid carried out by the Division was on May the 7th, and, by an extraordinary coincidence, that night was also chosen by the enemy to raid the troops of the 32nd Division on its right, at a point about 200 yards west of that of the British raid. The German barrage opened at 11 p.m.; the British "zero" was midnight. Major Peacocke,** second-in-command of the 9th Inniskillings, had his party already out in the sunken Thiepval-Hamel Road when the German bombardment began. He spoke on a telephone which he had taken out with him to his commanding officer, Colonel Ricardo, and it was decided to carry through the raid. The British guns, trained on the barrage lines selected for the raid, held their fire, and a most uncomfortable hour had to be endured in Thiepval Wood. At midnight the British barrage opened and the raiders charged in. The enemy was on the alert, and a fierce struggle followed. The raid was successful in inflicting heavy casualties on the enemy. No prisoners were taken, as the Germans in the deep dug-outs showed fight, firing up the steps. The raiders thereupon bombed the dug-outs till all sounds of life below had ceased. The casualties were trifling, but there were a good many more in the sunken road, where the raiding party had to

---

* The writer can recall working parties when the allotted task was completed a full hour before the allotted time, owing to the fact that the big countrymen of his company were able to carry two sandbags full of chalk, one in either hand, at once.

** Afterwards Lieutenant-Colonel Peacocke, D.S.O., who was foully murdered at his home near Cork, on June the 1st, 1921.

lie two hours before it could return to its trenches, so heavy was the German barrage.

Meanwhile, the enemy's intentions with regard to the troops on the right of the 36th Division being only too clear, six platoons of the 10th Inniskillings, two from dugouts on the reverse slope of Thiepval Wood, and a company from Authuille, moved up to their support. The former body arrived in the front line of the 1st Dorsets in time to assist them in repelling the enemy, who left a dead officer and a wounded prisoner in the hands of the English battalion. The company from Authuille and two guns of the 109th Machine-Gun Company also pushed up through a very heavy barrage to the front line. The Dorsets had suffered very considerable casualties, and the troops of the Ulster Division assisted to man their line till morning. The appreciation of the 32nd Division was warmly expressed by the G.O.C.

In May took place the first reorganization of the Divisional Artillery, the object of which was to divide the howitzers among the Brigades, to overcome the disadvantages of which there has been mention. Three of the Brigades, the 153rd, the 172nd, and the 173rd, were made up of three four-gun 18-pounder batteries and one four-gun 4.5 howitzer battery. The fourth, the 154th Brigade, which had been the Howitzer Brigade, thus lost all its howitzer batteries, and was made up by three 18-pounder batteries, one from each of the other Brigades, in exchange for the howitzers. Brigade Ammunition Columns were abolished and the Divisional Ammunition Column largely increased.

At the end of May Brigadier-General Hickman, commanding the 109th Brigade, returned to England, being succeeded by Brigadier-General R. Shuter, D.S.O. General Hickman, whose part in the formation of the Division has been recorded, was the last of the Infantry Brigadiers who had accompanied the Division to France. General Hacket Pain, commanding the 108th Brigade, had been succeeded by Brigadier-General C. R. J. Griffith, C.M.G., D.S.O., on December the 4th.

With the month of June began those more detailed preparations for the offensive which must be reserved for the chapter that deals with it. By this time all ranks had become aware of what was brewing. A keen sense of expectation was in the air. The Division had become a living soul ere ever it crossed the Channel. The months of trench warfare had strengthened it to an inestimable extent. The men were keyed up to a very high pitch of daring and determination. The infantry had the utmost confidence in itself, and in the artillery which was to support it. Officers and men of these two arms had known each other but a short time, but already a personal liaison, unusually close, to grow even closer during the comparatively quiet months in Flanders, had been established between them. The Division was to do great deeds in after days, and upon other fields of battle, but never was there quite the same generous and noble enthusiasm with which it entered upon this, its first offensive. That which it was about to accomplish will live in memory as long as there is a British Empire to honour the exploits of British arms.

## CHAPTER III

### THE BATTLE OF THE SOMME: JULY 1ST, 1916

On the first day of June, 1916, the front of the 36th Division was held by the 107th Brigade, the 108th being in support in the neighbourhood of Martinsart, and the 109th training. To permit the two latter Brigades to train together, the 147th Brigade of the 49th Division was ordered to relieve the 108th and take over its working parties. The 108th Brigade then moved back to Varennes, and the neighbouring villages of Harponville and Léalvillers. Training was carried out over an elaborate system of dummy trenches marked out with plough and spade, near Clairfaye Farm, to represent those of the German system to be attacked. It was largely due to this preparation that the men knew their task so well, and were able to push on to their objectives when their leaders had fallen. On the 5th a raid was carried out by a party of the 12th Rifles, sent up from the training area, on the German sap that ran parallel with the main railway line north of the Ancre.\* The wire was cut by an ammonal torpedo. This was a zinc tube, three inches in diameter, filled with ammonal. Each tube was about six feet in length, but tubes could be connected up with bayonet joints, and any length of torpedo thus made. It was generally fired by a sapper accompanying the raiding party. The Germans had run back or taken to their dug-

\* See Map I.

outs under the fire of our artillery, and few were seen. The dug-outs were bombed, and an officer shot. Two tunnels leading toward the British lines were discovered, one containing fourteen high-tension copper wires, which seemed to point to mining with a mechanical digger. The heads of these saps were blown in by the engineers who accompanied the raiding party. Five nights later the Germans retaliated upon the little salient in the British line opposite, known as the William Redan, then held by the 15th Rifles. After our trenches had been pounded by a bombardment of half an hour, the raiders advanced. They suffered loss from our barrage, and not more than half a dozen ever actually entered our trench. Half a minute's bitter hand-to-hand fighting, and they were out of it again, bearing with them the leader of the raid, who had been shot by a British officer. Our trenches were considerably damaged, but casualties were not heavy.

The weather now took a turn for the worse, there being a sort of cloud-burst on the 12th. Cross-country tracks were impassable for infantry, and the carriage of ammunition to the new gun positions was a very heavy task. The rain came at an unfortunate moment. Battalions of the 109th Brigade were moving up to Aveluy Wood, south of Mesnil, to complete the work of preparation. The 16th Rifles (Pioneers) were there already. These troops had to endure the gravest discomfort from the weather. Little canvas shelters were all their protection, and for days together their clothes were not dry. Yet their work was magnificent. When, almost at the last moment, a Regiment of French Field Artillery joined the Division to assist in the attack, the 11th Inniskillings were ordered to help them in the construction of gun-pits and shelters, with little enough time to do it. The men threw themselves into the task with splendid enthusiasm. It seemed that they worked the harder because their work was for strangers, who would be left half-protected if they failed them. There was a fine flavour of international courtesy in the manner of their toil, for they gave of their free will energy that not the most

## NEW ASPECT OF WARFARE 43

skilful of taskmasters could have wrung from them. General Nugent sent to Colonel Brush, then in command of the Battalion, a letter of warm congratulation upon their efforts.

In the battle that was about to begin, General Sir H. Rawlinson's Fourth Army was taking the offensive along its whole front, with the Sixth French Army of General Fayolle on its right. The Battle of the Somme, the first in which our New Armies of volunteers were engaged in great numbers, concerned the 36th Division but at its opening. Its general aspects were, however, of the highest importance to all the Allied troops. It differed broadly from such an action as that of Loos. There an immediate strategic result was sought from a small offensive. Here, while a break through was sought on the first day, and would doubtless have been possible had the whole German trench system been captured all along the front, thereafter the aims became quite other. On the vast plateau of Picardy, an advance of ten miles or thereabouts had small strategic importance. The nearest first-class railway junction, Cambrai, was thirty miles away. The new phase was the "limited offensive." The plan was to push forward infantry behind artillery fire of overwhelming weight upon a broad front, step by step, smashing down resistance. The plan was made possible for us by the huge development of our munition factories. It was the war of attrition. It was a mighty assault battle, wherein England and France hurled man and gun and material upon German man and gun and material. It had manifold and obvious blemishes. Its cost was prodigious, particularly in its early stages, before certain needful lessons had been learnt. It stereotyped attack and robbed commanders of initiative, and was in this respect the text-book of all the lessons Ludendorff impressed upon his troops in the first three months of 1918. But—and of this there can be no shadow of doubt to-day—it laid the foundations of final victory.* The German

* For a brilliant appreciation of the Somme Battle and its lessons, General Mangin's book, *Comment finit la Guerre*, should be read.

troops were never quite the same after it, while our young levies, dreadful as were their sacrifices, were to arrive at a far higher standard of military value.

The 36th Division was the left Division of the X. Corps, having on its right the 32nd Division and on its left the 29th Division, not long arrived from the East, which was in the VIII. Corps. The 49th Division was in X. Corps Reserve. The 36th Division was to attack astride the Ancre. On the left, or southern bank, its objective was the fifth line of German trenches, known as the " D " line.* The right flank boundary ran from the north-east corner of Thiepval Wood to D 8. On the right bank the objective was a triangle of trenches enclosed between the left boundary line and the Ancre, beyond Beaucourt Station. The left boundary ran from the point of the salient in our lines, known as the Mary Redan, to two houses half-way between Beaucourt and its railway station, thence along the river to the railway bridge. The ground rose sharply on either side from the deep-cut bed of the Ancre, but while on the northern bank it was cut by a gorge running down from the village of Beaumont-Hamel, at right angles to the river, and parallel with the German trenches, on the south it swelled up in a great convex curve, rising two hundred and fifty feet in a thousand yards. The crest was crowned by a parallelogram of trenches, extending from the German " B " line to the " C " line, that will live long in history as the Schwaben Redoubt. The trenches were defended by masses of wire. An artillery officer, who made a careful reconnaissance with a good glass from " Brock's Benefit," on the Mesnil Ridge, counted sixteen rows guarding the front line just south of the river, and an average of five rows along the second line. The dug-outs, most of them at least thirty feet deep in the chalk, were to all intents and purposes shell-proof, and were numerous enough to house the whole trench garrison. The enormous activity behind our lines had taught the Germans long before that an attack

---

* The boundaries of the 36th Division, with all names that occur in the description of the battle, will be found in Map I.

## PLANS FOR THE ATTACK

was brewing. They trusted to their fortifications and awaited it with confidence.

For the purposes of attack, the front was divided into four sections. The right and right centre sections were allotted to the 109th and 108th Brigades respectively. The left centre section, bounded by a line drawn from the north corner of Thiepval Wood just north of B 19, C 11, and D 11, and the Ancre, was, owing to the great frontage of the 36th Division, not to be attacked directly. The left section, on the right bank of the Ancre, was allotted to the 108th Brigade. This Brigade had attached to it one battalion of the 107th. It was to employ three battalions in the right centre section, and two in the left section. The 107th Brigade (less one battalion) was in Divisional Reserve.

The task of the 109th Brigade in the right section was to attack the "A" and "B" lines within its section,* and to advance to a line drawn from C 8 through B 16 to the Grandcourt-Thiepval Road at C 9 ; there to halt and consolidate. For this purpose General Shuter was attacking with two battalions, the 9th Inniskillings on the right, the 10th on the left, in first line ; and the two remaining, 11th Inniskillings on right and 14th Rifles on left, in second. The two first were to take and consolidate the final objective, the rear battalions to hold the "A" and "B" lines and to send up liaison patrols to get touch with the leading battalions. The most important task of the 11th Inniskillings was the fortification of the Crucifix on the Thiepval-Grandcourt Road.

The task of the 108th Brigade in the right centre section was to clear the "A" and "B" lines within the section, and advance to the "C" line, halting and consolidating on the salient C 9, C 10, C 11, the north-east corner of the Schwaben Redoubt. A special detachment, with one Stokes mortar, one Lewis and one Vickers gun, was to act as left flank guard, to clear the communication trench from B 19 to C 12, holding the latter as a defensive post, and

* The "A" line consisted of a double line of trenches, a front line, and immediate support. The second was alluded to as the "A.I." line.

sending a detachment down to C 13, to ensure observation and fire on the Grandcourt - St. Pierre Divion Road. In addition, two officers' patrols, each a platoon in strength, with a Lewis gun, were to reconnoitre and clear the left of the "A" and "B" lines up to St. Pierre Divion. General Griffith was attacking here with the 11th Rifles on the right, the 13th on the left, and the 15th Rifles of the 107th Brigade, attached, in support.

North of the Ancre, in the left section, the task allotted to the two remaining battalions of the 108th Brigade was to assault the German salient on the left of its objective and clear the trenches down to the railway, to establish strong points at B 26, B 24, and B 21, and to occupy Beaucourt Station and the trenches immediately behind it. It was afterwards to occupy the mill on the river bank and the two houses beyond the station. Here the 9th Irish Fusiliers were attacking on the right, and the 12th Rifles on the left. Of the latter battalion one platoon was detailed to attack the railway sap, of which mention has already been made, and one to patrol the marsh.

The assault on the "D" line, the final objective, was to be carried out by the 107th Brigade with its three remaining battalions. The Brigade was to advance through Thiepval Wood, following the 109th Brigade, pass through the leading Brigades on the "C" line and attack the "D" line from D 8 to D 9; then to extend its left to D 11. General Withycombe disposed the 10th and 9th Rifles in first line, the former with its right on D 8, the latter with its left on D 9. After the capture of this objective, the 9th Rifles were to extend to D 10 and the 10th to D 9. The 8th Rifles, moving up in rear, were to occupy and hold from D 10 to D 11.

The assaulting battalions were to advance, each in eight successive waves, at fifty yards' interval, but the 107th Brigade, passing through to the attack on the final objective, was to advance in artillery formation till compelled to extend.

The artillery consisted of the 36th Divisional Artillery,

## ARTILLERY PROGRAMME 47

one Brigade of the 49th Division, a Regiment of French Artillery, and, under the orders of the X. Corps, a greater concentration of heavy artillery than had been made in the course of the war till now, except perhaps in the latter stages of Verdun. The preliminary bombardment was to last five days, from the 24th to the 28th of June. Owing to wet weather the attack was postponed two days, and there were two extra days of bombardment. The results, as witnessed from our observation posts, were magnificent. All wire that could be seen was effectively cut. As one watched the big shells bursting, sending up huge columns of earth, day after day, it appeared as though no life could continue in that tortured and blasted area. The barrage for the attack was not the true "creeping barrage" which was to become universal later on, and was, indeed, employed that day by the French. After a final intensive bombardment of sixty-five minutes, it fired upon each German line in succession, lifting from the "A" to the "A.I." at Zero, from the "A.I." at Zero plus three minutes, from the " B " at Zero plus eighteen minutes, to a line 400 yards east of this objective. Then at Zero plus twenty-eight minutes it moved on to the " C " line, and at Zero plus one hour eighteen minutes off the " C " line to the " D." There was then a long halt to permit of the passing through of the 107th Brigade. At Zero plus two hours thirty-eight minutes the barrage moved up to a line three hundred yards east of the " D " line. At each lift, sections of 18-pounders and 4.5 howitzers "walked up" the communication trenches to the next barrage line. Stokes mortars were to take part in a final hurricane bombardment prior to Zero, while medium* and heavy mortars were also employed, the former on special points, the latter moving with the artillery barrage to the extremity of their range. The French artillery joined in the preliminary wire-cutting, using high explosive instead of shrapnel according to its custom, but its main task was the drenching of the Ancre valley with gas shell.

* Z/49 Trench Mortar Battery was attached to the 36th Division for this operation.

Two machine-guns were to accompany each battalion in the attack, the remaining eight of each Machine-Gun Company being in Brigade Reserve. Guns were allotted to all the principal strong points that were to be consolidated. Eighteen Stokes mortars were to go forward, the personnel of the remaining eighteen acting as carriers. Two sections of the 150th Field Company were allotted to the 109th Brigade, and one section of the 122nd Field Company to the 108th Brigade on each bank of the Ancre. The remainder of the Field Companies were in Divisional Reserve.

The medical arrangements were of peculiar difficulty, particularly on the southern part of the front. The two Main Dressing Stations, for stretcher cases and "walking wounded" respectively, were at Forceville, manned by the 108th Field Ambulance, and Clairfaye Farm, further west, manned by the 110th Field Ambulance. The Advanced Dressing Station was situated close to the Albert-Arras Road in Aveluy Wood. Evacuation of wounded from the Regimental Aid Posts in Thiepval Wood and Authuille had to take place over Authuille Bridge, or by the trench tramway which crossed the Ancre to the north of it. The motors of the Field Ambulance were parked on the Martinsart-Albert Road, south of the former village. For "walking wounded" there was a collecting station west of Martinsart, whence horsed wagons carried them by a cross-country track through Hédauville to Clairfaye. From Hamel evacuation was simpler, though even here it had to follow a specially dug trench from the village to a point where the Hamel-Albert Road was screened from observation.

On the 22nd and 23rd the infantry took up the positions it was to occupy during the bombardment; the 9th Inniskillings in the right section of Thiepval Wood, the 11th Rifles in the left, and the 9th Irish Fusiliers in the Hamel trenches. These troops had a purgatory to endure. For the most part in the narrow slit assembly trenches, with the rain pouring steadily down upon them, they were under furious German bombardments that wreathed the wood in smoke and flame, and made the crashing of great trees the

## A SUCCESSFUL RAID

accompaniment to the roar of bursting shells. On the night of the 26th gas was liberated by us from cylinders in the wood after a great bombardment. It was the first time the Division had had to do with the abominable stuff, which brought no good fortune. Many cylinders were burst by the heavy German barrage, and serious casualties suffered by the men of the Special Brigade responsible for opening the cocks, and by the infantry assisting them.

Two hours later a raid was carried out in this sector by a party sent up by the 13th Rifles. The men, now at a pitch of excitement and enthusiasm that rendered them resistless opponents in hand-to-hand fighting, swarmed into the battered German trenches, shooting right and left, and bombing dug-outs. They returned with one German officer and twelve other ranks as prisoners, the first captured by the 36th Division. Their own casualties were six killed and nine wounded, suffered for the most part in the Sunken Road, where, like the 9th Inniskillings, they had to lie for some time ere it was possible to return to their trenches. Captain Johnston, the leader of the raid, brought in all his casualties, as well as his prisoners. He was to fall five days later in the greater venture. The prisoners denied knowledge of our gas, nor did their respirators smell of it. It was occasionally the experience of the Division that the British gas services rated too highly the effects of their devices.

On the 27th, " X " day, it rained in sheets, and " Y " day was little better. It was accordingly decided by the Higher Command to postpone the attack for two days. This necessitated a postponement of the assembly also. Instead, inter-brigade reliefs were carried out in the trenches to give some rest to the troops that had endured the early hammering. Their rest, unfortunately, was in huts in Martinsart Wood, huts that trembled and creaked to the terrific roar of siege howitzers firing night and day beside them. Yet it was better than that other wood across the river, which was the following day, now " Y.1 " day, visited by the heaviest bombardment yet seen. The trenches were in a terrible state, and the men of the medium trench mortar batteries, engaged in cutting the German wire, suffered more even than the infantry, and earned the admiration of the latter by their devotion to their task.

In all the circumstances it must be said that the total casualties for the month of June, approximately seven hundred and fifty, were not heavy. They included the results of a veritable calamity that befell the 13th Rifles. On the evening of the 28th, " Y " day, the battalion was relieving the 11th Rifles in Thiepval Wood, and marching out of Martinsart by platoons at two hundred yards' interval. As number 11 Platoon and battalion headquarters were about to march out together a shell fell right in the midst of the party. Fourteen were killed on the spot, and ten more died later. Almost all the rest were wounded, including the second-in-command, Major R. P. Maxwell, and the adjutant, Captain Wright. The confusion in the pitch darkness, with scarce a man on his feet, was appalling. Fortunately a platoon of the 11th Rifles, just relieved from the trenches, appeared on the scene, and the street was speedily cleared. But the Germans could have had far bigger hauls than this at " Lancashire Dump " on the Albert-Hamel Road in Aveluy Wood any night they had chosen to shell it.

This was the *rendezvous* of a mass of transport immediately after dusk, bringing up munitions and rations for the offensive. Large stores of the latter were placed in specially constructed dug-outs on the river bank. The work of the Divisional Train was here most admirably organized by its commander, Colonel Bernard. So close were the big convoys to the German trenches that extraordinary precautions to avoid noise had to be taken. Wheels were bound with straw and old motor tyres, steel chains replaced by leather straps, boots, like those used in rolling a cricket ground, placed over the horses' hoofs. And it was an amusing sight to see an A.S.C. driver frantically clinging to the nose of some sociable horse that desired to greet new acquaintances with a friendly neigh.

## ANNIVERSARY OF THE BOYNE

The reward of waiting came in a fine day on "Y.2" day, the 30th. Divisional Headquarters moved up to their report centre on the Englebelmer-Martinsart Road. At night the approach march took place, and assaulting battalions returned to their positions in the trenches. The assembly positions of the 107th Brigade (less 15th Rifles) were in slit trenches in Aveluy Wood. The battalions marched up by cross-country tracks, marked, one by red lanterns, the other by green. The night was fine, and the artillery on either side rather less active, though lachrymatory shell was falling in the wood. In a curious complete lull that fell before dawn, men heard with astonishment a nightingale burst into song, pouring out her bubbling notes one upon the other, as though this had been still the pleasant copse, deserted by man, but a kingdom of the birds, of two years gone.

The two days' postponement had had upon the men an effect contrary to that which might have been attended. The extra strain of waiting was more than counterbalanced by the coincidence of the date. For it was upon July the 1st, the anniversary of the Boyne, that the sons of the victors in that battle, after eight generations, fought this greater fight. To them it had a very special significance. A stirring in their blood bore witness to the silent call of their ancestors. There seemed to them a predestination in the affair. They spoke of it as they waited, during the final intensive bombardment, while the German counter-barrage rained upon their trenches.

Day had dawned clear and sunny. Zero was at 7-30 a.m., when it had been light for four hours. Far better had it been had the conventional dawn attack been carried out. However, the first movements were concealed by the intensity of our fire, and by smoke barrages put down by 4-inch Stokes mortars in the valley of the Ancre and in front of Thiepval village. The troops formed up in "No Man's Land," facing their objectives, following for the most part, on the left bank of the Ancre, the line of the sunken Thiepval-Hamel Road. At 7-15 a.m. the leading companies issued from the gaps cut in our wire, extended to two paces' interval, and moved forward to within one hundred and fifty yards of the German trench. The hubbub of the British bombardment was terrific; over their heads the Stokes mortars, firing at highest rate, were slinging a hundred shells into the air at once.

Zero! The hurricane Stokes bombardment ceased. The artillery lifted off the first line. The whistles of the officers sounded, and the men sprang up and advanced at steady marching pace on the German trenches. Those who saw those leading battalions move to the assault, above all their commanding officers, forbidden to accompany them, who waved to them from the parapet, received one of the most powerful and enduring impressions of their lives. Colonel Macrory of the 10th Inniskillings speaks of " lines of men moving forward, with rifles sloped and the sun glistening upon their fixed bayonets, keeping their alignment and distance as well as if on a ceremonial parade, unfaltering, unwavering." General Ricardo, then commanding the 9th Inniskillings, wrote a few days later : " I stood on the parapet between the two centre exits to wish them luck. . . . They got going without delay; no fuss, no shouting, no running, everything solid and thorough—just like the men themselves. Here and there a boy would wave his hand to me as I shouted good luck to them through my megaphone. And all had a cheery face. Most were carrying loads. Fancy advancing against heavy fire with a big roll of barbed wire on your shoulder ! " So they bore upon the German lines, while behind them, from Thiepval Wood, rocked by exploding shells, sheeted in the smoke and flame of bursting shrapnel, fresh troops issued and followed upon their advance in little columns.

It is the custom, kept throughout this History, to describe the course of battles from the right hand to the left. If here it is departed from, it is only because the action on the north side of the Ancre was separate from the other and of lesser importance. Its description, alas! will occupy small space enough. There was here in " No

Man's Land " a deep ravine, which the map contours show without giving an idea of its abruptness. The first wave of the 9th Irish Fusiliers reached this with little trouble, but those which followed met with very heavy machine-gun fire, and suffered terrible loss. Advancing at Zero with splendid dash, the survivors of a battalion which Colonel Blacker's training had made one of the best in the Division, swept through the enemy's front line trenches. One small body of the right centre company in particular carried all before it, and was last seen advancing upon Beaucourt Station. On the left the 12th Rifles had worse fortune. The wire round the German salient over the hill-brow, less easy to observe, was less completely destroyed than on the rest of the front. Many gaps were cut, but machine-guns were trained upon them. Beaten back at the first rush, and having lost the barrage, the remnants of the battalion were twice re-formed by devoted officers under that withering hail, and twice again led forward. It was of no avail. On their left the leading troops of the next Division crossed the front line trenches, but were assailed from the rear by machine-gunners emerging from dug-outs. At eight o'clock the 36th Division was informed that the enemy had retaken his front line. The attack north of the Ancre was a failure, though gallantry every whit as great as that of the battalions on the left bank was behind it.

Elsewhere, for all its losses, the attack was a complete success. Every objective was reached. Had it been possible to attain the same results all along the front, the day would have ended with the greatest British victory of the war.

The leading waves, still moving as on parade, reached the German front line trench and moved straight across it. They did not suffer heavily. Hardly were they across, however, when the German barrage fell upon " No Man's Land," upon the rear companies of the first line battalions, and upon those of the second line. And immediately the barrage left it, flanking machine-gun fire burst out from the dominating position of Thiepval cemetery. The 11th Inniskillings and 14th Rifles, as they emerged from the wood, were literally mown down, and " No Man's Land " became a ghastly spectacle of dead and wounded. On the left of the line the 13th Rifles, under long-range fire from the Beaucourt Redoubt across the river, suffered at this stage most heavily of all. They had lost the bulk of their officers ere ever they reached the German trenches. The Division on the right was never able to clear Thiepval village, and it was that fact which was responsible for the gravest losses of the 36th.

Under this deadly punishment the men never hesitated. They went straight forward across the first two lines, sending back the few prisoners they took. The " B " line was to be reached at 7-48. Despite the gaps in their ranks the first wave swept upon it at precisely that moment. There was not much fighting here, but a large number of prisoners was taken, the German infantry surrendering as our men came upon them. The 15th Rifles, the supporting battalion of the 108th Brigade's attack, had, however, to deal with some Germans who came up out of unnoticed dug-outs after the leading battalions had crossed the "A" lines, the bombing squads told off to clear the trenches having been destroyed by machine-gun fire. On pressed the leading waves. Never losing the barrage, they took the " C " line, including the north-east corner of the Schwaben Redoubt, at 8-48. Even in the trenches they suffered loss from the flanking machine-guns, while movement from front to rear was now all but impossible. The supporting battalions, or their survivors, were also upon their objectives. Every man had done what he was set to do, or dropped in his path. And, to the eternal credit of our artillery, no man appears to have needed his wire-cutters.

Let us turn to the 107th Brigade, which had meanwhile advanced to the "A" line. It had moved from Aveluy Wood and across the Ancre to the western skirts of Thiepval Wood, almost at the bottom of the valley, assembling at 6-30 about the track known as Speyside. It had an hour to wait, shell after shell passing just over the heads of the troops and bursting in the marshes beyond them.

At Zero, led by the 10th Rifles, it moved back east for a short distance, to reach the rides which were its paths to the front line. Here the men could see the troops of the Division on the right issuing from their trenches, and each platoon, as it extended in " No Man's Land," disappearing before the blast of machine-gun fire that met it. The ride used by the 10th Rifles on the right had been denuded of its foliage by the bombardments of several days, and w s in view. The battalion came under machine-gun fire from front, right, and right *rear* simultaneously. The commanding officer, Colonel Bernard, was killed, and casualties were high. The final passage had to be carried out by rushes to the front line. The leading men could even see the German machine-guns firing at them, so that it is easy to imagine what sort of target they offered to those guns. Lewis guns were brought forward to engage them, but their teams were destroyed. The other battalions suffered considerably less, being screened in their rides, and further from the Thiepval guns. Before ten o'clock, runners, with the skill and devotion of their kind, had come back to report that the " C " line had been reached. Eight minutes past, it may be remembered, was the hour for the assault upon the " D " line.

To General Nugent it had appeared long before probable that his troops, if they went forward further as a wedge into the enemy's defensive system, with not a yard gained on either flank, would go only to their own destruction. At 8-32 his G.S.O.I., Colonel Place, had asked the X. Corps whether the 107th Brigade might be stopped from advancing upon the last line. The reply was that a new attack was being made on Thiepval, and also by the VIII. Corps north of the Ancre, and that the 107th Brigade must do its part by continuing its advance. But three-quarters of an hour later, at 9-16 a.m., instructions from the Corps to withhold the 107th Brigade till the situation upon the flanks had been cleared up were received. General Withycombe was ordered to stop his troops, and employed every means in his power to do so. But all the telephone lines taken forward had been cut by German fire, while for a runner to reach the line now held by the troops was a very long affair. Fortunate was he if he crossed that zone of death without scathe. The message arrived too late; the troops were committed to the attack. With them went forward some men of the other Brigades.

Of that last wild and desperate venture across a thousand yards of open country, few returned to tell the tale. Those that did tell of an entry into that last entrenchment, of desperate hand-to-hand fighting, and then, when the odds were too great, for the trench was full of German reserves, of a stubborn retirement to the next line. And now the German bombers surged up the trenches from St. Pierre Divion, to be beaten off again and again by the 8th and 15th Rifles, and the handful of the 13th remaining on that flank. Pressure on the other side did not come so soon: in fact, Lieutenant Sanderson, of the 9th Rifles, reconnoitred the trench "Mouquet Switch," on the front of the 32nd Division, and found it unoccupied. But Thiepval's machine-guns were still firing, and " No Man's Land " was a land of death. Two companies of the Pioneers were sent up to dig a communication trench across, which would have permitted the sending up of bombs and water. But at two o'clock Colonel Leader, their commanding officer, reported that the machine-gun fire rendered the task impossible. Supplies had run out, and the little parties that strove to bear them across were annihilated by fire. After noon attacks came upon the right flank also, the 11th Inniskillings at the Crucifix, and the 9th in the Schwaben Redoubt, being hard beset. The French artillery was ordered to put down a flank barrage on the right, and carried out its task admirably.

The 146th Brigade of the 49th Division had crossed the Ancre during the morning. At three p.m. it received orders to attack Thiepval village under a barrage, after an intense bombardment. The attack failed completely under terrific machine-gun fire. It was, in fact, stopped after the leading battalion, the 1/6th West Yorks, had seen the platoons which strove to deploy wither away. It was about this time that the Germans launched a counter-attack in the open on the left flank. Two companies emerged from the trees of the river valley and advanced on C 11. Caught on the hill by our artillery and the Lewis guns of the 8th Rifles, they were destroyed. There was a grave misunderstanding about the employment of the 146th Brigade. At four o'clock the 36th Division was informed that it was at its disposal. General Withycombe, the senior Brigadier in Thiepval Wood, was ordered to send two of its battalions to the Schwaben Redoubt, to rally the troops beginning to be forced back. But two battalions of the Brigade were already committed to the attack on Thiepval, while the two others had moved up behind them into the trenches of the 32nd Division. Not till 7-18 did six companies move up towards the " C " line, and now it was too late. On this flank it was already lost, and the Yorkshiremen were beaten off by German machine-gun fire.

Meanwhile the situation had grown desperate. Major Peacocke, second-in-command of the 9th Inniskillings, had managed to cross " No Man's Land " at noon into the front line about A 12, and after beating off attacks by Germans bombing their way up from Thiepval, collected a little bodyguard and worked forward to the Crucifix. He speedily discovered that the holding of the ground here, now slipping from our hands, was an impossibility unless Thiepval were taken. The men were still determined, but at their last gasp from fatigue. There was scarcely any ammunition or water for the Vickers guns, and it was all but impossible to send it up. A similar report was brought to General Griffith by Major Blair Oliphant, second-in-command of the 11th Rifles, who carried out an admirable reconnaissance. A final counter-attack, launched in the dusk by fresh troops that had come into Grandcourt by train during the evening, drove our men in from the " B " line. By ten o'clock it did not appear that we had any troops in the German lines. That which had been won at a sacrifice so vast, had been lost for lack of support.

Fresh troops for a further attack on Thiepval were put at the disposal of the 36th Division in the middle of the night. General Withycombe, at 11-30 p.m., received the 4th York and Lancs, of the 148th Brigade, with the intimation that the 4th and 5th K.O.Y.L.I.'s of the same Brigade would follow, to retake the Schwaben Redoubt, with the assistance of the remnants of the 107th and 109th Brigades. At one o'clock the latter battalions had not arrived. General Withycombe made the following appreciation of the position :

It was doubtful if it would be possible to organize an attack before daylight. This was a vital consideration, since an advance by daylight would be swept by fire from Thiepval, which was not being attacked that night, and the inevitable result would be a repetition of the previous day's experiences.

If the troops did succeed in moving off before dawn, it would be almost impossible for them to keep direction in the darkness, on ground they did not know.

Lastly, General Withycombe submitted that, if the Schwaben Redoubt were taken, it could not be held while Thiepval was still in German occupation.

General Nugent was fully in accord with these views. He submitted the matter to the Corps Commander, who replied that in such a case the man on the spot must decide. The proposed operation was therefore cancelled, and General Withycombe sent the 4th and 5th K.O.Y.L.I.'s to Aveluy Wood, retaining under his hand the 4th York and Lancs, in case of emergency.

At seven a.m. next morning, as sun dispersed the first summer ground-mist, observers on the Mesnil Ridge saw that there were yet British troops in small numbers in the first two lines of German trenches. General Nugent ordered General Withycombe to support and reinforce these troops, and to send forward supplies of bombs, ammunition, and water. General Withycombe collected a force of four hundred men of the four battalions of his own Brigade, together with two guns of the 107th Machine-Gun Company. Under the command of Major Woods, of the 9th Rifles, this devoted band moved across " No Man's Land " at two o'clock in artillery formation. It lost a third of its numbers from the enemy's fire, but it reached its objectives. Two small parties of the 16th Rifles (Pioneers), with bombs and ammunition, crossed later in the afternoon, going through the German barrage in most gallant fashion. On the left flank Major Woods found Corporal Sanders, of the 7th West Yorks, with a party of forty men, whom he described as "played out, but full of fight." He had been beating off German bombing attacks all night, had rescued several wounded Ulstermen, and taken a number of prisoners. This stout-hearted N.C.O. was subsequently awarded the Victoria Cross.

That night the 36th Division was relieved by the 49th. The 148th Brigade relieved the 107th in the two lines of trenches now held, between A 12 and A 19. The relief was not complete till after ten o'clock the following morning, when a weary, tattered, pitiful remnant marched into Martinsart and flung themselves down to sleep. They had brought back to Thiepval Wood fourteen prisoners. The total number captured by the 36th Division in the offensive was five hundred and forty-three. Its casualties in the two days amounted to five thousand five hundred officers and other ranks killed, wounded, and missing. The whole Province was thrown into mourning for its sons. Among the dead were Colonel H. C. Bernard, of the 10th Rifles; Major G. H. Gaffiken, of the 9th, who had led his company to the final objective; Lieutenant G. St. G. S. Cather, Adjutant of the 9th Irish Fusiliers, awarded a posthumous Victoria Cross for his services in bringing in wounded under machine-gun fire, in the course of which he lost his life; Captain E. N. F. Bell, 9th Inniskillings, attached 109th Trench Mortar Battery, who likewise had bestowed on him that last honour. Captain Charles Craig, M.P. for South Antrim, was wounded and taken prisoner. Some battalions had almost disappeared. The 9th Irish Fusiliers, for example, had at the end of the first day none of the officers and only eighty other ranks left unwounded of the force that took part in the attack. The figures of the 8th Rifles, as of a battalion below rather than above the average in casualties, may be given in full. Officers: fifteen wounded, five missing. Other ranks: twenty-four killed, two hundred and sixteen wounded, one hundred and eighty-six missing. And of the "missing," it must be recorded that three-fourths at least were in reality dead, somewhere out in front of the line finally handed over.

Of the deeds of heroism that day accomplished, it is not possible to enumerate one-hundredth. Notable among them were the achievements of junior officers and N.C.O.'s when their seniors had fallen. Lieutenant H. Gallagher, 11th Inniskillings, was the sole officer of his battalion to cross the German front line. With his orderly's rifle he killed six Germans holding up the advance, and then, at the Crucifix, organized the resistance, being one of the last to quit the German trenches at night. Lieutenant Sir Harry Macnaghten, 12th Rifles, twice reformed the tatters of his company in "No Man's Land," and led them against gaps in the German wire, to fall himself on the second occasion. Corporal John Conn, 9th Inniskillings, came upon two of our machine-guns out of action. He repaired one under fire and annihilated a German flanking party. He carried both guns himself most of the way back, but had to abandon one at last owing to utter exhaustion. These are but examples, picked at random. Another very remarkable Victoria Cross was that won by Private Quigg, 12th Rifles, Sir Harry Macnaghten's servant. He had, on July the 1st, advanced thrice to the attack. Next morning he heard a rumour that his officer was out wounded in "No Man's Land." Seven times he went out to look for him, and seven times he brought in a wounded man, the last dragged on a waterproof sheet from within a few yards of the German wire.

All arms had supported the infantry finely in their great, heroic achievement. The work of the artillery could not have been bettered. It carried out its long and gruelling task to perfection. Even in front of the " D " line the wire was well cut. One forward battery of the 172nd Brigade in Hamel, in full view of the enemy, enfiladed his lines across the Ancre, doing great execution and being handled with extreme gallantry. The Engineers suffered very heavy casualties in their devotion to duty, working in the marsh at keeping repaired the vital pipe-lines, regardless of the shells that all day fell about them. The stretcher-bearers of the R.A.M.C. were tireless. Often, owing to break-down on the trench tramway due to shell-fire, they had to carry wounded right down from Thiepval Wood and across the Ancre at Authuille. Many dropped from sheer exhaustion, and many refused to rest when reliefs arrived. The Army Service Corps drivers of the ambulances kept their cars continuously on the roads for thirty-six hours. There was throughout no hitch in the medical arrangements, though at one period of the day the overcrowding of the Main Dressing Station at Forceville, due to the strain upon the Motor Ambulance Convoy which evacuated the wounded to the Casualty Clearing Stations, gave rise to much anxiety.

A volume might be written—the extent of many a volume probably has—upon the causes of the failure, for such the whole northern section of the attack undoubtedly was. This is not the place for a detailed discussion of them. It may at least be said that, while the work of the artillery could not have been excelled, the whole scheme of its employment had not reached anything approaching the science of the following year. Artillerymen of the higher ranks were to some extent carried away by the weight of metal for the first time at their disposal, and carried away other arms by their new enthusiasm. The heavy gunners believed and proclaimed that no life could endure their fire, and that the battle would resolve itself into an advance by the infantry to take over shattered and undefended trenches. They had not realized that the machine-guns would be comparatively safe under their bombardment, and that it would take but a few seconds to bring them into action when the barrage was past. It is probable that at a later stage of the war a fortress such as Thiepval would not have been attacked directly by infantry till it had been first encircled and isolated by its advance, being kept the while under such artillery fire as would have forced the machine-gunners to lie low, and then rushed from all sides by bombing parties. It may be said that our organization at the beginning of the Somme Offensive was in a transitional stage. We had realized that defence with the machine-gun had beaten attack, and had begun the process of increasing the quantity and improving the quality of mechanical accessories. It was still, however, to cost thousands of lives before the factories could produce sufficient of the latter, or the higher commands reach the ratio between infantry force and mechanical aids necessary to the prosecution of a given operation. But no explanations that can be found stand without ample tribute to the fighting qualities of the German soldier. The dash and bravery of the counter-attacks of the bombers moving up from the valley merit high praise. The highest, however, must be reserved for the machine-gunners, who had sat for days in their dug-outs without fresh food, the very earth shaking to the thunders of our artillery, and then came up and brought their guns into action at the right moment.

On July the 5th the Division moved back to Rubempré and the neighbouring villages, and five days later to the Bernaville area. The Artillery remained in line under the orders of the 49th Division, while the Pioneers, 121st and 122nd Field Companies, were left several days at work, the former having, amongst other unpleasant tasks, to make a communication trench across " No Man's Land " to the new-won ground.\* The 150th Field Company had a yet harder time. It was sent to the 12th Division, further south, in the neighbourhood of Ovillers, where a slight advance had been made. Its work here was the consolidation of strong points, " before they were taken," as its commander, Major Boyle, remarks.

\* It was not held for long, nor was the Schwaben Redoubt to come again into British hands for several months.

Orders came at Bernaville for a move to Flanders. The Engineers, relieved of their task, marched north. The rest of the Division, less the Artillery, was moved by train from Auxi-le-Château, Frévent, and Conteville, to Berguette, Thiennes, and Steenbecque, between Aire and Hazebrouck, on its way to the training area west of St. Omer. The infantry battalions were but shadows of their former selves. Well might commanding officers feel appalled at the magnitude of the task before them in building up anew, without the best of their officers and N.C.O.'s. The men were very silent in these first few days after the battle. Not one of the survivors but had lost companions who had been two years at his side; many, friends of a lifetime. But if ever gift be God-given, it is the healing effect of time. And in days of war a week even is a long period. These men, moreover, felt that in all that had happened there was no reproach for them. They, at least, had accomplished their task in the face of incredible difficulties. On the 12th of July, General Nugent and his Staff saw the battalions of the 107th Brigade marching from the station of Thiennes into Blaringhem. Sun was shining on the old Flemish village. Officers and men wore marigolds in caps to honour the day; the bands played " King William's March." The least practised eye could tell that to these men confidence was returning; that the worst of the horror they had endured had been shaken from their shoulders. They marched like victors, as was their right.

# CHAPTER IV

## FROM THE SOMME TO MESSINES : JULY 1916 TO JUNE 1917

ON July the 13th the Division moved into the well-known training area west of St. Omer, with headquarters at Tilques. Those of the 107th Brigade were at Bayenghem, of the 108th at Eperlecques, and of the 109th at Boisdinghem. Here training and reorganization began, and here reinforcements arrived in considerable numbers.* Five days later the Artillery, which had remained in line covering the 49th Division, rejoined, having moved north by march route. R.A. Headquarters were established at the château at Recques. The troops were much refreshed by this return to civilization, and units had leisure to absorb their drafts. Unfortunately it did not last very long. On July the 20th Headquarters moved to Esquelbecq, to a famous and beautiful moated château, that bore at the door rings to which Marlborough's troopers had tied their reins, and had been occupied by General Grant after Waterloo. Meanwhile the 108th Brigade moved forward, by 'bus and lorry, to Kortepyp Camp, south of the village of Neuve Eglise, and Red Lodge, on the southern slopes of Hill 63, and west of the famous Bois de Ploegsteert, that will go down to Britons for all time as "Plug Street Wood." On the 23rd Headquarters moved to the château on Mont

* In the month of July the Division received 193 officers and 2,182 other ranks. These reinforcements left it still, of course, considerably below strength.

Noir, a couple of miles north of Bailleul, and that night the 108th Brigade re-entered the line in relief of two battalions of the 20th Division. By the end of July the 109th Brigade had come in on the right, in relief of troops of the 41st Division, and the 107th had relieved the 108th Brigade. The front line now held ran from a ruin on the Neuve Eglise-Warneton Road, known as Anton's Farm, on the right, to another known as Boyle's Farm on the Wulverghem-Messines Road, on the left. The frontage was some three thousand yards in a straight line, but there were over two and a half miles of front-line trench. On September the 1st the headquarters of the Division moved from Mont Noir to the village of St. Jans Cappel, near Bailleul.

The Division was to remain for upwards of a year in this part of the line, but it seldom held precisely the same section of front for more than a few weeks at a time. The various moves cannot be treated in detail. There were changes in August, all three Brigades entering the line, and early in September a "side-step" to the north, the right boundary now being the River Douve, and the left "Piccadilly Trench," south of the Kemmel-Wytschaete Road. The 108th Brigade was now on the right, the 107th in the centre, and the 109th on the left. The characteristics of the various parts of all this front were similar, the conditions of the soil the same throughout, so that a general description will hold good for all the period passed by the Division in the neighbourhood.

The trenches and dug-outs, to begin with, were not such at all in the sense in which the troops had been wont to use the names on the Ancre. The fighting trenches consisted, everywhere save on the highest ground, of parapets built of sandbags filled with clay. In places there was a parados similarly constructed, but over long stretches the men in the front line simply stood behind the wall, with no protection against the back-burst of shells. Water in this country appeared everywhere just below the surface, and it was useless to dig trenches in the real sense for any purpose other than drainage. Even the communication

F

trenches were sunk not deeper than a foot, and piled high on either side with earth, which made them satisfactory enough as cover from view, but very vulnerable to shell-fire. These communication trenches were longer than those to which the troops had been accustomed, the approaches to the front line being much more exposed than among the folds of the Somme country. As for dug-outs, there were none. Little wooden-framed shelves in the parapet, a few "baby elephants"—arched steel shelters, which, if covered thickly enough with sandbags, afforded protection against the shells of field guns—served for the troops in line, while further back, for battalion headquarters and forts, there were ruined farms, which often had good cellars, and in the frame-work of which concrete structures could be hidden. It was hard for troops used to the Somme chalk to accustom their minds to the spongy nature of this soil. In the dry weeks of August, for example, the R.E. built one very fine dug-out, twenty feet deep, and were proud of their handiwork. In September there was in it a foot of water, in October two; November found the water level with the top of the stairs, and a sarcastic notice, "The R.E. Swimming Bath," at the entrance.

When it rained, which was not seldom, all the low-lying ground flooded. The valley of the Douve, above all, from Wulverghem to the front line, became a muddy swamp, in which the water lay in sheets. At such times, and indeed during a great part of the winter, many trenches simply could not be occupied. No adequate idea of the impression conveyed upon the mind of a man coming up north from the clean, white trenches of the Somme can be obtained of all this area unless it is conceived as dirty, mournful, and disconsolate; haunted by the evil stench of blue clay, and brooded over by an atmosphere of decay.

Since the days of the first Battle of Ypres and of the rival turning movements which had ended in the present deadlock, the Germans had had the best of the ground in the Messines sector. Behind the salient of their front trenches it rose sharply, with a dip half-way up, formed by the shallow valley of the Steenebeek, to a dominating ridge, crowned south and north by the fortress-villages of Messines and Wytschaete. The road joining these was the limit of our observation, except for telescopes on Kemmel Hill. To the south we had a fair observation point in Hill 63, but the one great boon granted to us was Kemmel. Had it been a thousand yards nearer the front line, it would have done much to counteract the advantage of the Messines-Wytschaete Ridge. It is scarcely necessary to add that the enemy had, in his long possession of the ridge, fortified it with all his wonted industry and art. It was protected by four general lines of well wired trenches west of the road, and peppered over with little forts, wired all round, the garrisons of which were provided with concrete structures, miniature houses rather than dug-outs, proof against anything up to an eight-inch shell.

General Plumer's Second Army was at this time playing the *rôle* of Cinderella among the British forces. Its front was lightly held, even at Ypres, which had grown strangely quiet of late. Certain preparations had been made for an offensive in the summer, but had been largely abandoned for lack of labour. The Army Commander, however, insisted on pushing on his mining, in which he had great faith, a faith amply to be justified the following year. Throughout the winter and spring the Division furnished large parties for work under the various Tunnelling Companies in the shafts that were being driven under " No Man's Land," and beneath the strongest portions of the enemy's front line. The German miners were skilful enough, and on other parts of the front often gave rather more than they got, but here, from first to last, they were out-manœuvred and out-fought in an underground war. A striking instance of this was at La Petite Douve Farm, on the Ploegsteert-Messines Road, where the British tunnellers succeeded in pumping a fair proportion of the muddy Douve into the Germans' shaft, whence they could be heard, night after night, frantically ejecting it with a motor-pump. One "camouflet," as a defensive explosion was called, did indeed blow in our gallery here and undo months of work, but the enemy probably did not know what he had achieved, and the temporary check availed him nothing in the end. No Ulsterman who served in Flanders in that winter and the following spring will forget the skill, patience, and absolute contempt for danger displayed by those tunnellers. The 171st Tunnelling Company, with which the Division was most closely associated, will be remembered with particular affection and admiration.

The Second Army has been called the Cinderella of our forces. Not only was it holding a long line lightly, and with few reserves, but the main flow of ammunition and material passed it by and went down to the Somme, where the British were creeping forward in desperate fighting to Bapaume. There were weeks in August and September when the allowance of shells dropped to two and even one round per 18-pounder a day, with heavier calibres proportionately rationed.* The Germans were in this respect similarly situated. Their ammunition also was wanted on the Somme to put down those eternal barrages with which they opposed our assaults. When the Division first arrived in Flanders the artillery shell-fire was very light indeed. That of the trench mortars did a good deal to replace it. The Germans had concentrated on these weapons as their chief means of offence, and, possessing the advantage of the ground, they used them cleverly and with great effect. With that curious regularity that appeared to form part of the German mentality their bombardments generally took place almost precisely at 3-30 p.m. They were particularly severe in the neighbourhood of the Spanbroek salient.** " In this sector," writes a machine-gun officer, " I have seen five or six large 'minnies' in the

---

* Men who served do not need to be told, but perhaps civilians may, that there was no parallel between these conditions and those of early days, when there were often, literally, only a few rounds per gun available. At this time the ammunition was there, in the gun-pits and echelons behind, and could be used quite unsparingly at a sign of danger. When, however, there was no danger, it had to be conserved.

** See Map II.

air at one time—really fearsome things. You could see the fuses of the bombs alight in the air and follow their flight most of the way, only to lose it when straight overhead; and then there was nothing to do but wonder where it would fall!" These long aerial torpedoes exploded with shattering effect and made huge craters. It is useless to disguise the fact that, during the first few weeks of the Division's acquaintance with these trenches, the enemy had an ascendancy in trench-mortar warfare. That ascendancy had to be fought down. In the first place the German mortars, or rather their emplacements, were carefully marked down from observations taken in the line, and by the study of aeroplane photographs. Maps were then issued by the staff, upon which each active emplacement was shown by name. The names began with the letter of the map square; all in the " S " squares with S, and in the " U " squares with U. The names chosen were generally feminine—doubtless without ironic intention. A certain number of the emplacements were allotted to each howitzer battery of the Divisional Artillery, and also to such 6-inch howitzer batteries of the Corps Heavy Artillery as were available. When the mortar opened fire, all that was necessary was for the words " Susie active," or " Ursula active," to be wired back to the batteries. Susie, or Ursula, as the case might be, was instantly engaged, while any machine-guns that could be brought to bear upon her neighbourhood also took a hand in the game. By this means it was generally found possible to silence any individual mortar in about a quarter of an hour at most, and to prevent it from getting the exact range, and then knocking in a whole section of trench at leisure.

On the British side, also, big trench-mortar bombardments, aided by the Divisional Artillery, were periodically arranged. In these affairs the leading *rôle* was played by that terrific weapon, the heavy trench mortar, firing a projectile of 180 lbs., and highly dramatic it not infrequently was. One of these monsters dwelt at R.E. Farm, on the Wulverghem-Wytschaete Road, and it was from this locality that the principal "hates" were discharged. For perhaps ten minutes the fire would continue, the "flying pig," as it was called, sending over its giant shells, the medium mortars firing their 60-lb. "plum puddings," and perhaps two batteries of light Stokes mortars discharging twenty or twenty-five rounds a minute from every gun. Meanwhile the 18-pounders and howitzers behind joined in, while machine-guns fired upon communication trenches. The German retaliation was frequently heavy, and the teams of the mortars, heavy, medium, and light, showed grim determination in carrying out their tasks under punishment. General Brock, the C.R.A., did not believe in sending to the mortar batteries weaklings who were not wanted with the guns, and these trench mortars acquired a peculiar type of artillery officer,* resolute, hard-bitten, perhaps often careless and unconventional, but capable in great moments of the most splendid courage, lightly worn and taken for granted between comrade and comrade.

Few who have known anything of it can recall the "flying pig" without a smile. There was a pleasing uncertainty about this weapon. When the first round was fired from R.E. Farm, the charge did not ignite properly, and the big shell went forth, flaming gun-cotton marking its path, to land three hundred yards away just behind the British front line, making a huge crater and demolishing the local company headquarters! Thereafter the propellent was improved, but it was thought wiser temporarily to evacuate the front line over which the mortar was firing. It was typical of the infantryman's good humour that the incident was greeted everywhere with laughter and treasured as an excellent jest. War, indeed, has a curious effect upon the sense of humour, and far grimmer pleasantries than this were the subjects of mirth. When a IX. Corps intelligence summary remarked that a German cemetery behind the ridge "appeared to be filling nicely," it was hailed as the joke of the season.

* The heavy and medium batteries were manned by artillery, the Stokes mortars by infantry, personnel.

## THE POLICY OF RAIDS

It was the aim of the Army Commander to harass by all means in his power the troops that faced him, to prevent divisions that were sent down to the Somme from going as fresh troops, and to prevent those others that had been withdrawn from the hell-broth from recovering too quickly and easily from its effects. The intense bombardments with trench artillery were but one weapon in this campaign. Another, as autumn drew on and supplies of ammunition came more freely to hand, was the shelling of approaches and, above all, the railway terminus in Messines, by night. But the principal weapon in this minor offensive was the raiding party. So long as men who took part in the war are alive, the subject of raids is like to crop up whenever two or three are met together. But the conclusion of such discussions is invariably the same. Raids were frequently useful, and sometimes imperatively necessary; but the British raided too often. Raids to obtain identification of troops opposite, and even to keep the enemy "on the stretch," were justifiable; those with the object of raising the moral of our troops were not, because they did not succeed in their object. "No doubt," writes one of the Brigadiers of the 36th Division who was responsible for many raids, "no doubt a successful raid had a good effect in a unit, but not always among the raiding party. The meticulous preparation made the 'waiting-for-the-dentist' period hard and trying. And the raiders were always picked men, who in a battle were of inestimable value. Many units had to deplore the loss of the very cream of their officers, N.C.O.'s, and men in raids. And the cold-blooded courage demanded of all concerned took heavy toll of the nervous energy of even the biggest thruster." The Higher Command, also, often called for raids immediately troops had taken over a line, before they had learnt their way about in "No Man's Land" by dint of patrolling, and before they had recovered from the effects of an attack delivered on some other part of the front.

The record of the 36th Division with regard to raids was from first to last a very high one. The failures were few in comparison with the successes. It was also the case that, while the troops of the Division carried out a great number of successful raids, the number of occasions on which they themselves failed to repulse German raids or lost prisoners to the raiders can be numbered on the fingers of both hands. In the eleven months between the opening of the Somme Offensive and the Battle of Messines, the Division carried out over a dozen raids; but the first hand-to-hand encounter with the enemy took place, not in his trenches, but in "No Man's Land." It is a curious little episode, and deserves to be treated at some length.

It may be mentioned that only a short time before the Somme Battle was the efficacy of the German apparatus for overhearing telephone conversation realized by the British. Till then it had been our easy custom to talk of such important matters as reliefs over the telephone from the front line. It was established that these casual conversations could be picked up by the enemy's instruments, especially in chalky ground. They were accordingly banned, and, after the British manner, from the extreme of imprudence we rushed to a comical extreme of caution. It was currently believed that all conversations within three miles of the line could be heard by the Germans, and brigadiers sometimes found themselves precluded from using the telephone. It was still possible to send telegraphic messages, using the "fullerphone," an invention which greatly diminished the risk of tapping. And an instrument of torture, known as the "B.A.B. Code Book," became part of the equipment of every officer. How many company commanders have sat in their dug-outs translating a series of numerals into amazing gibberish, to discover that they had wasted half an hour by using last month's correction!

On the occasion in question, an officer of the 9th Irish Fusiliers, Lieutenant Godson, conceived the idea of using the listening set of the enemy as a bait to take some of his men. On the afternoon of the 14th of August, he announced in the clearest possible tones, on a telephone at company headquarters in the front line, that an officer and three men would leave the trench at midnight, and move out on the right of the Le Rossignol-Messines Road to reconnoitre the clump of willows in " No Man's Land." At 9-30 p.m. he moved out to this spot with a party of two officers and sixteen other ranks. By 10 he had his force in prearranged formation near the willows, and waited for what might happen. But he must be allowed to tell in his own words, as they were written next morning, the story of his sensations and of his achievement.

"At 11 p.m. I see, I see—what do I see ? A little black mark in the grass forty yards in front that was not there when I looked before. O yes, it was. I look about. The moon is very full out now on our right front. What a nice night, and so quiet! Not a sound from the German lines. I look to the front again. I am getting fed with this. I am wet from head to foot crawling through the wet grass. . . . This is not a job for one man to be at day after day. Everyone ought to take his turn at this. The discomfort is beastly. It is all right till I move, then I have to warm a new place on the dank grass. Hullo! by Jove, I've forgotten that black spot, the only thing in sight I had made a mental note to look at again. . . . It's growing bigger. What the devil is it ? There's another behind, and another. They're coming! I have heard of hearts leaping into the mouth. It meant nothing to me, but by Jove that's what mine did. It nearly made me dizzy just for two seconds. I collect myself Twenty-five yards off and coming, oh, so slowly and cautiously, moving down a little ditch in the open that I had not noticed. . . . I sign to the sick scout to stop his noise and lie close to the ground. I level my revolver. They're coming. And one of the other men is sure to make a noise or cough. . . . I see the first distinctly now, ten yards off,—nine, eight, seven, six, five. He sees something, he whips round, all turn behind him; as far as I can see, three, four, five, six, seven—how many ? Bang, bang, bang, ring out the rifles! I let off five with my revolver, and they have disappeared as if by magic. 'Come on, boys!' I'm up and out. I see a figure on his back. I leap at his throat. 'Kamerad, Kamerad!' he shouts, and waves his hands. Clements whips by me and Ervin and Breen."

The net result of the ambuscade was two Germans killed and four prisoners. That the false message had been overheard could never be exactly proved, but the probabilities seemed to be in that direction.

To summarize the raids carried out or attempted during autumn and winter, there were two on the night of September the 15th, two on September the 30th, three on October the 12th, two on the 31st, and one, the most important, on November the 16th. Of these ten, six were successful in varying degree. The two first were carried out by the 9th Rifles, just east of the Wulverghem-Wytschaete Road, and by the 11th Inniskillings some five hundred yards north of it. The former, by reason of its neatness and the fact that the raiders suffered no loss, must be accounted the best of the series. It was sent to obtain an identification, and it obtained one, a single prisoner. In addition, the officer who led it shot two Germans as he entered the trench, and a third was shot by the flank guard on the left. But the great achievement of the raid was the work of Rifleman Kidd, the champion long-distance bomber of the battalion, a man worth a platoon in such an affair. By his long-range bombing he kept off, single-handed, the German bombers moving up to the rescue, killing three. The British casualties were three men so lightly wounded that they remained at duty. The other raid was notable for very pretty work by the Artillery. At this point, opposite Kruisstraat Cabaret, the British lines jutted out into a work known as the "Bull Ring," which commanded some relatively high ground, about seventy yards from the enemy's trench. The raid was just north of this work, on an enemy trench almost on the same longitudinal line, yet a machine-gun was able to fire from the "Bull Ring" two thousand rounds on the enemy's trenches, while the "box" barrage of the Artillery was put round the raiding party, and no shell came near it. Over thirty Germans were estimated to have been killed,

## A SERIES OF RAIDS

but, unfortunately, the Inniskillings, besides ten wounded, had three wounded and missing. One prisoner was taken as an identification.

The raids on the 30th were part of a series on the whole IX. Corps front. On the right the 11th Rifles did not start, owing to an accidental bomb explosion; in the centre the 10th Rifles were held up by the depth of the wire; on the left the 10th Inniskillings entered the enemy's trenches—after the fuse of their ammonal torpedo had failed to ignite, and the sapper in charge had affixed and lit a new one under the very noses of the German sentries—killed a number of the enemy, blew up dug-outs, took a machine-gun, rifles, and equipment. In the raids of the 12th of October the 108th Brigade had again no fortune at the strongly wired Petite Douve Farm, but the 107th and 109th Brigades each took prisoners. Of the latter raid, carried out by the 9th Inniskillings, it is related that, just before it took place, the two officers who planned it were out in " No Man's Land " having a look round, and lost their way, the trenches being here only fifty yards apart. Having seen some wire they could not agree whether it was "ours or theirs," and tossed a coin in a shell-hole to decide which view should prevail. The winner approached the wire, put up his head, and was fired at at four yards' range—and missed! He bobbed down. Again he took a look, and again there was a miss by the sentry. Finally he heard footsteps approach on the trench-boards, and a voice demand: " Jasus, what what are ye shootin' at ? " That was a welcome and homely sound. *Sotto voce* explanations followed, and he and his companion came in. The raids of October the 31st were held up by showers of bombs from the stout-hearted Swabian peasants of the 26th (Wuertemberg) Division. But the Wuertembergers were wanted on the Somme. On November the 16th the 11th Inniskillings, raiding the Spanbroek salient on a front of two hundred yards, came upon their less formidable successors, a Saxon Division, before they were accustomed to the new trenches, and dealt with them in terrible fashion. Twenty-three dead were counted in the trenches, and more than twice as many must have fallen. The terror-stricken Saxons deserted their front line on a wide front, and the Inniskillings had their pleasure with it for half an hour, looting everything which they could carry over, blowing up all the dug-outs, to the accompaniment of tunes played in " No Man's Land " on mouth organs. Three prisoners were taken. Our losses were slight. One of the few successful raids carried out against the Division in all its career took place on February the 14th, when the enemy obliterated the trenches on the Wulverghem-Messines Road and apparently captured two prisoners.

It will be remembered that the Divisional Artillery, which had come to France consisting of three 18-pounder and one 4.5 howitzer Brigades, had been reorganized in May, the howitzer batteries being divided among the other three Brigades. A second reorganization took place in September, to a basis of six-gun instead of four-gun batteries, though the howitzer batteries did not receive their extra section of two guns till the New Year. The 154th Brigade was broken up, and in February 1917 the 172nd Brigade became the 113th Army Brigade, and left the Division. The details can best be shown by a tabular statement which appears in the " Order of Battle." Henceforth the Artillery consisted of two Brigades only, the 153rd and the 173rd. A large number of Army Brigades were created by the reorganization, and were used to increase the artillery at the disposal of divisions for offensives or in dangerous sectors. The change had some tactical advantages, but the lot of the new Army Brigades, "nobody's children" as it were, and constantly moved from one lively front to another, could not be described as happy.

The Division always worked hard, but there was probably no part of the front in which it attempted and accomplished so much as here. Just at first there was shortage of material, as there was of ammunition, but the situation soon improved. By the labours of the Pioneers and Infantry, working under the supervision of the three Field Companies, the whole trench system was transformed. Parapets were

built stout and strong; parados, where none had been before, appeared to match them. The communication trenches were strengthened and improved by the famous "A" frame, the greatest single blessing that authority provided for troops in Flanders. The deepening of the bed of the Douve, and the removal of obstructions by the Engineers, did much to lessen the winter floods. Trench tramways were laid, good shelters constructed, reinforced concrete being largely employed. Of these the most interesting was the battalion headquarters at La Plus Douve Farm.* As one approached the place, one saw no sign of human occupation, nor of its possibility. There was nothing but a huge roofless farm, built round three sides of a square, as is common in Flanders. But inside one of the wings was an unobtrusive concrete structure thirty feet long, wherein the commanding officer and his staff dwelt in great comfort, above ground, with ample head-room, real windows, and protection from "five-nines." The courtyard remained as it had been when the farm was finally destroyed by bombardment eighteen months before, and its smashed reaping-machine, half a bicycle, and old umbrella, seemed to have grouped themselves after a Bairnsfather drawing.

Mention must here be made of the remarkable underground barracks, made on the southern slopes of Hill 63 by the Australian Tunnelling Company, to which the troops of the Division acted as carriers. Driven into the steep flank of the hill, it was proof against any artillery, lit all through by electric light, and capable of holding two battalions at a pinch. There its charm ended, for it must be confessed that it was damp, close, and malodorous, and that it was impossible to leave a battalion long in it without ill effects upon its health.

For the first three months of 1917 the Division was without its Pioneers, filched by the new "railway king," Sir Eric Geddes. The Pioneers worked with their wonted

---

\* Local names were frequently transformed by British troops, followed by the map-makers. This was probably La Plus Douce. When the Douve overflowed its banks the new name was certainly the more suitable.

vigour on 60 c.m. light railways between Ouderdom, south of the Salient, and Kemmel, and between Busseboom and Dickebusch, and also on broad-gauge work. In their absence it was very difficult to continue the elaborate programmes of construction. A temporary " Works Battalion," one company from each Brigade, with a nucleus of one hundred trained Pioneers, who had been retained, was formed to replace them. It was intensely unpopular with the men, and cannot be said to have been a success. In February practically all work of other natures ceased, so that men might be put to that of wiring. The intense frost had converted the Belgian inundations into solid ice ! They were no obstacle to the enemy, who for some weeks was suspected of the preparation of an offensive. Certainly his artillery had become very aggressive, carrying out heavy bombardments of our trenches and batteries, and shelling camps in rear. The country was literally sown with wire, " Plug Street Wood " being such a tangle that it has always been a mystery to those who saw it how the Germans passed through it in 1918. The alarm died down presently. It had never very serious foundation, but the frost in the ground constituted a risk.

There was one advantage in holding the line in the same area for a long period. It was possible to provide some comfort and recreation for the troops. There were a football competition, boxing competitions, a horse-show, many sports meetings. A large hut was put up at Dranoutre for concerts and other entertainments. Over a long period a 'bus ran daily from " Hyde Park Corner," just outside Ploegsteert village, to Bailleul, which represented with its shops and eating-houses comparative civilization. Many will recall with regret its fine square and beautiful *Hôtel de Ville*, all smashed to powder in 1918. Probably the worst hardships of the troops were due to the intense cold of that winter. Life in the trenches was bad enough, but there were many men who found it easier to sleep there than in their rest camps. A bare, draughty wooden hut, a temperature of fifteen degrees below zero, insufficient fuel ; it does not

## A GROWTH OF ACTIVITY

require much imagination to conjure up the misery implied by such conditions.

With early spring came a great burst of activity. In the last days of the old year the Division had been reorganized on a two-brigade frontage, so that the troops of one Brigade might obtain some rest and training. Now, in mid-March, it closed down to a small front, from the Wulverghem-Wytschaete Road on the right, to a point opposite Maedelstede Farm* on the left. This was held by one Brigade, the second being well back about Flêtre, while the third trained in the pleasant neighbourhood of Lumbres, west of St. Omer. No longer was the Second Army Cinderella. Its area was packed with troops. Even the private soldier, who saw the opening of the splendid new railhead at Haagedoorne, outside Bailleul, with its maze of sidings, saw the country covered with transport lines, saw the dumps grow full, saw the digging of new communication trenches and the laying of light railways, must have realized that something was toward. It is certain at least that the enemy did. On the morning of March the 24th he bombarded the lines of the 107th Brigade on the right flank and those of the New Zealanders, its neighbours, for an hour and a half. Just before dawn his men were seen to issue from their trenches. Caught by our artillery barrage and the fire of machine and Lewis guns, the party was swept away like chaff. He made other unsuccessful attempts to raid the Division. That, however, represented but one aspect of his alertness. The more serious was his persistent shelling of billets and horse-lines, and his bombing of Bailleul. It was also observed that he had large parties at work on his rear lines.

The Second Army was preparing the capture of the Messines-Wytschaete Ridge.

The raiding activity of the Division was renewed in those last weeks of preparation. On several occasions men slipped across in broad daylight to the nose of the Spanbroek salient and threw bombs into the German trenches. On May the

\* See Map II.

19th a raid was attempted from the "Bull Ring," but beaten off by the enemy, who in turn sent over parties in the early hours of the morning, which were beaten off with loss. On May the 23rd the 14th Rifles raided the trenches on the Kemmel-Wytschaete Road, taking a prisoner and confirming the suspicion that the Germans had reinforced their line. On the 29th a very big party of Germans, estimated at a hundred strong, made three attempts to enter the "Bull Ring," but was kept out by the barrage and the fire of the Lewis guns. These raids were without doubt attempts to reach and destroy the mine-shafts in our front line.

Meanwhile there had come into the divisional area, and moved quietly, battery by battery, into the positions already prepared, the Divisional Artillery of the 32nd Division, with four Army Artillery Brigades, making a total of 192 field guns and howitzers on the front. All the positions for the incoming batteries had been constructed by the 36th Divisional Artillery, and much of their ammunition stacked in them ready for their use. Upon this General Brock was most insistent. To him and to the hard work of his subordinates the newcomers owed provision such as incoming batteries all too rarely met with. A great mass of heavy artillery under the orders of the IX. Corps had arrived also, and was bombarding the slope of the Messines Ridge, doing great execution upon the concrete shelters with which it was studded. The Germans could play at this game also, and they had some tempting targets. All over the back areas were horses piqueted in the open, troops in tents. Against these the Germans did much damage with a railway gun, which, as it could easily be moved, was safe from our fire. On the night of May the 27th Divisional Headquarters, which had moved up to their new Ulster Camp, west of Dranoutre, were bombarded by a 10 c.m. gun. A direct hit was obtained on one of the huts, and several clerks were wounded. The shelling continued for two hours, during which the staff and personnel of the headquarters had to take to the fields. That which would have been pure comedy—for such the spectacle of a whole divisional headquarters running about in the dark must undoubtedly appear to the troops—was turned to tragedy by the death of Lieut.-Colonel W. A. de C. King, the C.R.E., who was killed on the spot by one shell. On the following morning General Nugent moved, with his advanced Headquarters Staff, to the command post that had been prepared on the western slope of Kemmel Hill.

On the 31st of May the preliminary bombardment opened.

# CHAPTER V

## MESSINES : JUNE 1917

THE Battle of Messines has more than one claim to a prominent position in the history of the war. It was, in the the first place, the first completely successful single operation on the British front. It shares with the action of Malmaison, fought four months later, the distinction of being the most perfect and successful example of the limited offensive. Lastly, it was by far the most elaborately and carefully "mounted" action ever fought by British arms. Fine as were the fighting qualities of the formations and units that took part in it, the most remarkable aspects which stand out when we look back upon it are the perfection of its organization and of the liaison between all arms. It represented a triumph of staff work. Every man in the huge force under his command was made to feel the guiding hand of the Commander of the Second Army, and of one of the most brilliant staff officers the war discovered. The troops entered upon it with high heart. The capture of the Vimy Ridge had seemed of good augury for the year's campaign. The doubtful success of the French offensive in Champagne, which might have acted as a check upon this optimism, was not generally known.

Before no other battle was there such an infinity of detail to be mastered as in the preparation of this. It would not be difficult to write fifty pages about the plans.

## PREPARATION FOR THE OFFENSIVE 83

Since space permits of about six only being allotted to them, it is impossible to do more than outline them in the briefest manner.

Some idea of the thoroughness of the training for the assault may be gained when it is recorded that not only were attacks practised over ground marked out to represent the German trench system, but officers from the flanking battalions of divisions attended each others' field days to ensure that in the minutest details there was harmony along the line. An elaborate model of the Messines Ridge, with all its trenches, forts, roads, and woods, was constructed by the C.E. of the IX. Corps on the slopes of the Scherpenberg Hill, between Locre and La Clytte. It was surrounded by a wooden gallery and trench-board walks, so that at least a company could examine it at one time. The men took great interest in it, while all day long little knots of officers were to be observed studying it. Another new feature of the attack was the message-map served out on a large scale to officers and N.C.O.'s. This had on one side a map of the German trenches, on which the position could be marked; and on the other a skeleton message-form, bringing forcibly to the mind of the sender those details in a message that were of importance to the recipient, which, in the heat of battle, a young and inexperienced officer might forget.

Nothing was studied more carefully than the provision of food, water, ammunition, and stores for the advancing troops. In front of the huge divisional dumps at Lindenhoek cross-roads and "Daylight Corner," on the Lindenhoek-Neuve Eglise Road, there were an advance dump, a dump for each of the attacking brigades, six battalion dumps, and many smaller in the trenches. An elaborate system of pack transport was devised, two hundred extra pack-saddles with special crates attached being issued. Two hundred and fifty "Yukon packs"—a Canadian device which enabled a man trained in its use to carry a very heavy load—were also issued. Arrangements were made to serve in the trenches a hot meal at midnight prior to the assault. A special ration of oranges, Oxo cubes, chewing gum, and lime juice was issued to every man, and a tin of solidified alcohol for cooking to every fourth man.

Means of communication, by visual signalling, pigeons, wireless, the fullerphone, runners, and the rocket for S.O.S. calls, were worked out in detail. For the fullerphone there were two lines of buried cables, with cable-heads in our front line trenches. Forward stations were selected in the enemy's line at Spanbroekmolen and Peckham, to which armoured lines were to be laid across " No Man's Land," from the cable-heads, by the brigade forward parties. As soon as the final objective was reached, these forward stations were to move to the crest of the ridge. Working independently of this machinery, which was in the hands of the Signal Service, were the brigade and battalion intelligence sections, the former of which were to establish observation posts at Spanbroekmolen and Peckham, while the latter moved up behind their battalions, selected observation posts to follow their movements and cover their final position, and sent out scouts to obtain touch with flanking battalions and bring information as to their progress. For visual signalling a divisional signal station was established on Kemmel Hill, which had a clear line to the brigade forward stations, so that messages could be sent either forward or back by the Lucas lamp.

The Second Army was to attack the Messines-Wytschaete Ridge, and the ground east of it as far as the Oosttaverne line.* The IX. Corps was allotted from the Wulverghem-Wytschaete Road to the Diependaal Beek, a distance of six thousand four hundred yards along the front line of the enemy's salient. It was to attack with three divisions in line : from right to left the 36th (Ulster) Division, the 16th (Irish) Division, and the 19th (Western) Division. These troops were to advance to the Black Line, east of the Messines-Wytschaete Road, after which the 11th Division, in Corps Reserve, was to pass through to the final objective. A glance at the map will show how the frontage

* The boundaries of the 36th Division, the successive objectives, and all the names used in the following description are shown on Map II.

of attack narrowed with every thousand yards of the advance. On the right of the 36th Division was the 25th, in the II. Anzac Corps.

The attack of the 36th Division, of which the final objective was from Lumm Farm to a cutting on the Wytschaete-Oosttaverne Road east of Staenyzer Cabaret, was to be made by two Brigades, the 107th on the right and the 109th on the left, each having one battalion from the 108th Brigade attached. Each Brigade was to attack with two battalions in front, which advanced as far as the Blue Line, the ground in rear of that objective being "mopped up" by the attached battalion of the 108th Brigade. The remaining two battalions of each Brigade were to pass through on the Blue Line for the advance to the Black, providing their own "mopping-up" parties. The 107th Brigade was to use the 8th Rifles on the right and the 9th on the left for the attack on the Blue Line, with the 15th and 10th Rifles to pass through to the Black Line. The 12th Rifles, from the 108th Brigade, carried out the work of "mopping up" and consolidation in rear. The 109th Brigade was to use the 14th Rifles on the right and the 11th Inniskillings on the left to take the Blue Line, and the 10th and 9th Inniskillings to take the Black Line. The 11th Rifles were attached for consolidation and "mopping up." The boundary line between the 36th and 16th Divisions ran, it will be noticed, along the main street of Wytschaete, half the village being in the objective of each Division.

The date of the attack was designated "Z" day, the five days of preliminary bombardment being designated "U," "V," "W," "X," and "Y." There had been considerable bombardment of the ridge before "U" day, but from this day onwards it became more intense. Its object was not the total destruction of the hostile trench system, but the disorganization of the defence by the smashing of concrete emplacements and shelters. It took nothing short of an 8-inch howitzer to destroy the German concrete, while 12-inch and 15-inch howitzers fired on Wytschaete. The cutting of wire was performed by the 18-pounders, assisted in the case of the front line by trench mortars. Further to disorganize the enemy, a programme of barraging night and day his communications, and shelling his billets, was carried out, while bursts of fire with lethal and lachrymatory gas shell of various sorts took place throughout the period. Special half-hour hurricane bombardments of Messines and Wytschaete, during which every gun available, from largest to smallest, was in action, were carried out. The barrage for the advance consisted of, firstly, a creeping barrage of 18-pounder shrapnel, moving in advance of the infantry, with average lifts of a hundred yards, at the rate of a hundred yards in three minutes; and, secondly, a standing barrage of 18-pounders, 4.5 inch howitzers, and medium and heavy howitzers, established in succession on trenches and strong points. For the creeping barrage there was one gun to twenty yards, firing at maximum rate. One gun a section fired smoke shell, to screen the infantry. The barrage was highly complicated, as, owing to the configuration of the German salient and the varying rate of the advance, it lifted off none of the objectives at the same moment all along the line.

Meticulous care was taken by Army Headquarters to ensure that the preparation was as complete as human forethought could make it. Each morning air photographs, showing the effect of the previous day's bombardment, were circulated to Divisions in the line. Each Division was required to state, day by day, what further special bombardment it desired. From its observation post on Kemmel Hill the Staff of the 36th Division could see practically all the slope of the Messines Ridge, from just above the dip of the Steenebeek valley to the crest. Day by day it studied the ground during the bombardment. A trench or concrete work which did not appear to have been sufficiently shelled was noted, and request made that it should receive further attention next day. Such requests were invariably met. Trenches and dug-outs were shelled again and again, till Divisional Headquarters declared itself satisfied. Many of the concrete structures were revealed only when the bombardment of the trenches had blown away the earth about them. They were then subjected to the fire of heavy howitzers till destroyed. Finally, each Division was asked to state if it were satisfied with the preparation. In the case of the 36th Division at least, the answer was an enthusiastic affirmative.

The sympathy and understanding which existed between the Staff of the Second Army and the man in the fighting line created a moral tone of incalculable value to the Army's efficiency as a striking force.

The work of the preliminary bombardment threw a great strain upon the personnel of the artillery, though such rest as possible was given by carefully organized reliefs. The infantry was greatly impressed with the results it could witness. In particular the liaison between infantry and heavy gunners, hardly thought of before this action, was of the closest, the artillery officers bringing battalion commanders aeroplane photographs to show the results of the bombardment on their front.

Stokes mortars and machine-guns were assigned important *rôles* in the early part of the attack. The 3-inch mortars belonging to the Division, less four a brigade, to be taken forward in the attack, were to open a hurricane bombardment for three and a half minutes at "Zero." A battery of 4-inch Stokes mortars, specially attached, was to preface the assault with a bombardment of the Spanbroek salient, with two lifts, using the highly demoralizing incendiary shell known as "thermit." Six guns of the Machine-Gun Companies of the attacking Brigades were to go forward with them; the rest of the guns of these companies, with those of the 108th, the 32nd, two sections of the 33rd, and six guns of the 19th Motor Machine-Gun Battery,* a total of sixty-six guns, were to be employed to provide a creeping barrage beyond that of the artillery, a standing barrage on the main defences of the ridge, and fire on strong points,

---

* The 32nd, half of the 33rd Machine-Gun Companies, and the 19th Motor Machine-Gun Battery, were at the disposal of the 36th Division for the attack.

woods, and ravines. One section of Tanks* was allotted. They were not to catch up the infantry till the Blue Line was reached, and in the advance to the Black Line were to concentrate mainly upon Wytschaete.

All the successive lines, with the exception of the Green, were to be consolidated, special strong points being established at such positions as L'Enfer Farm, Skip Point, and Jump Point, in the Blue Line; and Lumm Farm, Pick House, and Torreken Farm in the Black. The infantry was to start the work of consolidation; then, when the Black Line had been taken, the 121st and 150th Field Companies were to move up to work upon the principal strong points. After dusk on the evening of "Z" day, the 122nd Field Company was to move up and construct a wire entanglement along the whole front of the Black Line. Small opportunity, it will be seen, was left for successful counter-attack if the assault reached its objectives.

Two contact aeroplanes were to be in the air at once throughout the battle, calling at fixed hours, by the sounding of a Klaxon horn and the firing of a Vérey light, for the signals by which the infantry was to mark its progress. The latter consisted of green flares, lit in bunches of three, and the turning of Watson fans, marked white on one side and black on the other.

A whole series of mines, the greatest ever used in war, was to be fired at "Zero." Of these there were three on the 36th Division's front: one at Kruisstraat Cabaret, one at Spanbroekmolen, and one at Peckham. The second had been doubtful up to the last minute. The passage to the charge had been cut some time before by a German defensive "camouflet," and it had seemed as though the toil of a year and of thousands of men had been wasted. The tunnellers of the 171st Company had laboured unceasingly to cut a new gallery. On the eve of the action a scribbled note from the commanding officer to Colonel Place, G.S.O.I. of the Division, announced that the work was accomplished and that it was "almost certain" the mine would go up.

* *i.e.*, four Tanks.

## MEDICAL ARRANGEMENTS

In case there might be failure with this or any other charge, the assaulting infantry was instructed not to wait more than fifteen seconds after the opening of the barrage before leaving its trenches.

For the evacuation of the wounded there was an Advanced Dressing Station at Lindenhoek, close to the main road, skilfully prepared by the 109th Field Ambulance. Wounded could be carried into the main shelter by the entrance on the north side, from the trench tramway, given what attention was necessary, and conveyed out by the exit on the west side, where the motor ambulances of the Division arrived by a specially constructed semi-circular road. This relieved the main road at that point, and enabled the cars to sweep round without turning. The cars bore the wounded to the Main Dressing Station just east of Dranoutre, manned by the 108th Field Ambulance, while "walking wounded" were sent by a specially-marked track to the Main Dressing Station prepared for them and manned by the 110th Field Ambulance a mile east of the village. From these Dressing Stations the Motor Ambulance Park had the task of carrying the wounded to the two Casualty Clearing Stations in Bailleul. Distances were shorter and roads better than on the Somme; and, had the casualties been as many as on that occasion, they would have been removed in less than half the time and with far less discomfort to the wounded. As it most happily chanced, the casualties were less than a fourth of those at Thiepval.

So much for the preparations. Any of importance which have not been mentioned will appear in the account of the actual battle.

The 108th Brigade held the line during the period of preliminary bombardment, employing for the purpose the two battalions which it was to retain during the battle as divisional reserve. It having been decided to carry out some practice barrages in broad daylight, to note the effect of the smoke shell, and see whether any guns were shooting short, these seemed to offer good opportunity for big raids. The first of these raids took place at 3 p.m. on June the

3rd. A party of three officers and seventy other ranks of the 13th Rifles entered the enemy's trenches at Peckham behind the barrage, and after a short bombing fight captured nineteen prisoners of the 2nd German Division. On the following afternoon at 2 p.m., a larger party of the 9th Irish Fusiliers followed the barrage into the Spanbroek salient, returning with one officer and thirty men as prisoners—a remarkable haul for a raid. Their casualties were two killed and six wounded. It was a fine, sunny day, and, despite the haze of dust caused by the shelling, the whole operation could be seen in detail from the observation posts on Kemmel Hill. The barrage, though the rate of fire was but a third of what it was to be on the great day, was very impressive. It appeared a wall of curling smoke creeping slowly up the ridge. The figures of the infantrymen following it could be seen distinctly; there was the flash of bombs, and there were Germans coming from their dug-outs holding up their arms. As the party returned one man was seen to break away from it, walk back fifty yards in most leisurely fashion, summon forth two Germans whom he had evidently observed hiding in a hole, and bring them in at the point of the bayonet.

The day of battle was at hand. Nothing could have been more favourable than the elements to the British cause. The weather was clear for observation, dry, and not unduly cold at night.* The infantry which was to make the attack was bivouacked in tents and shelters, the 107th Brigade south of Locre, the 109th S.W. of Dranoutre, thus avoiding the shelling, particularly with gas, wherewith the Germans visited all our hutted camps. After dusk on June the 6th, "Y" day, these Brigades moved up to their positions of assembly, which consisted partly of our front and support line trenches, and partly of slit trenches specially dug. As on the occasion of the assembly for the Somme Battle, cross-country tracks had been prepared to avoid the congested roads. East of the Neuve Eglise-Lindenhoek Road there were no less than four

* One officer records that, two evenings before the attack, he played bridge in the open air till midnight.

tracks available for each brigade. It was reported that the assembly was complete, without a hitch, by 2-30 a.m. on June the 7th.

The reader must strive to imagine the emotions of the men who waited in the dark for the fateful moment. Some, the luckier ones, those of the battalions and attached troops that were to take the Blue Line, had but another forty minutes, though those forty minutes must have seemed long enough. The battalions which were to pass through them on that objective had two hours after that. It was eleven months since the Division had made its first great attack. Despite its heavy losses on that day and since, there was here a large proportion of officers and men who had taken part in it, including many who had then been wounded. They must have recalled, as they waited for the crash of opening artillery, with what high hopes they had gone forward on the banks of the Ancre. The task must have appeared to them almost equally formidable to-day. And yet there was a general feeling of confidence, and confidence not unreasoned. The British Army had learnt much since then, and the men in the line realized the growth of that knowledge and had their part in it. They had watched the stage prepared for the triumphant *dénouement*, prepared with matchless industry and forethought, and they were ready to play their part fitly when the curtain rose. There was among the men, it may be, less of that spirit of gay, generous, headlong valour, ready to spill itself without a thought of the cost, but there was a greater store of the soldier's craft; the craft which seeks to save itself that it may inflict the more loss upon the opponent. In fighting efficiency the Division, war-tried, but not war-weary, was probably, in the small hours of that June morning, at the highest pitch it ever attained.

Zero was at 3-10 a.m. It had been fixed, after long consultation with Divisions, by the Army as the hour at which men should be able to see just one hundred yards ahead. In the conferences after the battle the general opinion seemed to be that it had been put five or ten minutes too early. It had been arranged that a normal programme of harassing fire should be carried out, as a cessation of this would have appeared suspicious to the enemy. It seemed, nevertheless, to those who watched and waited, that the night was unusually quiet. A few of our howitzers spoke now and again, and from the German lines came regularly the hiccoughing double thud of their great gun, followed by the whine of its missile overhead, on its course to some objective as far back as Hazebrouck.

Then, with one monstrous roar, every British gun upon ten miles of front opened fire. At the same time the great semi-circle of mines exploded, spewing up, as it seemed, the solid earth, of which fragments fell half a mile away, and sending to the skies great towers of crimson flame, that hung a moment ere they were choked by the clouds of dense black smoke which followed them from their caverns. There came first one ghastly flash of light, then a shuddering of earth thus outraged, then the thunder-clap. That opening uproar was heard quite distinctly in England. General Nugent, returning to his command post on Kemmel from the observation post a hundred yards away, declared that the sight he had seen was "a vision of hell."

Amid a gloom still thick and intensified by a smother of dust, the first wave of the infantry sprang from its trenches and went forward. The second followed at twenty-five yards' interval to avoid the German barrage. One of the mines was fifteen seconds late. Curiously enough, it was the doubtful one at Spanbroekmolen. The infantry had obeyed instructions and had not waited for it. A few of the leading men of the 14th Rifles, out in "No Man's Land," were thrown off their feet by the force of the explosion. But there were no casualties, and the men quickly closed in to the barrage. The size of the craters to be skirted and the darkness made the keeping of direction a matter of difficulty. It would have been impossible but for the use of compasses by the platoon commanders. There was considerable overlapping by the troops of the Division on our right, at least two companies of which swung across our front. The body of one of their officers was subsequently found in the bed of the Steenebeek, at L'Enfer Wood, over two hundred yards within the 36th Division's boundary.

There was no resistance by the enemy in his front or support trenches. Dazed and disorganized by the mines and the tremendous weight of artillery, the few survivors surrendered. Two machine-guns only, firing through our barrage, are recorded to have come into action at this stage, on the front of the 109th Brigade. They came into the open when it had passed, on the extreme left flank, and were put out of action, one by a section of rifle grenadiers, the other by a Lewis gun of the 11th Inniskillings. The enemy's barrage was unaccountably light and ragged, even when the violence of our counter-battery fire is considered, and fell upon the British front line. The assaulting troops went straight forward to the Red Line, close upon the barrage, leaving to the "moppers up" the task of taking prisoners. It was reached at Zero plus 35; that is, at 3·45 a.m. Here there was a halt in the barrage of a quarter of an hour, and here the third and fourth company of each battalion "leap-frogged" the first and second for the assault of the Blue Line. The serious business of the attack was but beginning.

As in almost every action of the war, the stoutest-hearted German was the German behind the machine-gun. The artillerymen, with shell hailing upon their positions, were more anxious to withdraw their batteries than to support their infantry, but the machine-gunners lived up to their reputation. As the new waves swept on, dipping now on the right brigade front into the marshy bed of the Steenebeek, guns came into action directly the barrage was past at L'Enfer Wood, Earl Farm, Skip Point, and Scott Farm. At Skip Point, in particular, two guns were handled with boldness, firing till the work was rushed with the bayonet by the 9th Rifles, assisted by a platoon of the 14th, which swung in from the left. There was still resistance in this veritable fortress, and some bombing of its dug-outs. Upwards of a hundred and fifty prisoners were taken in it. At Scott Farm an officer was seen standing on top of the work, encouraging his men. He was shot at long range by a sniper, whereat the defence at this point collapsed. There yet remained, however, Jump Point, the strongest position short of the road. By this time the Intelligence Officer of the 109th Brigade was on the high ground beyond Peckham, in touch with his Brigadier on the telephone. He reported that he saw a yellow flag at Jump Point. Now, the battalion flag of the 14th Rifles was *orange*, a far more significant shade. " I said," writes General Ricardo, " ' Yellow be damned ! ' slammed down the 'phone, called the Division on the other, and said I wished to report that Jump Point was occupied. Corps was informed accordingly, within a few minutes of schedule time. I was asked by B.G.G.S. Corps next day how we managed our information and communications. I told him, ' by orange flags.' " And so the first flag moved forward from the border of the map at IX. Corps Headquarters, which was to mark the progress of the battle, and was stuck into Jump Point.

All along the front the leading waves, well closed up to the barrage, reached the Blue Line at the appointed hour, 4-50 a.m. The troops of the 36th Division were in touch with those of the 25th and 16th Divisions on right and left, both of which also reached their objectives successfully. Here there was a halt of two hours, during which consolidation was begun, during which also the battalions attacking the Black Line, the 15th and 10th Rifles and the 10th and 9th Inniskillings, moved up in artillery formation. The two former battalions had to pass through a light barrage which the enemy had now put down upon the valley of the Steenebeek, but had not many casualties. At 6-50 a.m. the barrage moved forward once more, the fresh troops following it with great dash.

The severest resistance was not met here till the Green Line was past and the troops were almost on the famous road, upon which they had looked so long. Pick House was strongly held. With the rifle grenade it was attacked, while a captured machine-gun was brought into action against it from the flank.* The garrison, which included a battalion commander, then surrendered. A little further north the 10th Inniskillings were held up by a machine-gun. A tank was just in front, but the occupants apparently could not see the gun, nor could the infantrymen attract their attention to it. A sergeant of the Inniskillings ran up to the tank, beat upon its side with a Mills bomb, and so gained the attention of the crew. The tank then bore down upon the machine-gun and put it out of action. Still further north, on their extreme left flank, the 10th had trouble from a line of riflemen behind a ditch. A platoon of their neighbours, the 9th Inniskillings, outflanked this party, killing three and making prisoners of the rest. In their half of Wytschaete the 9th Inniskillings had some "mopping up" to accomplish, and took about fifty prisoners. Their neighbours, the Munsters of the 16th Division, had a like task in the northern half of the village—a village that was now a crumbled rubbish-heap of bricks, nowhere more than a few feet high.

But the point at which resistance was most dogged was on the extreme right, and it was the 15th Rifles which had the heaviest casualties among the infantry. The following graphic account is taken from a letter written by Captain P. K. Miller, who commanded the right flank company of this battalion:

"About a hundred, or perhaps two hundred, yards short of the Messines-Wytschaete Road we came into a lot of machine-gun fire, and the men went to ground to find out where it came from, so I crossed the road and lay down on the other side for about five minutes and got my field-glasses going. Very warm spot, as our barrage was dropping about there ! Beat it back to the company, and ordered Lieut. Falkiner to take his platoon, less Lewis-gun team, and put out of action the strong point which I had spotted

* Our own Vickers gun teams had dropped behind the infantry here. Vickers guns, tripods, and belt boxes are very heavy loads on ground cut to pieces by shell-fire.

on my right. Got the L.G. in action to spray the place meantime (had three out of five riflemen killed doing this; however, they kept the gun going). Then I went along to left of line and started Lieut. —— of 'B' Company (forget his name, but he got the M.C. for it) to attack another S.P. which was plugging at our left. (O.C. 'B' Company had got a 'blighty' coming up hill.) Then I went back to the right of the line and found that Lieut. Falkiner had got Lumm Farm. The Huns put up a fight here. However, one of the concrete places was bombed by Riflemen Aicken and Cochrane. In the other the Hun officer and Lieut. Falkiner had a rough-and-tumble fight. The Hun collared him somehow round the waist, but he managed to get an arm free and shot him, and his men came tumbling down after him and finished the rest of them. About fifteen were left alive and surrendered. . . . I then pushed all the men on a hundred yards and started them digging. . . . Some time later the commander of the (25th Division) company on my right came along and asked me if I would let him use Lumm Farm as a company headquarters, as he had no dug-outs in his sector. So I gave him one of the rooms—there were three or four in the dug-out."

The final part of this first-hand narrative is inserted because, in a book recently published, the capture of Lumm Farm is attributed to the 25th Division.*

Consolidation of the Black Line was started. At 8·40 a.m. patrols pushed forward in touch with those of the 25th and 16th Divisions, and established themselves without much difficulty a thousand yards ahead, on what had been known on the preliminary plans as the Dotted Black Line, afterwards called the Mauve Line, which was held as an outpost line. Meanwhile, in the lull that followed, the field artillery was moving forward. Most of the batteries moved to the neighbourhood of the old British front line, but batteries of the 153rd and 173rd Brigades crossed " No

\* *The 25th Division in France and Flanders.* By Lieut.-Colonel M. Kincaid-Smith.

Man's Land," and established themselves as far forward as the Red Line. The gunners, in the enthusiasm of victory, forgot their fatigue and the strain of those sleepless nights of bombardment, and rushed their guns forward over the difficult ground with the delight of schoolboys. At 10-5 a.m. it was reported to General Nugent that batteries of the 173rd Brigade were in position. A few minutes later came a similar report with regard to the 153rd Brigade. Not for upwards of two hours was there sign of a counter-attack in force. Then the IX. Corps announced that long columns of troops and transport had been observed by balloon and aeroplane moving west from the canal at Houthem. The German command had, however, been too slow. By this time good progress had been made with the work of consolidation of the Black Line, and of the strong points in rear of it, the latter of which the engineers of the 121st and 150th Field Companies had already taken in hand. In addition to the wire brought forward on pack mules, far greater quantities of German wire had been found, particularly at one big dump near Guy Farm. All the twelve Vickers guns which had gone forward with the infantry had arrived successfully. There were now three in position north of Lumm Farm, three between Guy Farm and Staenyzer Cabaret, three some hundred yards west of the main road, and two in reserve. All the sixteen guns of the 108th Machine-Gun Company were in position in their rear, a battery of eight east of L'Enfer Wood, four at Jump Point, and four on Hill 94, at the south-west corner of Wytschaete. A big counter-attack would have driven in the outposts on the Mauve Line; it appeared improbable that it would dislodge our troops from the Black. When it came, a little after one o'clock, it was not on the front of the 36th Division, but on that of its right-hand neighbours, the 25th and New Zealand Divisions. The Germans came forward stoutly enough across the open ground, but the attack got nowhere near the British lines. Before the terrific blast of our barrage it withered away and dispersed.

The heat was now very great and the stench round

Wytschaete from the many horses that had been killed by our bombardments of the past week was almost overwhelming. The troops were suffering from fatigue. It was the hour at which reaction from the strain he has endured, and the high pitch to which he has keyed himself, begins to creep upon all but the very strongest of men. They solaced themselves during the intervals of digging and wiring with the doubtful joys of German ration cigars, found in great quantities in some of the dug-outs. The Germans had begun to shell Messines and Wytschaete heavily.

The hour of the " New Zero "—that is, for the passing through of the troops of the 11th Division—had been fixed meanwhile at 3-10 p.m. At 12-20 p.m. came an order from the IX. Corps that the Mauve Line was to be held in force and consolidated, so that a good second line of defence should be prepared by the time the 11th Division had captured the Oosttaverne Line. Each Brigade was accordingly instructed to garrison the Mauve Line with a battalion. Each Brigadier decided to use the attached battalion of the 108th Brigade which had been employed for " mopping up," and so was fresher than his other battalions. Before three o'clock the 12th and 11th Rifles were upon the Mauve Line, and at work putting it into a state of defence.

Punctually at 3-10 p.m. the 34th Brigade of the 11th Division moved through the Mauve Line, behind a splendid barrage and with four tanks. Though less artillery was firing, the barrage was even thicker than had been that of the 36th Division, owing to the frontage having been reduced to less than one half. It reached its objective, the Oosttaverne Line, but was subjected to intense bombardment from the German artillery, now all east of the Canal. The IX. Corps Cavalry went through at 6 p.m.—too late, even if it had ever had a chance. It suffered casualties from machine-gun fire, and could make little or no progress.

The 16th Rifles (Pioneers) had attacked their heavy task of road-making. Bridges for the trenches had been prepared and were set in position. Shell-holes were hastily filled. With such a will did the two companies on the road work, that before dusk wheeled transport could move on the Lindenhoek-Messines Road beyond the great crater in the Spanbroek salient. Another company cleared tracks for pack transport up to the Black Line, marking them out with white stakes and notice-boards. After the taking of the Oosttaverne Line the battalion turned its attention to the top of the ridge, clearing old communication trenches and cutting new ones. The 122nd Field Company put up a fine obstacle along the whole length of the Black Line, using, for the most part, German wire. This task was completed by 3 a.m. on June the 8th.

It was an ideal opportunity for the employment of pack transport. Once the enemy had been pushed off the ridge it was secure from ground observation, while, as for German aeroplanes, they had no chance to cross our lines, so complete was the British mastery of the air. The pack was one of the successes of the battle. Officers commanding battalions had in most cases picked their headquarters in the enemy's lines days before, and told their transport officers they would expect them at such an hour with the rations, just as if they had been holding the most placid trenches on the front. They were not disappointed. Indeed, mules were moving up with grenades, water, and wire, before ever the Black Line was reached. The transport officers of the battalions showed in this action that long months of stagnation in the war had not robbed them of their initiative.

The forward slopes of the Messines Ridge, ere dusk put for a while a decent veil upon it, presented a ghastly spectacle to bear witness to the destructive power of modern artillery. The ground had been literally ploughed up. L'Enfer Wood, which had remained a considerable copse of stunted trees through years of shell-fire, was now but an indeterminate collection of stumps. Some of the concrete structures had disappeared. The Steenebeek stream was a stream no more. Its path was marked by mud thicker than elsewhere, and where its bed had been the shell-holes were full of water. There were a number of dead Germans in the valley, with their faces turned toward the hill. They had run back before the dreadful moving wall of the British barrage, and had been caught by it in the marshy ground. Some lay on their faces, arms outstretched. It was a sight that, at normal times, would have filled the breast of everyone who witnessed it with pity and horror. But in such moments the wells of these emotions are almost dried up.

At night the 108th Brigade relieved the 107th and 109th in the line; that is to say, its remaining battalions, which had been in divisional reserve, relieved the troops holding the Black and Blue Lines, while General Griffith took command of the front. The relieved troops moved back to the comparative comfort of the old British trenches. The night was very disturbed. On more than one occasion the S.O.S. rocket went up on the right of the Division, and at 10 p.m. a counter-attack on Messines was reported. If counter-attack there was, it was of small account. No big attack could, in fact, have been carried out in the darkness. Morning dawned, leaving the British in secure occupation of the battlefield and all their objectives. The ridge was, however, subjected to very heavy shelling all that day and at night, when the 150th Field Company had a very wild task in wiring the whole of the Mauve Line. On the afternoon of the following day, at 4 p.m., command of the sector, the actual front line of which had been held for upwards of forty-eight hours by his troops, passed to the G.O.C. 11th Division. That night the 32nd Brigade of the 11th Division relieved the 108th Brigade in the Mauve, Black, and Blue Lines, the weary battalions moving back to bivouac on the slopes of Kemmel Hill. On the 16th the Headquarters of the 36th Division returned to their old village, St. Jans Cappel.

The total number of prisoners captured by the 36th Division in the offensive was 31 officers and 1,208 other ranks. Against this its casualties, to the night of June the 9th, when it was relieved, were 61 officers and 1,058 other

## DEATH OF CAPTAIN GALLAGHER

ranks. In the actual assault, the losses were probably not above seven hundred. Other divisions, notably some of the Australians of the II. Anzac Corps, suffered more severely than the 36th; but, on the whole, it seems safe to presume that the German losses were more than thrice our own. One prisoner stated that practically all his company was destroyed by one of the mines, while the tenor of the letters found upon others was that it had been " far worse than the Somme." No German field guns could be withdrawn by our troops before the Division was relieved, but a number were captured between the Black Line and the Mauve. Among the comparatively few officers killed was Captain H. Gallagher, D.S.O., of the 11th Inniskillings, whose gallantry and fine leadership upon the Somme have been recorded. At the beginning of the action his right arm was shattered by a fragment of shell. Urged to go back, he laughingly refused, threw down the rifle he was carrying, and took his revolver in his left hand, saying : " This will do me rightly." He led his company to its objective, and was returning later to have his arm dressed when he was killed instantly by a shell. He was buried in the old " No Man's Land," just outside the " Bull Ring," which he had so often held, from which he and his company had repulsed a big German raiding party a short while before.

The 16th Division lost one distinguished man in Major William Redmond, M.P., who was brought in by stretcher-bearers of the 36th Division, and conveyed to its Main Dressing Station. He had been attached to Divisional Headquarters, but had insisted on rejoining his regiment for the battle. His wound was light, but he was no longer a young man, nor in a state of physical fitness to withstand such a strain. He died some hours later.

The 36th Division had by no means finished with the Messines-Wytschaete Ridge, even for this year; but before dealing with its last days in the area, it may be not unprofitable to speculate upon the causes of this triumphant success. If this account has achieved its object, the majority of them will stand out clearly enough. In the conferences after the battle, and in reply to *questionnaires* issued by the commanders, there were very few criticisms made. Zero, as has been stated, was considered to have been too early, though by not more than a few minutes at most. All the infantry was enthusiastic about the manner in which the artillery had been handled, and about the effect of the barrage. Some battalions considered that it had been set to move rather too fast, but the general opinion was that the infantry had been able to keep up with it comfortably enough, and that the pace was a factor in the success. The mines, it was agreed, had been decisive in the capture of the front-line system, and had exercised a great moral effect much farther back. The tanks had been a success. They were useful in incidents such as that which has been described, and they probably saved the infantry some casualties on the top of the ridge. Broadly speaking, however, they did not appear to have exercised any great effect upon the course of the battle. Brigadiers and battalion commanders were unanimous in praise of the smoothness with which the machinery worked from behind. The services of supply—the Divisional Train, Supply Column, and Divisional Ammunition Column—were at their best, and their standard of excellence was high. The Ordnance had responded to every demand made upon it for the multifarious material used in the offensive.

With regard to the infantry itself, the most interesting feature of the Battle of Messines was the triumph of the platoon. Each platoon had now a Lewis-gun section and a section of rifle grenadiers. It was converted thereby into a little self-sufficing force, an army in miniature, with every weapon necessary for the carrying out of the minor operations likely to confront it in such an assault. Some of the platoon leaders displayed in this battle a high order of tactical skill.

But let us glance also at the affair from the other side, where a German Army Commander, the famous Sixt von Armin, was seated at his map-table. What were the problems that confronted him, and how did he face them ?

## GERMAN COMMANDER'S PROBLEM

The Germans meant to hold the ridge if they could. It was a valuable position that had cost them dear in the winning. They knew an attack was coming, but they put it one or two days later than it was delivered. The Higher Command was well aware that the troops in the trenches were in no fit state to meet it, after days of terrific pounding, heavy losses, and shortage of food. It was in the act of relieving them when the attack was launched. The relief of one Division was incomplete when the mines went up and the British bayonets came in the dark upon the columns in the communication trenches. The confusion must have been indescribable. Again, the German position, admirable for trench warfare, had weaknesses in such a battle as this. It was a sharp salient, with a semi-circle of artillery about it. The artillery had excellent observation. Had the weather been misty, Kemmel would have been of little avail, and the work of destruction comparatively ineffective. But the atmosphere was wonderfully clear. The British fire upon the forts was overwhelming. The counter-battery work was the best accomplished in the war. An average of one gun to every German battery in action was destroyed by our fire, according to the evidence of captured artillerymen. The loss in horses alone constituted a severe blow. As to the counter-attack, which was made in the afternoon with the 7th and probably regiments of the 24th Divisions, it was launched late, and met the full weight of our barrage. With its failure the High Command appears to have decided, wisely no doubt, to abandon the struggle, and made all haste to get every gun left to it east of the Canal d'Ypres. It must have appeared to it that the position held by the British offered doubtful results to a counter-attack in force. The latter had now all the best of the ground, and a great counter-attack upon the re-entrant held by them would have required more troops than the enemy probably had available.

On the 13th of July the 36th Division, less its Artillery, which remained in position, moved to the area between Mont Noir and Bailleul. A certain amount of rest was obtained, but large parties of infantry had to work under the Chief Engineer of the IX. Corps. However, better things were in prospect, the Division being under orders to move back to Merris. These orders were suddenly cancelled. On the night of the 19th, the 107th Brigade on the right, and the 109th on the left, took over from the 11th Division the whole front now held by the IX. Corps, from the Blauwepoortbeek at Deconinck Farm, just north of the village of Gapaard, on the right, to Rose Wood, north of the Roozebeek, on the left. The length of the front was about three thousand yards. The Headquarters of the 107th Brigade were established in a company headquarters of our old trenches, those of the 109th Brigade in enemy dug-outs in the northern part of Grand Bois. On the 20th, 36th Divisional Headquarters opened at Ulster Camp.

The holding of a new-won position after a great attack was always an unpleasant task. In this case the conditions were, from some points of view, more difficult than those of the capture of the ridge. "Jerry was angry," said the men, with justice. The Germans now had a mass of heavy artillery behind the Canal d'Ypres, and day and night they shelled the British forward positions and the western slope of the ridge. On their second day in the line the Headquarters of the 109th Brigade in the Grand Bois were so heavily bombarded that General Nugent decided they should be withdrawn to a company headquarters in our old lines. The troops in the front trenches were on a forward slope, very exposed to observation, and suffered heavily. At night ration parties on the roads had many evil experiences. Casualties rarely amounted to less than a hundred for the period of twenty-four hours, and several battalions had considerably greater losses in ten days of this experience than in the period from the 7th to the 9th of June.

Nor was it alone upon areas over which he had observation from the ground that the enemy was able to bring to bear accurate fire. Parties on railway work, lorries on the Wytschaete Road, suffered very heavily also. The reason was that the situation in the air had altered.

## VON RICHTHOFEN

British supremacy there had been absolute. Not a German aeroplane had been seen during the battle. Since then certain of our squadrons had moved north to the Salient. The German air force, on the contrary, had been heavily reinforced. In particular the famous Richthofen, with a squadron of very fast single-seater scouts, painted bright red, raged up and down the front, catching many of our comparatively slow photographic and artillery aeroplanes, and shooting them down. Another favourite device of his was to sweep low over our trenches, firing belt after belt upon the infantry in them, who retorted, without much effect, by the fire of machine-guns on anti-aircraft mountings. But his most spectacular feat was undoubtedly the burning of our balloons. Of these there was a great number on the front. From Kemmel about fourteen could be counted, stretching almost to the coast on one side, and perhaps to Estaires on the other. For men in the neighbourhood of the hill it became one of the interests of those sunny afternoons to watch the balloons. The programme was always of a similar nature. There would be a sudden uproar of anti-aircraft fire, a fast-moving dot would approach one of the balloons, two silver dots below the latter would represent the observers making their way earthwards in their parachutes. A tiny flicker of fire would appear atop of the balloon, swiftly growing and spreading. Within a few seconds the flaming mass would sink slowly. Sometimes the aggressor would dart straight off to the next balloon in the line, and repeat the process with that. On the afternoon of June the 23rd, three balloons in succession were brought down by one aeroplane. It must, however, have been displeasing to the Germans to observe how swiftly every balloon burnt by them was replaced.

. The German infantry, it must be added, was entirely unaggressive, nor was it easy to locate its positions. It held the ground west of the Canal d'Ypres with isolated posts, and made no effort to improve the half-dug trenches already existing. All labour was concentrated upon the positions east of the Canal.

On the 29th a welcome relief of the 36th by the 37th Division took place. On the following day the G.O.C. 37th Division took over command of the front, the whole of the 36th Division, less Artillery, Engineers, and Pioneers, moving to the Merris area. The Headquarters of the Division and that of the 108th Brigade were in that village; the 107th Brigade at Outtersteene, and the 109th at Strazeele. The batteries, which had withdrawn to their forward wagon-lines for rest on the 19th, had returned to the line by the 27th in relief of the 11th Divisional Artillery, and remained there till July the 5th, under heavy hostile shelling, in indifferent weather with poor visibility. The Pioneers and Field Companies had but a day's rest before being moved to the Salient to begin new work.

The first week of July was given to rest and training at Merris.

## CHAPTER VI

### THE BATTLE OF LANGEMARCK: AUGUST 1917

ON July the 7th the Division, less Artillery, Engineers, and Pioneers, moved to the training area south-west of St. Omer, headquarters being established at Wizernes. The area was considerably smaller than that occupied the previous summer after the Somme fighting, being in fact the southern portion of the latter. Billeting accommodation in the villages was inadequate, and had to be augmented by tents. Small hardship this in such weather and such surroundings. Many officers whose lodging was entirely comfortable chose for preference to sleep in the open air, or in tents in the cherry orchards. The men were soaked in sunshine. Old friendships of 1916, and of the early spring, when Brigades had been training for Messines, were renewed. Fishermen obtained some excellent trout-fishing. In fact, the Division probably never had, during all its service in France and Flanders, a pleasanter period than these twelve days of rest and training. They ended with a great gymkana at Acquin on the 23rd, with horse-races, mule-races, jumping, transport competitions, wrestling on horseback, and sports of all kinds. A feature of the afternoon was the "divisional drag," whipped by Major S. H. Green, the D.A.Q.M.G., with a team of horses borrowed from Signals, trained and mannered to a point not unworthy of the Coaching Club, but undoubtedly on the heavy side—and the hairy!

On moving to Wizernes the 36th Division had come under the command of the XIX. Corps, Fifth Army, General Gough having moved north from Artois for the impending battle. The Artillery, Engineers, and 16th Rifles had not shared the good fortune of their comrades. Relieved at Wytschaete on July the 5th, the former had marched straight to wagon-lines off the Poperinghe-Ypres Road, coming under the orders of the C.R.A., 55th Division. By the night of the 7th one section of each 18-pounder battery was in action in the northern part of the Salient, on the Ypres-Poelcappelle Road. A week later all the batteries were in positions allotted by the 55th Division for the opening attack, the preliminary bombardment for which began on the 16th. The Field Companies and Pioneers moved first to the region about Watou, half-way between Cassel and Poperinghe, where they were engaged in digging new wells to improve the water supply for the great numbers of troops that would be passing through during the offensive. This was hard work but safe. After three weeks of it, however, they moved forward, and were henceforth employed on road repair and the making of cross-country tracks for men and animals. At this work they suffered much from shelling, and particularly from gas shell. The 150th Field Company, of its complement of six officers, had three killed and two wounded within a week; as well as losing a high proportion of its sappers.

The Division moved up at the end of July in huge brigade convoys of 'buses and lorries, and by the 30th was in the back area of the XIX. Corps, between Watou and Poperinghe. Headquarters were established temporarily in the latter town at two houses in the rue d'Ypres. The following morning began the terrible struggle which is generally known as the third Battle of Ypres.*

The great attack launched that morning was the second stroke of a campaign which had begun triumphantly at

---

\* The official title of the campaign is " The Battles of Ypres, 1917 "; that of the action of August 16th, in which the 36th Division took part, " The Battle of Langemarck."

Messines. The plans made for 1917 by the Allied Command had been thrown into some confusion by the retirement of the German armies on the Somme to their Hindenburg system, in March, and later by the stopping of General Nivelle's great offensive in Champagne.* The British had certainly played their part at Arras and Messines. The British Command could obviously now not count upon another great French offensive for some little while, and it was under the vital necessity of keeping the German armies heavily engaged. Its greater object was to strike at the Belgian coast, where the submarine bases of Ostend and Zeebrugge were becoming a menace so serious to the very existence of the nation. That scheme has not been made public, and its details can be no more than a matter of surmise to any but those in the confidence of the British Command, or the Imperial General Staff. It will not be discussed here. It is known, however, pretty generally, that it involved an attack upon the coast-line and a landing. Camps had been formed near Dunkirk, surrounded by barbed wire, where divisions were to be assembled in greatest secrecy. And as for the attack in the Salient, a glance at a railway map will show how serious an advance across the Passchendaele Ridge upon Roulers would have been to the German communications. A threat to the next great railway, the main Brussels line between Ghent and Bruges, would probably have led to the abandonment of the coast by the enemy. Ludendorff, in mid-July, while the 36th Division was enjoying its repose in peaceful country, had made one move in the game—no more than the move of a pawn in such a struggle, but a clever and effective one. At Lombartzyde, outside Nieuport, he had launched an attack against our troops upon the little slice of ground held by them north of the Yser Canal, driving them back into the river. Two divisions had very serious losses, including over a thousand prisoners, and, worst of all, the

* The attack, after very heavy losses, was stopped by the orders of the French Government. History will decide whether the stopping was right or wrong. General Mangin, who commanded an Army in it, has given his reasons for the belief that the attack should have continued.

"jumping-off" ground for an attack on the coast line had been snatched away.

Even if they failed in the ambitious venture, the British could at least hope, beside continuing their policy of striking blow upon blow at the enemy, to make an end of the accursed Ypres Salient, and drive the Germans from the dominating semicircle of higher ground from which they had so long harassed our troops. Half of this task had indeed been accomplished by the Battle of Messines. The southern curve of the Salient had almost disappeared. It remained to cut away the northern. The great part of the fighting of Ypres, 1917, was to take place north of the Zonnebeke Road.

The attack launched on July the 31st by the Fifth Army of General Gough, and the First French Army of General Anthoine on his left, met with a considerable measure of success. At its outset, indeed, the success appeared complete; but the Germans, holding their positions lightly and in depth, with the local counter-attack as one of the main weapons of defence, retook much of the ground won. The Pilkem spur was, however, in our hands. Great as had been our losses, the attack upon a position of tremendous strength had gone well enough for a beginning. But the weather, so pitiless on the Somme, that had almost startled pessimists by its unwonted mercy at Messines, broke that very day. Ere afternoon was over rain began to fall in torrents. By the following morning the ground, ploughed up by weeks of shell-fire, was a sea of mud.

The 55th Division, in the fate of which the 36th Division was particularly interested, since its artillery was supporting the attack, and its other arms were to relieve their Lancashire comrades in that sector at a later date, had fared as well as any other. The troops had gone forward with great dash and had almost everywhere reached their final objective, known as the Green Line, east and just south of St. Julien. The leading battalions had, however, suffered very heavy loss from the fire of German machine-guns, distributed in depth, and had not been sufficiently strong to resist the counter-attack when it came. They were driven in upon the second objective, or Black Line, which followed, roughly speaking, the line of the road running south-east from St. Julien to the farm known as Pommern Castle, in the Pommern Redoubt.* It was an advance of fifteen hundred yards. To the south affairs had gone less well, and the Black Line remained to be taken.

It had been the intention of the Commander of the XIX. Corps to keep the assaulting troops in line after they had made their attack, till the eve of the next. The result of the Battle of Langemarck was greatly affected by the fact that this resolution was not kept. The 55th Division had suffered so greatly, and its infantry was in a state of such fatigue, that it was decided to withdraw it at once. The decision may have been inevitable; on that point the Corps Commander, General Watts, was alone in a position to form a judgment. For him and the 36th Division alike, it was disastrous. It meant that for his next attack he had in his hands a Division jaded, weary, shaken by deadly shell-fire, having lost a good third of its infantry strength ere ever it left its trenches for the assault.

On the morning of August the 2nd, the 107th Brigade entrained at Poperinghe and detrained at the famous Goldfish Château, west of Ypres, coming under the orders of the 55th Division, to which it had been allotted as a reserve. While his Brigade was on the move, General Withycombe received orders from the 55th Division for it to relieve the 164th Brigade in the old British front-line trenches. The General reached Wieltje, the Headquarters of the 164th Brigade, at 12-45 p.m. Three-quarters of an hour later he received a telegram from the 55th Division ordering a further relief, that of the much-depleted 165th and 166th Brigades in the captured German positions. His men had a long march in heavy rain, and had not completed the relief of the 164th Brigade till 3-40 p.m. The new relief was entirely unexpected, and was not in accordance with the intimation received by General Nugent that his troops

* See Map III.

were to be used as a reserve. It was carried out in continuous rain, through mud eighteen inches deep, under heavy fire from howitzers of heavy calibre, and in the midst of bombing attacks launched against the right flank of the 55th Division. Not till six o'clock on the morning of August the 3rd was its completion announced. The Brigade had had heavy casualties, particularly the 10th and 15th Rifles, which had taken over the Black Line. After that night's work, in fact, there could be no question of employing those battalions in the coming attack.

That night two battalions of the 108th Brigade, the 13th Rifles and 9th Irish Fusiliers, relieved the 165th Brigade, which had moved back to the old British front and support lines; and two battalions of the 109th Brigade, the 11th Inniskillings and 14th Rifles, the 166th Brigade; the whole force under the command of General Withycombe, G.O.C. 107th Brigade, who had his headquarters in the great mined dug-outs at Wieltje. Divisional Headquarters were established at Mersey Camp, north of the Poperinghe-Ypres Road, and about mid-way between the two towns, taking over command at 4 a.m. on August the 4th. On taking over the line from the 55th Division, General Nugent decided that, in view of the dreadful conditions, it might be held more lightly, and withdrew two of the supporting battalions to camps about Brandhoek and Vlamertinghe, replacing them by companies of the supporting battalions of the 107th Brigade. There were other reliefs during the period of waiting, all the battalions having a turn, though the six which were to lead over on August the 16th were saved as much as might be. The headquarters of the Brigades also took turn about in command of the line, in the filth and stenches of Wieltje dug-outs.

Wieltje dug-outs! Who that saw it will forget that abominable mine, with its "town major," its thirteen entrances, the water that flowed down its main passages and poured down its walls, its electric light gleaming dully through steam-coated lamps, its sickly atmosphere, its smells, its huge population of men—and of rats? From behind sack-curtained doorways the coughing and groaning of men in uneasy slumber mingled with the click of typewriters. In the corridor one would fall over a runner, slimy from head to foot with mud, resting while he waited for a return message to the front line. One advantage only it had : it was safe within. And that was in part counterbalanced by the danger of exit and entrance, constantly menaced by storms of fire. The cross-country tracks, simply paths from which wire had been cleared, behind it, were more horrible still. Their object was to allow troops and pack animals—even the shells for the field artillery had to go forward by pack—to avoid roads under constant shellfire. But the Germans now knew them every whit as well as the roads, and shelled them all day with every calibre up to 8-inch howitzers. No one who used them but had at some point to lie crouched on his belly, watching huge columns of earth and water spout up with the burst of the big shells. Horrors were not new, nor did the sight of dead bodies affect men overmuch, but there was one vision upon one of these tracks, the mangled remains of a complete party of artillery carriers, six men and twelve horses, which burnt itself upon the brains of those that saw it.

The war had in those days reached its worst stage. Gas shelling and aeroplane bombing were at their height. The infantry resting in the camps between Vlamertinghe and Elverdinghe had to endure, night after night, the crashing of great bombs among the huts and tents. The casualties to horses were very high, a horse being ten times as vulnerable as a man to bombs. The Casualty Clearing Stations probably suffered higher losses than in any other battle of the war. The counter-battery work was ferocious on both sides. For our batteries there was little concealment, and for their guns and teams little shelter. The gunners of the 36th Division, who had been in action at the opening of the Battle of Langemarck for over a month, suffered from strain and discomfort perhaps even more severely than the infantry on this occasion. And, day after day, fell the rain.

In the trenches the mud and the artillery fire were the most serious foes. The German infantry could easily be held. There was one counter-attack on the 8th, on the extreme left. Our bombing squads moved up and drove the enemy out. On the 10th the II. Corps on the right attacked to establish itself upon the Black Line, the artillery covering the 36th Division co-operating. The attack was in the main successful, and the way was prepared for a further advance. On the night of the 14th the troops of the 107th Brigade, then in front line, were relieved, and those which were to carry out the attack moved up, picking up their bombs and special equipment at battle stores previously established as far forward as possible, past which the platoons moved slowly in single file.

The final objective of the 36th Division was from a point on the Zonnebeke-Langemarck Road near Gallipoli Copse, on the right, to Aviatik Farm on the left. This was represented by a series of strong concrete forts, and known as the Red Line. The 16th Division was attacking on the right and the 48th Division on the left of the 36th. The attack of the 36th Division was to be made by the 108th Brigade on the right and the 109th Brigade on the left, with the 107th Brigade in reserve. Each Brigade was to attack with two battalions in front line, one in support, about a thousand yards in rear, and one in reserve, in the old British front and support lines. Each battalion was to attack on a two-company front, in four waves. The second and fourth waves were to be only half the strength of the first and third, owing to companies having been reduced for the time being to three platoons. The objective of the leading companies was the line Gallipoli-Schuler Farm, the old Green Line of the first offensive, still so-called. On this line the rear companies were to pass through to the final objective, the original leading companies following in close support. The supporting battalions were then to move up and take over the Green Line. A company from each of the supporting battalions was allotted to the leading two battalions on each brigade front as "moppers up."

Special platoons were given as their objectives such concrete strongholds as Somme, Pond Farm, Hindu Cott, Green House, Schuler Farm. Four guns of each of the Machine-Gun Companies of the attacking brigades were to go forward with the infantry, the remainder being used for the barrage. No Stokes mortars could be taken forward owing to the state of the ground. The task of the R.E. was the consolidation of the Dotted Green Line. This was to be a defensive system on our side of the wire running from Gallipoli Copse through Green House, using that obstacle for our own purposes. That of the Pioneers was the clearance of the Wieltje-Gravenstafel Road.

The field artillery, under the orders of General Brock, the C.R.A., consisted of the 36th and 61st Divisional Artilleries and the 108th and 150th Army Field Artillery Brigades. For the creeping barrage there were fourteen 18-pounder batteries, giving, as at Messines, about one gun to twenty yards. There were four 18-pounder batteries for distant barrage, to search hidden ground, and deal with strong points beyond the creeping barrage, while the six 4.5 howitzer batteries fired a hundred yards ahead of the latter, resting on all known strong points and machine-gun emplacements. The pace of the barrage was a hundred yards in five minutes, with a pause of thirty-five minutes in front of the Green Line. This seems as slow as could well be, but events were to prove that it was too fast in the conditions. There were three gas-shell bombardments prior to the attack, the last being on the night of the 15th, "Y/Z" night. For these there was allotted a hundred rounds per 18-pounder and fifty rounds per howitzer. One section of tanks was to take part in the attack, but there was at no time a probability of tanks reaching our front line. Zero was at 4·45 a.m.

There was very heavy shelling of the assembly trenches and the roads in rear during the night of the 15th. A small dug-out occupied by the headquarters of the 14th Rifles near Spree Farm was hit repeatedly, and it was impossible to keep alight a candle inside it. So excellent, however, was the German concrete, that it held out. Between midnight and 2-30 a.m. the four leading battalions must have suffered on an average fifty casualties apiece.

The story of the attack, alas! is not a long one. The German barrage came down swiftly, but, as it was for the most part on the assembly trenches and behind them, it had small effect upon the leading waves. But enemy machine-guns all along the front opened fire almost simultaneously with our barrage. Gallipoli, Somme, Aisne House, Hindu Cott, Schuler Farm, Border House, and Jew's Hill, were held in strength by the enemy. The concrete "pill-boxes," containing in some cases half a dozen separate compartments, seemed to be entirely unaffected by the pounding of many weeks. Moreover, strong wire entanglements running down obliquely from Gallipoli were encountered. The lanes cut by artillery fire were covered by machine-guns. The ground was a veritable quagmire. The "mopping-up" system was found to be impossible. The concrete works had to be fought for; they could not be passed by and left to "moppers up" in rear. The inevitable result was that the men quickly lost the barrage. The strength of the attacking force had become inadequate to its frontage of one thousand five hundred yards. So heavily had the battalions lost since the Division took over the line, and particularly during the last twenty-four hours in the trenches, that seventy men was about the average strength of the company. There were assuredly not two thousand infantrymen in the force which went "over the top." The foremost wave must have consisted of less than three hundred men, probably reduced to a third within half a minute. Not unfitting was the description of a sergeant who took part in the attack: "It looked more like a big raiding party than anything else."

In the circumstances, after what they had endured, with ranks so thinned, against such opposition, it may be said, without calling upon superlatives or high-flown words, that none but troops of excellent quality would have gone forward at all. The troops of the 36th Division did much more than this. On the extreme right the 9th Irish Fusiliers, attacking from the Pommern Redoubt, pressed up across Hill 35, driving the Germans before them from the gun-pits on its forward slope. The 13th Rifles on their left advanced equally well. Somme, one of the strongest forts on the front, was passed by the leading wave, but the platoon detailed to take and hold it was unable to do so, though the rifle-grenade section strove gallantly to work round and take it in flank. The adjutant, Captain Belt, made an attempt to dig in in front of the place with a handful of men, but was severely wounded and fortunate in being able to crawl back to our lines. On the right of the 36th Division, the 16th had at first made good progress, but a counter-attack drove its troops back to their original line. From six o'clock onwards men began to fall back. Colonel R. P. Maxwell, commanding the 13th, seeing what was happening, led forward his battalion headquarters to a desperate attack upon Somme. He was unsuccessful, being himself severely wounded. It will be remembered that Colonel Maxwell, who had two sons on active service, had been wounded in Martinsart on the eve of the Somme attack. He was to reappear, none the less, in France in 1918. Colonel Somerville, commanding the 9th Irish Fusiliers, had already been mortally wounded. With the failure of Colonel Maxwell's forlorn hope, it may be said that the attack on the front of the 108th Brigade collapsed, though the 9th Irish Fusiliers made an effort to cling to the top of Hill 35.

On the right of the 109th Brigade, the 14th Rifles had to cross ground far worse even than the ordinary, completely under water, in fact. In their passage they came under withering machine-gun fire from Pond Farm. Lieutenant Ledlie made a fine attempt to capture this place, surrounding it on three sides with the few men remaining to him when he reached it, and killing any Germans who showed themselves. With his numbers so greatly depleted, he waited for support before making an attempt to rush it, sending back two messages. But no supports came; the men could not face the machine-gun fire. They had already suffered greatly from the artillery barrage, which the leading waves had avoided. At eight o'clock, seeing that his position was hopeless, he withdrew his men a hundred and fifty yards, covering his retirement by Lewis-gun fire. The best work of the day was accomplished by the men of the 11th Inniskillings. They also had heaviest casualties on the right, where a mere fragment was left glued to the ground in front of the Green Line, the men crawling in to our line after dark. On the left the usual blast of fire came from Border House and Fort Hill. One officer and seven men, by doubling when they fell behind the barrage, reached the Green Line, but none could move up to their support, and they were compelled to withdraw. The men of the supporting companies rushed Fort Hill with bomb and bayonet, killing a number of Germans and taking some prisoners. This was the one appreciable gain, an advance on the extreme left of some four hundred yards. The 48th Division had not been able to accomplish even as much on the flank. From Fort Hill a rough line to the original position in Capricorn Keep was consolidated. The reserve battalions of each Brigade, the 12th Rifles on the right and the 10th Inniskillings on the left, had moved up to the Black Line, where officers busied themselves in reorganizing the men and making preparations for a possible counter-attack by the enemy. The latter may have had such intention. He was at least observed to reinforce his position strongly behind Pond Farm. On an S.O.S. rocket being sent up, our barrage fell upon his platoons moving up at this point, and scattered them with heavy loss.

General Nugent for a time contemplated a second attack with a new barrage, to take at least the Green Line. The reports of Brigadiers and Staff Officers visiting the line in the afternoon made it clear that the troops were in no fit state for any such attempt. Disorganization was still considerable; a high proportion of officers and N.C.O.'s had fallen, and the men were utterly exhausted. Moreover, neither the 108th nor the 109th Brigade could have mustered

## THE DIVISION'S LOSSES

five hundred men for a new attack. General Nugent accordingly decided against this course, and instead ordered the relief of the two attacking Brigades by the 107th that night. This was carried out in circumstances of great difficulty, some platoons not quitting the front line till after five o'clock next morning. The weary remnants were moved straight back by 'bus to Winnizeele, and that night a Brigade of the 61st Division relieved the 107th Brigade in the line.

It is impossible to arrive at the exact casualties during the hours of the actual assault. Between 6 a.m. on the 16th and 9 a.m. on the 18th, however, there passed through the Divisional Dressing Stations 58 officers and 1,278 other ranks, wounded or gassed. These casualties do not include those of the attached artillery. They are very high if the depleted state of the infantry prior to the attack be taken into consideration. But they are almost insignificant if compared with the total casualties suffered in the holding of the line in the Salient, from August the 2nd to the 18th. In that period the 36th Division lost 144 officers and 3,441 other ranks killed, wounded, or missing. That is to say, it had more than two thousand casualties ere launched to the attack. Two other commanding officers, besides Colonels Somerville and Maxwell, were among the casualties. Colonel A. C. Pratt, 11th Inniskillings, had been killed at the entrance to Wieltje dug-outs early on the morning of the 16th, while Colonel Macrory, 10th Inniskillings, had been severely wounded a few days earlier. The difficulties of evacuating wounded during the action were extraordinary. Stretcher cases had to be brought by hand at least two thousand yards, and it took eight men to each stretcher. There were 433 stretcher-bearers, of whom rather more than half were R.A.M.C., the remainder being men of a Tunnelling Company and the Divisional Salvage section. Among many who displayed great bravery in the work of evacuating wounded under heavy shell-fire was the Assistant Chaplain-General of the Division, the Rev. F. J. Halahan, M.C., who by precept and personal example encouraged the stretcher-bearers to new efforts. Search parties, sent out after dark, brought in about a hundred wounded men from in front of our line. The conduct of the medical officers with the battalions, tending their wounded under the very heavy shell-fire that was maintained throughout upon the Black Line, was beyond praise. Captain Gavin, R.A.M.C., attached to the 14th Rifles, did splendid work at Rat Farm, where two other medical officers were killed. This gallant officer, who earned a bar to his Military Cross on that occasion, and had escapes little short of miraculous, was to be killed a few months later by no more serious an accident than a fall from his horse.

Among those good dumb soldiers, the transport animals, the casualties were the highest ever suffered by the Division. The pack mules, the use of which was even more necessary than at Messines, but infinitely less favoured by the *terrain*, were pushed forward too soon, and came under heavy machine-gun fire. Many were killed, and a far greater number had to be destroyed, though a few survived their wounds, and, like gallant veterans, bore their scars till the war was over. The loss among artillery horses was also very great.

This action was the only attack made by the 36th Division which suffered complete reverse, for that on the Ancre had been a local victory, of which the fruits were lost through no fault of its troops. It is important to consider what were its causes and what its lessons.

Many of the former will have become apparent in the course of this sketch of the battle and of the days preceding. They may be summarized as, firstly, exhaustion and attrition of units; secondly, weather; thirdly, lack of essential preparation.

The Division had been holding the line for thirteen days. Owing to the dreadful state of the trenches and the heaviness of the German shell-fire, constant reliefs had been necessary. From the "resting" battalions parties totalling sometimes as much as a thousand men a day had been furnished for work on forward areas under constant fire from artillery of the highest calibres. Apart from the question of the huge losses, there were no troops really fit or in a normal state of efficiency when the day of the assault arrived. The personal equation had been overlooked, with disastrous results. The water-logged condition of the ground was another prominent factor. What it was only those who have seen the Flanders plain strewn with shell-holes, sometimes almost lip to lip, can imagine.

But it was the machine-guns in the "pill-boxes," and the excellent fashion in which they were defended, that were by far the most fatal obstacles. The new German methods of defence in depth depended, in Flanders, upon the concrete structures built in and around the foundations of the destroyed farms with which that countryside is studded. They served their purpose admirably. Few that were captured by us were found to have been damaged by artillery. The British heavy artillery was firing from a salient, instead of, as at Messines, upon a salient. It had against it a far greater weight of German metal than in that battle, and suffered far more heavily from counter-battery. The German artillery dominated ours in the early stages of the battle, certainly in position, probably also in actual gun-power. The observation of the latter was almost worthless. And where any could be obtained it was well-nigh impossible to identify the "pill-boxes" from map to ground. An instance given by the G.O.C. 109th Brigade, General Ricardo, is illuminating. A few days prior to the attack he arranged with a liaison officer from the Corps Heavy Artillery a series of three-minute bombardments of certain strong points, with pauses between, so that it should be clear to the observers exactly which was being shelled, to correct the many various readings of maps and photographs. In several cases, he states, the concentration, nominally upon one strong point, covered many hundred yards. The same considerations applied to the cutting of wire, not nearly so effective as at Messines, through no fault of the gunners of the Division and of the batteries working beside them.

The "pill-boxes," which were mainly responsible for the losses of the troops in the attack of July the 31st, were standing intact and garrisoned on the 16th of August. The claims of counter-battery sometimes prevented demands for re-bombardment being fully met.

"We felt," said a distinguished officer after the action, "that the Battle of Messines was won at Zero, and that the Battle of Ypres was lost long before it." In the vast armies of the late war the Army Commander, and even the Corps Commander, was a shadowy personage, not alone to the private soldier, but to the Colonel commanding a battalion in the trenches or a brigade of artillery behind them. But the Second Army and the IX. Corps, under the orders of which the 36th Division fought at Messines, had a subtle power of making their presence felt. The system of liaison was practised by the Second Army as in no other. General Harington's car stopped at every door, and the cheerful young staff officers, who knew every communication trench on the Army front, who drank with company commanders in their front-line dug-outs before coming back to tea with a Brigadier, or with General Nugent at his Headquarters, formed a very real link between the Higher Command and the troops. The private soldier knew the Army Commander and his eyeglass as he knew no Corps Commander under whom he fought. His personality was a real accretion of strength. The difficulties at Ypres were infinitely greater than at Messines; that everyone recognised. But in the former case they did not appear to be met with quite the precision, care, and forethought of the latter. The private soldier felt a difference. He may have been unfair in his estimate, but that estimate was none the less of importance. For what the private soldier felt had a marked effect upon what the private soldier, the only ultimate winner of battles, accomplished.

Of the lessons the most obvious was that the barrage must be slower and of greater depth. General Nugent, in notes written after the battle as a comment upon captured orders of the Fourth German Army, made some interesting suggestions in this regard. He stated in the first case that the Germans could now no longer shell the area over which our troops were advancing, since their own troops were distributed in depth upon it. However much damage their barrage did to our supports, it did little or none to the leading troops. It was, however, more important to facilitate the advance of the latter than to protect the rear area during an attack. If both could not be accomplished, the artillery covering the front of assault should be strengthened at the expense of counter-battery groups. The creeping barrage, he suggested, might be slightly reduced to one 18-pounder per twenty-five yards, and augmented by a sweeping barrage, concentrated to cover about ten yards a gun, each group sweeping right and left along the front allotted to it, with a higher burst and greater searching effect upon shell-holes. The pace of the creeping barrage must be reduced, and there must be more frequent pauses. During these the sweeping barrage and a 60-pounder barrage in front of it might sweep and search. He also made some remarks upon the possibility of control of the barrage by the infantry, the advantages of which are too obvious to merit discussion, and the difficulties of which are equally apparent.

But the most interesting of General Nugent's suggestions were with regard to the formations of the infantry. " With the adoption," he wrote, "of a new form of German defensive tactics, consisting of small parties dotted about a wide area, the disadvantages of long lines of attack are that lines have small manœuvring capacity and lack depth. It is for consideration whether mobile company columns echeloned in depth on a narrow front, each a self-contained tactical unit with a machine-gun and trench mortar, each operating within an allotted zone, would not be a more suitable tactical formation than the present system, which breaks up under machine-gun fire and in badly shelled ground into a number of isolated groups without cohesion or leaders."

It is to be noted that when, on September the 20th, the 9th (Scottish) Division attacked at Frezenberg, the creeping barrage advanced the first two hundred yards in eight minutes; then slowed to a hundred yards in six minutes; halted on the first objective—four to five hundred yards—no less than an hour, and went forward again at the snail pace of a hundred yards in eight minutes. As regards the infantry, the attack was carried out by lines of sections in file at about twenty yards' interval. The system of "leap-frogging" was also employed instead of special groups for "mopping up." This attack was a complete success.*

---

\* *History of the 9th (Scottish) Division.* By John Ewing.

## CHAPTER VII

### YPRES TO CAMBRAI: SEPTEMBER TO NOVEMBER 1917

HAVING once more left its Artillery and Pioneers in line, under the orders of another division, the 36th Division, after four days' rest about Winnizeele, moved south by train. The troops detrained at Bapaume and Miraumont, ruins now, upon the church steeples of which some of them had looked from the Mesnil Ridge a little over a year before. With the Division moved the 1st Battalion Royal Irish Fusiliers. This regular battalion had joined the Division in the Salient before the Battle of Langemarck, but had not taken part in that dolorous affair. Its arrival was highly significant. It was a sign of the shortage of recruits from home. The 36th Division had not been made up to strength between Messines and Langemarck, and was now deplorably below it.

The country into which the troops stepped from their trains was of a like they had not yet seen in all their active service. Behind them lay the "shelled" area; that in which they now stood was the "devastated" area. The former was featureless to an indescribable degree. Marks of battle there were few, save for the stumps of trees. All the countryside, its débris and its shell-holes, was covered with a mass of very coarse grass. There were not even ruins, for buildings had been blown flat and their rubble carted away to help maintain the excellent main roads with which the area was now traversed. It was hard to discover the sites even of villages. Most people who used the Albert-Bapaume Road will remember a wooden cross whereon was written: " This is the site of Le Sars Church." For that statement it was necessary to take the writer's word. There was no other evidence.

The devastated area, on the other hand, had not been fought upon. It represented the ground evacuated by the enemy in his retreat to the Hindenburg Line. It had, however, been cleared of civilians and scientifically demolished to make it as difficult and comfortless as possible for our troops. All houses had been blown up by explosives, bridges destroyed, fruit-trees cut down or gashed to death. Yet it was far from being as dreadful or as ugly as the battle-field. The ground was unbroken and covered with good grass or crop run to seed. There were still woods and copses. It was depressing, yet far less so than the Salient. It resembled primeval prairie, and the hutments springing up here and there might have been the encampments of bold pioneers.

Between the 28th and 30th of August the Division relieved the 9th (Scottish) Division in the line. The right boundary was marked by a communication trench, " Queen Lane," on the Beaucamp-Ribécourt Road, a thousand yards north of the former village; the left was on the Demicourt-Graincourt Road. The frontage was very considerable, upwards of six thousand yards in a straight line. All three Brigades were in line, the 107th on the right, in what was known as the Trescault sector; the 108th in the centre, in the Havrincourt sector; and the 109th Brigade on the left, in the Hermies sector. The men of the Scottish Division made a very good impression upon their comrades of the 36th by working on their trenches till the moment of relief. As the troops of the 107th Brigade filed up the long communication trenches they saw the men of the 9th Division's South African Brigade carrying up the last sacks of chalk from the deep dug-outs under construction. It was a friendly gesture, typical of the good sportmanship of this fine Division.

## THE HINDENBURG LINE

It was an interesting and remarkable front that was taken over by the 36th Division. Its principal feature was the Canal du Nord, designed to link up the Canal de la Sensée with the Canal de la Somme at Peronne. The Canal du Nord had been about half completed at the outbreak of war. It ran due south to the northern skirts of Havrincourt Wood, the height from its bottom to the ground level varying from fifteen to a hundred feet, dry where it crossed the Bapaume-Cambrai Road, but with a few feet of water in it further south. North of Havrincourt Wood it turned west along the Grand Ravin, then south again, disappearing at Ruyalcourt, and reappearing a couple of miles further on north of Etricourt. Just at the destroyed railway bridge between Hermies and Havrincourt it formed a barrier between British and German.

The other important feature was the Hindenburg system of trenches, two great lines, from five hundred to two thousand yards apart, each consisting of front and support trenches. The system constituted in all probability the most formidable fortification constructed in the course of the war. The Germans had sited and dug it at their ease, to a great extent with gangs of Russian prisoners and forced civilian labour. The trenches were wide, deep, and well revetted. The mined dug-outs were all designed to a pattern; the stairways, supports, and all timber used in them having been turned out by the sawmills in replica by the thousand pieces. They represented the first successful application of mass production to the construction of dug-outs. The wire defences were of huge extent, generally in three or four deep belts, at least twenty feet apart. The system had already been pierced by our troops at Bullecourt, but on a tiny front and at vast cost. It appeared practically impregnable.

From the village of Mœuvres the front system of the Hindenburg Line* followed the western bank of the Canal

---

* The expression "front Hindenburg Line" was applied loosely either to the front-line trench of the first system, or to the whole of that system. The word "system" will be used in this and succeeding chapters to avoid misunderstanding.

du Nord for four thousand yards, then crossed it, sweeping in a bold curve round the village of Havrincourt and south of that of Ribécourt. It did not, however, represent by any means the line held by the German outposts, which were in general a thousand yards in advance of it, and frequently in themselves stout and well-wired positions. Along the banks of the Canal du Nord there were at intervals spoil heaps, consisting of the chalk dug from its bed. Of these, two were of great importance to the Division. The northern spoil heap was on the front of the 109th Brigade, on the west bank of the Canal. Sixty feet in height, it was strongly wired and had machine-guns mounted on its flat top which swept our trenches. The southern spoil heap was smaller, at the sharp bend west of Havrincourt, where the Canal turned westward along the Grand Ravin. It was known as Yorkshire Bank. There was a British trench on the top of it, but on its eastern rim the Germans had established posts, rather unaccountably in view of the aggressive character of the troops of the 9th Division. They, too, seemed to feel that such a legacy to a relieving division was unworthy their fame. On the night of August the 30th, before General Nugent had taken over command of the front, a party of Argyll and Sutherland Highlanders, advancing after the German part of the spoil heap had been shelled with gas, drove out the enemy piquets and established posts of their own. The 9th Division, therefore, was able to leave an honourable legacy here after all, but a peculiarly lively one. Next evening, after General Nugent had taken over the command and established his headquarters in Little Wood, outside the village of Ytres, the Germans hit back. After a bombardment of Yorkshire Bank, they drove in our posts and re-established their own. At 4-15 a.m. next morning they were re-ejected. Next night they came again, two parties bombing their way up simultaneously from either side. At 1 a.m. on the 2nd the 12th Rifles retook the posts, with bomb and Lewis gun. That evening at dusk an officer visiting the posts saw Germans looking over the edge of the bank. They were rushed immediately and driven out, leaving a wounded prisoner. Two nights later they tried yet again, with typical German persistence. A shower of bombs from the top of the spoil heap drove them off, and as they were retreating a shell from a Stokes mortar was seen to drop in the centre of a group. One other attempt was made, to meet with like decisive failure. It was not an important affair, though it caused the name of Yorkshire Bank to appear in the British *communiqué* three days running. The 36th Division had had the better of the exchanges, but did not unduly pride itself thereon, having a manifest advantage in position.

For the rest, the area was rolling, well watered, and fairly thickly wooded. In the big Havrincourt Wood, which had originally covered some four square miles, the Germans had cut down much timber and used it on the Hindenburg trenches, besides leaving a great many trees lying on the ground. It still contained enough, however, to afford excellent cover. The Hindenburg System was admirably sited, and afforded to the enemy good observation of the area held by us, particularly from the dark mass of Bourlon Wood, crowning the height of the hundred-metre contour north of the Bapaume-Cambrai Road. In such country as this, however, it was impossible for the Germans to deny to us all the good ground. From the Hermies Ridge, from trees in Havrincourt Wood, from the very front line on the Trescault spur, the British had admirable views of their positions. Very tantalizing they were to men who dwelt among ruins, for the villages on the German side were intact, save for the nearest, which had been slightly damaged by our shell-fire. Very distinct from one point, and little more than eight miles off, were the steeples and roofs of the beautiful city of Cambrai.

There was a striking contrast between the trenches in the Trescault and Havrincourt sectors, and those in the northern or Hermies sector. The former consisted of a whole series of lines, so many trenches that they had to be occupied and defended at intervals only, by a system of " localities," each manned in general by a platoon. These trenches had, in fact, been prepared in the spring for assembly with view to an offensive which did not eventuate. In the Hermies sector, on the contrary, there were practically no defences at all, save a shadowy front line and some trenches round the village. This northern sector had been held by the 27th Brigade of the 9th Division, commanded by the celebrated Brigadier-General F. A. Maxwell, V.C., who was killed in the Salient shortly after his Division had moved north. He, apparently, was not a believer in trenches, and relied on holding his position by counter-attack from the Hermies defences and from behind the high ridge along which ran the Hermies-Demicourt Road. The plan did not appeal to General Nugent or to General Ricardo, commanding the 109th Brigade, and a heavy programme of trench-digging and wiring in the Hermies sector was at once drawn up.

Meanwhile, in the Salient, the Artillery and 16th Rifles endured a bitter period. Indeed, it is to be doubted whether any Divisional Artillery, since the second Battle of Ypres in 1915, had been subjected to strain such as that which now fell to the lot of the 36th Division's gunners. They had gone into action on July the 14th, in support of the 55th Division. They remained in action after the 36th Division had departed, and on August the 21st supported an unsuccessful attack by the 61st Division on the same front. They were not relieved till the night of the 23rd. And these six weeks had represented battle conditions in their worst form, a huge expenditure of ammunition, heavy and continuous hostile counter-battery, shelling of wagon-lines, the scantiest of accommodation, mud and indescribable wretchedness. A great proportion of the personnel had disappeared, new officers were commanding sections and junior officers batteries, when they detrained at the end of August at Bapaume. The lot of the Pioneers was not quite so hard, but their period in the Salient was longer. Two companies worked on the ruins of the infantry barracks at Ypres, the remainder on screening the Menin Road, on a trench tramway to Railway Wood, on the construction of strong points

on the Westhoek Ridge, and like tasks, till September the
30th, when the battalion was entrained at Vlamertinghe and
sent to rejoin the Division.

The line now held by the Division was on the whole
the pleasantest it had ever known. This does not imply
that the troops were allowed to take life easily. On the
contrary, the fighting arms displayed considerable aggression, with important results. The German methods of
defence, with outposts far in front of the main Hindenburg
System, not always very strongly defended, and sometimes
held at night only, offered considerable opportunity for those
little silent raids upon isolated piquets which the Canadians
had perfected, and knew by the expressive term " winkling."
The first affair was on a scale rather bigger than this implies,
parties of about sixty being engaged on either side. The
scene was Wigan Copse, north of Yorkshire Bank, and the
result the retirement of the Germans, leaving a wounded
prisoner in the hands of the 12th Rifles, who had an officer and
four men slightly wounded. That was on October the 6th.
Three days later, at dusk, the 10th Rifles cut the wire of
a post on the edge of the eastern arm of Havrincourt Wood,
known as Fémy Wood, waited for the garrison to arrive,
captured its leader, a corporal, and killed the remaining ten.
On the 23rd, a party of the 11th Rifles, covering work on
our wire, made a neat capture of six men who approached
it, closing in on them from either flank, and taking them
without a shot fired. Another prisoner was captured by
the 1st Royal Irish Fusiliers, now in the 107th Brigade,
when one of its saps north of Trescault was unsuccessfully
attacked by the enemy. Various other deserters and single
wanderers were also taken from time to time. On the British side was one minor disaster. A patrol of one officer
and nine other ranks of the 1st Irish Fusiliers, examining
the results of trench mortar fire on the German wire, was
ambushed by a party of about thirty Germans. After
heavy fighting, in which they inflicted numerous casualties
on the enemy, the Fusiliers were forced to withdraw, three
wounded men being captured. But the most heroic of

these little episodes was when a party of Germans approached a sap-head held by a section of four men of the 15th Rifles, calling out in English: "It's all right. We're coming to visit you." Deceived by the ruse, the Riflemen's first warning was a shower of bombs, which wounded one of them. At the same moment the Germans jumped into the sap. The three remaining Riflemen might well have been excused had they retreated down the sap. Instead, upon the instant, they charged the enemy with the bayonet. The Germans ran, but the plucky defenders laid hands upon one that they had wounded, and kept him. The prisoner stated that his party had consisted of an officer and eight men. And at dawn the body of that officer, dead from a bayonet wound, was found outside the sap-head. It was in truth a gallant exploit.

In two or three other cases our men were unsuccessful in entering posts, finding the enemy on the alert. One raid only on a big scale was carried out, on the trenches south of the Hermies-Havrincourt Road and east of the Canal. At 7-30 p.m. on November the 3rd, three parties of the 9th Irish Fusiliers, numbering in all, with stretcher-bearers and sappers, four officers and sixty-seven other ranks, moved out from Yorkshire Bank and passed through gaps in the German wire. They then sent up a red flare, which brought down a heavy barrage on all approaches. The raid would have been a complete success had not the right party come upon some wire repaired by the Germans since it had been reported destroyed by our artillery. Eventually they stormed the obstacle and cut down the defenders, but not without heavy loss to themselves. Our total casualties were one man killed, three missing, believed killed, and one officer and fourteen men wounded. The Germans were estimated to have had forty killed. Had the men, for the most part newly transferred troopers of the North Irish Horse, not been more eager to kill than to capture, a considerable number of prisoners might have been taken.

Among other offensive methods employed must be recorded a new horror of war, the Livens projector, which

## THE LIVENS PROJECTOR

the troops of the 36th Division now saw for the first time. It was simply a large steel drum filled with lethal gas, under compression, fired from a short tube. Its range was upwards of two thousand yards. Six hundred of these mortars were dug in at the bend of the Canal, and on the night of the 14th of September fired into Havrincourt. It was definitely established by the evidence of prisoners captured the following month that the losses in the village were very heavy. The battalion which held it had to be relieved that night. In two dug-outs alone twenty men were killed by the gas.

The artillery also was active. The ammunition allotment was high. It was, indeed, the huge increase in the supply of 18-pounder ammunition that had made really "quiet bits" almost unknown upon the British front. For when the British had ammunition they fired it off. The French, on the other hand, on a quiet front, preferred to live quiet lives. The IV. Corps ordered that two-thirds of the allotment should be expended at night, in harassing fire upon roads. As most of our batteries had little flash-cover, such shooting betrayed gun positions. Recourse was therefore had to single guns for night-firing, pushed forward at dusk and withdrawn before dawn. Some of these forward guns had an unpleasant reception. One was destroyed by accurate enemy fire. The Germans, for their part, paid greater attention to our batteries than to our trenches. Their favourite method, which the 36th Division had experienced in Flanders, was a deliberate "shooting-up" of a single battery, beginning with aeroplane observation, and continued by the aid of high shrapnel bursts, which could be "spotted," for five or six hours at the rate of about a round a minute. These bombardments did some damage and caused some loss to the gunners, but the latter had more than once the satisfaction of drawing fire upon dummy or abandoned positions, while those in use went scatheless.

Mention has already been made of the arrival of the 1st Irish Fusiliers from the 4th Division. This battalion was, on August the 27th, posted to the 107th Brigade. To make place for it two other battalions of that Brigade, the 8th and 9th Rifles, were amalgamated, becoming the 8th/9th Royal Irish Rifles. It was a sad occasion, above all for such officers and other ranks of these original battalions as still survived with them. It meant the end, or well-nigh the end, of a cherished tradition. The next arrivals were over three hundred all ranks of the North Irish Horse, a regiment of which had been dismounted. This large draft was posted to the 9th Irish Fusiliers, thereafter officially known as the 9th (North Irish Horse) Battalion Royal Irish Fusiliers. Then came the 7th Irish Rifles from the 16th Division, and a regular battalion, the 2nd Royal Irish Rifles, from the 25th Division. The 7th Battalion, of a total strength of less than four hundred all ranks, was broken up, and its personnel transferred to the 2nd. The latter was then posted to the 108th Brigade, while to make place for it the 11th and 13th Rifles were amalgamated, becoming the 11th/13th Royal Irish Rifles. In each case surplus personnel was drafted to the remaining battalions of the 107th and 108th Brigades, which were now over strength. The 109th Brigade, which received considerable reinforcements during the month of September, was little below it.

The work of the 36th Division in this area almost equalled that of Flanders. The "localities" in the front line trenches soon resembled model fortifications, such as might have been made for the instruction of an engineering school. Curving round the village of Hermies, the Pioneers dug perhaps the best trench ever made in entirety by the Division, which was christened in their honour "Lurgan Switch." The best deep dug-outs the Division had ever known, with thirty feet of cover, were dug in the chalk under the instruction of the Field Companies, now no mean experts in such work. Here, too, what were known from their shape as "champagne" dug-outs were constructed, on a pattern invented by that artist in trench warfare, the enemy. In these the team of a single machine-gun could shelter from the heaviest bombardment, and bring its gun into action in the time it took two men to run up a ladder.

Behind the lines work was equally hard. In such country as this, with not a solitary house standing, the troops had no other accommodation than that which they constructed for themselves. This was the land of the "Nissen" hut, too well known even to people who never saw the Front to merit description here. They sprang up everywhere, these ugly but useful buildings, with their arched roofs of corrugated iron. Excellent Divisional Headquarters were built in Ytres, to replace those in Little Wood. Fine new Brigade Headquarters appeared in Neuville and Bertincourt, to which the two northern Brigades moved back from unsafe and uncomfortable headquarters further forward. Bertincourt represented perhaps the best example of scientific work upon a ruined village. It was parcelled out between the various units, each being allotted its own section, on which no other might encroach. General Ricardo offered prizes for the best designed and best kept billets. Under the stress of this competition Bertincourt had become, when the 109th Brigade reluctantly quitted it, a model village.

So, in line and behind it, the troops were as comfortable as conditions on any part of the British front allowed. They would have been as happy as was possible under any conditions of active service had it not been for the desolation about them, which bred a feeling of loneliness. The British soldier had grown used to being billeted in villages, or lodged in encampments within reach of them. He missed vaguely the sights of village life, the gallant old men and the women setting about their endless toil, the clatter of the farm, the children who watched him falling in for parade, and came in the afternoon to listen to the band. More definite was the loss of the shops, the eggs to be bought from the villagers, the warmth and comfort of the *estaminet*, where he drank his beer, solaced himself with bacon or fried potatoes if he had gone short of a meal, joked with the daughter of the host, or played "House" with his friends on benches about the fire. Officers of the Provost Staff have stated that in their experience there was almost always

less crime and unrest among troops in inhabited regions
than among those living upon the Teuton-made *veldt*.
There was among the men of the Ulster Division little
crime at any time, but undoubtedly they also were in some
degree a prey to the inevitable nostalgia born of desolation.
They would have come far more completely beneath its
influence but for the efforts that were made to afford them
distraction and increase their comfort. " Peace hath her
victories," and a comparatively peaceful life afforded as much
opportunity as battle for the Quarter-master General's
Staff—" Q "—to prove its ingenuity and resource. In this
sector the work of the 36th Division " Q " was certainly
triumphant in this respect; first of all under the direction
of Colonel Comyn, for eighteen months A.A. and Q.M.G.,
and then, on his transfer to the War Office, under his successor, Colonel S. H. Green, who had worked under him
as D.A.Q.M.G. It organized in the first place daily trips
to Amiens. Three lorries, one to take twelve officers, the
remaining two each twenty other ranks, left Ytres at an
early hour each morning for Achiet-le-Grand. Thence the
party went by train to Amiens, being met again by the
lorries at Achiet in the evening. The trips allowed of six
hours or more being spent in the city. Beer was provided in
great quantities to replace the supplies of the lost *estaminets*.
In September the Division was buying from brewers of
Amiens no less than two railway truck-loads of forty-five
barrels a day. A soda-water factory was established on the
Canal bank at Manancourt. Soda-water, labelled " Boyne
Water," a fancy which appealed to the troops, was sold
at a penny a bottle, and various other aerated concoctions
at twopence. The Divisional Canteens, always of the
greatest benefit to the troops, became then of incalculable
importance. Added to their usual " lines "—tobacco, biscuits, chocolate, tinned foods, books, candles—were now
sold in great quantities fruit and vegetables, eggs, bread and
cake, and, when procurable, fresh fish and even oysters;
while special orders for anything required in Amiens by
officers or men were taken, the goods being procured by

## BRITISH ORGANIZATION

the following evening, and sold to the buyer at cost price. The Division had long had a cinema, a concert party—"The Merry Mauves"—and an excellent band. These passed up and down the front, all units taking turns in the pleasures of their performances. Football and boxing competitions reappeared. There was one very exciting race meeting and horse show, with numerous classes for transport turn-outs. For animals at least the area was a paradise, there being unlimited grazing and great fields of clover. Some agriculture was attempted, over a hundred acres being ploughed and sown. A few headquarters purchased cows, and many units pigs and chickens.

To those who cared to ponder such things, the wonders of the great, creaking, rather clumsy machine, in which it took a thousand men to form the tiniest cog, never ceased to appeal. The British organization for war was assuredly by now amazingly thorough. Was there required some newfangled and complicated Lewis-gun-mounting for trench warfare; a message and a tracing to some workshop behind brought a hundred in a week. Copies innumerable of an enlarged aeroplane photograph wanted in a hurry for a raid could be printed off at Albert in twenty-four hours. The little press of the IV. Corps, the Intelligence Branch of which officers of the 36th Division will remember with gratitude, seemed to pour forth up-to-date maps. If there was the slightest hitch about rations, it was the topic of conversation for a week. The post-office was an unceasing marvel. In Flanders, Divisional Headquarters had had their newspapers the day they were published, and the rest of the troops next morning. The letters for men in the saps reached them in two or at most three days. A letter to Hermies would probably take longer now.

But, there was no doubt about the matter, the organization was expensive in man-power, and man-power at that moment was a problem that engaged G.H.Q. almost as much as did the enemy. The writer of this book can well remember being sent, in Flanders, when the Division was very weak, to investigate the number of men a certain battalion had in the trenches. The "paper strength" of that battalion was just six hundred men. It had in the line, exclusive of its headquarters, one hundred and seven men. He went through the state with the adjutant. That revealed, indeed, a remarkably strong battalion headquarters, and an undue number at the transport lines, but no other leakages which the adjutant had power to stop. There was a number of men at Divisional Headquarters, clerks, draughtsmen, orderlies, a cook, five attached to the Signal Company; and about three times as many at Brigade Headquarters. The rest followed varied avocations. Five were on traffic control, a number attached to a Tunnelling Company. There were clerks to town majors, camp wardens, guardians of coal, straw, and ration dumps; cooks and servants at the Rest Camp. There were about forty on leave, and twenty sick not evacuated.

There were also twenty at various schools. Schools were a vital necessity; but who at this period can doubt that they were ludicrously overdone? Every formation had its schools—G.H.Q., the Army, the Corps, the Division, the Brigade. There were infantry schools, artillery schools, and trench-mortar schools; machine-gun schools, Lewis-gun schools, bombing schools, gas schools; schools which taught horse-mastership, shoe-making, brick-laying, carpentry, sanitation, butchery, cooking. For a weak Division, schools became a nightmare. Divisional commanders had to protest that they had either to man their trenches inadequately, or refuse vacancies allotted. And vacancies refused raised a vast to-do, because they threatened the existence of the school, and the school naturally appealed to the formation of which it was the *protégé*. Up to the Division headquarters this did not so largely matter. The Division may have been inconsiderate at times, but it did know precisely how its line was held, how strong its posts, how far separated. But above the Division the situation was not always so quickly grasped. The Corps was an impersonal affair, encamped, sometimes for years, upon the same front, changing its Divisions week by week. And when a Corps headquarters, as happened before Cambrai, resting out of the line, sent out appeals for students to attend *its* schools, so that they might not be idle, the most longsuffering were inclined to protest and to feel that, after all, for the idle, there was a certain work which might have been accomplished somewhat further forward. The jests of most humorists are based upon exaggeration, but there is just a kernel of truth in them, or they are not good jests. Of such nature is the dictum of M. André Maurois,* the French interpreter who loves the British so well and pokes such clever fun at them—that a school " is a plot of ground traversed by imitation trenches, where officers who have never been near the line teach war-worn veterans their business."

The swarm of writers which, under the influence of the reaction from war, has so bitterly criticised the higher staff officers for the waste of man-power, has been hopelessly astray in its estimation of the reason. It was not inefficiency or carelessness. It was rather the Englishman's passion for organization, for orderliness and smoothness. That passion for perfecting the machine put too many cogs and fly-wheels upon it, made it over-complicated, clumsy. Ever eager to expand their business, these directors put into it too much of the one form of capital which they could not afford—man-power.

In October began preparations for a great new offensive, a surprise offensive, which was to depend entirely upon the use of tanks. The scheme and the plans for the Battle of Cambrai must be left for discussion till the next chapter. Here will be detailed only some of the preliminary moves. The part of the 36th Division in the first day's attack was to be confined to the capture of the German trenches bounded by the Bapaume-Cambrai Road and the Canal du Nord. This was the task of one Brigade only, and the other two were to be withdrawn from the Trescault and Havrincourt sectors, each being replaced by a Division. These Divisions, the 51st

* Author of two classic books on the humours of war: *The Silence of Colonel Bramble* and *General Bramble*.

(Highland) and the 62nd (West Riding), were to be kept in rear as long as possible. It fell, therefore, to the 36th to do much of the work of preparation in their areas; the repairing of forward roads, the excavating of new dug-outs, the construction of bridges over trenches. The C.R.E.'s of these Divisions, with their Pioneer battalions and some Engineers, moved forward early in November to work under the general control of the C.R.E., 36th Division. Havrincourt Wood was crammed with little wooden hutments, which its trees and scrub rendered invisible to the enemy. One of the most important tasks was the metalling of the roads, and the dumping of metal beside them in parts where it was impossible to lay it, in order that work might commence with the assault. The surface of the roads was good, but only because the Division had been holding a front so wide, which made the traffic upon them relatively light. It was quite obvious that a single day of traffic such as an offensive entails would cut them to pieces. It was frontline roadmaking upon which the C.R.E., Colonel Campbell, was required to exercise his ingenuity. Work upon tracks in Havrincourt Wood was easy; silence was all that was necessary. But work upon what was to be the most important communication of the IV. Corps in the offensive, the road from Metz to Ribécourt, was of great difficulty. In Trescault, half-way between these villages and almost in our front line, there were, to begin with, two enormous craters blown by the enemy before his retirement. These had to be filled in by night, and it took chalk by the ton to do it. Road-metal also was stacked by night almost up to the front line, and covered with camouflage before dawn. Wooden bridges were prepared for all the trenches crossing the roads which would be required, and most of these for British trenches set in position. The problem of gun positions on the northern part of the front was difficult. Cover there was none reasonably far forward, save among the ruins of Hermies and Demicourt. Among these the positions were prepared, and by night seven hundred rounds per 18-pounder borne up to them.

## WORK IN THE MIST

During the first sixteen days of November, the 36th Division had also to provide parties of from two to six hundred men daily for unloading trains at Ytres station, for the Heavy Artillery ammunition dump at Bus, and for the Field Artillery dump in Vallulart Wood. Trains frequently did not arrive within six hours of the advertised time, and the men had to sit about and wait for them, frequently half through the night—as ill a preparation for troops on the eve of an offensive as could well be imagined. Amid much confusion and unnecessary hardship, one officer earned the gratitude of the infantrymen by his foresight and consideration, the Staff Captain of the IV. Corps Heavy Artillery. He required parties up to seventy-five men, and always at short notice. He kept three of his lorries always standing by at his headquarters, telephoned when he wanted men, and fetched them from Ytres, Neuville, Ruyalcourt, or Bertincourt, as detailed by the General Staff of the Division. Better still, he generally gave them tea before sending them home, to supplement their haversack rations.

The weather favoured the British arrangements amazingly. It was fine, but morning after morning dawned with a thick ground mist which hung about all day. Foden lorries carrying stone and light steam rollers to lay it were enabled, beneath this shelter, to work at a proximity to the Germans that had otherwise been out of the question. Night after night the tanks, upon which all hinged, moved up into Havrincourt Wood. Here again the mist was a godsend, for the track of a tank across country is plain enough on an aeroplane photograph, and not hard to distinguish with a glass. Contrary to the general belief of those who have not heard them on the move, the tank is not very noisy. It was the artillery tractors, dragging up the big howitzers, which frightened everyone by their clatter.

The relief of the 107th and 108th Brigades took place on the nights of the 17th and 18th of November. To deceive the enemy as to the great concentration in front of him, a screen of the troops of these Brigades remained to hold the outpost line. These men knew only that a raid on a large scale was intended. In the early hours of the 18th, the Germans, evidently somewhat suspicious, raided a sap held by the 1st Irish Fusiliers behind a heavy "box" barrage, and took six prisoners. From the evidence of German prisoners taken subsequently, it appeared that the most the enemy gathered from the examination of his captives was that an attempt to capture Havrincourt might be expected. This aroused in the German command no great uneasiness. On the 16th, the 14th Rifles had taken over the whole front of the 109th Brigade to permit the other battalions to train for their task. This training was carried out by General Ricardo over trenches laid out to scale with the plough, upon a front of four thousand yards.

Accommodation was so limited that much marching and counter-marching was necessary to provide billets for the 51st and 62nd Divisions moving up. In its course the 108th Brigade moved back as far as Barastre, upwards of eight miles from the front line. By the night of the 19th, however, the eve of the attack, the infantry was concentrated well forward. The whole of the 109th Brigade was in assembly positions, the 108th Brigade in Vélu Wood, and the 107th Brigade in the area Ytres-Lechelle. The 16th Rifles were in Havrincourt Wood.

These details have been here given in order that the next chapter may proceed with the scheme of the Battle of Cambrai, without interruption to explain the moves which preceded it. It is in itself one of the most interesting actions in which the 36th Division took part during its combatant career, and, at the same time, measuring final result by the standard of early achievement, one of the most disappointing. The material results that it produced were small, but it opened a new era in the history of war. No adequate conception of the victories of 1918, first of the Germans, then of the Allies, can be reached without a close study of its lessons.

# CHAPTER VIII

### CAMBRAI AND AFTER (I):
### NOVEMBER 20TH TO 22ND, 1917

THE year 1917 had drawn to its close leaving unfulfilled most of the high hopes that had buoyed men's spirits in the opening months. Some, at least, of the causes of their downfall were far away from the Western Front, and beyond the control of Generals Nivelle, Pétain, and Sir Douglas Haig. Russia, that strong-armed but weak-headed and weak-legged giant, had collapsed, leaving Roumania to its fate—complete overthrow. At Carporetto the Italians had been heavily defeated by the Austro-German armies, and France and England had been forced to send divisions to Italy to act as rallying points of resistance. In France the Champagne offensive had left a legacy of doubt and exasperation among soldiers as well as civilians, and it had taken all the fostering skill and care of General Pétain to restore his troops to the standard at which they had begun the year. The Flanders offensive, vitally necessary, crippling to Ludendorff, as he has admitted in his book, had been unduly prolonged in conditions far more dreadful even than when the 36th Division had taken part in it. Not men only but horses were drowned in the shell-holes ere it was over, and by the time Poelcappelle and Passchendaele had been reached the evacuation of wounded had become all but impossible. The heights were won, indeed, on the southern flank, though at Westroosebeke the enemy still had the best ground, but, broadly speaking, the strategical value of the advance was *nil*.

Passchendaele, indeed, had resolved itself into a terrible object-lesson. Here was the point to which a mechanical conception of warfare had led us. Was there not, the keenest minds in every army were asking, was there not some outlet ? Were men to be forever at the mercy of the munition factory and the mud of its making, the roll of barbed wire, the slab of reinforced concrete ? Was the real genius of the soldier never to have the chance to display itself outside this war of fortifications ? Often one heard the question, academic enough, but of extraordinary interest : " Could supreme genius, could the greatest captain that ever lived, could Napoleon have freed his hands from the deadlock ? " The greatest soldier of this war has revealed, in the incomparable language that is his gift, that he also had asked himself that question, and answered it unhesitatingly in the affirmative.* As affairs were now marching, it did indeed appear as though we were reverting to the mere tactics of the battering-ram, as though, metaphorically speaking,

> " Elephants
> And barbèd horses might as well prevail
> As the most subtle stratagems of war."

And a way out from mechanism was found, as might have been expected, in mechanism.

Whose the credit for the conception of the surprise tank

---

* Aux moments sombres de la guerre, nous nous sommes souvent demandés : " Si Napoléon sortait de son tombeau aux Invalides, que nous dirait-il, que ferait-il de nos armées actuelles ? "

Il nous aurait dit : " Vous avez des millions d'hommes ; je ne les ai jamais eus. Vous avez les chemins-de-fer, le télégraphe, la télégraphie sans fil, les avions, l'artillerie à longue portée, les gazs asphyxiants ; je n'avais rien de tout cela. Et vous n'en tirez point parti ? Vous allez voir ! "

Et, dans un mois ou deux, il aurait tout renversé, réorganisé, mis en œuvre de quelque façon nouvelle, et culbuté l'ennemi désorienté.

MARSHAL FOCH : *The Times* (Napoleon Supplement), Thursday, May 5th, 1921.

assault, whether General Tudor's or General Ellis's, or another's, it is not here pertinent to speculate. The germ of the idea was inherent in the tank itself, and must have been present, vaguely or clearly, in the minds of all who contributed to its design and organization. Here, at any rate, had been found an ideal testing-ground for the scheme, good ground, obstacles which it would have, at that date, been madness to attack in the conventional manner, the prospect of inflicting upon the enemy a swift and signal defeat. Moreover, a blow that would prevent the massing of more German divisions on the Italian front, where every German division put new life and dash into at least two Austrian, was urgently needed. The striking of the blow was entrusted to General Byng's Third Army.

The plan was simple. The tanks were to roll out gaps in the wire of the Hindenburg System, through which the infantry columns could push. The aim was to overcome the enemy holding the line between the Canal du Nord and the Canal de l'Escaut, which runs parallel with it at a distance of from six to eight miles further east; to secure possession of the area bounded by these Canals on east and west, and by the marshes of the Sensée River to the north; and, as a consequence, to clear the whole area west of the Canal du Nord of hostile forces. It must be remembered that the German line, running north from Havrincourt to Mœuvres, there turned west by north. Had the British, pressing northward, reached Oisy-le-Verger and the banks of the Sensée River, they would have been ten miles behind the German front line at that latitude. A precipitate retreat would have been certain, and a very large haul, if not of prisoners, at least of material, almost equally so. Even if the advance to the north accomplished no more than the consolidation of the high ground round Bourlon Wood, the Germans would have to abandon the Drocourt-Quéant Switch, a very strong position. The battle was to have three stages: the first, a surprise infantry attack assisted by tanks and an unregistered artillery barrage to capture the crossings of the Canal de l'Escaut at Masnières and

Marcoing, and a German trench east of them known as the Masnières-Beaurevoir Line; the second, the advance of the Cavalry Corps to isolate the city of Cambrai, and seize the crossings of the Sensée River, while the troops of the IV. Corps captured Bourlon Wood; and the third, the clearance of the area and of Cambrai itself. The attack was to be carried out by the III. Corps on the right and the IV. Corps on the left, with the V. Corps in reserve. The right flank of the attack lay upon the great spur, crowned by the Bois Lateau and the hamlet of Le Pave, running from Gonnelieu to the Canal de l'Escaut at Crèvecœur; the left roughly upon the Canal du Nord. There was to be a subsidiary attack to the north upon the Hindenburg Line at Bullecourt. If one were to search for a key-word to define the general idea of the offensive, that key-word would probably be "exploitation." It was not intended merely to break through the enemy's defences, to strike him a heavy blow; it was designed to exploit a preliminary success, to clear a great tract of country of hostile troops, to turn a flank; for, be it remembered, the advance to the Sensée marshes would have involved not merely a headlong retreat or wholesale capture for the German troops south of them, but an eventual retirement of several miles at least to the north. The Drocourt-Quéant Switch, the main Hindenburg Lines, would be gone. Cambrai was, for the Western Front, a small battle, but great events hung upon it.

In the previous accounts of battles it has not been necessary, for the purpose of writing the History of the 36th Division, to do more than glance at the progress of the Divisions fighting upon its flanks. In this battle, on the contrary, if any adequate conception is to be reached from the account, the plan and the action of the IV. Corps, that is, of the two Divisions on the right of the 36th, and the 56th Division, which was under the orders of the IV. Corps for the greater part of the action, must be studied in some detail. The right boundary of the IV. Corps was the Trescault-Ribécourt Road; thence north of Noyelles. It

## TASK OF 109TH BRIGADE

was to attack with three Divisions, the 51st on the right, the 62nd in the centre, and the 36th on the left. The 51st and 62nd Divisions, the left of the latter on the Canal du Nord, were to advance north from the skirts of Havrincourt Wood. The normal northern objective of the first day was the Bapaume-Cambrai Road. If, however, there was little opposition, the 51st and 62nd Divisions were to press on and take the high ground crowned by Bourlon Wood and village, or take them over from the Cavalry if the latter had occupied them, while the 107th and 108th Brigades of the 36th Division moved parallel with them east of the Canal, formed a flank-guard facing west, and seized the passages of the Canal at Mœuvres and Inchy-en-Artois. In the event of serious opposition this later programme was to be that of the next day. The primary task of the 36th Division was to capture the German trenches west of the Canal du Nord and south of the Bapaume-Cambrai Road. For this it was to employ one Brigade, the 109th, one of its Field Artillery Brigades, the 173rd, together with the 280th Brigade and the 93rd Army Brigade R.F.A. Its other Artillery Brigade, the 153rd, was at the disposal of the 62nd Division, to take part in its preliminary barrage. The plans were entrusted to General Ricardo, who worked them out with his Artillery Group Commander, Lieut.-Colonel H. C. Simpson, D.S.O., and had thus an almost unique opportunity for a Brigadier on the Western Front of fighting his own battle in his own fashion. Communication across the Canal was to be established by the erection of a bridge on the Demicourt-Flesquières Road, to take wagons and field guns, at the earliest possible moment. Materials for this were, of course, prepared in advance, as were some for a minor bridge, for infantry and pack transport, to be thrown across at a suitable point some fifteen hundred yards further south.

A glance at the map* will show that the German defences west of the Canal began at the northern spoil heap, consisted for the greater part of their length up to the

* Map IV.

Bapaume-Cambrai Road of two main lines, and at their greatest depth, on a frontage of fifteen hundred yards, of three. No tanks were allotted to the 36th Division, so a frontal attack without artillery preparation was out of the question. It was decided, therefore, to capture the northern spoil heap, wire in front of which had been cut over a long period by artillery and a 6-inch trench mortar with instantaneous fuse—the latter the best wire-cutter the 36th Division ever discovered—and work up the trenches from south to north. It appeared that this sixty-foot pile would enable machine and Lewis guns to cover the infantry in their advance. On paper the task of working up these trenches, traversed at frequent intervals by rays of wire, appeared of well-nigh insuperable difficulty. And, indeed, no planning and no gallantry in execution could have accomplished it had not the enemy troops been much demoralized by the advance of the tanks behind them east of the Canal, as it was intended they should be. The attack of the 36th Division was, therefore, not to take place till the main attack had drawn level with its point of departure. Zero for the former was at 6-20 a.m.; for the 36th Division at 8-35 a.m.

The attack carried out by the 109th Brigade has been officially described as a " bombing action," and such, doubtless, to a great extent it was. But there was no fear more constantly present with General Nugent and General Ricardo than that of its developing into the conventional bombing action, which progressed at snail's pace at best, at worst reached an early deadlock, and always required bombs by the dozen for every yard of ground gained. In this case four thousand yards, covered by two or three parallel lines of trenches, with numerous communication trenches at right angles to the attack, had to be taken. And speed was essential; for, much as the attack depended upon the advance east of the Canal, that in its turn could have been taken in flank by machine-gunners on the west had not the 109th Brigade kept pace with it. And so the order was—no bombing till other methods failed. At the head of the platoon columns to move up the trenches was to be not a bomber, but a Lewis gunner. A Lewis gun could be used by a man of large physique—and of these the Ulster Division still possessed plenty, if not such numbers as a year back—with a sling over the left shoulder, the gun resting above the right hip. It was heavy and clumsy, but its tremendous moral effect in such broad trenches as those of the Hindenburg System can readily be imagined. It was to be the spear-head of the attack along each line of trenches. General Ricardo had learnt the idea from the Canadians, who had employed it at Vimy. Moreover, when it was found possible, riflemen were to move on top, outside the trench. The question of artillery support was not easy, since no preliminary registration, here, or on any other part of the front of attack, was possible. Colonel Simpson, who took up his position with General Ricardo at a command post in the sunken Demicourt-Havrincourt Road, just short of the British front line, planned and controlled the artillery support in most brilliant fashion, well worthy the fame he was winning as one of the most scientific and least conventional junior artillery commanders in the British Army. It must not be supposed that the part played here, or on the whole front, by artillery was negligible, nor that the barrage was inconsiderable. On the contrary, the artillery support for the main attack was of vast weight. In Havrincourt Wood, along the rides, guns stood almost wheel to wheel. But these guns had not registered. Consequently the barrage might be expected to be somewhat ragged, and was to keep considerably further in front of the tanks and infantry than would otherwise have been the case. Still, a barrage does not cut wire. It was the tanks which were to accomplish this. Had they failed, the whole scheme would have collapsed. During the night of November the 19th, the whole line of tanks on the front of the III. and IV. Corps moved to a general distance of a thousand yards from the German outpost line. The noise of their advance was covered by long bursts of machine-gun fire.

At 6-20 a.m. the great assault was launched. The tanks went forward behind the barrage, followed by their infantry columns. From the first moment it was evident that the calculations of the British staffs had been correct. The surprise was complete, showing that the Germans had learnt nothing of importance from their prisoners. The advance had the precision of clock-work, the infantry following the tanks without difficulty through gaps in the most formidable wire entanglements in the world. It was 7-15 ere observers of the 36th Division upon the ridge east of Hermies could penetrate the mist and smother of smoke. Then they saw the tanks going forward over the ridge north of Havrincourt, well up to the barrage and waiting for each lift, the columns of the 62nd Division behind them, meeting with small opposition and suffering few casualties. It was a very impressive sight. To the Germans it must have been appalling, this line of great engines rushing through their magnificent defences as they had been of paper, checking an instant to put down huge brushwood-bound bundles to enable them to cross the wide trenches, then moving steadily and remorselessly on. Here and there a stout-hearted officer organized momentary resistance, but for the most part the affair was on one side a rout, on the other a procession. German barrage there was none; only some desultory and ineffective shelling. By eight o'clock the first objective, which included the villages of Havrincourt and Ribécourt, and Couillet Wood, and, of course, the front system of the Hindenburg defences, was in our hands all along the line. In Havrincourt and its château park fighting continued till ten o'clock or later, but it was without importance.

Upon the first objective there was a pause to allow troops for the next to pass through. At 8-35 a.m. the new advance began. Here again all went well—save at one point. The 62nd Division swept on unchecking; on the front of the III. Corps all resistance was easily overcome. But the 51st Division had no such fortune. The Highlanders were baffled by the village of Flesquières, perched upon its hilltop. Field-guns, dragged from their pits on the north side of the village, came into action as the tanks approached, firing over open sights, at point-blank range, crumpling them up, one after the other. The front line of the Hindenburg Support System was pierced; but as the tanks could not cut the wire of the second line, the infantry could not penetrate it. For the moment there was deadlock here. We must turn to our more immediate problem, the attack of the 109th Brigade, launched simultaneously with the general advance from the first objective.

For the assault upon the spoil heap a battery of four-inch Stokes mortars to fire "thermit" shell, which had been used with effect at Messines, had been procured. For four minutes these mortars and the covering artillery bombarded its south-west side. Then the 10th Inniskillings charged home and took it. There was no serious fighting here. The effect of the "thermit" shell was terrific morally. The defenders ran northwards up the trenches. A number were, however, killed by machine-gun fire, while seventy prisoners and two machine-guns were taken. The prisoners belonged to the 20th Landwehr Division, which had not been identified, and had come into line but two days before. This discovery was of good augury for the attack, since by this period of the war Landwehr troops were not of high quality.

The necessary point of entry into the German trenches having been won, the 10th Inniskillings pushed up them according to plan, behind their barrage. A second doorway was forced when, directly the barrage lifted from it, a company of the 14th Rifles, attached to the 10th Inniskillings, entered the communication trench on the Demicourt-Flesquières Road, fifteen hundred yards north of the first one. The clearing of the captured trenches was carried out most systematically. The leading platoons dropped a man at the entrance to each deep dug-out, to be picked up by the fourth section following in rear, which was allotted the duty of "mopping up." As each dug-out was cleared, a noticeboard was set up at entrance bearing the significant inscription "Mopped"! When the leading platoon exhausted its men, another moved through to the front, the first reorganizing behind it. A single flag with the battalion colours was carried by the leading platoon, and never displayed save at the head of the advance. The 10th Inniskillings reached their objective just north of the Demicourt-Flesquières Road at 9-30 a.m., or a few minutes behind schedule time. This, however, was of no significance, since the line now held was part of the general second objective of the whole attack, and there was a pause upon it of twenty-five minutes. The second objective had been reached upon the whole front, save only at Flesquières.

Meanwhile, the 9th Inniskillings, responsible for the next phase of the attack after the 10th had captured Hill 90, had moved in. Those only who have seen the Hindenburg trenches can realize how comparatively easy it was to pass one body of troops through another in them. In ordinary trenches such methods would have resulted in hopeless congestion. Here all went smoothly owing to the great breadth of the trenches. The 9th Inniskillings had one platoon moving along the bed of the Canal, here dry. Craters on the Demicourt-Graincourt Road, defended by machine-guns, caused trouble, but the right companies pushed on, and gradually the situation cleared. The 11th Inniskillings, for the final stage of the attack, had now moved in. This battalion met with somewhat stronger resistance. On the right some determined German bombers held up the advance for a while, the Lewis gunner not being able to see them. Here, as was generally the case, the Germans with their stick bombs outranged our men with the Mills, but the Mills rifle grenade more than restored the balance, and the Germans were driven steadily back. This company of the 11th Inniskillings was also able to give material assistance to the men of the 186th Brigade, across the Canal, by its Lewis-gun fire. Lock 6 was the last centre of strong resistance. Eventually the garrison fled across the Canal, though few of them reached the other side. About half-past three the Inniskillings crossed the Cambrai-Bapaume Road, and were soon after-

## DEFENCE OF FLESQUIERES

ward consolidating their position, with their outpost three or four hundred yards north of it. The bridge across the Canal here, it may be added, had been blown up hours earlier. It had never been doubted by the British that the enemy had prepared it for demolition.

On the left of the 109th Brigade the 56th Division now prolonged the line along the Bapaume-Cambrai Road. On its right the 62nd Division, working up the Hindenburg Support System and over open country, had met with complete success. Graincourt had been reached and taken at 1-30, and the long communication trench north of the Bapaume-Cambrai Road was consolidated at the same time as the final objective of the 36th. On the III. Corps front Noyelles had been reached. But the failure of the 51st Division to capture Flesquières constituted a serious menace to the whole scheme of the attack. It would have been greater had the village been strongly held by the Germans, for then the troops of the 62nd Division could never have advanced past it as they did. The fact seems to be that it was the supreme gallantry of one German officer, aided by the merest handful of men, that withstood the attack. The attack was renewed with fresh tanks during the afternoon without success, that one heroic officer, it is said, firing his last gun with deadly effect with his own hands upon the tanks, the wreckage of which, horribly twisted and maimed, strewed the steep slope at nightfall. A patrol of King Edward's Horse, attached to the 62nd Division, had early in the afternoon ridden into the village from the north-west, and reported it clear as far as the Marcoing Road. An attack from this direction by quite a small force would probably have overcome what opposition there was.

The fact that Flesquières remained untaken caused some alteration in the employment of the cavalry. The 1st Cavalry Division was to have been passed through Marcoing, but at 4-30 p.m. the 2nd Cavalry Brigade was ordered instead to occupy Cantaing, which should have been already captured had all proceeded according to plan. But the village was strongly held and the cavalrymen were beaten off. The Brigade therefore remained that night in Noyelles. Just before dusk a company of the 186th Brigade\* and two squadrons of King Edward's Horse made an attack upon Anneux, but were unsuccessful, owing to wire about the village and machine-gun fire from within it.

At 1-30 the 107th and 108th Brigades moved forward, the former to the northern slope of the Grand Ravin about Square Copse, the latter to Yorkshire Bank and the old British trenches south of it. It had now begun to rain heavily, and these troops, particularly those of the 107th Brigade, which were without any shelter, were drenched to the skin. At 8 o'clock the 107th Brigade was ordered across into Havrincourt and the trenches and dug-outs about it. The men were not finally settled with an opportunity for rest till 3 a.m. the following morning. The 10th Inniskillings of the 109th Brigade, which had carried out the first stages of its attack, was moved across the Canal to Kangaroo Alley, south of and parallel with the Bapaume-Cambrai Road. Patrols pushed forward on the west side by the 11th Inniskillings got within five hundred yards of the southern outskirts of Mœuvres, where they encountered resistance enough to compel them to withdraw. There is no reason, however, to suppose that Mœuvres was at this time strongly held, or that a determined attack would have failed to take it. The progress east of the Canal did not appear to warrant such an attack. The Engineers meanwhile had progressed excellently with their bridge-making. By 4 p.m. their bridge for infantry and pack transport, about a thousand yards north of the Hermies-Havrincourt railway line, was available. Half an hour later a still more important task had been accomplished; the existing causeway on the Demicourt-Flesquières Road having been repaired to enable field-guns and wagons to cross. The 36th Division would have been glad to have had at this stage its Pioneer Battalion to work upon its own roads, now being churned up by heavy traffic, but it was employed upon a similar task between Havrincourt and Ribécourt.

\* 62nd Division.

The Signal Service, admirably organized by Major Vigers, who on this occasion excelled, if that were possible, his successes at Messines, had opened up telephone communication, utilising the Canal bed to lay its wires. So good was this that it was a matter of no difficulty to speak from Divisional Headquarters, which still remained at Ytres, to Lock 6, just south of the Bapaume-Cambrai Road.

When dusk came down to bring operations to a halt, the situation was as follows. The 36th Division held a general line five hundred yards north of the Bapaume-Cambrai Road, in touch with the 56th on its left. East of the Canal the 62nd Division held the trench north of the road and the factory. Thence their line curved down just west of Anneux, with a long flank running east of Graincourt to the west of Flesquières. The line of the III. Corps ran well to the north of Noyelles. This left, as will be seen from the line roughly marked on the map, an extraordinary little German salient, in the midst of which there were still apparently German guns in action in Orival Wood.

During the night there was great movement of guns. Most of the heavy artillery of the IV. Corps, since it was difficult to move it through Havrincourt, and would have been harder to feed it, took up positions about Hermies and Demicourt, with the heaviest pieces back at Doignies. Here it could easily be served with ammunition, and here it proved invaluable in the days that were to come. The 153rd Brigade had a very long march. After covering the advance of the 62nd Division from Havrincourt Wood, the guns were withdrawn at midnight and moved, *via* Ruyalcourt, Hermies, and Demicourt, to positions in the old " No Man's Land," east of the last-named village. The batteries of the 173rd Brigade also moved to this neighbourhood, to be prepared to cover a further advance. The bad, narrow roads were, as may readily be imagined, in a state of much congestion. Batteries of the 153rd Brigade were not in action till 7-30 a.m. on the 21st.

In the course of the day's fighting the IV. Corps had

taken over two thousand prisoners, of which the share of the 109th Brigade was five hundred and nine. The latter had also taken a great deal of booty, particularly at Lock 6, which had been used as a general store-house for the forward area.

So ended the first day's fighting. The cavalry action on a grand scale had been a complete failure. Whatever chances of success it may have had were extinguished by the failure to take Flesquières. For the rest, all had gone according to plan. The Bourlon Ridge had not, it is true, been taken. That, however, was really, except in the case of unexpectedly sweeping good fortune, to be the second day's objective. Hopes still stood high.

At dawn on the 21st the German salient was eaten up in a flash. The 51st Division, advancing through Flesquières, swept up to the Graincourt-Marcoing Road, upon which it was established by 11 a.m. A number of guns in Orival Wood were captured. Cantaing, too, fell, after stiff fighting, before the 2nd Cavalry Brigade, assisted by battalions of the 51st Division. Late in the afternoon the Highlanders, who made tremendous efforts to atone for the failure of the previous day, stormed Fontaine-Notre-Dame, on the road from Bapaume to Cambrai, a mere two and a half miles from the latter city. The right flank of the 62nd Division also did well. Anneux was taken, and, after heavy fighting, Anneux Chapel, on the skirts of Bourlon Wood. But the attack on Bourlon Wood was a failure. The troops went round the western slopes in gallant fashion, but were woefully thinned out by machine-gun fire and unable to hold their ground. They advanced, however, to the south-west corner.

West of the Canal the attack was pushed forward by the 109th Brigade, with the 9th Inniskillings, who reached the point where the Hindenburg trenches swung west, a thousand yards north of the Bapaume-Cambrai Road. Here the battalion was held up by heavy machine-gun fire from Lock 5 and east of the Canal. At noon the 14th Rifles and 10th Inniskillings resumed the attack. In face of steadily-increasing opposition they penetrated to the outskirts of Mœuvres, but could not maintain their position under withering machine-gun fire from the village and the Hindenburg trenches west of it. The day's advance was one of less than a thousand yards, after considerably heavier casualties than those of the 20th.

The ground won appeared considerable on paper, but the day had not been successful. The advance had fallen very far short of the programme. It had been intended that the 62nd and 51st Divisions should reach Bourlon, while the 1st Cavalry Division followed through and seized the Canal crossings from Sains-lez-Marquion northward. The two reserve brigades of the 36th Division were to have pressed up on the east side of the Canal, and held its line from Mœuvres to Sains-lez-Marquion. All this had gone by the board. The 40th Division from the V. Corps had moved forward to the area Beaumetz-Doignies-Boursies, to be ready to take over Bourlon Wood when captured, and resume the advance. It did not come into action that day any more than the 107th and 108th Brigades.

The orders for the 22nd were for the 51st and 62nd Divisions to improve and consolidate their positions, while the 36th and 56th gained ground on their left. The 109th Brigade had now shot its bolt, having accomplished its task with every credit. In the early hours of the morning the 108th moved up to relieve it, and by 7 a.m. the 12th Rifles had taken over its advanced positions, the 9th Irish Fusiliers being closed up behind the leading battalion in the trenches about the Bapaume-Cambrai Road. The relieved Brigade withdrew to the old British trenches about Hermies.

East of the Canal the *rôle* of the 107th Brigade was to clear the first and second lines of the Hindenburg Support System up to the Canal, while the 108th took Mœuvres. This task was allotted to the 15th Rifles. A second battalion, the 10th Rifles, was then to pass through and continue the attack along what was known as the Canal du Nord Line to Lock 4, opposite Inchy. General Withycombe moved up to a German dug-out west of Graincourt. Eight guns of the 107th Machine-Gun Company were to assist in covering these attacks east of the Canal. The general rate of the barrage was to be fifty yards in five minutes east of the Canal, and fifty yards in seven and a half minutes west of it. The attack was further to be supported by four Siege and one Heavy Battery, and one 9.2-inch howitzer. It was to be launched at 11 a.m.

It was anticipated by the enemy. At 9-20 he counter-attacked upon the front of the 51st and 62nd Divisions. The latter lost no ground on its right, but its extreme left flank fell back for a short time on to the Bapaume-Cambrai Road, subsequently reoccupying its position. Worse fortune met the British further east, where the 51st Division lost Fontaine. During the counter-attack there occurred one very remarkable incident. A battery of machine-guns of the 36th Division was in action in the open, pushed forward much too far, half-way between Lock 5 and the factory on the Bapaume-Cambrai Road, when it was attacked at close quarters by a company of the enemy. The officer and section sergeant were killed and the guns surrounded. Two guns of another battery were brought into action by Major Miller, the Divisional Machine-Gun Officer, at little over a hundred yards' range. The effect was withering, the Germans melting away before the fire, saving themselves by jumping into trenches or crouching in shell-holes. When quiet had supervened, a machine-gun officer counted forty-two dead Germans about the recaptured position.

The attack of the 36th Division was launched at 11 a.m., after a forty minutes' bombardment. On the right the leading company of the 15th Rifles reached its objective, gaining upwards of five hundred yards of the Hindenburg trenches. The companies which passed through it had a more difficult task. The trenches of the second line were here but half dug, and this, seeing that the attack was working up along them, was to the advantage of the defenders. The Germans established a block above a length of trench about a foot deep, and beat off every attempt by machine-gun fire. At dusk the 10th Rifles made an attempt to rush the machine-guns, but could not get near them, losing six officers in trying to do so.

West of the Canal things went better at the opening. The 12th Rifles attacked Mœuvres with three companies in line. The two on the left penetrated the village, but the right company was held up by machine-guns in the Hindenburg Support System. On the left, troops of the 56th Division, bombing up the Hindenburg Front System, captured Tadpole Copse. Colonel Goodwin, commanding the 12th Rifles, now handled his battalion with great skill. He ordered his right company to bomb its way up the trench leading from the sunken Mœuvres-Graincourt Road to the Hindenburg Support System, while the other companies exploited their semi-success in the village. The right company did succeed in reaching the front trench of the Support System, and in clearing it, but the second line was full of Germans and could never be reached. Meanwhile the centre and western side of the village had been cleared, many Germans being killed in dug-outs and cellars. Pushing on through the village, the Riflemen took the trench on the western edge, fringing the cemetery, and began to consolidate it. Then came the counter-attack.

At 4 p.m. the enemy was seen assembling in great force in Hobart Street, half-way between Mœuvres and Inchy, and in the Hindenburg Support System north-west of the former village. Messages were sent back for support and for an artillery barrage. Both were procured, the former in the shape of a company of the 9th Irish Fusiliers, but, unfortunately, neither of them in time. The counter-attack, launched just before dusk, appeared to be made by two battalions, one working parallel with the Hindenburg Support System and one down the Canal, in several waves. The company in the trench east of the cemetery was forced to withdraw to avoid being surrounded. Our men fell back from position to position, in orderly fashion, taking toll of the enemy with their Lewis guns. There was no trace of fluster, still less of panic. It took the Germans, in fact, an hour and forty minutes from the launching of their attack to drive the 12th Rifles to the southern outskirts of the village. It was a piece of evil fortune after a fine achievement in village fighting. It must be remembered that there was a heavy German barrage south of Mœuvres and machine-gun fire from either flank, which delayed the supports of the 9th Irish Fusiliers.

The action once again demonstrated the disadvantages inherent in attacks on narrow fronts. The Hindenburg trenches west of Mœuvres, on higher ground, overlooked the village and permitted intense machine-gun fire to be concentrated upon it. They were outside the area of operations. In the same way, from the Hindenburg trenches east of the Canal, heavy machine-gun fire was kept up on the village and its approaches. This ground also was, for practical purposes, outside the area of operations, since it could not be taken without artillery preparation or tanks. There had been no artillery preparation, and no tanks were available.

The close of this rather unsatisfactory day may fittingly mark the end of a chapter. After wonderful initial success the action had not continued as planned. Little has been said of the extreme right flank because space does not permit. Nor does it in any way concern the 36th Division. But here also, though Masnières, across the Canal de l'Escaut, had been taken, the great cavalry "drive" had been a failure. Henceforth the battle was to be fought in other circumstances. Fresh German troops were up now, and resistance all along the line was fierce. Every yard of ground had to be won by hard fighting. The idea of exploitation to the Sensée River must have faded from the mind of the Commander of the Third Army. Indeed, he permitted a Division intended for that purpose, the 40th, to relieve the 62nd, now very weary. But much had been won. It was of the highest importance now to take the Bourlon Ridge. While it remained in German hands all our positions were overlooked, and could have been made in time almost untenable. In our hands, on the contrary, it would have been a veritable thorn in the side of the Germans, and would soon

# A NEW PHASE

have compelled an important retirement to the north, if neither so swift nor so great as that which would have been involved by our reaching Oisy-le-Verger.

A new phase was opening, of powerful forces on either side battling fiercely for position. And the crown of battle, looming up above the combatants, was the great circular mass of the Bois de Bourlon.

## CHAPTER IX

### Cambrai and After (II):
### November 23rd to December 31st, 1917

THE conditions under which the attack was continued were difficult in the extreme. From the 23rd of November onward the enemy artillery fire increased enormously, while the ground appeared to be powdered with machine-guns skilfully and tenaciously fought. The troops of the 36th Division were weary. Even such battalions as had not already been in action were suffering from the long exposure to bad weather. And the weather was worsening. Hitherto it had been wet, but, for November, not cold, though the nights were trying enough for troops in fighting kit and with small shelter. Now it began to appear as though the rain would turn to snow. The most formidable difficulty of all was that of communications. The light railways, of which so much had been hoped, were useful certainly, but had not come up to expectation. The roads were bad beyond expression. The main communication of the 36th Division was the Hermies-Graincourt Road. Over the greater part of its length it was sunken, as were those from Hermies to Demicourt, and from Demicourt to Graincourt. Being sunken, it was impossible to widen these mere country lanes, nor was there anything approaching a sufficiency of metal to sustain the huge volume of traffic upon them. On the Hermies-Graincourt Road there were frequent serious blocks in the traffic during the early days, when a limber broke a pole or a cooker lost a wheel. Eventually the road itself ceased to be used at all, traffic proceeding on either side of the banks, and chalk being hastily tumbled into the holes which it speedily made.

The plans of the IV. Corps for November the 23rd were ambitious enough, yet more modest than those of the preceding day. On the right the 51st Division was to retake Fontaine, and secure the high ground east of Bourlon Wood. The 40th Division, which had relieved the 62nd, was to take Bourlon village. The 36th and 56th Divisions were to advance up the Canal and roll up the Hindenburg Support System. Tanks were to assist the attack of the 36th Division for the first time during the operations.

The advance of the 36th Division was again to bestride the Canal du Nord. The 107th Brigade was to attack on the east side, the 108th Brigade on the west. The former was to be supported by the 93rd Army Field Artillery Brigade and a Siege Battery; the latter by the Division's own Artillery Brigades. The sixteen tanks available were allotted to the 107th Brigade. General Withycombe held a conference of commanding officers and officers of the Tank Battalion at his headquarters near Graincourt. The attack was to have two phases: the first, the capture of the Hindenburg trenches up to the Canal, of Round Trench and Lock 5; the second, an advance northward to Hobart Street from the Canal to the north corner of Quarry Wood, the northern and eastern skirts of which were to be held. To the first phase eleven tanks were allotted; to the second five, with any survivors of the first. An hour and a half was considered sufficient for the carrying through of the first phase; after which there was to be an hour's pause before the opening of the second.

West of the Canal the capture of Mœuvres was to coincide with the first phase. The second was to be the capture of the trench running westward from Lock 4 to the Hindenburg Support System. Zero for the first phase was fixed at 10-30 a.m., the earliest moment possible, seeing that General Withycombe had not been able to issue his orders till 8-30, owing to the difficulty in collecting the tank officers. One company commander in the 107th Brigade has informed the writer that he had less than fifteen minutes to assemble his men and explain the attack to his officers.

The task of the 15th Rifles was the rolling up of the Hindenburg Support System to the Canal, and on the success of that battalion the whole scheme of the 107th Brigade depended. It was nothing less than a calamity that of the two tanks that should have led the troops, one broke down, while the other turned off to the right and left them. As they went forward they met overwhelming machine-gun fire. One company made an advance of some hundred yards, while one of its platoons most gallantly rushed an enemy crater-post in the road running north from the factory. But the company was inadequately supported, being neither reinforced nor supplied with ammunition and rifle grenades, and, far from being able to improve its position, had eventually to abandon some of the ground won. The 8th Rifles, assisted by a tank, captured and consolidated Round Trench, also Lock 5, where a few prisoners were taken. A frontal attack upon the Hindenburg System was here out of the question, and these minor successes represented all the ground gained. It is doubtful whether more than two tanks out of the eleven ever crossed the Hindenburg Support System, the rest having either broken down or been put out of action by the German artillery fire, now very heavy. Without them, advance was all but impossible. It was the more unfortunate since the 40th Division had made a very fine attack and captured Bourlon, while the 51st again took Fontaine. Repeated and heavy counter-attacks drove the 40th from Bourlon, but the Germans could never penetrate the wood. The 51st were also driven out of Fontaine, and the line of the 40th was represented by a very dangerous salient.

In the attack on Mœuvres, the 12th Rifles, with the 9th Irish Fusiliers on the right, made small progress till

## THE GRAPPLE AT BOURLON

the fresher 2nd Rifles was thrown in to support them. Stubborn village fighting lasted all day. By dusk three-quarters of the village had been cleared, and four machine-guns captured by the 2nd Rifles. But while the Hindenburg trenches either side of the village remained untaken, consolidation was impossible. At dusk the troops were withdrawn to the southern houses. Before the next dawn the 108th Brigade was relieved by the 109th.

That day's fighting represented the last attack made by the 36th Division. The 107th Brigade was to have made on the morrow another attempt to advance, and would doubtless this time have captured at least the Hindenburg Support System, since it was to have had the co-operation of practically all the IV. Corps Heavy Artillery. The day began, however, with a violent German assault on Bourlon Wood, which drove the troops of the 40th Division back to a general line about half-way through it. The artillery was in consequence switched right to put down a barrage against this attack, and later to support the highly successful counter-attack of the 40th Division and some dismounted cavalry squadrons, which more than restored the original line. The attack of the 107th Brigade, without the necessary artillery assistance, could have achieved no more than that of the previous day. Colonel Clements, commanding the 1st Irish Fusiliers, took the responsibility of ordering his men not to advance, in which he was entirely justified. During the counter-attack, a body of sixty Germans which essayed to advance down the Hindenburg Line was almost annihilated by the fire of machine-guns and the Lewis guns of the 15th Rifles. A machine-gun was captured here by this battalion. West of the Canal, Germans debouching from Inchy, apparently to launch a counter-attack here also, were dispersed by artillery fire.

In the afternoon Bourlon village was taken once more. The IV. Corps had cancelled the attack, owing to the shortage of tanks. But communication between the 40th Division and its 121st Brigade having broken down, the latter attacked and took Bourlon with the twelve tanks at its disposal. On the front of the Guards' Division, which had relieved the 51st the previous night, there was no fighting of importance.

The 25th was an eventless day for the troops of the 36th Division, but for heavy shelling, particularly of its batteries. On the right the Germans again attacked Bourlon, as it was inevitable they should, while they had a battalion to go forward or artillery to cover its advance. After hard fighting they retook it, but could not penetrate the wood, which was in fact now almost impassable, owing to the haze of the gas with which it had been drenched among the trees. The 40th Division had suffered heavy casualties, and was relieved at night by the 62nd. On the following night the 36th Division was to have taken over a wider front, extending its line to within a thousand yards of the western edge of Bourlon Wood. The 107th Brigade had suffered appreciable casualties and its troops were jaded, so the 108th Brigade was to relieve it. At the last moment, however, these orders were cancelled. The Commander of the IV. Corps decided to relieve the 36th Division by the 2nd, which had been put at his disposal, and ordered that the relief should take place that night. The Artillery, Engineers, and Pioneers were to remain at the disposal of the 2nd Division. The machine-guns were to be relieved twenty-four hours later.

The night of November the 26th will remain an unpleasant memory to the survivors of the troops who were then relieved. The snow had come now, and swept almost horizontally before a wind that rose at times to tempestuous force. The relief took a very long time. When it was over, and the men staggered through the blizzard to the very indifferent havens that were to be their lodgings for the night—Beaumetz for the 108th Brigade, Doignies for the 109th, Hermies and the trenches about it for the 107th—they found this shelter, such as it was, packed with odd units. Doignies, in particular, had scarce a corner, being full of details of another Division. The besetting sin of the British Army, the accumulation of what might

## RELIEF OF 36TH DIVISION

almost be described as camp followers, was on such occasions as these a curse. A good many men spent what was left of the night in the open, in the snow.

The following day the Division, less Artillery, Engineers, and Pioneers, moved to the area Barastre-Rocquigny-Beaulencourt, where the men had at least some comfort and the chance to sleep. A day was spent here in the usual tasks of cleaning, refitting, and reorganization.

The Division, to which the 121st Field Company had now been returned, was transferred on November the 29th from the IV. to the XVII. Corps, which was holding the line east of Arras. It was to move to the area round Fosseux by tactical trains from Ytres and Bapaume, the transport moving by road, staging on the night of the 29th at Gomiecourt, Achiet-le-Petit, and Courcelles-le-Comte, ruined villages of the Somme area, in which some shelter for men and animals had been constructed. An agreeable prospect was held out by Staff Officers of the XVII. Corps of some weeks at least out of the line. How far it was realized will shortly appear. For the explanation we must turn once more to the line at Cambrai.

The IV. Corps made another attempt upon Bourlon, the morning after the relief of the 36th Division. Aided by tanks the 62nd Division captured half the village, but could not hold it against powerful German counter-attacks. It clung still, however, to the eastern houses and to the wood. Three battalions of the Guards' Division penetrated Fontaine, but were unsupported and had to be withdrawn at dusk. The resources of the Third Army permitted no further attack. On the evening of the 29th the IV. Corps relieved the Guards' Division by the 59th and the 62nd by the 47th. It had thus in line on the 30th three comparatively fresh Divisions.

On the morning of the 30th was launched the great German counter-offensive. It is called counter-offensive advisedly. It was, in effect, the greatest attack made by German forces on the Western Front since Verdun had died down, more than eighteen months before. Counter-attacks on a large scale had been expected, and preparation made to meet them, but this was something far more serious. It was a deliberately prepared attempt, supported by a great weight of artillery, to apply pincers north and south to the large salient formed by our recent advance. Its effect was curious, since on the south it was completely successful, while on the north it gained scarce a yard.

Of the northern blow the weight fell mainly from Bourlon Wood westward, upon the 47th, the 2nd, and 56th Divisions. The resistance of these, one an "Old Army" Division, the others London Territorials, stands high among the achievements of the British Army in the war. Here and there a section of trench was lost, a portion of a line slightly withdrawn, a position temporarily abandoned, but, broadly speaking, the great assault, launched in eight or ten successive waves, followed by columns in artillery formation, preceded by a whirlwind bombardment of all calibres, with gas and smoke, was a total failure. Repeated attacks throughout the day met a like fate. And not since the early days of the war had our artillery and machine-guns seen such targets. The fact that the IV. Corps Heavy Artillery had not been moved into the German lines, but was about Doignies and Demicourt, was now of incalculable value. It took the advancing host in enfilade. The field artillery likewise did enormous execution. The Left Group covering the 2nd Division consisted of the 153rd and 173rd Brigades, under the command of Colonel Simpson, who was with the Infantry Brigadier in the old headquarters in "Scotch Street." The 153rd Brigade alone fired ten thousand rounds that day. Many large parties of the enemy were caught in the open by its fire. Enemy batteries were seen following up the attack, unlimbering and coming into action. Several sections of 18-pounders and 4.5 howitzers of the 173rd Brigade were run up on to the crest of the Demicourt Ridge, whence they annihilated these batteries with direct fire. Ere nightfall a situation which had had critical moments was restored.

But, as all the world knows, no such rebuff met the

## THE GERMAN COUNTER-OFFENSIVE 169

southern arm of the pincer. Here the Germans broke through the British lines; Masnières, defended by a brigade of the 29th Division, held out, but to the extreme south of the original advance the front collapsed. La Vacquerie was retaken by the enemy. Further south he bit deeply even into our old line, taking Villers-Guislain, Gonnelieu, and Gouzeaucourt, all of which had been ours before November the 20th, and the last-named of which had then been over two thousand yards from our front line. The prisoners captured by the enemy ran into many thousands, and the guns into hundreds. It was a woeful affair, of which the main causes were the lack of an organized defence in depth, and that of training in junior officers and men.

It is pleasanter to turn to the very fine counter-attack by troops of the Guards' Division, fortunately out of the line and still in the neighbourhood. It was made at midday, and drove the Germans headlong through Gouzeaucourt and a thousand yards east of it. Further attempts were made that night and the following day to retake Gonnelieu and La Vacquerie, but without success. The enemy maintained his foothold in these villages and upon the edge of the Welsh Ridge. How far precisely the German advance progressed it is not easy to determine. It is certain at least that it was far east of Gouzeaucourt, and that the main communication of the IV. Corps, the Trescault-Metz Road, was seriously threatened at a time when that Corps' own troops were maintaining their positions. That calamity was averted by the action of the Guards' Division.*

It was at mid-day, while staffs were reconnoitring camps in the neighbourhood of Arras, that news reached the 36th Division of the break-through. Accompanying the news

---

* On the return of the 36th Division to the Cambrai area, the writer was informed that there was a dead German in Dessart Wood. The wood being ten thousand yards from the German line before the counter-attack, he found this hard to credit, and rode over to see. He could find no German. There were, however, undoubtedly some in Gouzeaucourt Wood, half-way between Metz and Gouzeaucourt.

came orders that it should instantly retrace its steps. There was no time now to provide trains upon the congested railways. The troops were to march back through the devastated area, Brigade Groups staging the night at Achiet-le-Petit, Courcelles, and Gomiecourt. They were on the move by half-past two that afternoon, cyclists having been sent out to meet the transport and turn it back. The following night saw the Division in the area Lechelle-Bancourt-Rocquigny. The men were very fatigued after ten days of what was practically open warfare, followed by marching and counter-marching. As for the transport horses, they too were feeling the strain of dragging heavy loads over atrocious roads, and had in many cases not been unhitched before their heads were turned south again. Moreover, the accommodation for men and animals in the Lechelle area was of the scantiest.

At 4 a.m. on the morning of the 23rd, the III. Corps informed the 36th Division that the latter had been placed at its disposal from noon on the following day. Officers from the 108th Brigade were ordered to reconnoitre the area then held by the 88th Brigade of the 29th Division, and from the 109th Brigade part of the area held by troops of the 61st Division on its right. Later in the day, after the reconnaissance had been carried out and invaluable lives lost in its course, these orders were modified. The Germans made a fresh attack at Gonnelieu. For a time the situation on the VII. Corps front was highly critical, but the attack died down after the enemy had made a certain advance. The 108th Brigade was put at the disposal of the 61st Division, and ordered to send up a battalion to hold an old British trench near Beaucamp. Later in the afternoon the whole of the Brigade was moved up to the neighbourhood of this village.

On December the 4th the 107th and 109th Brigades moved up from Lechelle and Bertincourt, halting in Havrincourt Wood for dinners *en route*. The 107th Brigade was disposed in old British trenches between Beaucamp and Villers-Plouich, the 109th in the old German front line north of the former, where it was in reserve to the 6th Division. The two Field Companies left behind, and the Pioneers, rejoined the Division, moving to a camp near Dessart Wood. Headquarters of the Division were established in an infantry camp at Sorel-le-Grand. That night the 108th Brigade relieved the 88th in the line, in the Couillet Valley. The next night the 109th Brigade followed, taking over the important plateau known as Welsh Ridge from the 182nd Brigade of the 61st Division.

On this night G.H.Q. carried out a grave but inevitable decision. The success of the German attack on the southern face of the Bourlon-Noyelles-Masnières Salient had made that salient so narrow in proportion to its depth that its maintenance would be a constant source of attrition. A considerable portion of the ground here, including Bourlon Wood, Cantaing, Noyelles, Graincourt, and Marcoing, was evacuated, all dug-outs within the area being systematically destroyed. This withdrawal was to have an effect upon the relief to be carried out by the 36th Division.

The new line, of which General Nugent assumed command on the relief of the 182nd Brigade, was curious and somewhat indeterminate as to exact position. It represented an acute salient, of which the nose pointed due east. Behind this ran, from south-west to north-east, the deep, densely-wooded Couillet Valley. At the south-west end was the ruined village of Villers-Plouich, at the north-east the little damaged village of Marcoing, captured by the British in the Cambrai battle, but now again in German hands. On either side of the Couillet Valley were the two ridges destined to become famous, Welsh Ridge on the south-east, and Highland Ridge on the north-west. Across these, at right angles to the Couillet Valley, ran the two Hindenburg Systems, which on Welsh Ridge drew to within two hundred yards of each other, forming a single system of defence. That fact proved how highly the men who had sited those trenches rated the importance of Welsh Ridge. To the British at this moment it was well-nigh as valuable as it had been to the enemy.

It will be remembered that the evacuation of Marcoing had taken place on the night of the 4th. There was still some uncertainty as to the position of the British outpost line. There was more before the relief was complete. The 9th Inniskillings of the 109th Brigade sent its No. 3 Company in advance up on to the Welsh Ridge in the afternoon. This company arrived in the midst of a tremendous bombardment, amid which the bursts of captured English 18-pounder high explosive were only too apparent to the experienced eye. It was greeted by the unpleasant news that the Germans were bombing up the Hindenburg Support Systems, had already made considerable headway, and that the troops awaiting relief, demoralized by utter weariness and exposure, and by the bombardment which had reduced them to a handful, were at that moment retreating only too fast. The company, as was natural in such a bombardment, was spread out with very long intervals between the platoons. The leading platoon was at once pushed along the front line. It had few bombs and no artillery support, so had to rely upon rifle fire. But it stopped the German advance. Three times the enemy pressed up the trench, and thrice was driven back. Moreover, on the report that the enemy was advancing also up the second line, two sections, perhaps ten men, were despatched to the assistance of the troops in that trench. Here likewise the German bombers were checked. The remainder of the battalion moved up, and the whole line was taken over. The night passed fairly quietly.

The heroism of this action is not to be measured by ordinary standards, since the men were in a state of fatigue and depression when it started. It was surpassed on the morrow, when the 9th Inniskillings, assisted by a platoon of the 14th Rifles, counter-attacked to restore the ground won by the enemy before their arrival. They were enabled to carry this out by the action of the Brigade transport officer, Lieutenant Vaughan, who had brought up, in the course of the night, by the road through Villers-Plouich, officially reported impracticable for any transport, fourteen

## DEFENCE OF 9TH INNISKILLINGS 173

limber-loads of ammunition, grenades, and Stokes mortar bombs. The attack was at first successful, winning back most of the lost ground and capturing nine prisoners, but the Inniskillings followed the retiring enemy too far, and parties of Germans, pushing down a sunken road which had been overlooked, cut off and captured the leading men, as well as a section of the 109th Machine-Gun Company, and drove the attack back to its starting point. Of what followed, a graphic account is given by Captain (then Lieutenant) Densmore Walker, of the 109th Machine-Gun Company, who had heard that his guns had been lost and had come forward with the company commander to investigate.

"We went up the main front Hindenburg Line. This really was a filthy place. Corpses were touching, laid along the fire-step, all men of the 61st Division. I expect the *strafe* of the afternoon previous accounted for a great many. . . . On and on we went and then cut to the left, where we found an officer called Emerson, of the 9th Inniskillings. Emerson said we couldn't get further as the Hun was thirty yards away bombing down the trench. Poor fellow, he thought his whole company was wiped out, and he had been hit on the head by a bomb. There was a hole in the top of his tin hat. . . . He was right about the Huns. Moore said we were still one hundred and fifty yards from the machine-gun positions. Some stick bombs fell around us, several on top of the parapet and one or two in front of us in the trench. We had about six men slowly falling back—they had no bombs. One was hit while I was there. I took a squint over the top and saw the Huns throwing many bombs. They had a light machine-gun in case we attacked over the open. We threw our few bombs, and that stopped them for a few minutes. When we stopped throwing they came on again. They can throw their stick bombs further than a Mills can be chucked by a normal man. We went on retreating quite slowly. We could have stopped them all right with bombs. Mulholland\* ran off to get some, and finally some reinforcements of the 14th Rifles

\* O.C. 109th Machine-Gun Company.

came up and held the cross trench, the Hindenburg Line. Here we could easily hold the Boche as we were right across his front. As there was nothing to do here, we decided to try to get to the machine-gun positions from the left flank, the right being effectually closed to us. Just as we were pushing off, Emerson gathered some men together, got out on top, and chased the Huns back up the trenches. It was uphill."

This heroic young officer, who had led his company in the original attack that morning and captured four hundred yards of trench, had, as Captain Walker remarks, been severely wounded in the head. For three hours he had rallied the remnants of his company to withstand the German bombers. He had made a previous attack over the open and captured six prisoners. On this last occasion of which Captain Walker speaks, having driven back the Germans at least a hundred yards, he fell, mortally wounded. He was awarded the posthumous honour of the Victoria Cross.

It may be added that Major Mulholland and Captain Walker, working their way round to the left flank, found two of their gun teams intact, though two men had been killed and thirteen captured by the enemy. The guns had been posted where no machine-guns should ever have been, in an outpost line very lightly held by isolated infantry sections, owing to the previous troops not having realized exactly how the land lay. The men had taken over their positions in the dark, no reconnaissance having been possible, not realizing whither they were being led by their guides, and had suffered the inevitable consequences when the German bombers attacked them. A Vickers machine-gun in a crooked trench is an indifferent weapon with which to repel an attack along that trench.

It was found necessary to relieve the 9th Inniskillings after twenty-four hours, so heavily had the battalion suffered. It had lost all four company commanders. The 11th took its place. Stokes mortars and rifle grenades had now been brought up, and at 6 a.m. on the 7th the new battalion made a very fine bombing attack, clearing three hundred yards of trenches on a front of two hundred yards, straightening out the line, and driving the Germans off the crest of Welsh Ridge. It avoided the mistake of the 9th in going too far. Two local counter-attacks upon the Inniskillings, within four hours of their establishing themselves upon their objectives, were beaten off. The trenches were blocked and Stokes mortars put in position to cover the obstructions. Germans massing for a further assault were dispersed by a concentration of artillery. The achievement of the 109th Brigade, when the condition of its troops and the state of the trenches are taken into consideration, must be held to rank high among the exploits of its career. Weary and sorely tried handfuls of men had made a most stout-hearted resistance to well-organized and determined attacks, and the bombing counter-offensives had been carried out with a dash that fresher troops could not have excelled. Welsh Ridge had been denied to the enemy.

The position was even slightly improved by the 107th Brigade, which took over the sector on the night of the 8th, and won some further ground in the first Hindenburg Line the following morning. The 107th Brigade also constructed new blocks. This work was carried out by the permanent Brigade Works Party, under the command of Lieutenant Haigh, who had earned the *sobriquet* of " Sandbags " by many similar achievements. The defence, an affair of makeshift at first, was now thoroughly organized, with machine-gun batteries linked by telephone to the Brigade Headquarters in Couillet Wood and on Highland Ridge.

On the front of the 108th Brigade there were fewer alarums and excursions. In the Couillet Valley its troops had even room for movement, the Germans contenting themselves with the establishment of posts in the sunken roads leading from Marcoing. Two prisoners were captured by the 2nd Rifles, and one by the 9th Irish Fusiliers. One post on the higher ground, at the very nose of the salient, was driven in by the enemy, but promptly re-established. One of the German prisoners reported that an attack was to be launched at dawn on the 14th. All troops and reserves "stood to," and an hour before dawn a great bombardment was opened by all the artillery on the III. Corps front. If attack were contemplated it did not develop. Until two days before its final relief the Division's front was covered by the 17th Artillery Brigade of the 6th Division, and three Army Field Artillery Brigades, under the command of General Brock. On the 14th the personnel of its own Artillery came in, taking over the guns *in situ* of two of these Brigades.

Welsh Ridge was safe now from anything but a "full dress" attack. But that was precisely what appeared to be coming. The Germans were plainly in aggressive mood. Their aeroplanes swept continually down upon our frontline trenches, firing upon the men in them. Areas in rear, about Metz especially, were bombed night and day. Their artillery was very active. Havrincourt Wood was rendered uninhabitable by its constant shelling. And it was increasingly plain that the infantry and machine-gunners of the 36th Division were in no fit state to withstand a new offensive in force.

Never since it landed in France had the troops of the 36th Division been reduced to a physical ebb so low. The men became indescribably dirty; lungs, throats, and hearts were affected. High as were battle casualties, the sick wastage was higher still, which had not been the case even at Ypres in August, because then the weather, if wet, was warm. The troops had, in fact, been exposed to three weeks of winter in the open, with almost continuous fighting, while it is doubtful if those of the 36th Division had fully recovered from the effects of the Ypres episode, three months earlier. The great captains of old times, who decided that long spells of open warfare in winter were impossible, were not fools. Man born of woman cannot withstand for long that combined strain and exposure without appalling physical and moral deterioration. Morally the infantry had survived far better than the authority which left them in line had right to expect. The men kept surprisingly good

## RELIEF IN A BLIZZARD

hearts. Walking round these much-harassed outposts one was still greeted with a grin when one inquired how many "pine-apples" had come over in the last twenty-four hours from the German blocks a little further down the trenches. But physically they were wrecks. They were living on their nerves.

A strong report as to the condition of the troops, sent up through the chain of the medical services, added weight to General Nugent's representations, which, realizing the embarrassments of the Higher Command, he had not made till they were absolutely necessary. Relief came at last. On the night of the 14th it began, the 189th Brigade of the 63rd (Royal Naval) Division relieving the 107th Brigade on the right. Two battalions of this latter Brigade had been exchanged with two of the 108th, which had endured a continuous spell in the line, though not in its worst portion. The following night it also was relieved. Ere they came out, the 9th Irish Fusiliers bombed an enemy machine-gun post, killing one man, driving off the others, and bringing in the gun. This parting fling was, in all the circumstances, it will be admitted, a *beau geste*.

Rest had come at last, but it had to be won after a last battle with the elements. The Division was to concentrate in the area round the delightful little village of Lucheux, near Doullens. It was now that there swept over Northern France—indeed over much of Northern Europe—a blizzard of snow that may almost be called historic. Dismounted personnel moved by train, and reached its destinations after long delays. Most of the lorries allotted to formations were, however, "snowed up," and did not arrive for two or three days. The transport struggled through in face of extraordinary difficulties. The snow banked itself up on the hedgeless roads. In those which were sunken it lay frequently six feet and more in depth. Units were obliged to march miles out of their courses, bringing the vehicles through drifts in relays with double teams, trace horses being sent back for a second batch when the first was upon firmer ground. Some of the country tracks off the Doullens-

Arras Road simply could not be found. One staging area had been allotted to two Divisions at once. The mounted personnel of the Signal Company, turned out by newcomers, marched fifty miles in these conditions.

Finally all troops reached their quarters and settled down, the chief work being the clearance of the roads and the making of tracks past the most formidable drifts where this was impracticable. By Christmas the men were in fair comfort, and, good cheer being easily procurable, a pleasant enough Christmas was celebrated. The troops had reason to congratulate themselves when they learned the fate they had narrowly missed. On December the 30th the Germans launched a heavy attack upon Welsh Ridge, and drove the 63rd Division off a great part of it.

General Ricardo returned at this time to England. The strain of the Battle of Cambrai and the counter-offensive had told severely upon his health. Except for a few weeks when he commanded another Brigade, he had been with the 36th Division from the beginning, had indeed, as has been elsewhere recorded, assisted at its birth. His brilliant powers of organization and his concentration upon the whole aspect of any problem presented to him, made him an ideal Brigadier in what has been described as a war of material. He was succeeded by his friend and brother-officer of the Inniskilling Fusiliers, Brigadier-General W. F. Hessey, D.S.O. General Hessey also had been one of the original commanding officers of the 109th Brigade, and had come to France with the 11th Inniskillings, leaving that battalion to command a brigade before the opening of the Somme battle. General Ricardo's organizing abilities were not lost to the British Army. He ended the war as Commandant of the large base of Dieppe.

The lessons of the Battle of Cambrai are clear enough, though some of its aspects will remain mysterious till all the secrets of the war are revealed. The piercing of the Hindenburg fortifications was to a certain extent a gamble, since no such operation had yet been attempted in such manner. The very fact that its surprise was complete was perhaps the most remarkable feat of all. It was a triumphant success, though it must be remembered that the Germans were ill equipped with either armour-piercing ammunition or anti-tank guns to oppose it. But, if the break-through was wonderfully achieved, the ensuing exploitation was not. The resistance of Flesquières and a broken bridge at Masnières checked the cavalry in its eastward thrust, but, after all, the Canal de l'Escaut was won, and exploitation east of it, including the capture of Cambrai, was of less importance than the northern advance to the Sensée marshes. "Cambrai," the writer heard a distinguished soldier say, "was either a surprise or it was not. It opened as a surprise, but it was not continued as a surprise should be." It appears probable to-day that had two fresh Divisions been passed through after the troops had reached their objectives—disregarding Flesquières, which actually did very little harm—they could have been firmly consolidated on the Bourlon Ridge by next morning, and possibly reached the outskirts of Cambrai. Mœuvres likewise would probably not have been a hard nut for the teeth of one of the reserve Brigades of the 36th Division that afternoon. As it was, these troops on that first day sat in the rain and were not employed. The supreme difficulty, which was not surmounted, was the passing through of new formations in a fresh state. This difficulty was due to the scanty accommodation in the forward area, which could not be largely augmented without robbing the attack of one of its most essential features—surprise. It was probably this cause which kept the Divisions in the V. Corps so far back. This question of accommodation was as important as any tactical problem. There was no rest for troops in reserve; they were scarcely better off than those in the fighting. The organization of billeting during reliefs broke down. No provision was made for surplus personnel of incoming Divisions. As a result, each area became congested with their details, and other Divisions, when allotted such areas, found no accommodation left. Another great difficulty was the lack of tolerable roads. The work done upon the roads before and during the battle was insufficient to preserve them, but it had the effect of wearying the front-line troops. The preliminary work, the exposure, cold, dirt, lack of rest and hot food, told very speedily upon the health of the infantry engaged, and diminished its fighting value.

The tanks were magnificent. They accomplished all that their commanders had promised. But their employment after the first day caused a tremendous strain upon their teams, which, when not fighting, were greasing and " tuning up." It is possible—though this is pure speculation—that the number used on November the 20th might have been reduced by a third, which would have left a really large reserve for subsequent operations. As it was, many tanks in the later stages of the battle broke down before reaching their starting line.

And once more, in conclusion, we must pay our meed of praise to the German machine-gunner. Machine-gun battalions were reported by airmen to have detrained at Cambrai on the evening of the 20th. If so, these picked troops were doubtless in action all along the front the following day. It was machine-gun fire alone that delayed the British advance till fresh troops were on the ground to bring it to a halt. Of the German machine-gunners General Nugent wrote : " It is not too much to say that the failure of our offensive to achieve the objectives laid down, was entirely due to the devotion and fighting spirit of these troops of the enemy, practically unsupported by their own infantry and artillery, during the first forty-eight hours."

This fact proved, if proof were needed, that no troops, however devoted, could, without mechanical assistance, face machine-guns in being, handled by really determined defenders.

## CHAPTER X

### THE GERMAN OFFENSIVE ON THE SOMME (I):
### JANUARY TO MARCH 22ND, 1918

SNOWBOUND as they were, the troops of the 36th Division passed several days in the most agreeable conditions. One day there might be snow-fall; the next might succeed with keen frost, but there was no lack of timber for fuel, and the amenities of civilization were very welcome to men who for five months had dwelt amid devastation. Training was practically impossible owing to the depth of the snow in the fields, but some musketry was carried out on a good rifle-range near Lucheux. The Artillery, having been relieved by that of the 63rd Division on Christmas Day, got no further than the Beaulencourt staging area, where it remained hemmed in by drifts.

The rest was, as usual, all too short, particularly in view of the exhausted condition of the troops. Immediately after Christmas the Division was again on the move, to the area Corbie-Boves-Moreuil. Brigade groups went by rail, the transport by road, staging at Puchevillers and Contay. The latter met with difficulties equal to those following the relief. Many lorries were stuck in drifts. In some cases the trains even were considerably delayed.

The British Army was extending its flank, taking over from the French a front far greater than it had ever held, even at the time of the German retirement of 1917, when its right had been on the Amiens-St. Quentin Road. This is not the place to discuss the wisdom of that extension, or supposing, as few will deny, that it was in itself reasonable, of its magnitude. Suffice it to say that Sir Douglas Haig now found himself seriously short of reserves. The relief of successive French divisions was being slowly effected, and the progress of the 36th Division was leisurely. It remained five days at rest in the Corbie area, where it was joined by its Artillery. Then it went slowly forward, *via* Harbonnières, to the area of Nesle, a town left undamaged by the Germans in their retirement, into which they had herded civilians, old men, women, and children, from other towns and villages destroyed by them. Here Divisional Headquarters were established on January the 12th. That night the 107th Brigade relieved a regiment of the 6th French Infantry Division astride the Somme before St. Quentin, remaining under the orders of the French Divisional Commander. The night following the 109th Brigade relieved the other French regiment in line, command passing to General Nugent at 10 a.m. on the 14th, when Headquarters took over from those of the 6th French Division at Ollézy. The 108th Brigade was billeted in villages on the Ham-St. Quentin Road, with headquarters at Dury. The Divisional Artillery had been joined by the 14th Army Field Artillery Brigade. The relief of the French artillery was not complete till the 15th.

Reliefs of French by British formations always presented great difficulties, owing to the fact that reserves of munitions of every sort had to be transferred, instead of being simply handed over as when Briton relieved Briton. Differences of language and of method were scarcely less important. Yet it often happened that reliefs on such occasions were the most satisfactory of all. Each side was on its mettle. Staff work was meticulously careful, reconnaissances were thorough, guides of proved intelligence chosen. This case was no exception. There is hardly a diary of the formations and units of the 36th Division in which is not expressed high appreciation of the arrangements made by the French, and of the kindness with which advance parties were treated by them. One officer writes of his own reception by a French regimental commander: " The most amazing dinner I ever did have in the line ! We had course after course of wonderful things, with suitable wines, till it was hard to think that the Huns could be only a thousand yards distant, but that was all they were." And not the officers only were entertained, for his men informed him that "the *poilus* made them eat the whole time and absolutely bathed them in coffee."

The front taken over ran from Sphinx Wood, some twelve hundred yards west of the village of Itancourt, to a point on the St. Quentin-Roisel Railway a thousand yards west of Rocourt Station. Rocourt is a suburb of the city of St. Quentin, at the gates of which the British Armies now sat. The position and its defences will have to be described later in some detail. Here it need only be said that the latter were already considerable, but that, the relief taking place in the midst of a thaw following upon weeks of snow and frost, the 36th Division succeeded to a legacy of fallen-in trenches and mud. For the rest, it was on the whole a quiet front and not uncomfortable. The destruction of the villages behind our lines did not appear to be as complete as before Cambrai. A few French civilians had trickled back to villages such as Ollézy and Douchy, while the town of Ham, where were the Headquarters of the XVIII. Corps, was intact and was full of them.

The Germans, who had excellent observation, were, of course, quickly aware of the relief, and evidently received orders to obtain identifications of the new troops in front of them. After several fruitless attempts they succeeded in obtaining them. On the night of January the 22nd they entered our outpost line on the front of both Brigades, capturing in each case a wounded prisoner. A small patrol of the 10th Rifles was also waylaid by superior numbers, and an officer and sergeant taken. This appeared to content them, and thereafter, for a considerable time, the front became of a placidity such as the troops of the 36th Division had seldom known.

For the moment—a fleeting moment, indeed—the enemy had second place in the minds of officers and men of the Division. Its first concern was with its reorganization. The shortage of man-power had been talked of long enough. Its fruits had now to be plucked, and bitter they were. The whole British Army was now cutting down its divisions to nine infantry battalions, and its brigades to three. From the tactical point of view, apart from the fact that it entailed a loss of some hundred and seventy-five battalions, the change had serious inconveniences. The brigade of four battalions was the traditional British formation, just as the regiment of three was the Continental. It was the formation which British commanders had handled in training and practice, upon which their conceptions of infantry in war were based. The moral loss was no less great, particularly in divisions and brigades with strong territorial associations and sentiment. It meant that battalions in every division disappeared, and that either their personnel was transferred to others, or that they became "Entrenching Battalions," pitiful, nameless ghosts, robbed of their pride and their traditions. Such changes could not be without their effect upon moral, working through the loss of *esprit-de-corps*, the very life's blood of a combatant unit.

The 36th Division, it will be remembered, had already received two regular battalions, the 2nd Royal Irish Rifles and the 1st Royal Irish Fusiliers. It was now joined by three more, the 1st and 2nd Royal Inniskilling Fusiliers, from the 29th and 32nd Divisions respectively, and the 1st Royal Irish Rifles, from the 8th Division. To make place for them, the 10th and 11th Inniskillings, the 8th/9th, 10th, and 11th/13th Rifles had to disappear. Three Entrenching Battalions, the 21st, 22nd, and 23rd, were formed from the disbanded battalions after the remainder, including the newcomers, had been brought up to strength. The 2nd Rifles in the 108th Brigade, and the 1st Irish Fusiliers in the 107th, were exchanged. The infantry of the Division was now as follows:

# VICTORIA CROSSES OF THE 36th (Ulster) DIVISION – 1917 and 1918.

The late 2/Lt. E. DE WIND
15th Royal Irish Rifles.

The late Corp. E. SEAMAN
2nd Royal Inniskilling Fusiliers.

2/Lt. C. L. KNOX
Royal Engineers.

Pte. N. HARVEY
1st Royal Inniskilling Fusiliers.

## REORGANIZATION OF DIVISION

**107TH INFANTRY BRIGADE.**
1st Royal Irish Rifles.
2nd Royal Irish Rifles.
15th Royal Irish Rifles.

**108TH INFANTRY BRIGADE.**
12th Royal Irish Rifles.
1st Royal Irish Fusiliers.
9th Royal Irish Fusiliers.

**109TH INFANTRY BRIGADE.**
1st Royal Inniskilling Fusiliers.
2nd Royal Inniskilling Fusiliers.
9th Royal Inniskilling Fusiliers.

The new arrivals were all regular battalions of Ulster regiments, but the characteristics of the Ulster Division were entirely changed. Its infantry, formed originally from the U.V.F., had now Ulster-Scot and Celt intermingled, and received English recruits as well.

At the same time the 16th Rifles (Pioneers) was reduced, with other Pioneer battalions in France, to three companies. One accretion of strength the Division received, as some small compensation. The 266th Machine-Gun Company arrived from England on January the 18th, and was formed, with the three existing Machine-Gun Companies, into the 36th Machine-Gun Battalion. The tendency had been for the machine-guns of a Division to come more and more directly under the control of the Divisional Commander during active operations. A Divisional Machine-Gun Officer had long been employed, but he was rather an *attaché* to the staff than a commander. Under the new system there was a lieutenant-colonel commanding the battalion who received his orders from the staff of the Division.

On February the 22nd the 30th Division, hitherto the reserve of the XVIII. Corps, was interposed between the 36th and 61st, taking over the front held by the 36th

Division north of the Somme, in the Forward System. In the second position, or Battle Zone, the 36th Division continued to be responsible for a sector north of the Somme, behind the village of Fontaine-les-Clercs.* The frontage was thus reduced to about six thousand yards. The relief of French troops by British had meanwhile extended further south, and the 36th Division had on its right the 14th Division of the III. Corps.

The Battle of Cambrai had been the last fling of the Allies for the time being. They were now definitely upon the defensive, awaiting a great attack in some uncertainty as to the precise point at which it should be launched. The victories of the Central Powers upon other fronts, above all the collapse of Russia, had freed German troops which, if not for the most part of high quality, would be able to man defences while attack was delivered elsewhere by the superior troops they relieved. Not a week passed without the announcement of the arrival of new divisions from Russia or Italy. Between November the 1st, 1917, and March the 20th, 1918, the number of German divisions in the Western theatre had increased from one hundred and forty-six to one hundred and ninety-two.** The total continued to grow for some time after the launching of the offensive. The heavy artillery had also been greatly increased, while a number of Austrian artillery regiments had come to the aid of their allies. The forces of the Allies were now considerably outnumbered, though not nearly to the extent which many writers, then and since, have pretended. Moreover, they were without unity of command, and there was among them divided opinion as to the point at which they would have to meet the onslaught, though Sir Henry Wilson had insisted that it would be at the junction of British and French. There had been preparations for an advance in Flanders. The French had apprehensions of one in Champagne. On both these fronts there came, indeed, great attacks at subsequent dates. Even if the attack were to come, as seemed most probable, on

* Map V.   ** Lord Haig's Despatches.

the front of General Gough's Fifth and General Byng's Third Armies, its exact scope was uncertain. The final opinion appeared to be that, while the opening assault would extend further south, the main weight of the attack would be north of the Somme, along which would be formed a defensive flank. There is little doubt, from the writings of German staff officers since published, that such was the original intention, and that only unexpectedly great success south of the Somme induced Ludendorff to modify it. It appears also that the Crown Prince, in whose Group of Armies were the forces in the left of the German advance, urged him to adhere to his first plan even after the battle had been several days in progress.

Lord Haig in his Despatches has revealed that, not being able to hold all his extended front in adequate strength, having to take risks somewhere, he took them on the front of the Fifth Army, where there was most elbow-room, and where loss of ground was likely to have least serious effects. It had become more and more apparent that defence in depth offered the best means of checking and breaking up an advance, and it had been laid down by G.H.Q. that all preparations must be based upon that system. Unfortunately, with the slender forces at the disposal of General Gough, defence in adequate depth implied a very shadowy defence in breadth.

The system of defence of divisions in line comprised a Forward Zone and a Battle Zone. The object of the former was to withstand a minor attack, and to check and, so far as might be, disorganize and disintegrate a major one. On the Battle Zone the Army Commander was to oppose the enemy's advance with all the forces at his disposal. The Forward Zone comprised a front and intermediate system; the former consisting of outpost line, line of resistance, and counter-attack companies; the latter of a system of isolated forts, wired all round, known as the Line of Redoubts. The Battle Zone likewise consisted of two main lines of defence, organized internally with counter-attack units and wired-in redoubts. The description of these defences may sound formidable till it is explained that there was but one battalion for the defence of each of them to two thousand yards on the front of the 36th Division, and even less density further south. There were likewise Rear Zone defences, notably behind the Canal de St. Quentin and Canal de la Somme. Here it may be added that confusion has been caused in the minds of many by the fashion in which the names " Somme River," " Somme Canal," " St. Quentin Canal," and " Crozat Canal " have been used by various writers in their descriptions of the battle; because the canalized Somme, giving birth to different canals at different parts of its course, was also the main obstacle in two successive lines of defence. The Somme runs south-west from St. Quentin to St. Simon, west for nine miles to Voyennes, then more or less due north to Peronne. Over the first of these three sections it is canalized under the name of the Canal de St. Quentin; over the second two, under that of the Canal de la Somme. Where confusion is apt to arise is in the fact that at St. Simon the Canal de St. Quentin leaves its parent river and runs down to the Oise at Terguier. In the account that follows, the river, a winding, branching stream, will be disregarded, and the Canals, which formed the real obstacles, alluded to always as the Canal de St. Quentin and Canal de la Somme.*

The front held by the 36th Division was in its natural features not ill adapted for defence. It was crossed by a series of ridges and valleys running east and west, parallel to the front line. Behind the front-line system, which was on the same ridge as the German outposts and on its reverse slope, was a deep valley known as Grugies Valley, from Grugies to the St. Quentin-La Fère Road, north of Urvillers, thence curving northward into " No Man's Land," towards Neuville - St. Amand. Grugies Valley had therefore its advantages and its dangers. On the one hand it afforded good masked positions for machine-guns; on the other, it was a conduit, from the north-eastern end of which attack

* Map VI.

might flow down behind the line of resistance of the Forward Zone. Behind it was another ridge, upon which was the Line of Redoubts. Behind this again the ground sloped away gradually, rising to a slighter ridge, along which ran the Essigny-Contescourt Road. Upon the forward and reverse slopes of this last ridge were the positions of the two southern sectors of the Battle Zone, four thousand five hundred yards behind the front line. The northern sector, as has been explained, was north of the St. Quentin Canal. These positions were good, but they had one great failing. The front line of the 36th Division ran roughly from west to east to Sphinx Wood, while thence the line of the 14th Division ran more nearly north and south. The right flank was therefore very insecure. Should Urvillers fall, the right of the 36th Division's Forward System would undoubtedly crumple, while should such a calamity as the capture of Essigny occur, the defences of the Battle Zone would be turned.

The night of February the 22nd, which saw the entry into line of the 30th Division, saw also a reorganization of the system of defence. All three Brigades now entered the line, the 108th on the right, 107th in the centre, and 109th on the left. Each had one battalion in the Forward Zone, one as garrison for the Battle Zone, and one in reserve. In each case the Forward Zone battalion had two companies in the line of resistance, finding their own outposts, one company for counter-attack in the front system, and one "passive resistance" company, with battalion headquarters, in a large fort in the Line of Redoubts. This unfortunate description implied that the last-named company was not allowed to counter-attack to retake ground lost in the front system. The Battle Zone battalions were billeted close to their battle stations, that of the 108th Brigade in dug-outs at Essigny Station, along the railway cutting, of the 107th Brigade in quarries near Grand Séraucourt, and of the 109th at Le Hamel, on the other side of the St. Quentin Canal. The artillery was disposed in two groups covering the Forward Zone, with one of the three Brigades, the 153rd, in reserve as supporting brigade. On February the 28th, when XVIII. Corps announced a "state of preparation," the batteries of this brigade took up positions south-east of Grand Séraucourt to cover the Battle Zone, with a section per battery pushed forward to temporary positions covering the Line of Redoubts.

Upon these positions a vast amount of work had to be accomplished, an amount so vast that it permitted of very scanty time being allotted for training. The Battle Zone had practically to be created. The lines had been merely sited by the French, and a little wire put up. Work was concentrated first of all upon this; secondly, upon the fortresses which were to contain battalion headquarters and "the passive resistance" company in the Line of Redoubts—known, from right to left, as "Jeanne d'Arc," "Racecourse," and "Boadicea"; and lastly, upon making good the main communication trenches, and making wired-in platoon keeps in the Forward Zone. There was shortage of wire in February and the early part of March, and bad indeed would have been the state of the defences but for the large dumps left behind by the French, for which the countryside was scoured. As it was, no-one in the 36th Division can be said to have been satisfied with the state of the Battle Zone by mid-March. Most of the trenches were no more than eighteen inches deep, it having been ruled that there would be time to dig them out when it became necessary to occupy them.

Uncanny work it was awaiting, in the silence of quietest of quiet lines, a mighty attack of which for very long there was scarce an indication. In the earlier days, save for reports from higher formations of aerodromes, hospitals, and railways far behind the German lines, the sole warning sign was in the large numbers of officers, maps in hand, observing day by day the British trenches and the country behind them. There was no great increase of movement on forward roads till about the 12th of March. Aeroplane photographs taken about this date showed that a large number of shell-holes a few hundred yards from the outpost line

## THE WEEKS OF WAITING

had been worked upon. It was surmised that these were being prepared for trench mortars, for the destruction of the British front-line system, as that of the Russians had been destroyed before the last great German advance at Riga. Significant also, in this connection, was the fact that Oskar von Hutier, who had carried out that attack, was now in line opposite, in command of Eighteenth Army. His known character and antecedents were food for reflection.

New military roads were also discovered behind Itancourt. But it was a few clear mornings and evenings, from the 15th of March onwards, that brought most conclusive evidence of what was impending. From the dovecote in Essigny, the best observation post on the XVIII. Corps front, which was manned by the 36th Division's excellent observers, an enormous amount of traffic could now be observed. Along the main road from Guise-Mont d'Origny to St. Quentin, in particular, huge convoys of lorries and horse transport were seen, as dusk drew in, moving towards the last-named city. Small place for doubt now remained.

On March the 4th occurred a curious incident. The Germans had apparently come to the conclusion that the British front line had been abandoned; and, indeed, it was held lightly enough by isolated sections. Strong patrols, amounting in general to a platoon, suddenly issued from the German trenches all along the 36th Division's front, in broad daylight. The outposts might be weak, but they could resist an attempt of this sort. Under the fire of Lewis guns all the patrols were stopped and dispersed with heavy loss. Patrols sent out in turn from the outpost companies captured in all one officer and ten other ranks. It was a sharp lesson, and thereafter, till the opening of the attack, was no move by the German infantry.

From March the 12th onward was instituted a series of nightly bombardments, in which the now considerable heavy artillery at the disposal of the XVIII. Corps took part, of valleys and dead ground forming probable assembly positions. Tests of the action to follow the preconcerted Corps message, "Man Battle Stations," were carried out. Bridges had long been prepared for demolition and allotted to particular sections of the Field Companies. Small mine-fields had been constructed in case of the employment of tanks by the enemy. Grugies Valley was starred with machine-guns, to sweep its length with zones of flanking fire. It was felt by officers and men of the Division that what the limited means at its disposal permitted had been accomplished. The worst misgivings were with regard to the gaps between keeps and redoubts in the Forward Zone, owing to the paucity of numbers available for its defence. There was no touch between the battalion headquarters forts in the Line of Redoubts; they were in no sense mutually supporting. There was little to prevent the enemy from breaking through in the intervals, pushing forward his main advance almost unembarrassed by them, while special detachments swallowed them at leisure.

Much noise of enemy traffic was heard at night from the 17th onward. On the evening of the 18th two Germans entered our lines on the front of the 107th Brigade to give themselves up. They declared they had deserted to avoid the coming battle, which would not now be long delayed. They confirmed the suspicions of massed trench mortars on the front. They had seen great numbers of troops, particularly of artillery. St. Quentin, they said, was packed with men. On the night of the 20th a raid was carried out by the 61st Division, resulting in the capture of prisoners who stated that the attack was to be launched the following morning. A special bombardment was therefore carried out from 2·30 to 3 a.m., with heavy rolling barrages on likely positions of assembly.

The great moment, for which, it is scarce exaggeration to say, men were waiting all the world over, came at 4·35 a.m. on the morning of March the 21st. The infantry of the 36th Division was then disposed as follows:

## MORNING OF MARCH 21ST

RIGHT BRIGADE: 108TH BRIGADE.

Forward Zone: 12th Rifles.
Battle Zone: 1st Irish Fusiliers.
Divisional Reserve: 9th Irish Fusiliers.

CENTRE BRIGADE: 107TH BRIGADE.

Forward Zone: 15th Rifles.
Battle Zone: 1st Rifles.
Divisional Reserve: 2nd Rifles.

LEFT BRIGADE: 109TH BRIGADE.

Forward Zone: 2nd Inniskillings.
Battle Zone: 1st Inniskillings.
Divisional Reserve: 9th Inniskillings.

The artillery had begun moving a large proportion of its guns to new positions on the night of the 17th, having taken a hint from the fate of batteries on the front of the Third Army, which had just been subjected to the heaviest "mustard" gas bombardments experienced in the whole course of the war. The moves of batteries of the 173rd Brigade were actually not complete till a few hours prior to the launching of the attack. The dispositions were then as follows:

RIGHT GROUP. (Covering front of 108th and 107th Infantry Brigades.)*

Headquarters, 173rd Brigade, R.F.A.
"A," "B," "C," and "D" Batteries,
  173rd Brigade, R.F.A.
462nd Battery, R.F.A.
464th Battery, R.F.A.

---

* Four of the six batteries of this Group moved on the night of the 20th. It is reported that their evacuated positions were assailed with destructive fire so heavy that they would have been completely neutralized from the first had they remained in them.

LEFT GROUP. (Covering front of 109th Infantry
    Brigade.)
  Headquarters, 179th Army Brigade, R.F.A.
  383rd Battery, R.F.A.
  463rd Battery, R.F.A.
  "D" Battery, 232nd Brigade, R.F.A.

BATTLE ZONE GROUP.
  Headquarters, 153rd Brigade, R.F.A.
  "A," "B," "C," and "D" Batteries,
    153rd Brigade, R.F.A.

With one great crash there opened a tremendous bombardment, of trench mortars by the hundred and every calibre of artillery save the 77-mm. field gun. Its continuous roar was punctuated, to those a little distance from the line, by the explosions of huge single shells upon objectives in rear. So far as can be ascertained the German programme consisted of a concentration mainly of trench mortars on the front system; a bombardment with high explosive and phosgene gas of the Line of Redoubts, the valley in rear of it, the trenches of the Battle Zone, and Battery Valley, which ran behind its ridge; for which 105, 150, and 210-mm. howitzers were employed; and fire on villages in rear, and upon the crossings of the Canal de St. Quentin, with the largest howitzers and high-velocity guns. Particularly heavy fire was directed upon the redoubts and battery positions. The proportion of lethal shell to high-explosive gradually decreased, till the barrages were composed entirely of the latter. There was, according to the reports of artillerymen, a remarkable absence of 77-mm. shell and of instantaneous fuses.

Five minutes after the opening of the bombardment the order, "Man Battle Stations," was sent out by the General Staff. Dawn had broken in a dense mist. Morning mists at this season and in this district are the rule rather than the exception, but this was far thicker than the ordinary.

## THE GERMAN ASSAULT LAUNCHED 195

It was at five o'clock impossible to see more than ten yards ahead, and visibility increased very slowly till the afternoon. All the battalions in the Battle Zone appear to have reached their stations, upon ground thoroughly known to officers and men, in good time, but, as communications were constantly cut and runners were slow amidst the fog and the shelling, reports were long in coming to hand. This loss of telephone communication rendered it almost impossible to issue barrage orders to the artillery.

The German infantry attack was launched at 8-30 a.m. That the enemy attacked the major part of the line of the 36th Division frontally is disproved by the reports of survivors and returned prisoners. The main assault of the Germans, it must be remembered, was due west, almost parallel to the 36th Division's outpost line from Sphinx Wood to Gauchy. The advance must have swept straight up the Grugies Valley. There is evidence that Racecourse Redoubt, which contained the battalion headquarters and one company of the 15th Rifles, was attacked before the companies in the front system. Hopeless indeed was the position of the men in this front system, outnumbered three or four times, taken in rear by parties which came upon them without warning. The case of the machine-gunners, from whom, in the defence of the valley, much had been hoped, was equally desperate. The Germans swept on them, as it were, out of nothingness. Few can have had opportunity to fire a shot ere they were rushed.

It was believed at the time that all troops in the front system had been speedily overwhelmed. The evidence of returned prisoners, however, has established that there was at least one magnificent defence in this area, which, though then unknown, must have had invaluable results. The three companies of the 12th Rifles in the front system of the 108th Brigade were, as will be seen from the map, astride the national road running from St. Quentin to La Fère, which for several miles south of this point ran roughly parallel with the British front line. Captain L. J. Johnston, who commanded " C," the counter-attack company, states that though the preliminary bombardment smashed up their trenches and cut huge lanes in their wire, though owing to the mist and the fumes of gas-shell it was impossible to see more than a few feet ahead, the casualties were relatively light. Though all communication to rear was cut, the telephone line held as far back as Le Pontchu Quarry, "C" company's headquarters. Captain Johnston thus received word when the attack was launched, and began to move his company into Foucard Trench. In its progress up the communication trench it met a small party of Germans, who were shot or bayoneted. The fact was, however, thus made unpleasantly apparent that the enemy had broken through the line of resistance. The keeps held by "A" and "D" companies, farther forward, were still resisting, but by 11 a.m. were completely surrounded, and finally overwhelmed by weight of numbers. For four hours constant bombing attacks were launched on Foucard Trench. On several occasions parties of Germans entered the trench, but in savage hand-to-hand fighting were ejected. About thirty prisoners were taken and sent back under escort to Le Pontchu Quarry. About noon a most determined assault was carried out with *flammenwerfer*, to be bloodily repulsed.

An hour later the fog suddenly lifted. It was then clear to "C" company what progress the enemy had made. More than a mile to rear the Germans could be seen swarming about Jeanne d'Arc Redoubt, which held the battalion headquarters and "B" company. On the front of the 14th Division German cavalry could be seen advancing, and, what was even more astonishing, a column of transport, three hundred yards long, moving down the main St. Quentin-La Fère Road, about four hundred yards to the right of "C" company's position. Lewis-gun fire opened upon this body in a few seconds killed or wounded every man and horse in it, leaving the whole column in a welter of confusion.

By now, however, the company was being attacked from both flanks, and a withdrawal to Lejeune Trench, five hundred yards in rear, was ordered. The enemy followed up

## DEFENCE OF LE PONTCHU

the withdrawal fiercely and with the greatest gallantry, a rather pathetic incident occurring when a single German with bayonet fixed charged the whole line! The incident is instructive, as it reveals the high state of training in the offensive spirit of the attacking troops, and helps to account for some of their successes in later days, when our men were wearied out. "C" company, reinforced by the forward headquarters, which had been in Le Pontchu Quarry, now numbered nearly a hundred and twenty men. A further magnificent stand was here made.

About 3 p.m. a company of the enemy, evidently believing they had to deal with but a handful, was seen marching up in fours from the rear. The men held their fire till the Germans reached point-blank range. Then such a blast burst forth as brought the whole body to the ground. Captain Johnston believes that not a man escaped.

The position, however, was now hopeless. All thought of cutting a way through was out of the question, so thick were the enemy to rear. The end came at 4 p.m. A German tank came down the main road, firing into the trench in enfilade. At the same moment a whole battalion advanced from the front. There were about a hundred men only alive, many of them wounded. There was no course open but surrender. As the prisoners were marched back toward St. Quentin they had the grim satisfaction of seeing the column of transport they had annihilated still strewn in indescribable confusion about the road.

This most valorous defence was, as has been stated, unknown at the time. After the Armistice one Military Cross, two Distinguished Conduct Medals, and four Military Medals were awarded to the survivors of the company. The defence of "C" company of the 12th Rifles, against hopeless odds, when all seemed melting about them, must be held to rank with the very finest episodes of that month of March, the blackness of which is gilded with so many deeds of imperishable courage and fortitude.

The front system pierced, the enemy wasted no time upon the Line of Redoubts. The leading battalions pushed through the gaps between them, leaving it to their successors to attack them deliberately, with the aid of trench mortars and *flammenwerfer*. At 11-45 a.m. a report was received from the 30th Division, on the left, that the enemy had broken through on either side of the Epine de Dallon Redoubt, and that the special "redoubt barrage" was being put down. At 12-10 p.m. the "redoubt barrage" was ordered on the 36th Division's front also. That the enemy had passed through the Line of Redoubts before the barrage was put down is now certain. Twenty minutes later the 107th Brigade received a message from its Intelligence Officer, Lieutenant Cumming, whose work in reconnaissance was extremely gallant and useful, that the attack upon the Battle Zone was developing. At 12-15 p.m. Artillery Groups were warned to be prepared to withdraw their batteries to the Battle Zone positions. The personnel of the 18-pounder batteries of the 173rd Brigade was, however, obliged to withdraw from its guns, being attacked at close quarters by riflemen and machine-guns. Breech blocks and sights were carried away by the gunners in their retirement. The most serious report of all came from the 107th Brigade. The enemy was in Contescourt, in the section of the Battle Zone held by the 1st Rifles. It appears that the platoon of this battalion told off to defend the northern part of the village, was almost destroyed by a shell on the way up. A company of the 2nd Battalion moved forward in an attempt to eject him, but suffered heavily from machine-gun fire and failed to achieve its purpose.

The position was now very dangerous, but not irretrievable. Save at Contescourt, where the enemy made no further progress, the Battle Zone was intact. So, likewise, was that of the 30th Division on the left, and of the 61st Division further north, save at one point. At noon all three battalion headquarters on the Line of Redoubts were most manfully holding out, beating off attack after attack. General Nugent had refused to allow more than one company from a reserve battalion on the 107th Brigade's front to reinforce that holding the Battle Zone. He had still, therefore, with

# BREAK-THROUGH TO THE SOUTH 199

his Pioneer Battalion, reserves to fill a gap. Moreover, there was in rear the 61st Brigade of the 20th Division, allotted to the support of the 36th Division's front, though not yet at General Nugent's disposal. Up till now it might be said that, their superiority in numbers and their advantage from the mist having been taken into consideration, the Germans had been held as effectively as could have been expected. The mist was now clearing, and machine-gunners in positions of the Battle Zone were beginning to cause loss to the enemy.

But from the right there came news most disquieting. The Germans had captured Manufacture Farm, in the front line of the 14th Division's Battle Zone; soon afterwards they were in Essigny. It is difficult to ascertain precisely at what moment this important point, on dominating ground, was occupied by the enemy. The reports of the 108th Brigade would seem to put it about noon. On the other hand, an air report to the 14th Division stated that at 1-30 p.m. all the roads south of Urvillers were "teeming" with Germans, and that batteries were in action in the open south-west of the village. Now, in an attack, roads do not begin to "teem" with troops until supports and reinforcements move up, some time after the leading waves. Moreover, the detachments of two guns of the Machine-Gun Battalion, with positions near Essigny, state positively that there were Germans in that village considerably earlier, and that they themselves were in action against parties advancing upon the railway station from it. One gun dispersed an important attack with great loss before it was destroyed by artillery fire. The second covered the railway cutting, up which the enemy presently began to press from the *south*. Later it was withdrawn to a point fifty yards west of the cutting, whence it continued to engage the enemy advancing from Essigny. It remained in action till ordered to withdraw at night.

At whatever hour precisely the enemy penetrated Essigny, it is certain that by one o'clock, whilst all along the front the Germans were attacking the Battle Zone, the right

of the 108th Brigade was completely turned. At this time
the telephone line to Station Redoubt, wherein were the
headquarters of the 1st Irish Fusiliers, which had been cut
long before, was repaired, and General Griffith learnt that
fierce fighting was in progress here in the front line of the
Battle Zone, and that the 41st Brigade on the right had
been driven back. By 2-30 p.m. the enemy was in Fay
Farm, south of Essigny, three thousand yards behind the
front line of the 14th Division's Battle Zone. On the front
of the 1st Irish Fusiliers the enemy forced an entry at the
railway cutting, but every attempt to advance was defeated
by the Lewis-gun fire of the garrison. General Griffith
now moved up the 9th Irish Fusiliers to form a defensive
flank. A veritable break-through had occurred on the right,
extending a considerable distance south over the front of
the III. Corps. The general situation, from being men-
acing, was become suddenly desperate.

At 4-5 p.m. General Nugent ordered the 108th Brigade
to form a flank along the railway line, half-way to the village
of Lizerolles, to which it should be prolonged by the 14th
Division. On the left flank of the 36th the 1st Inniskillings
was holding stoutly. General Nugent therefore put at
General Griffith's disposal the 9th Inniskillings, the reserve
battalion from the 109th Brigade. This battalion was swung
across the front. Colonel Peacocke, its commanding officer,
reported, however, that the troops of the 41st Brigade were
now holding on, and that he had accordingly taken up a
position behind the 9th Irish Fusiliers. So the position
remained, more or less, till dusk began to draw on. The
enemy was in Contescourt, but the 1st Rifles clung to the
cross-roads south-east of the village. The right company
of the same battalion maintained its position in desperate
fighting. Enemy troops massing along the canal bank
between Dallon and Fontaine-les-Clercs, for the attack upon
the Battle Zone positions of the 1st Inniskillings north of
the canal, were heavily engaged by the batteries of the Left
Group. The fire was observed and controlled from Ararat
Observation Post, on the high ground north-west of Quarry

## DEFENCE OF RACECOURSE REDOUBT

Redoubt, with which telephone communication was maintained. At length the Germans succeeded in running a forward gun into Fontaine, but all efforts to serve it were frustrated by the fire of the 463rd Battery R.F.A.

Up forward, meanwhile, the three Redoubts of the Forward Zone, hopelessly beleaguered, completely surrounded by the enemy, had fought a battle that may be described as epic. The enemy pounded their trenches with trench mortars, attacked, was beaten off, bombarded once again, again attacked. Jeanne d'Arc, on the right, was the first to fall, about noon. The other two fought on, in the hopes of effecting a break-through after dusk. But it was out of the question, so thick was the enemy now in their rear. Trench after trench was taken by the enemy in Racecourse Redoubt, till at last only a corner round the railway cutting remained. Attacks with *flammenwerfer* were repulsed, largely through the skill with the rifle grenade of Captain Stewart, the Adjutant. Such a battle against incredible odds could not continue for ever. At half-past five, almost simultaneously, though they had of course no communication with one another, Colonel Cole-Hamilton, commanding the 15th Rifles, and Lord Farnham, commanding the 2nd Inniskillings, decided that further resistance was impossible. Both were highly complimented upon their resistance by the German officers who took over the forts. Colonel Cole-Hamilton was told that a battalion had been attacking him all morning, and that a second had been brought up during the afternoon. He himself had about thirty men unwounded. In the case of the headquarters of the 2nd Inniskilling Fusiliers, the Germans released two pigeons in Boadicea Redoubt with messages announcing its capture. The messages were received by the Headquarters of the 36th Division. The resistance of Racecourse and Boadicea Redoubts affords a rare example of that "cold courage," unsupported by the ardour and excitement of an advance or the hope of ultimate victory, which has been so often displayed by soldiers of British race in all periods of the history of British arms.

At 4-15 p.m. the 61st Brigade of the 20th Division, placed at the disposal of the 36th Division, was ordered to man the St. Simon defences, an arc covering the hairpin bend in the Canal de St. Quentin, and including the villages of Avesne and the Pont de Tugny. General Cochrane, commanding the Brigade, established headquarters at St. Simon.

The position on the right flank grew still more serious toward evening. Finally the Commander of the Fifth Army decided to withdraw the III. Corps behind the Canal de St. Quentin, in conformity with which move it was necessary for the 36th Division to be swung back also, pivoting upon the 1st Inniskillings, which battalion still clung to its Battle Zone. The 61st Brigade was ordered to withdraw across the Canal, obtaining touch on the right with the troops of the 14th Division, east of Avesne. From its left, half-way between Tugny and Artemps, the 108th Brigade was to hold up to the cemetery at Happencourt. Thence, up to and inclusive of Le Hamel, was to come the 107th Brigade. Then the 9th Inniskillings was to prolong the line to the Battle Zone defences of the 1st Inniskillings. The 61st Brigade was not to withdraw from the arc of the St. Simon bridgehead till the troops of the other Brigades had completed their retirement. When this had been effected, the 61st Brigade was to be in touch not only with the 108th, along the Canal, but with the 60th Brigade of its own Division, now at the disposal of the 30th Division, which had outposts on a line from the Canal south of Happencourt to Vaux, north of the Ham-St. Quentin Road.

The retirement began at 10-30 p.m., being covered by small rearguards. In the darkness the troops were not seriously pressed by the Germans. Long before dawn all battalions were established in their new positions, the three Brigade Headquarters of the 36th Division being at Lavesne, and that of the 61st Brigade in the old Divisional Headquarters at Ollézy. General Nugent had meanwhile transferred his headquarters to Estouilly, north of Ham. It must be remembered that each Brigade had by now had one bat-

## HEROIC ACTION OF LIEUT. KNOX 203

talion almost completely destroyed, and that the Battle Zone battalions were at an average strength of about two hundred and fifty men. There was an accretion in artillery strength. Two batteries, A/91st and C/91st, of the 20th Divisional Artillery, together with the 232nd Siege Battery, were put at the disposal of the 36th Division, and remained with it throughout the retreat, though there were constant changes in the formation of Groups. The Siege Battery was later transferred to a special Heavy Artillery Group, with two others, directly under the orders of the 36th Divisional Artillery.

The destruction of bridges and pontoons allotted to the Engineers of the 36th Division was carried through without hitch. Shortly after noon the pontoon and foot-bridge at Fontaine were destroyed by the 121st Field Company, which in the small hours of the 22nd of March blew up the whole group of bridges between Grand Séraucourt and Le Hamel. Later, in daylight, the 150th Field Company blew up the Artemps Group. The Tugny and St. Simon bridges had been allotted to other sections of the company. Lieutenants C. L. Knox and J. B. Stapylton-Smith were each responsible for twelve bridges. The first warning received by the former was when the débris of the Artemps bridges floated down-stream. He at once commenced his task. Several of the bridges were destroyed under machine-gun fire. At Tugny, the Germans were advancing on the main steel-girder bridge when the time-fuse failed. The night dew or the mist had spoiled it. As Lieutenant Knox rushed forward the foremost of the enemy were upon the bridge, a long one. He tore away the useless time-fuse, clambered under the frame-work of the bridge, and lit the instantaneous fuse. The bridge was destroyed, and, by some miracle, Lieutenant Knox was uninjured. He received the Victoria Cross. Among many heroic actions performed by officers and men of the Division in the course of the war it would be difficult to point to one of finer calibre. At St. Simon, Lieutenant Stapylton-Smith blew up a large number of the enemy with one of the three main bridges.

## 204 HISTORY OF 36TH (ULSTER) DIVISION

The early hours of March the 22nd, which dawned in thick mist like the day before, passed fairly quietly. For the moment, the right flank of the Division and the III. Corps on its right being behind the barrier of the Canal de St. Quentin, the greater pressure was shifted to the north. In bitter fighting the troops of the 1st Inniskillings held their ground in the forward positions of the Battle Zone, till 2 p.m., when, completely outflanked, they were ordered to withdraw to Ricardo Redoubt, the headquarters redoubt in the Battle Zone, upon which attack after attack was launched, to be beaten off with heavy losses by the defenders. The Germans across the Canal were meanwhile far in their rear, having batteries in Artemps by now. Finally, Ricardo Redoubt was surrounded, the 9th Inniskillings being compelled to fight a rearguard action back to the Happencourt-Fluquières Line, upon which, as has been recorded, were troops of the 60th Brigade. On the right the Canal Line held, though the enemy had brought up batteries, trench mortars, and machine-guns under cover of the mist, and was bombarding it heavily.

At noon General Nugent was informed that, in consequence of the decision of the Higher Command to hold the line of the Canal de la Somme and its continuation southward, the Canal de St. Quentin, a further withdrawal was necessary. The 36th Division, with the 61st Brigade attached, was now to hold this position from the present right flank of that Brigade to Sommette-Eaucourt. The 61st Brigade had already a battalion, the 7th D.C.L.I., holding from the Canal junction to a point west of the Dury-Ollézy Road, less one company, which had been moved down to the right flank to fill a gap between its right battalion, the 7th Somerset L.I., and the troops of the 14th Division. Its other battalion, the 12th King's, was driven out of Tugny at dusk by the advance of the enemy north of the Canal de St. Quentin, crossed the Canal de la Somme at Dury, and was withdrawn through the 7th D.C.L.I. to support on the railway behind that battalion. The withdrawal of the Brigades of the 36th Division was complete

## THE SECOND WITHDRAWAL 205

at 11 p.m., when the last troops passed through Pithon. The 108th Brigade took over the defence of the Canal bank from the left of the 7th D.C.L.I. to Sommette-Eaucourt. The 107th Brigade moved to Eaucourt and Cugny, the 109th to Brouchy in support. As no touch could be obtained with the 30th Division, which was to have prolonged the line westward, by the 108th Brigade, the 21st Entrenching Battalion, which had now come under General Nugent's orders, was put in on the left of the Brigade.

Ricardo Redoubt, in which the heroic resistance of Colonel Crawford's 1st Inniskillings continued all day, was now, of course, completely isolated. At three o'clock the commanding officer sent away a detachment, some men of which succeeded in making their way back to our lines. The remainder fought to the end. Finally driven to the north-western corner of the Redoubt, they ejected the enemy bombers who had now a footing there. Two men alone, Privates Bailey and Conway, drove out one group of the German bombers. Trench mortars pounded them from all sides, which they could not reach. A mere handful was taken prisoner with Colonel Crawford about 6 p.m. It is difficult to overestimate the value of this magnificent stand against overwhelming odds.

The position at two o'clock on the morning of March the 23rd may be summarized for the sake of clarity. The 36th Division, with attached troops, held the line of the Canal de St. Quentin and Canal de la Somme from a mile and a half north-west of Jussy to a mile west of Sommette-Eaucourt. Upon this line it had, from right to left, the 61st Brigade (7th Somerset L.I. on right, 7th D.C.L.I. on left, 12th King's in support); the 108th Brigade (9th Irish Fusiliers on right, 1st Irish Fusiliers on left; with a composite battalion of details and men returned from courses finding the outposts, to allow some rest to the other battalions); 21st Entrenching Battalion. The length of the front was upwards of five miles. The 16th Rifles (Pioneers) was at Sommette-Eaucourt, where the battalion had been working since before noon on a line of strong points. The

109th Brigade, consisting now of the 9th Inniskillings, was at Brouchy, in reserve. The 107th Brigade Headquarters and the 2nd Irish Rifles were at Cugny. The other battalion of this Brigade, the 1st Rifles, now very weak, was at Eaucourt. Divisional Headquarters were at Fréniches.

The artillery position is somewhat complicated, owing to early losses and subsequent changes. The Potter Group (A/153rd Brigade R.F.A.; B/153rd Brigade R.F.A.; D/173rd Brigade R.F.A.; D/91st Brigade R.F.A.; and 383rd Battery R.F.A.) had been ordered to join the 20th Division. It was in action in Bacquencourt during the day, rejoining the 36th Division in the afternoon after a big march. The front was now covered by the Erskine Group (A/91st and C/91st Brigade R.F.A.; and D/173rd Brigade R.F.A.) on the right, in positions in and around Aubigny; and the Eley Group (463rd and 464th Batteries R.F.A.; C/153rd and D/153rd Brigade R.F.A.; B/91st Brigade R.F.A.; and two howitzers of B/232nd Army F.A. Brigade) on the left, in positions near Brouchy. The Heavy Artillery Group was out of touch, and could no longer cover the divisional front.

The Machine-Gun Battalion had disappeared as a unit, but there were still detachments with each of the Brigades, acting as a rule under the orders of the battalion commander on the spot.

During the afternoon the Engineers of the 36th Division had taken over from the XVIII. Corps the destruction of bridges in Ham and along the river and canal to Ollézy. They were all effectively destroyed, save the main railway bridge at Pithon, which was found not to have been prepared. French railway troops, working in haste and with insufficient explosives, did all the damage in their power to it, but it is believed to have been swiftly repaired by the enemy.

The battle had been till now an attack with great superiority of numbers upon partially-prepared positions, or naturally formidable obstacles, such as the canals and the marshy bed of the Somme. From the morning of the 23rd open warfare developed, from the moment the enemy, as happened early, had driven the 14th Division back from the Canal de St. Quentin at Jussy. That accomplished, the Canal de la Somme at this point formed no real obstacle to the German advance, because, from St. Simon to Voyennes, it was parallel with it. For the 36th Division there were no more defences till the front line of 1916 was reached. It had to fight its battle of the 23rd and 24th of March in open country. The account of that battle and of the remainder of the retreat must occupy a chapter to itself.

## CHAPTER XI

### THE GERMAN OFFENSIVE ON THE SOMME (II): MARCH 23RD TO 30TH, 1918

IN the account which follows, it is scarcely to be hoped that all the confusion arising from reports that often conflicted can be eliminated. The resistance made by the 36th Division and its attached troops was one in which a large number of units, some existing, some hastily improvised, took part. But, for the most part, they were very small units, except for the battalions of the 61st Brigade, less depleted and less wearied by the morning of March the 23rd than those of the 36th Division. This chapter opens with events occurring forty-eight hours after the beginning of the great German bombardment. In that period the troops of the Division had been constantly engaged in fighting, or, when not fighting, on the march, or upon the alert for a fresh attack. On the nights neither of the 21st nor the 22nd had more than a couple of hours' sleep been snatched by any of the infantry. Many units had had absolutely none. The men were already wearied out. The 1st Rifles, to take one example, after fighting all day on the 22nd in the neighbourhood, first of Le Hamel, then of Happencourt, had marched by night to Pithon, there crossed the Canal de la Somme, then continued its march to Eaucourt, which was reached at three in the morning. The distance covered was nine miles. Even on arrival there was not rest for all, as piquets had to be posted round the village.

It is hard for those who have not seen a great retreat of this nature to imagine how depressing are the circumstances and the sights which he sees about him to the soldier entrusted with the fighting of delaying actions, how great his mental and moral, apart altogether from his physical, strain. The flood of civilians pouring out of towns and villages was in itself a pathetic and depressing sight. At three o'clock on the afternoon of the 22nd the nurses of the C.C.S. in Ham were walking down the Guiscard Road, carrying bundles, some of them assisting wounded men. Lorries and ambulances had already taken the worst cases, but at this stage there was not transport enough for all. Such sights as these were calculated to prey upon the mind and react upon the moral of the stoutest hearted. Allied with great physical fatigue and the sensation of being three or four times outnumbered, their effect was even more dangerous.

The exploits of the troops of the Fifth Army are great enough without straining the note. Some writers had made it appear as though the men were of triple brass. Men are of less durable material. Each has what may be called his "weakening-point," which is arrived at sooner in some men than in others. There were cases of weakness in the days that followed among troops of the 36th Division, as among other troops. But their achievements must be measured by the standard of their cruel and heart-breaking task. With that as gauge, these achievements, viewed as a whole, stand out in their magnificence, a shining monument to the spirit of the race that bred them.

The 21st Entrenching Battalion, interposed on the left of the 108th Brigade to find touch with the troops of the 30th Division, had not succeeded in its object. It was discovered at dawn that the line of the 30th Division turned back from the Canal about Verlaines. The 23rd Entrenching Battalion, consisting of men of disbanded battalions of the 36th Division, under the orders of the 30th, beat off all hostile attempts to cross the Canal in the neighbourhood of Offoy. Lieutenant-Colonel the Hon. Odo Vivian, the officer commanding that battalion, reports that at 7 a.m. troops fell back on his right from Ham, saying that they had been driven out by the enemy. About eleven, two Canadians informed him that they had slept the night in the town and seen no sign of the Germans. Be this as it may, it seems certain that the crossings at Ham, of all places on the front, were least effectively guarded, and that the enemy had some troops over the Canal here by noon. To cover the left flank, the dismounted sections of the Engineers and a battalion of divisional details were put into position north of Golancourt.

It was, however, on the other flank that danger first appeared. The enemy, according to the reports of the 14th Division, effected a crossing at Jussy at 3-30 a.m., but was counter-attacked and driven back by the 7th K.R.R.C. This respite was temporary only. By 11-15 a.m. the enemy was over the Canal de St. Quentin at many points, though the 7th Somerset L.I. clung stoutly to its position. Half an hour earlier the 2nd Rifles had been ordered to take up a defensive line east of Cugny, in touch with troops of the 14th Division, which had fallen back astride the road from that village to Flavy-le-Martel. By noon the troops on the right were falling back from Flavy-le-Martel and Annois, hard pressed by the enemy. The retirement continuing, the 1st Rifles was moved up on the right flank of the 2nd Battalion. On its right were at first no British troops, but a line was hastily taken up by dismounted French dragoons. In this position the line remained on this flank for some hours. The 1st Rifles was constantly engaged and managed to hold its ground. The 2nd Battalion did not come into action till later in the afternoon, as there were still in front of it a few men of the 14th Division who had retired from Flavy.

Meanwhile, in the centre, the line from Sommette-Eaucourt to Ollézy, and that of the 61st Brigade upon the Canals, held in splendid fashion. It was now the turn of the left flank. The 9th Inniskillings was heavily attacked from the north-west at Aubigny. One company fell back in disorder from the village. Thereupon the Brigade-Major, Captain G. J. Bruce, rode forward, rallied the men, and galloped into the village at their head. The Germans were driven out. It was a wonderful example of the inspiration of personal gallantry and leadership upon weary and disheartened men. Gradually, however, the line at this point fell back under severe pressure. Sommette-Eaucourt was lost, and a little later Brouchy. Both flanks of the Division were now completely turned.

At 4-30 p.m. General Cochrane, commanding the 61st Brigade, ordered the 7th D.C.L.I. and the 7th Somersets to withdraw to the line of the Ham-Terguier Railway, from the brook west of Annois to the Ollézy-Eaucourt Road. The Somersets, however, upon the Canal de St. Quentin, lost the better part of three companies, which fought on when surrounded till all their ammunition was gone ere surrendering. The D.C.L.I. extricated itself under great pressure, and took up position upon the new line.

And now upon the right the attack was renewed in great force. Enemy battalions passed through Flavy and deployed on either side of the Cugny Road. At about 5 p.m. the Germans attacked that village, using trench mortars to cover the advance, to be repulsed by the 2nd Rifles. A gap had now formed between this battalion and the 1st, through which the enemy pushed at dusk. The 1st Rifles was also attacked at 7 p.m., and also drove off the enemy, but this mere handful of brave men was now menaced both from south-east and north-west, and, to avoid being surrounded, withdrew towards Beaulieu, a mile south-east of Cugny. The 2nd Rifles also was compelled to evacuate the village, taking up a position astride the Villeselve Road at its western outskirts.

When night fell the line ran east of Beaulieu, to the western edge of Cugny, to the railway south-east of Ollézy, and along it to the Ollézy-Eaucourt Road, thence along the road, including the village of Eaucourt, a thousand yards south of Brouchy, to north of Golancourt. Behind it was a line of French infantry, pushed up hurriedly, without artillery or more ammunition than was carried on the men, roughly from Esmery-Hallon, through Flavy-le-Meldeux and Villeselve, to Beaumont-en-Beine. The Headquarters of the 36th Division were withdrawn from Fréniches to Beaulieu-les-Fontaines, north of the Roye-Noyon Road, at six in the evening.

In the course of the day all arms of the Division had been constantly in action. The 16th Rifles, which had been put at the disposal of the officer commanding the 9th Irish Fusiliers, had been fighting all day upon the Somme, and had fallen back in the general withdrawal on the left flank. Details of the Machine-Gun Battalion, under the second-in-command, Major Low, had, as has previously been recorded, also been in action on the left. All details, men returning from courses and leave, had been pushed into the battle. The clerks and runners of the 109th Brigade Headquarters had fought at Brouchy.

Great steadiness and devotion to duty had been shown by the Artillery. Two batteries of the 91st Brigade (from the 20th Divisional Artillery), A/91st and C/91st, are specially mentioned in the report of the C.R.A. When infantry, in the first case that of the 109th Brigade, in the second that of the 61st Brigade, fell back upon their positions, the battery officers rallied the men, and the gunners aided them to dig in in front of the guns.

Amid all the confusion food supplies had not failed, though no rations could be distributed to the troops in line till the small hours of the morning of March the 24th. The 107th Brigade was able, besides keeping its own troops supplied with tools for entrenching, to send a number of picks and shovels to Rifle Brigade battalions of the 14th Division in the neighbourhood of Cugny. On this day and throughout the retreat the work of the Train and Supply Column was most praiseworthy, while the Staff Captains of Brigades showed forethought in their arrangements. The medical services, under great difficulties, had done all that was possible in the evacuation of wounded.

The night passed fairly quietly. It was doubtless em-

## DAWN OF MARCH 24TH

ployed by the Germans to bring up fresh guns, for upon the morrow the volume of artillery fire was noticeably greater. There was no German infantry attack with the light, as might have been expected, on the morning of March the 24th. It did not come on either flank in any strength till about ten o'clock. Very probably the enemy had been relieving his front-line battalions, and their successors were not ready to renew the struggle till some hours after dawn.

It was, however, discovered at dawn that parties of Germans had entered Golancourt in the darkness, and that our men had evacuated the village. This was a very serious blow, as it threw into confusion schemes formulated overnight between General Hessey, commanding the 109th Brigade, and General Cochrane, commanding the 61st. These two commanders had planned a counter-offensive to ease the pressure on the left flank, and blunt the pronounced salient into which the line was being forced. General Nugent had put at General Hessey's disposal a composite battalion under Major Knox, and had later strengthened his line by sending up three hundred details from Beaulieu, servants, orderlies, grooms from Headquarters, and the personnel of the Signal School. These were formed into two companies, under the command of Captain W. Smyth, R.E., attached to the General Staff, and Captain C. Drummond, A.D.C. to General Nugent. Major Knox's detachment was to move *via* Golancourt, approach Aubigny as closely as might be in the mist, and attack the village at eight o'clock. Meanwhile the 9th Inniskillings, with a company of details, was to reoccupy Brouchy. General Cochrane arranged to retake Eaucourt with a hundred men of the 284th Army Troops Company, R.E., who had come under his orders, commanded by two of his own infantry officers. This he had succeeded in doing before midnight on the 23rd. Touch was obtained by the attacking force with the 7th D.C.L.I., on the railway where crossed by the Ollézy-Eaucourt Road.

But Major Knox came under heavy machine-gun fire

from Golancourt on his march, and was unable to make headway. The attacks upon Aubigny and Brouchy were therefore cancelled, and the companies of details thrown in on the left of the 9th Inniskillings. The position of the 7th D.C.L.I. on the railway was now impossible. The battalion was being pressed on either flank, and its right was in air. At eleven o'clock General Cochrane ordered it to fall back from the railway, and to take up a line in touch with the fragments of the 12th King's, a thousand yards west of Cugny, roughly parallel with the Cugny-Eaucourt Road. The right company of the D.C.L.I. had to fight a rearguard action to cover the withdrawal, and suffered considerable loss from machine-gun fire. Upon its heels the Germans pushed forward their machine-guns and a number of single field guns which had been brought across the Canal.

At this time the 2nd Rifles was still maintaining its position, three hundred yards west of Cugny. Behind it, between Cugny and Montalimont Farm, the 1st Battalion had dug itself in. It will thus be seen that there were two thin lines of men, literally back to back, with about a mile between them, one facing east toward Cugny, the other west toward Golancourt. Such a situation could not possibly persist. On the right there was intense confusion. Here the French had been relieving what was left of the troops of the 14th Division, between Cugny and Ugny-le-Gay, when the Germans attacked, and the two lines, relievers and relieved, had been rolled back before noon. La Neuville-en-Beine had been lost. The difficulties were not lessened by the fact that small parties of troops of the 14th Division, which had become intermixed with those of the 36th, received the order that they were relieved by the French, and were to fall back upon Guiscard. Their withdrawal left new gaps, of which the enemy, whose light machine-gun groups were handled throughout the day with consummate skill, was not slow to avail himself.

The salient held by the 36th Division suddenly caved. From all sides the semicircle fell back upon Villeselve, which was heavily bombarded by the enemy from noon onward. Desperate efforts were made by Brigade Staffs to rally the men in front of Villeselve, and get them into trenches with the French infantry. To a great extent they were successful, but the impossibility of co-ordination between troops which always fought in method so different was plainly apparent. When the trenches were shelled the French troops walked out of them. When the shelling ceased they walked back. Such procedure was all very well for formed units under their own leaders; it was impossible to make it understood by scattered details of men of a dozen units, harassed and strained by four days' fighting. Eventually, at about three o'clock, the French received orders to retire. Our men likewise fell back from the village.

Meanwhile upon the right had been enacted a drama truly heroic which has never been recorded, because, in the days when reports and despatches were written, there was no survivor to tell its story. On the morning of the 24th, the 2nd Rifles consisted of the following officers: Captain T. Y. Thompson, D.S.O., commanding since the officer commanding at the outset of the attack, Major Rose, had been wounded; Captain J. C. Bryans, Lieutenant M. E. Y. Moore, M.C.; Lieutenant R. B. Marriott Watson, M.C.; Lieutenant J. K. Boyle, M.C.; Lieutenant E. C. Strohm; and perhaps two hundred other ranks. Of these, Lieutenants Moore and Marriott Watson were old companions-in-arms. They had served together in the 13th Rifles; had together taken part in that battalion's great raid on June the 26th, 1916, and had both been wounded on July the 1st. Having withdrawn from the eastern to the western skirts of Cugny overnight, the battalion had steadfastly maintained its position, almost entirely unsupported. After beating off an enemy attack at ten in the morning, it was discovered that ammunition was woefully short, and orders were issued to fire at especially good targets only. Captain Thompson, deliberately exposing himself to encourage the men on the menaced right flank, which was being again attacked, was killed, as also was Lieutenant Marriott Watson.

Captain Bryans now assumed command. Messages sent up from the 1st Rifles in rear, ordering the battalion to withdraw, did not reach it. The men who bore them were killed or wounded. In any case, it was the opinion of Captain Bryans that a retirement across the bare, open country between Cugny and the village of Villeselve, with the Germans on three sides of him, was impossible.

From noon onwards was a lull, which was occupied in reorganization of the line. Then, about 2 p.m., preceded by a violent barrage of artillery and machine-gun fire, supported by an attack from low-flying aeroplanes, an assault was launched, the Germans sweeping in from the left in overwhelming numbers, despite the gaps cut in their ranks by fire. By the time the enemy was upon them there was scarce a round left to fire. "Many," writes Captain Bryans, "had only their bayonets left. Rather than wait for the end, they jumped from the entrenchments and met it gallantly. It was an unforgettable sight. We were overwhelmed, but not disgraced."

After a desperate hand-to-hand fight, the little band was simply engulfed. Lieutenants Moore and Boyle were killed. Of about a hundred and fifty men on their feet when the attack began, it is estimated that over a hundred were killed or wounded.

With the enemy pressing south-eastward from the direction of Golancourt, and westward from Beaumont-en-Beine, the situation was as acute as it had been at the worst moment of the morning. It was relieved by a great charge carried out at 3 p.m. by troops of General Harman's 3rd Cavalry Division, which had been assisting to maintain the line of the 14th Division during the morning. The 7th and Canadian Brigades had been moved in the direction of Beaulieu, to check the German pressure on the salient. A detachment of the 6th Brigade, about a hundred and fifty men, under Major Watkins Williams, 10th Hussars, charged from the neighbourhood of Collézy the enemy advancing through the two copses north-west of Villeselve. The detachment came under heavy machine-gun fire, and many saddles were emptied. But it achieved its object. The Germans were caught in the open, a considerable number cut down or shot, and over a hundred prisoners taken. Infantry of the 36th Division, weary as they were, followed up the charge cheering. It was a most brilliant little action. But it was, and could be, no more than a delaying action. There was no question of reoccupying Villeselve. The 9th and 62nd French Divisions had orders to withdraw before heavy attacks, holding the enemy where possible, but never risking a break in their line. Toward evening Berlancourt and Guiscard were heavily shelled. The enemy had now some 150-mm. batteries in action, and employed instantaneous fuse against Guiscard. Here Captain Rabone, Brigade-Major of the 108th Brigade was wounded. The Headquarters of the 9th French Division moved out of Quesmy, south of Guiscard, only just in time to avoid being surrounded. Patrols of the enemy, using white flares after dark as a guide to their artillery, were in Guiscard before 11 p.m.

At 11 p.m. the 36th Division was put at the disposal of the 62nd French Division, and ordered to withdraw its troops through its line. The 108th Brigade, leaving the remnant of the 9th Irish Fusiliers to fight a rearguard action on the ridge between Guiscard and Berlancourt, withdrew to Crisolles, and later to Sermaize, where the men had some rest. The 107th and 109th Brigades withdrew to Sermaize and Frétoy-le-Château, arriving about 2 a.m. in the morning of the 25th.

During the day the artillery attached to the 36th Division, to which the Potter Group, after having been in action under the 20th Division, had been returned, had actively barraged the roads leading south from the Canal de la Somme upon which the enemy was advancing. The Potter Group had bombarded the enemy massing for attack in the neighbourhood of the Esmery-Hallon—Golancourt Road, causing considerable casualties to parties in the open. The Erskine Group continued in action near Beines till French and British infantry had withdrawn through its guns. C/91st

Battery remained covering the retirement till after dark, and was fortunate to be able to extricate its guns after the Germans were in Berlancourt. The Eley Group had to make three withdrawals, first, before noon, to Berlancourt; then, at 2-30 p.m., to Buchoire, where it covered the French infantry; and at 6 p.m. to the neighbourhood or Frétoy-le-Château. In every case the retirement was delayed till the last possible minute. The men of "C" and "D" Batteries, 153rd Brigade R.F.A., displayed the highest courage and most dogged perseverance throughout this day.

At night the Erskine Group was put at the disposal of the 9th French Division, the Eley and Potter Groups at that of the 62nd French Division, under the control of the 36th Divisional Artillery Headquarters. General Brock, on return from leave, assumed command of the two latter Groups. Colonel H. C. Simpson, who had hitherto acted as C.R.A., became Liaison Officer with the 62nd French Division.

An order of the 62nd French Division, issued at 2-15 a.m. on March the 25th, contained the following information and instructions for the 36th Division. The general line held ran west of Quesmy, Bethancourt, Fréniches, to the Canal de Robécourt at Rouy, east of Nesle. The *rôle* of the 62nd Division was to check the enemy's advance, and prevent his crossing the Canal de Robécourt before, at earliest, the evening of the 25th. The British batteries were to remain in action under the orders of the 62nd French Division. The remaining troops of the 36th Division were to be withdrawn for reorganization, in readiness to assist the 62nd Division in case of emergency.

The reorganization, such as it was, was carried out in the course of a fifteen-mile march. The 21st Brigade, now reduced to less than five hundred of all ranks, was ordered to rejoin its own Division north of Roye. It was detached from the line of retreat at Avricourt, where it was met by a column of 'buses. Officers and men saw it go, to the further desperate fighting which awaited its survivors, with sentiments of the warmest admiration. During the whole

## HORRORS OF THE RETREAT

period of their attachment to the 36th Division, General Cochrane's men had displayed wonderful endurance and devotion. In the centre of a line which was turned upon both flanks, they had held each one of their successive positions till the last possible moment.

The troops of the 36th Division halted at mid-day in the neighbourhood of Avricourt, where they had a few hours' rest. They then received orders to resume their march. The 107th Brigade moved back to Guerbigny, on the banks of the Avre; the 108th Brigade to Erches, a mile north of that village; the 109th Brigade to Guerbigny and Warsy. Troops arrived between midnight and two o'clock, and, for the first time since the beginning of the attack, had a continuous sleep of at least six hours in comfortable billets. The 9th Irish Fusiliers, however, coming straight through from the neighbourhood of Guiscard, a distance of upwards of thirty miles, did not arrive till 8 a.m. General Nugent established his headquarters in Warsy.

The spectacle of the infantry upon that march was one that would have aroused compassion in the most war-hardened breast. Men's faces were deeply marked by overwhelming fatigue and lack of sleep. Some moved in a sort of trance, stumbling forward oblivious to their surroundings. In some cases their boots had given out. Many company officers, in the course of the last few miles, dispensed with the regulation halts, because they found it almost impossible to get their men on their feet again after them. They lay like logs, and had to be violently shaken before they could be recalled to consciousness. Fortunately more 'buses had been sent for the 61st Brigade than that scanty remnant required, and a few were able to assist in moving back the men absolutely unable to walk.

There were other sights upon that line of march perhaps even more moving. The men in this evil case were, after all, soldiers, undergoing such experiences as many soldiers have undergone in many great retreats. The spectacle of the civilians, turning out in haste from their homes, was often heartrending. Their big wains would be piled high with their household possessions, with perhaps the old grandmother of the family holding its youngest baby, perched perilously on top. Mile after mile, at the cart-tail, or driving cattle that became mixed up with the British transport, the children trudged in the rain. It was only the rich and comparatively fortunate that had horsed transport. The poorer struggled along with the most valuable of their things upon handcarts. The present writer remembers seeing a woman carried out on a bed and put on to a farm-cart. He was told she had given birth to a child two hours earlier. A little later he came upon an old woman pushing her paralyzed husband in a wheelbarrow. Let those who desire to realize what effort this requires for a woman of sixty, try wheeling a heavy man in a wheelbarrow even a hundred yards. For these room was found in a British lorry at the next village, but there were many cases where such relief was impossible.

The mien of these unfortunates was wonderful. Here and there a woman sobbed as she walked, a man cursed his chance. For the most part, about the most incongruous of these little cavalcades there was the high dignity of sorrow and suffering stoically and nobly borne.

In the course of the mid-day halt, details were as far as possible sent to their own units. In the 107th Brigade the 2nd Rifles, which had disappeared at Cugny, was reformed at about the strength of a large platoon. A company of the 15th Rifles, under Captain Miller, which had been a part of the first-formed battalion of details, was attached to the Brigade. The 109th Brigade formed small companies from the remnants of the 1st and 2nd Inniskillings.

The fighting of March the 25th exhibited in lamentable fashion the difficulties that occur in a retreat when two armies, using different methods, speaking different languages, based upon different lines of communication, with different apprehensions preoccupying the minds of their commanders, are being forced back before a victorious and more powerful enemy. The French were retiring south-west; the British west. Sooner or later a gap was inevitable. It occurred on this evening, at Roye. The 62nd French Divi-

## A GAP BETWEEN THE ALLIES

sion, covered by the Potter and Eley Groups under General Brock, fought an admirable delaying action. The Germans did not reach Libermont till 4 p.m., nor was the Canal crossed by them till about 6 p.m. Thereafter the 62nd Division, its left flank turned by the German advance at Nesle, withdrew to the line of the Roye-Noyon Road. During the remainder of the retreat the 36th Division saw no more of the artillery which had been attached to it, nor of its own C.R.A. and staff. An account of their action with the French must be left till a little later in this narrative.

The gap had formed, and in the early hours of the morning the enemy poured through Roye from the north-east, scarcely checked by the efforts of a French Cavalry Division, flung out upon a front of six miles. New French Divisions were about to detrain upon the Amiens-Montdidier Railway. If the Germans should strike home at that, a disaster far greater than any which the Allies had yet suffered would ensue. To close the gap there remained nothing but the remnants of the two original southern Divisions of the XVIII. Corps, the 36th and the 30th.

At 8 a.m. on the morning of March the 26th, the 36th Division received orders to take up a line from the neighbourhood of l'Echelle St. Aurin, on the Avre, where it was to obtain touch with the French, to the main Amiens-Roye Road, north of Andechy, linking up with the 30th Division. The 109th Brigade was ordered to take up a position from the river to Andechy, with the 108th Brigade on the left; the 107th Brigade remaining in reserve at Guerbigny. North and south of the western outskirts of Andechy ran a good trench, covered by a certain amount of wire, the second French line of 1916. Some three hundred yards north of the village, however, this line bent north-eastward, and could not be occupied. The advanced troops of the enemy were already at hand, and it was a matter of minutes whether the troops would be able to take up the position. The suddenness of the advance may be gathered from the fact that farmers from Guerbigny were yoking their horses to ploughs on the ridge north of the village when they were informed of the situation by troops moving forward. The present writer well remembers the gallant and dignified, " *Eh bien, monsieur, il faut partir alors,*" of one old man about to hitch in his team, when informed that the Germans were about a mile away.

By the time the troops of the 109th Brigade were in position the enemy was in Andechy. Those of the 108th were actually prevented from reaching their station on the Roye Road by machine-gun fire on their left flank. Touch with the 30th Division was never obtained here, but later on it was discovered that its right was at Bouchoir, a mile further back on the main road.

All through the morning small parties of the enemy attempted to work their way forward, but were held up by the fire of Lewis guns. The 122nd Field Company, under the orders of General Griffith, had been posted in echelon to protect the left flank. At 1 p.m., as the enemy appeared to be progressing slightly on the left, General Nugent ordered the 107th Brigade to hold the old French line following the road from Erches to Bouchoir. The 107th Brigade, to which was attached the 121st Field Company, the 16th Rifles, and the 21st Entrenching Battalion, as well as the personnel of its own Trench Mortar Battery, contained now the remnants of seven units. It was accordingly formed into three groups, the largest, under the command of Colonel McCarthy-O'Leary, 1st Rifles, consisting of its own three battalions. It was in position by 4 p.m., later pushing forward a line to gain touch with the left of the 108th Brigade.

The troops had now been in position for six hours; six hours of time the value of which no standard can measure. When their physical state is considered, the steadiness they showed on this occasion is equal to any of their achievements through the week that had passed. Every German attempt to advance was frustrated by their fire. No artillery was supporting them. Even a single battery of 18-pounders would have been of great service, and would have had many

## COLONEL PLACE CAPTURED

splendid targets round Andechy. The Germans, for their part, were now heavily bombarding the village of Erches, which the 108th Brigade Headquarters were obliged to quit, moving into the open fields behind it.

At dusk the enemy launched an attack in strength upon Erches, preceded by a bombardment. By eight o'clock he was in the village. The 108th Brigade Headquarters was attacked at close quarters, and General Griffith slightly wounded in the hand fighting his way clear of the German patrols. Colonel Place, the G.S.O.1 of the Division, going up from Guerbigny in a car, with Colonel Furnell of the 1st Irish Fusiliers, and Major Brew of the 9th, to ascertain the position, ran into a party of the enemy. A bullet stopped the engine of the car. Colonel Place jumped out, but before he could draw his pistol from under his coat was hit in the leg, and fell in the roadway. Instantly a German sprang upon him and stabbed at him with his bayonet. Fortunately for Colonel Place, the thickness of his "British Warm" saved him. The little party had no alternative to surrender. The car was subsequently recovered, towed back, and served the Division well in after days.

Colonel Place had been G.S.O.1 of the 36th Division for more than two years. As a staff officer he was far more than merely able and efficient. His sympathy and imagination enabled him to grasp all points of view, and to understand those which were different to his own. He never seemed to require, as do so many men engaged on difficult tasks, an hour free from interruption, but could switch his mind on to each new problem presented to him, and return to his own where he had left it. His loss in this unlucky fashion was much regretted.

Lieutenant Cumming, whose reconnaissance on the 21st has been mentioned, led a patrol of six men into Guerbigny, to see if the enemy had yet entered it. They had not, but on his way the patrol was attacked by a German patrol of five. As a result of the fight every single German was killed.

The remnants of the 108th Brigade had taken up a line

west of Erches, putting themselves under the orders of General Hessey, as their own Brigade Staff had been cut off from them by the German patrols which had burst through. There was now heavy shelling and trench-mortaring of the British positions, the enemy having moved up guns and mortars into Andechy. A patrol sent out at 1-45 a.m. on the morning of the 27th by the 121st Field Company, saw long columns of the enemy; infantry, transport, a troop of cavalry, and a battery of artillery, moving into Erches. Captain Miller's company of 15th Rifles, west of the village, was pounded with artillery and mortar fire, the trenches being obliterated and heavy casualties suffered. He had with him one machine-gun, and, as light appeared, this gun began to obtain many targets in Erches, inflicting considerable loss upon the enemy. At 8 a.m. the enemy entered a sap in front of his trench and began to bomb his way up. Lieutenant Young, with a handful of riflemen, promptly drove him out.

Meanwhile, clinging to a trench on the Erches-Guerbigny Road, was Captain Densmore Walker of the Machine-Gun Battalion, whose diary has previously been drawn upon in the course of this narrative, with a handful of men of his company, armed with rifles. Behind him was a party of the 107th Brigade with one machine-gun. Captain Walker had with him a rifleman of the old 14th Rifles, now in one of the Entrenching Battalions, named Gilmour, one of those curious individuals who, when all seems to be melting about them in moments of great emergency, suddenly display resource and coolness which amaze all who have known them. Together they had already carried out a patrol into Guerbigny, into which some of the enemy had been seen to move, in the course of which, Captain Walker cheerfully confesses, Rifleman Gilmour, rather than he, had been the leader. The counter-attack which followed may be described in Captain Walker's own words, because it succeeds, as no official account ever can, in picturing the exact details for the mind's eye.

"Things were looking as black as conceivable. I suppose

it would be about 7-30 a.m. when the attack came. We heard shouting straight behind us and saw about a dozen men a mile away, coming towards us in a line.* One waved a white flag and they all shouted. Some said they were English, and we were relieved; some said they looked like French; and I said that any way we would fire on them—which we did. They were perfectly good Huns! They took cover when we opened, and then, when we were really interested in them, the real attack came from Erches. He swarmed on to the road and came down the trench. This looked like the finish of it. There was a general movement backwards, but Evans prevented the machine-gunners from dismounting the one machine-gun with the 107th Brigade, and got it into action on the top of the trench. This changed the aspect of things, as the Huns checked. We all got out of our trench (most people with the idea of clearing over the open, I fancy), and there we stood for quite a while, our people firing towards Erches, and the Huns hesitating. Seeing this latter tendency, Gilmour and I moved slowly towards Erches, trying to urge the troops to attack, but they were too undecided. . . . Then we saw a Hun in the trench just below us. I fired my revolver at him and he ran back. So we chased him. This settled matters! The Huns turned tail and our men followed. As my particular Hun turned round traverses I got in another couple of shots, but didn't bring him down. When we reached the road—which was sunken— . . . the bank came up to his waist, and he looked scared—horribly—but I fired again. . . . I distinctly saw what I thought was a puff of smoke go out from his pack. Any way he at once went down behind the bank, and Gilmour rushed up with his bayonet. I said 'Leave him,' but I don't know whether he did or not. And now I didn't know what to do. Fritz was legging it for Erches hard enough, and by this time indeed they had all reached it. I don't know how big the village was, but we might have rushed it. On the other

---

* These men were evidently advancing from Saulchoy-sur-Davenescourt, into which a number of the enemy had filtered in the darkness.

hand, I didn't know what had happened on the left, or in what strength the enemy was. . . . At this stage I was delighted to see an infantry officer with an M.C. come up. I asked him if he thought it was any use trying to go on, and he said it would be better to make a line there."

Eventually Captain Walker, surrounded, except on the north-west, withdrew. He adds :

" I think on the whole the Erches scrap went in our favour. We were few in numbers compared with the Huns. They were backed up by victory, while our men were terribly tired, hungry, and dispirited. . . . Our ammunition was about gone. For our M.G. we had three belts left when we retired. We were entirely surrounded, if only by Hun patrols, and we only knew hazily what direction to make for. In the circumstances, to delay a force superior in numbers and moral for half a day after it attacked our position, was as much as could be expected. I reckon the Boche should have wiped out our party at Erches, but we turned on him severely enough to persuade him to let us go quietly." *

It was, then, at Erches that the enemy first broke the line on a serious scale. On the right, south of the Avre, the French posts were withdrawing. The 109th Brigade had no alternative but to cross. It was impossible to retire along the right bank. The crossing was superintended by the Brigade Major, Captain G. J. Bruce, and carried out in orderly fashion, with covering fire from successive sections. The line then fell back with the French outposts through the wood north of Lignières, which was heavily shelled by the enemy.

North of Erches, Captain Miller held his ground till noon, when his trenches were being blown in. On his left what remained of the 1st and 2nd Rifles had fallen back a little after Colonel McCarthy-O'Leary had been wounded

* Returned prisoners of war informed Captain Miller, whose diary has been drawn upon in this chapter, that the streets of Erches, through which they were marched, were littered with German dead. So, as he remarks in a letter to the writer, the affair " was not so one-sided as it looked."

## WHAT THE DIVISION ACHIEVED     227

—for the second time. Captain Miller therefore withdrew upon Arvillers, when he gained touch with Captain Patton, who had about sixty officers and men of the two other battalions. Finally, on the order of General Withycombe, the whole line withdrew upon Hangest-en-Santerre, since large columns of the enemy could be seen advancing towards Davenescourt, and disappearing in the wooded country in its rear. This withdrawal was complete at 5 p.m. By evening a French Division had moved up, and the remnant of the 107th Brigade was ordered to march back on relief, and rejoin the rest of the Division at Sourdon. One party of three officers and sixty-eight other ranks, however, out of touch with the Brigade, remained in action north-west of Arvillers till the morning of the 28th. Constantly pressed by the enemy, they kept him stationary by their rifle fire. Not till 11 a.m. were they relieved by the French.

The achievement of the troops of the 36th Division, a mere handful at this time, almost broken by fatigue, in many cases without food, must take a high place, not alone in the annals of the March retreat, but in that of the war. That men here and there, bowed beneath the weight of a burden almost unbearable, showed weakness, is not controverted. The account of Captain Walker has been purposely inserted—as an instance, to which many might be added—to show in what fashion weakness was overcome by leadership and example. It is the finest type of courage that, in the slang phrase, "comes up to scratch" again and again, beating down in the breast the inevitable weakness as it arises. The individual Briton is at least as brave as the individual of any other race; but men in the mass are not naturally heroic. It is discipline, training, pride in a unit or a formation, and, above all, in such crises as these, leadership alone which can instil into men who have undergone the strain these men had undergone, the courage to stand firm in the plight wherein they found themselves. These men had stood. Not only to the officers and picked men among them, who made the stand possible, but to the whole group spirit which they created for their weaker brethren in adversity, the adjective "heroic" may fairly be applied. Best of all, their object had been achieved. There can be no suggestion of hyperbole if that object be described in a phrase from Lord Haig's Despatch. The resistance, he said, of the 36th Division near Andechy played "no small part in preventing the enemy from breaking through between the Allied Armies." If we ponder that phrase and its inferences we shall have small need of further testimony.

After their long and trying march to Sourdon the troops had one more call to answer. An enemy column had found a gap at Montdidier and taken advantage of it. By 8 a.m. on the morning of the 28th it was over two miles west of the town. At 12-30 p.m. General Nugent received an order signed by General Débeney, commanding the First French Army, to the effect that he was massing artillery at Coullemelle, and that he required all infantry at his disposal to cover it. All troops of the 107th and 109th Brigades that could be collected were moved down to Coullemelle, and took up a position covering the French batteries. They were in position at about five in the evening. Subsequently came a message from the French requesting that they should be moved to Villers-Tournelle, two miles south-east of Coullemelle. But the French troops on the spot informed our men that the situation had improved, the enemy having been counter-attacked and driven back. Patrols sent out to Cantigny, another mile and a half east of Villers-Tournelle, found the French infantry solidly placed and unattacked. The night being very wet and cold, the majority of the force was therefore withdrawn into the houses of Coullemelle, piquets being posted south-east of the village, and patrols keeping touch through the night with the French in front.

The following day the march was continued. And now the weary troops saw heartening sights upon the route. Column after column of lorries, little Annamite drivers at the wheel, packed with the dark blue uniforms of the Chasseurs Alpins, roared by them. At some points there were serious blocks in the traffic. At Essertaux, where General

## ACTION OF THE ARTILLERY 229

Nugent had his headquarters for a few hours, he was succeeded by General Mangin, commanding the IX. French Corps. The French were really now in strength. Attack and counter-attack were to rage here a few days longer. Up north, upon the Scarpe, Below's great final thrust had been heavily defeated. The German advance was stayed at last.

On the morning of the 30th, after a night spent in the open in cold and wet, the troops of the 36th Division were entrained at Saleux, south of Amiens, now half-deserted and racked by bomb and shell, and moved north to the area of Gamaches, on the Norman coast, for reorganization.

Remains only to be related the last actions of the Artillery. On the evening of the 25th it had withdrawn with the 62nd French Division through the forest south of the Roye-Noyon Road, coming under the orders of a new French Division, the 77th, on the morrow. On that day, when the infantry was beginning its grapple at Andechy, an important battle opened against the Germans debouching from Noyon, upon the line Cannectancourt—Canny-sur-Matz. Here the Germans made little progress. Attack after attack on the afternoon of the 27th was beaten off, the barrage fire being very effective and earning high praise from the French commanders. On the 28th the Germans succeeded in entering Canny, but made no progress elsewhere. On the morning of the 30th desperate German attacks penetrated some distance into the French positions, taking the vital height of Plémont Hill. In the afternoon, however, a brilliant counter-attack was carried out, splendidly supported by our artillery. The whole line was restored, and over seven hundred prisoners taken.

The French now had their own batteries in action. On March the 31st the Artillery began its march back to Poix, the concentration area for refitment. It had carried out a great task in a manner worthy of the highest traditions of the Royal Regiment.

If this narrative has been faithful, and if—a task far harder to accomplish—it has appealed to the imagination, there remains little need to discuss the causes of the greatest defeat suffered by British arms since York Town. The German victory was a victory of superior numbers, but it was more than that. It was a victory of training. While our thin-strung battalions were digging, Ludendorff trained his great host, collected astride the Oise. He taught it what armies were forgetting, how to advance without barrage or tanks. He instilled into it the offensive spirit, and saw that it reached the very corporals commanding light machine-gun groups. They it was who won him his battle.

But, if the defence was overwhelmed by superior numbers, it seems clear that it broke down earlier than it need have done, and that the fault lay in its organization. The Forward Zone was little more than a screen, and was so regarded. Yet it was held by three whole battalions on the front of each Division. The orders were that the enclosed keeps, even in the front system, were to resist to the last. The whole position in front of the Battle Zone may be regarded as the outpost line. This outpost line, manned by a third of the infantry force of each Division, was not to retire and was not to be reinforced. The first shock of the attack swept this third away. It was defence in detail, not defence in depth, and in detail it was defeated. Defence in depth may be defined as successive lines of organized defence, upon which the defenders can fall back in succession, always finding some fresh troops on the new position, so that the line becomes gradually stronger as it falls back, until at last is reached the line upon which the real defence is to be made. Gallantly as they strove, much as they accomplished, the three battalions in the Forward Zone of the 36th Division were wasted under the Fifth Army scheme.

As for the lines of the St. Quentin and Somme Canals, which might have been very formidable, there had been no preliminary organization of their defence, nor even reconnaissance with that end in view. When the moment came the defence had to be improvised.

This does not detract from, but rather increases, the

magnificence of the defence of the 36th Division, and indeed of the whole of the XVIII. Corps, which had sixteen German Divisions, in front and second line, against its four. There is at least every reason to suppose that, had all gone elsewhere as on the front of the XVIII. Corps, the full weight of reinforcements would have arrived before the enemy had forced the lines of the St. Quentin and Somme Canals. In that case the war would undoubtedly have had a speedier ending.

## CHAPTER XII

### FLANDERS: THE 108TH BRIGADE IN THE MESSINES-KEMMEL BATTLE :* APRIL TO JUNE 1918

THE 36th Division had a glance only, infinitely tantalizing, at the beautiful valley of the Bresle, with its pastures and woodlands, and snug villages in which the troops were billeted, from Gamaches, several miles inland, to the little pleasure-resort of Ault on the coast. A short rest in these surroundings would have been delightful. But there was no rest for anyone for a long time to come, nor could be. The last trains did not arrive in the area till the morning of April the 1st; the last trains left it, bearing the remnants of the Division towards Ypres, on the 4th. For the old battlefield, still known as the Salient, was its new destination.

The interval had been spent in reorganization and the absorption of the Entrenching Battalions, originally formed in February from the surplus personnel of the infantry, which had accompanied the Division north. They did not go very far to fill the gaps caused by the prodigious casualties. The word gaps, in fact, is inapplicable. The infantry of the Division had disappeared. The 108th Brigade had

---

\* The official description of the fighting on April 10th and 11th is the Battle of Messines, 1918. It is safe to prophesy that the official nomenclature will never in this case, nor in many others, become the popular one. The 108th Brigade also took part in the action officially known as the Battle of Bailleul, dated from the 13th to the 15th of April, 1918.

been reduced to a little over three hundred, mostly transport and employed men. The total casualties in the Division in the ten days from March 21st were 7,252. Of these, 185 officers and 5,659 other ranks were reported missing. Perhaps four-fifths of these were prisoners of war, wounded or unwounded. It was a very weak Division which detrained at Proven and other stations further west.

From the day of its arrival, however, it began to receive very large drafts from the flood of recruits that now poured across the Channel. Bitter criticisms have been heard of the policy which had kept so many troops in England till then. Whatever their justice in some cases, they have none where the drafts now received by the 36th Division are concerned; for of these eighty or ninety per cent. consisted of boys of nineteen, with far from adequate training. In some cases these youths, almost before they knew their officers by sight, were to be put to the severest test, and were to emerge from it with quite astonishing credit.

Divisional Headquarters, in which Lieutenant-Colonel A. G. Thompson, D.S.O., Indian Army, had succeeded Colonel Place as G.S.O.1, were established at Ten Elms Camp, near Poperinghe, on April the 3rd. On the night of the 6th the Division began relieving the southern part of the front held by the 1st Division. By the morning of the 8th the relief was complete, the 107th Brigade being in front line, the 109th in support, and Divisional Headquarters on the Canal Bank a mile north of Ypres.*

The new front line included the village of Poelcappelle, which consisted now of a few "pill-boxes" and naught besides. The area behind it had been the scene of the most savage fighting on the British front, and was simply a waste of shell-holes, traversed by "duck-board" tracks. In rear, however, camps had sprung up amidst the desolation. Ypres, of all places under the sky, boasted an officers' club.

* On this date there died, at Rouen, of wounds received in March, one of the most gallant and popular C.O.'s the Division ever had, Lieutenant-Colonel P. E. K. Blair Oliphant, C.M.G., D.S.O., who had served with it from earliest days, first with the 11th Rifles, and later in command of the 11th/13th Battalion of that Regiment.

There was a railway station at St. Jean, which those who had seen the campaign of 1917 remembered as one of the most unpleasant spots upon the front, and a mass of sidings at Wieltje, which had been infinitely worse. Not for long was the area to enjoy these amenities, nor Ypres its unwonted isolation from the enemy. On the 9th the troops heard a tremendous bombardment to the south. The enemy's offensive on the Lys had opened.

From Givenchy, where they were magnificently held, to the neighbourhood of Gapaard, on a front of some twenty miles, the Germans had broken through. On the front of the Portuguese Corps the line was shattered, and the German wave flowed up the low valley of the Lys. The battered city of Armentières fell. For two or three days no real resistance could be organized across the gap, and the Germans pushed west upon Hazebrouck, a most important railway junction. Estaires, ten miles west of Armentières, was occupied by the evening of the 10th. By that time troops of the 36th Division were upon the scene of action.

The 108th Brigade was in II. Corps reserve. At noon on the 10th it received orders to move at once to Kemmel, with " C " Company of the Machine-Gun Battalion. 'Buses were provided for dismounted personnel. The 'bus column, moving *via* La Clytte, reached Kemmel village at 4-15 p.m., the Brigade coming under the orders of the G.O.C. 19th Division. That Division, with the 9th, had been fighting hotly for the defence of the Messines Ridge. The admirable steadiness of their young recruits and the gallant fashion in which their counter-attacks had been launched form a brilliant page in the history of the war, and helped to turn the Lys offensive, huge as were its gains, into one of the most expensive and fruitless of the great series of German assaults. General Griffith was ordered to put his Brigade into the Kemmel defences. His headquarters were established in Kemmel Château.

Shortly after midnight General Griffith received orders to move up to the Messines Ridge, in support of the weak South African Brigade of the 9th Division, which had been thrown into the battle under the orders of the 19th. The 1st Irish Fusiliers took up a line on the Messines-Wytschaete Road, from five hundred yards north of the former village to the neighbourhood of the 36th Division's old acquaintance, Pick House. The 12th Rifles was on the Spanbroek Ridge in support; the 9th Fusiliers about the old British front line on the Wulverghem-Messines Road. The morning passed fairly quietly, but there was ominous news as to the German advance north of Ploegsteert. General Griffith received a secret warning order that, in the event of the enemy capturing Hill 63, the whole line would have to pivot back across the Spanbroek Ridge and its prolongation east of Wulverghem, south of which village touch would be obtained with the 25th Division.

At half-past three, after heavy bombardment, the enemy launched an attack upon the crest-road. The South Africans on the left were pushed off it, and the line of the 1st Irish Fusiliers broken. A very gallant counter-attack by Fusiliers and South Africans, side by side, restored the position, though subsequent pressure on the left of the latter forced them to bend back somewhat from the road toward Hell Farm. At 7 p.m. came another assault, in face of which the Fusiliers lost not a yard of ground. None of the officers who took those raw boys into action can have dared to expect of them such steadiness and resolution as they now displayed.

At night, however, came orders to carry into effect the movement anticipated in the warning order. The advance of the enemy to the south had made it only too necessary. The ridge must go, though the 9th Division was still to cling to its northern crown, the village of Wytschaete. The retirement was carried out before dawn, but it was discovered on its completion that there was no touch with the left flank of the 25th Division. After a great deal of trouble, this was attained by withdrawing the right of the 108th Brigade some hundred yards.

All day was heavy shelling, but no infantry attack developed till after six o'clock. On this occasion, as always, the Germans placed great reliance upon a local assault delivered as dusk was falling, which just permitted attackers to consolidate a position won, and gave no time for a counter-attack before the pall of darkness descended. Such a night as this, which would be lit scarce at all by the thin sickle of a new moon, was peculiarly favourable to these tactics.

They were, however, unsuccessful. Once again the defence of the 108th Brigade prevailed. The left of the 9th Fusiliers was driven back. Quickly a counter-attack was launched. The reserve company of the 9th, led by the commanding officer of the battalion, Lieut.-Colonel P. E. Kelly, and a company of the 12th Rifles, led by Major Holt Waring, most gallantly restored the position. By eight o'clock all was quiet. But casualties had been heavy. The 1st Fusiliers in particular had had very serious losses the previous day on the Messines Ridge. This battalion was reorganized as a company, and attached to the 9th. During the night there was no touch with troops of the 25th Division, the gap having formed owing to the advance of the enemy on Neuve Eglise and the consequent lengthening of the line. In the early hours of April the 13th a battalion of the 178th Brigade, now attached to the 19th Division, was moved up to fill it.

The 13th was a day of continuous alarms. Parties of the enemy made attempts at dawn to advance by short rushes on the front of the 12th Rifles, east of Wulverghem, but were beaten off with loss by Lewis-gun and rifle fire. A couple of hours later fresh attacks appeared to be brewing. Parties of Germans were dispersed by the fire of machine and Lewis guns. The former were excellently placed by an officer who knew every foot of the ground, Captain Walker, in old positions which he had often held before the Battle of Messines in 1917. Then, all through the afternoon, small parties of the enemy strove to make ground under cover of the old camouflage screens upon the Messines-Wulverghem Road. They were counter-attacked and driven off, suffering considerable casualties from the fire of Lewis guns. The position on the right flank was, however, more desperate

## FIGHTING AT WULVERGHEM 237

than ever. At nine o'clock had come from the 25th Division the evil news that the Germans were in Neuve Eglise.

During the night the 9th Fusiliers was relieved by troops of the 178th Brigade, and withdrawn to the dug-outs on Kemmel Hill. The 12th Rifles remained in line. The relieved battalion was not given long to rest. Before noon it was ordered to man the Kemmel defences, and to send up its company of the 1st Fusiliers to dug-outs behind the old British front line opposite Kruisstraat Cabaret. The 14th may be accounted a quiet day, since it passed without infantry attack. But the volume of artillery fire was immense, and distributed to a great depth in rear of the positions held. "Green Kemmel Hill," as one officer wrote, "was turning brown before our eyes." And the enemy was definitely in possession of Neuve Eglise.

At 10-30 p.m. orders were received from the 19th Division for an immediate withdrawal west of Wulverghem. This was carried out before dawn, the line pivoting back on the left of the 12th Rifles, which joined up with the 178th Brigade west of the village. It was completed only just in time. With morning light the Germans opened an intense bombardment on the new position, which, for the greater part of its length, followed no old British trench. An infantry attack followed, and bodies of Germans broke through at the junction of the 12th Rifles and 178th Brigade. A counter-attack by the 1st Irish Fusiliers and the scanty reserves of the 12th Rifles, led by Major Holt Waring, failed to restore the position, but prevented the enemy gaining further ground on the left. Major Waring, a most gallant officer and a born leader of men, was killed. The left and centre of the 12th Rifles were very wisely withdrawn a few hundred yards to a famous communication trench of old days, known as "Kingsway." From this there was a fairly good field of fire. The 9th Irish Fusiliers had now been moved up from the Kemmel defences, and was ordered to send up two platoons to connect the right flank in "Kingsway" with the original line west of Wulverghem. These two platoons had an unfortunate fate. At dusk they were almost surrounded by groups of the enemy pressing forward, and were forced to fall back some hundred yards with heavy casualties.

At 2-15 a.m. on the 16th the little remnant of the Brigade began to withdraw on relief, covered by small outposts. It then marched back to a camp near La Clytte, suffering numerous casualties on its route from shell-fire. Four machine-guns remained near Kemmel village. The enemy was now indulging in what were known to artillerymen as area bombardments, concentrating upon half a square mile of country for half an hour, then switching his batteries to another. Such methods are ineffective unless based upon an enormous mass of heavy artillery. With this available, as it was on this occasion, they are extraordinarily noxious and demoralizing. Reserves, tired units withdrawn for a short rest, are kept constantly on the strain, ever wondering when their turn is coming, compelled hurriedly to shift position when it does. Severe loss and disorganization are caused to transport piqueted in the open or bringing up rations and munitions. A spot undisturbed at one minute becomes the centre-point of a hellish tornado at the next.

April the 16th, while the men of the 108th Brigade, wearied out and dazed by shell-fire, snatched what rest they could, was the occasion of furious fighting at Wytschaete. The village was lost in the morning, and retaken by a magnificent counter-attack of those veritable paladins of modern war, the Highland Brigade of the 9th Division. It could not be held on the morrow owing to its isolation, and the line had to be withdrawn to the neighbourhood of the old British trenches of 1917. The 17th, to many observers, appeared the blackest day they had seen. Almost everywhere the gains of years of desperate fighting had been lost. Passchendaele and Poelcappelle—to which there will be further reference when we return to the fortunes of the 36th Division—were gone. Huge slices of territory on which the Germans had never stood, or over which they had been hustled in retreat, were now in their possession. Bailleul, which had been at many periods a Corps Headquarters, had fallen. From villages such as Westoutre, where they had lived in comparative peace since 1914, the villagers were rushing out under shell-fire, pushing barrows, staggering under the burden of huge bundles, across the fields. Men asked whether we had any reserves remaining, whether the young American formations would ever be ready, whether the Channel ports could be saved.

And yet, though none who watched can have guessed it, hardly even the great soldier now in supreme command of the Allied Armies, or his British colleague, the day may have marked a turning-point. The French were hurrying north. Their troops were already in line on the right of the 9th Division; their field artillery, the " seventy-fives," rushed up, each at the tail of a lorry which carried the detachment, were lining the hills, the Scherpenberg, Mont Rouge, and Mont Vidaigne. The German infantry was suffering heavy loss. Black as was the night, there was, if as yet no faintest light of dawn, the paler gray on the horizon which is its herald.

On the evening of that day orders were received for the formation of the Brigade, which could now muster about four hundred rifles, into a composite battalion. This battalion, under the command of Colonel Kelly, was ordered to move down behind Kemmel Hill, in reserve, to be in position by 4 a.m. next morning. It encountered a storm of shelling on its way, having seventy casualties. Among the killed here was Captain Despard, 9th Irish Fusiliers, who had shown great tenacity and fine leadership during the retreat of the previous month. All day the battalion remained here, under very heavy fire, from which Kemmel now afforded but slight protection. At evening it was withdrawn, French troops having taken over the defence of this part of the line. The remnants of the Brigade marched all night, to Siege Camp and Hospital Farm, between Poperinghe and Elverdinghe, rejoining the 36th Division at 5-30 a.m. on the 19th of April.

The Brigade had, for the second time in a month, been cut to pieces. The 12th Rifles alone had had upwards of fifteen hundred casualties in that period. One often saw in our summaries of intelligence reference to reports that such and such a German formation had had particularly heavy losses, followed by a statement that it might be considered negligible for some time to come. Few can have had losses higher than those of the 108th Brigade, which had, as has been recorded, practically disappeared by the end of March. Yet in ten days' time this Brigade had entered another great battle, to prove itself very far from negligible. The admiration one feels for its achievements is mingled with surprise when one thinks of the youth and lack of experience in its ranks. Well did it merit its share of the commendation expressed in a telegram received from the G.O.C. IX. Corps the day before it was finally relieved. The message ran as follows :

" The C. in C. has just been at Corps H.Q. He would have liked to see all ranks now fighting on the 9th Corps front, and to tell each one of them of his personal appreciation of the magnificent fight they have made and are making. He would like to shake hands with each individual and thank him for what he has done. He has not time for this, but has asked me to give everybody this message."

The 36th Division, when the 108th Brigade departed on its desperate lone venture, was left with its front line east of Poelcappelle, and its headquarters on the Canal Bank. On that very day, March the 10th, the Army Commander decided to withdraw the II. Corps to its Battle Zone, here practically the British front line of 1917. The right of the 36th Division would now be just in front of Wieltje, so well known of old. An outpost line was, however, to be maintained upon the Steenebeek.

The retirement was absolutely essential, nor could it be delayed. By April the 11th the Germans were approaching the Forest of Nieppe. Passchendaele and Poelcappelle now protruded, an incredible salient, that made the old Ypres Salient unremarkable by comparison. Nevertheless, a few nights' respite was allowed, in order that the enemy might be deprived of the booty, and of the shelter for future operations, that had otherwise fallen to him. The heavy artillery was to move back first, bringing back all the ammunition that could possibly be carried, and tipping that which could not into shell-holes. An extensive programme of demolitions was planned by the C.R.E. Every dug-out or "pillbox" of importance was to be destroyed by explosives at the last possible moment. Craters were to be blown at important road-junctions. Light railways were to be, as far as possible, torn up or otherwise demolished.

There was a feverish rush by the Engineers, assisted by Infantry working-parties, to do the work in the scanty time available. Most of the forward demolitions were carried out by the 122nd Field Company, now commanded by Major W. Smyth, who had greatly distinguished himself during the March retreat as an *attaché* to the Divisional Staff. They were very effective. The 121st Field Company dammed the Steenebeek in an attempt to make it a more formidable obstacle, and began the construction of a new line behind it. The 150th Field Company prepared ten bridges over the Ypres Canal for demolition. The world knows that none of these bridges was ever "sent up," but may not know by how little their destruction was averted.

On the night of the 11th of April the withdrawal of the heavy artillery to cover the Battle Zone began, being completed three days later. The field artillery also moved back, leaving, however, forward guns in action by night, to deceive the enemy as to the British intentions. All was now prepared in rear. It remained only to withdraw the two battalions manning the outpost positions, firing the charges for the demolitions as they retired. This was carried out on the night of the 15th. Necessary as was the task, it was one which could not but inspire disappointment and regret. In a night the British Army was abandoning ground which had been profusely watered with its blood, and had taken long months in winning. The enemy advanced very slowly and cautiously on the morrow, heavily shelling Poelcappelle, now a mile and a half from the outposts, before he ventured to occupy it.

The Belgian Army was extending its front, as a helping hand in time of adversity. On the night of April the 18th the 4th Belgian Division relieved the 30th Division, on the left of the 36th, taking over the front of one battalion of the 107th Brigade. The next week passed quietly, the infantry showing aggression against the enemy outposts, capturing six prisoners in patrol affairs on successive nights. Divisional Headquarters were withdrawn from the Canal Bank to Border Camp, in the woodlands north of the Vlamertinghe-Poperinghe Road. For a couple of days the Steenebeek became the line of resistance, with outposts on the east bank. But Kemmel, so many miles in rear, had fallen, and the Germans were attacking north of it. General Plumer felt himself compelled to order a further withdrawal. The Ypres Canal was now to be the line of resistance. That decision, it is believed, has never been realized by people in England. Battered Ypres, small as was its actual importance of late, had been all through the war a sort of lodestar to the Germans. The best blood of England had been spilt in its defence. And now, theoretically, it was in the front line. Theoretically only, however, it may happily be recorded. An outpost line over two thousand yards east of it was maintained, and, as the German troops on the immediate front remained unaggressive—they had had a heavy defeat from the Belgians further north a few days previously—and the Lys Battle died down, lines in rear were gradually improved and dispositions altered, so that they might be held in greater strength in the event of an attack.

The second withdrawal of the 36th Division was evidently anticipated by the Germans, who followed it closely. An officer and two men of the 31st Landwehr Division, over impetuous, were captured. One party of the enemy, pressing swiftly on, entered Juliet Farm, a point which the 107th Brigade had been ordered to retain. Both the "pillbox" and Canopus Trench, in its neighbourhood, were retaken next night, together with an enemy machine-gun. The 109th Brigade on the right took five prisoners.

On the following day a great attack was launched by the Germans from south of Meteren to Voormezeele, upon the French D.A.N.* and the Second British Army. Everywhere it was completely and bloodily repulsed. To the enemy it was a terrible check. April the 29th, 1918, deserves to rank as high as the following 8th of August** in the history of the war. It marked the failure of the German northward offensive. For failure that offensive was, as the Somme offensive was not. The tenacity of troops on the flanks, such as the 55th Division on the right and the 9th on the left, had confined and narrowed the thrust. The curious formation of great hills, in almost straight line across the Flanders plain; Kemmel, the Scherpenberg, Mont Rouge, Mont Vidaigne, Mont Noir, Mont Kokereele, Mont des Cats, then, after a gap, Cassel, proved an impassable barrier in later stages of the battle. The first of the series alone fell. Upon the rest French artillery was now massed, pouring death into the Germans below. A few days earlier Ludendorff had, at a critical moment, struck again at Amiens. That offensive, which might have changed the whole position, had been pushed back before counter-attacks, and nipped in bud by the brilliant recapture of Villers-Bretonneux by the Australian Corps. The Germans were to make new offensives and gain much ground, notably near Rheims, where they cut the main Eastern Railway, and came all too close to Paris at Château-Thierry. But they were the blows of desperation. Week by week drew nearer the great retribution.

The next six weeks passed quietly for the 36th Division. The chief diversion was about a little dug-out near Juliet Farm, in the front line, formerly a Signals testing-point for overhead wires. Here there was constant bombing and raiding, largely to the disadvantage of the German troops, who were not of first quality and were unable to

* Détachement des Armées du Nord.
** The opening of the Amiens offensive.

withstand our men in close fighting. During the month of May fourteen prisoners were taken by the Division on seven separate occasions. One night a German wagon with rations drove into our outpost position in error and was captured, so indeterminate were the opposing front lines. The 36th Divisional Artillery had returned and taken over the defence of the front before the end of April. Early in May it received, with all other British divisional artilleries in France, a proportion of Indian personnel for its D.A.C., to replace English drivers. These were thereupon sent back for training as gunners.

During this period there occurred a great change in the command of the Division. Within three weeks three general officers long associated with it returned to England. On May the 6th Major-General O. S. Nugent, C.B., D.S.O., was succeeded by Major-General Clifford Coffin, V.C., D.S.O., in the command of the Division, General Nugent proceeding next day to England, preparatory to taking up a command in India. As long as the 36th Division is remembered, General Nugent's name will be associated with it. His whole existence was centred upon it; he was intensely proud of its achievements and jealous for its good name. It owed much to him, particularly to his training in the early days after its arrival in France. His successor, General Coffin, was an officer of the Royal Engineers, with a reputation for vigour, and a Victoria Cross gained for great bravery at Ypres. Just before General Nugent, General Withycombe and, just after him, General Griffith gave up command of the 107th and 108th Brigades respectively. General Withycombe had commanded his Brigade from within a few days of its arrival in France, except for a short period in 1917 when he had commanded a Brigade in England, and had inspired affection and trust in all its ranks. His headquarters was always a happy family, and a hospitable one, as the present writer would be ingrate were he to refrain from recording. The war leaves few pleasanter memories than those of meals at friendly boards after much perambulating of trenches. General Griffith had arrived a

Major-General C. C. Coffin, V.C., C.B., D.S.O.

little later, and his service with the Division was actually longer. His imperturbability and resource in moments of emergency had often served it and his own Brigade well. Their successors were Brigadier-General E. J. de S. Thorpe, D.S.O., in the 107th Brigade, and Brigadier-General E. Vaughan, D.S.O., in the 108th.

The 36th Division had indeed enjoyed the continuity of tradition and purpose which comes from a long tenour of command by senior officers. General Nugent, General Withycombe, General Griffith, General Brock, in the Divisional Artillery, had now commanded for two and a half years. In the 109th Brigade had been more frequent changes, but two of its Brigadiers, Generals Ricardo and Hessey, who between them commanded it for two years, had previously commanded two of its battalions.

In the early days of June came a most welcome relief, just when the country was at its best. Handing over the defence of the line to the 12th Belgian Division, the 36th moved back to the agreeable wooded area between Poperinghe and Proven. It was now in II. Corps reserve, ready if necessary to support the right flank of the Belgian Army. One Brigade, two Field Companies, and two companies of the Pioneer battalion, were at the disposal of the II. Corps for work on rear defences. There was now, men said, "wire from Ypres to Calais." Between Ypres and Poperinghe, six miles apart, were no less than four well-defended lines: the Brielen defences, and the Green, Yellow, and Blue Lines. In rear of Poperinghe were plenty more. The troops working upon these defences were relieved periodically, the other formations and units carrying out training. The Artillery put one section per battery into positions prepared for the defence of the Blue Line, in the event of another great attack, which still appeared not improbable.

The troops benefited very greatly from this welcome respite, the first the Division had had for a year, if the few days in the snow at Christmas be excepted. The young soldiers who now for the most part filled the ranks grew strong under the influence of good food, exercise, and life in the open under pleasant conditions. Their fitness for battle increased swiftly under that of steady training. There was plenty of sport, football, cricket, running, and boxing, in all of which their neighbours, the Belgians, took a hand. The only trouble was the extraordinary epidemic of influenza which swept over the world that summer, and visited all the armies in the field. Some German divisions, it was reported, were for a time not in a fit state to move or fight owing to its ravages. In the prevalent fine weather, fortunately, men recovered quickly from its effects.

The 36th Division had great tasks yet before it. It had to swing its hammer in the mighty line of destroyers that was to crush in the German defences and open the road to final victory. For those tasks that sunny month of June out of line was, as a prelude, of inestimable worth. After the dazing and deadening effect, the *abrutissement* of a battle, nothing told so much on the dash and energy of troops as long, dreary months of trench warfare, even in a line relatively quiet. They lost not only their physical agility, their power to march and run, but their mental power as well. A spell such as this gave them not only new strength, but new heart, new spirit, new hope. Affairs might be gloomy, but gloom was dispersed by the sun, like the Flanders mists. When the Division next entered the line, it was once again a fine fighting force.

That event came in the first week of July. The French, who, after losing Kemmel, had made a very fine stand at Locre, the vital gateway to the valley between the Scherpenberg and Mont Rouge, were now being relieved by the British along the line of the hills. After three days about Cassel, in reserve to the French XVI. Corps, the 36th Division relieved the 41st French Division on the northern skirts of Bailleul. Divisional Headquarters were established at Terdeghem, with a command post on the Mont des Cats prepared for emergiences. The sudden move had almost, but not quite, succeeded in spoiling a very fine Divisional Horse Show, held at Proven, in beautiful weather and surroundings, on July the 3rd. Upon this the officers of the neighbouring Belgian Cavalry Division, including an Olympic competitor, descended like wolves on the fold, giving a remarkable display of skill and horsemanship, and taking practically all the prizes for jumping events.

The Division was to hold this line for upwards of two months, then to go forward upon the enemy's heels. Nor was it ever again to be forced to give ground. The gray blur on the horizon was brighter now; the light was not far off.

## CHAPTER XIII

### BACK TO THE MESSINES RIDGE : JULY TO SEPTEMBER 1918

THE new sector was at the north-west corner of the great salient made by the Lys offensive. It ran from Fontainehouck, a hamlet north-east of Meteren, which was in the hands of the enemy, to the high ground south of the Croix de Poperinghe. It was about a mile and a half north of Bailleul. Here, as all along the line of hills, the enemy was at heavy disadvantage. His territory was overlooked. Every movement, every gun-flash, could be noted from Mont Noir and the other hills. Bailleul crumbled away before the eyes of our men. St. Jans Cappel, for so long Divisional Headquarters in days that now seemed very far away, was not far behind the front line. It was to a great extent destroyed. Many of the isolated farms, with which that countryside is bestrewn, were, however, undamaged, right up to the front line. The country was deep in crops, the wheat having to be cut round the outposts to prevent surprise attacks and provide a field of fire. As for vegetables, the men had all the potatoes and green peas they could eat without walking a hundred yards from where they slept. After Ypres, it was a very agreeable position. German artillery fire was not as a rule severe, owing to the fact that the battery positions were overlooked from the hills. The worst disturbance was caused by night bombing, assiduously practised by the enemy. Casualties were low. They would have been lower had our troops been as circumspect in following the hedges, and confining their movement to the night, as their predecessors, the French, had been. But the lesson of "lying low," so well learnt by Frenchman and German, never had been mastered by the British soldier, nor ever was.

On July the 19th the 9th Division, in line on the right, captured Meteren, the Artillery of the 36th Division cooperating in the attack. The 36th Division did not at first strive to improve its position in a similar way, but contented itself with raids on a large scale. One, by the 109th Brigade, resulted in very heavy fighting, the enemy being on the alert. Though the enemy's casualties were estimated at thirty, and a prisoner was taken, the raid hardly ranked as a success, since our casualties were seventeen, including four men missing. The 107th Brigade, on the left, had a more satisfactory venture. A strong patrol of the 2nd Rifles surrounded a farm in which there was an enemy garrison of ten. Two of these were taken prisoner, the rest killed. The patrol had not a casualty, despite heavy machine-gun fire. Further prisoners were taken by the 107th Brigade on a later occasion, while the only raid attempted by the enemy, from Haagedoorne, where his troops held the old railhead, was beaten off by rifle fire, even though the Germans got within twenty yards of the outposts before being seen.

An interesting event of this period was the visit of His Majesty the King to the area. On August the 6th, at Oxelaere, a little village on the slopes of Cassel Hill, he presented to Lieutenant Knox, 150th Field Company, R.E., the Victoria Cross won by him during the March retreat in circumstances that have been described. On the following Sunday His Majesty attended a parade service at Terdeghem, where were Divisional Headquarters.

The 36th Division, being in the Second Army, was not destined to take part in the early great counter-offensives that raised all men's spirits and showed the world that at last the tide had turned. The first of these had been French, though four of the best British Divisions had played their part in it. In what is now known as the Battle of Tardenois, beginning on July the 18th, the salient of the great German advance to Château-Thierry had been crushed in, and the enemy routed, with great loss of prisoners and booty. Then, on the 8th of August, came a second mighty blow. The Fourth British and First French Armies began a great offensive down the Amiens-Roye Road. The quality of the resistance with which it was met showed that German discipline and German steadfastness were weakening at last. On the 21st the British Third Army, and a little later the First Army, launched still greater attacks, sweeping swiftly across the waste of the old Somme battlefield, and once more approaching the Hindenburg Line. Before that was reached the 36th Division, up in Flanders, was again in action.

Various local offensives had been planned, to take from the enemy what little good ground he held near the point of his salient. The 9th Division's capture of Meteren has been mentioned. At the end of July, the 1st Australian Division, further south, had retaken Merris. On August the 18th the 9th Division carried out a further successful operation, capturing the important Hoegenacker Ridge, south-east of Meteren. It was now the turn of the 36th Division to improve its position. On August the 22nd an attack carried out by the 15th Rifles, on the right of the line, advanced it a quarter of a mile on a front of half a mile. Twenty-two prisoners and two machine-guns were captured. A curious and vastly effective ruse was employed in conjunction with this operation. The demoralizing effect of the Livens projector upon the enemy was well known, but its use, charged with gas, would have prevented any immediate attack by our troops upon the area bombarded. The drums were therefore filled with a scent which resembled the smell of gas. Many of the enemy had run back before our men advanced, while others were caught wearing their respirators.

Two days later an attack on the left by the 1st and 9th Irish Fusiliers, under a barrage of smoke and shrapnel,

## THE ENEMY WITHDRAWS 251

advanced the line to the Haagedoorne-Dranoutre Road on a front of upwards of a mile. So great was the surprise and so swift the assault, that the enemy was "smothered," and did not make a serious resistance. Sixty prisoners and eleven machine-guns were taken here. An enemy counter-attack in the evening was brought to a stop by rifle and machine-gun fire, though the 108th Brigade lost one small post. The line was now a thousand yards only from Bailleul, and the defences of the town were pierced. An attack upon the salient would now have resulted in a great German rout. The enemy did not await it. Under the skilful leadership, that was never more apparent than in the months of defeat and humiliation which were to follow, he flitted in a night.

The 36th Division, on the morning of August the 30th, was awaiting relief by the 35th Division, to be given a short period of rest and training before being launched upon the great series of final offensives in Flanders. Its right-hand neighbour, the 9th Division, had already been relieved by the 31st Division on the Hoegenacker Ridge, with a like object. That rest the 36th Division was not destined to enjoy. At ten o'clock that morning came a report from the 31st Division that the enemy was gone from its front, and that its men were entering Bailleul from the south. Before two o'clock patrols of the 36th were in the huge Asylum north of the town, and upon the Neuve Eglise Road. The relief was cancelled and an immediate advance ordered, to be carried out by the 109th Brigade.

This was not the first enemy retirement in the Western theatre. There had been that of 1917, in which some of the troops now in the 36th Division had been the pursuers. No doubt the men who had then tracked the retreating Germans had felt elation. But that had been false dawn. Now, as men sprang up eagerly to set about their preparations, a conviction spread among them that this was the true, that not again would they have to turn back. Some of our present-day pessimists pretend that by the summer of 1918 the horror, the iron ruthlessness, of the war had robbed men of their stores of latent enthusiasm, and that, even for victory, they had none to summon forth.

It is untrue. Were it true, they could not have so swiftly prevailed against an enemy, disheartened indeed, but still disciplined, tenacious and well led, still admirably equipped, and, above all, backed by a series of defences such as the Allies, in their days of adversity, had never dreamed of. All testimony, moreover, is to the contrary. Like a flame the spirit of victory, the bright-hued prospect of deliverance, spread among all ranks. Defeat and retirement had bred melancholy and bad temper. The new atmosphere dissipated them. To go forward, to strike, to make an end—those were the impulses and the hopes that swept through the waiting ranks.

The ground immediately to be recovered had a double appeal, a sentimental interest. It was that which had been the area of the Division for a year. The Château of St. Jans Cappel had been Divisional Headquarters for the greater part of that period. The remains of that pleasant villa—*heu quantum mutata!*—were to shelter General Coffin's staff during the advance.\* On the Ravelsberg Ridge, the first objective, had been the Divisional School. In Neuve Eglise, the second, had been a Brigade Headquarters. Not a house, not a lane, not a forlorn camp with shell-punctured hutments, not a machine-gun position further forward in the old battle-line, but was known to some of the officers and men now making ready to advance. There was triumph even, mingled with the pathos, in re-entering poor, battered Bailleul, which had been a good friend in time past. From a handsome town it was become a mass of ruins, so completely destroyed that, across a fine central *place* of several acres, there was now but a single narrow track for transport through the rubble. By midnight on the 30th the patrols were half a mile along the Neuve Eglise Road and a mile from the summit of Ravelsberg Hill. To capture that on the morrow was the task of the 109th Brigade.

---

\* General Coffin was at this time on leave, the Division being commanded by Brigadier-General Brock, the C.R.A.

The Brigade had a wide frontage, roughly a thousand yards north of the Neuve Eglise Road, and two thousand south of it. The advance was steady, but made in the teeth of considerable machine-gun fire. The Germans had evacuated their positions, but they did not want to be hurried, nor were they prepared to forego the opportunity of inflicting loss upon our troops which such a height as the Ravelsberg afforded. But, once that hill captured, the enemy rearguards were hustled down the further slope. By night the Brigade had reached the foot of the next hill, a mile east of the Ravelsberg. A mile and a half to the south the 1st Inniskillings had its right upon the main Armentières Road.

Neuve Eglise was the first objective for September the 1st. The 2nd Inniskillings was ordered to extend its left flank as far as the road from that village to Dranoutre, and advance with its left upon Wulverghem. The 108th Brigade had meanwhile moved up in support to Haagedoorne, the 107th being in the area of Mont Noir and Mont Kokereele. Great efforts were being made to bring artillery forward over the very bad roads. Kemmel Hill was once again in British hands, and good news came in the morning from the 30th Division, on the left, which had reached Lindenhoek and south of it as far as the valley of the Douve.

The severest resistance was met at Westhof Farm and De Broeken, both well known of old, where German machine-guns caused serious loss. German artillery fire was also heavy. The various strong points were taken one by one. The German rearguards slipped back in each case before our men came upon them, but a number were killed in flight and, outside Neuve Eglise, a machine-gun and two prisoners captured. By afternoon the enemy had been driven back to the western outskirts of the village. Some of the 2nd Inniskillings appear actually to have reached its houses, but the line finally taken up at night was five hundred yards short of it.

The 108th Brigade was ordered to pass through the 109th at night and resume the advance, its objectives being from Red Lodge, in the north-west corner of "Plug Street Wood," to South Midland Farm on the Wulverghem-Messines Road. The artillery was now in a position to give it adequate support. The attack was carried out by the 12th Rifles on the right and 1st Irish Fusiliers on the left. On its southern flank, Kortepyp Cabaret and the Custom House on the Steenwerck Road gave trouble.* A Stokes mortar here well repaid the labour of bringing it and its ammunition forward, enabling the infantry to rush these places after a short bombardment. Then the line pressed forward to the Nieppe Road running south-east from Neuve Eglise. Machine-gun fire from this village was at first galling, but, after it had been heavily shelled by the artillery, a company of the 12th Rifles took it in most gallant fashion, while two other companies made progress to the south of it. By four o'clock the line was east of Neuve Eglise.

The next obstacle was a fairly formidable one, an old British system, the name of which recalled the days when the British Army had been a very small force indeed—the G.H.Q. Line. The Germans had put up some wire to defend its support trench from the west. At 7-30 p.m., light being still good, our artillery bombarded these defences heavily for an hour, after which the infantry advanced to the attack. The trenches were not taken without fighting, though, in all the circumstances, the enemy's resistance must be reckoned feeble. Desultory encounters continued all night, but by morning the infantry was in possession of the G.H.Q. Line along the whole front. On the left, meanwhile, the troops of the 30th Division had entered Wulverghem.

On the 3rd, as resistance stiffened, the frontage was narrowed. A Brigade of the 29th Division had just relieved the 31st Division troops on the right for the assault on the very important position of Hill 63. The new objective of the 108th Brigade was from White Gates, at the western foot of this hill, to South Midland Farm.

* *i.e.*, the Belgian Custom House, Neuve Eglise being in Belgium, Steenwerck and Bailleul in France.

At 9-30 a.m. the 12th Rifles and 1st Irish Fusiliers went forward. In the early stages they had artillery support. Thereafter, owing to constant movement and the difficulty of ascertaining the position of the front line, the only assistance that could be rendered by the artillery was by fire on objectives far in rear, save for occasional opportunities that came the way of single mobile guns. The attack resolved itself into individual assaults upon German machine-gun positions, which were taken in flank by Lewis guns worked forward, and then rushed with the bayonet. Three were thus taken, and their detachments killed or captured, while none of the latter, which ran before the infantry came upon them, escaped without loss from our fire. By evening the line ran from L'Alouette, a mile east of Neuve Eglise, to La Plus Douve Farm, a famous old battalion headquarters of the 36th Division, south-east of Wulverghem. The whole of this front was taken over after dark by the 9th Irish Fusiliers, which battalion had not yet been in action.

The 108th Brigade's attack next morning began at 8-30 a.m. under a creeping barrage. Half an hour prior to it, on the extreme right, the 9th Irish Fusiliers advanced about a hundred yards toward Hill 63, to support an attack on the hill by troops of the 29th Division. The attack was completely successful. Hill 63 was of the greatest importance to the enemy, and was very strongly held, as was proved by the capture of nearly two hundred and fifty prisoners by the men of the 29th Division. The hill being in British hands made affairs far easier for the 108th Brigade. The advance of the 9th Irish Fusiliers met with considerable opposition. Gaps appeared, and there was some loss of direction, not astonishing when it is considered that the battalion was on a frontage of over a mile. Eventually a company of the 1st Irish Fusiliers had to be brought up on the right flank, on the Neuve Eglise-La Basseville Road. Before noon all objectives were attained. On the right the 1st Irish Fusiliers had advanced beyond White Gates. On the left, Gooseberry Farm, a mile east of the starting-line, was in the hands of the 9th.

All had gone excellently so far. But the British were now facing positions which the Germans desired to hold for some time longer, for which they were prepared to fight. An immediate local counter-attack down the Douve valley was repulsed with the aid of artillery fire. But at 4·15 p.m., after a heavy bombardment, the enemy launched a counter-attack from the south-west on this part of the line. Gooseberry Farm and Stinking Farm* were lost, and the line driven back five hundred yards.

On the following day the 36th Division actually lost a little ground instead of gaining it. An attack carried out at dawn by the 1st and 9th Irish Fusiliers, under a light artillery barrage, insufficient to keep down the very heavy machine-gun fire, was unsuccessful. A heavy hostile counter-attack drove our troops back beyond their original line. The 108th Brigade had now been fighting for four days, with no shelter but that of old and dirty trenches, in persistent rain. The men were in good spirits still, but fatigue was beginning to tell upon them. It was decided that the 107th Brigade should relieve them after dusk, to continue the attack upon the morrow. The 108th Brigade had captured thirty-five prisoners and three machine-guns. Its casualties, however, especially during the last two days, had been very heavy, numbering upwards of four hundred. The 29th Division, on the right, was again being relieved by the 31st.

The night of the relief was very unpleasant. The Germans, beginning about ten o'clock, deluged all the low-lying valleys with mustard and other gas shell. The new advance was to be supported by the fire of two Machine-Gun Companies, instead of the one which had been in action hitherto. Captain Walker describes how he rode out in the darkness to find his sections, scattered among battalions of the 109th Brigade in reserve, and came into the cloud at Neuve Eglise, forced to keep his eyes uncovered

---

* The farm had earned its horrible name in 1915 from the odour of a huge store of rotten potatoes in its cellars. These had been removed the following year by sappers of the 36th Division, wearing gas-masks. Thereafter it stank no worse than any other ruin in the Flanders front line.

## ATTACK OF SEPTEMBER 6TH

to find his way, but keeping the nose-clip and mouth-piece of his respirator in position. When dawn broke he discovered that the pool of gas lying in the basin in which 107th Brigade Headquarters were situated almost lipped the entrance floor of the dug-out. Most fortunate it was that the dug-out was half-way up the side of the basin. When, later, he walked down the main road to Wulverghem, he found the occupants of the dug-outs which bordered it "being sick by the score." A good many casualties were caused during the relief, but for the most part the gas was not of the most noxious sort, and many of those who had inhaled it were able to take part in the action of September the 6th. It had the effect, however, of delaying the relief. When dawn broke all the companies of the 2nd Rifles were not in position; nor was it possible to move them forward afterwards, owing to the forward slope on which that position lay being in full view of the enemy.

The 36th Division Artillery was now prepared to put down a really effective barrage, to advance at the rate of a hundred yards in three minutes, then to form a protective curtain two hundred and fifty yards in front of the objective, till an hour and a half after Zero. This objective was the old British front line, from the Douve on the right to the Wulverghem-Messines Road on the left.

At 4 p.m. the attack was launched. The companies of the 2nd Rifles not already in position began to move up in little columns as the bombardment opened, continuing this method of advance as the barrage lifted. On the right, troops of the 31st Division attacked simultaneously. Despite heavy German artillery fire the infantry went forward with great spirit. After heavy fighting, all objectives, except Gabion Farm on the right, were taken. Nineteen prisoners were captured, and many Germans killed. How strongly the line was held was shown by the capture of eight machine-guns, as well as a trench mortar. The troops of the 31st Division also had reached their objectives. Early on the morning of the 7th the advance was rounded off by the capture of Gabion Farm, where a post was established.

The enemy was not yet resigned to the loss of the position. At dawn on the 8th, after an intense bombardment, two groups advanced to recapture the advanced posts. They were literally annihilated by machine and Lewis-gun fire, a wounded survivor of each being captured. That night the 30th Division took over the front to Gabion Farm, while the 107th Brigade extended its right to Hyde Park Corner, in "Plug Street Wood," becoming responsible for the defence of Hill 63.

Comparative stagnation ensued, broken only by two small attacks upon the 15th Rifles, which had now taken over the line. The period was marked by one distressing accident. General Thorpe, commanding the 107th Brigade, had gone up with General Brock on the night of the 13th to visit Hill 63 and the sentry-posts north of it. Moving along "Winter Trench" he was suddenly fired at from point-blank range by one of his own men and severely wounded in the arm, his elbow-bone being shot away. It was a stroke of cruel ill-fortune, which prevented General Thorpe from leading the Brigade to final victory. He was able to return to the command of his regiment after the war, but with an arm well-nigh useless for life, from which he has since suffered incessant pain. Lieutenant-Colonel R. H. MacKenzie, C.R.E. of the Division, took over command of the Brigade till the appointment of his successor. That successor was General Brock, who, after bringing the Divisional Artillery to France and commanding it in the field for more than two and a half years, was to finish his career with the 36th Division by leading an Infantry Brigade with equal success. He was succeeded as C.R.A. by Brigadier-General C. St. L. Hawkes, D.S.O. Another senior officer of the Division lost to it a short time before was Lieutenant-Colonel J. E. Knott, D.S.O., commanding the 2nd Inniskillings, severely wounded by a shell which killed the Intelligence Officer of the 109th Brigade, Lieutenant J. J. Fox, and wounded the Brigade Major R.A., Major H. F. Grant Suttie, D.S.O., M.C., by his side. Another calamity was the bombing of the wagon lines of the Divisional

## MOVE TO YPRES

Train near St. Jans Cappel. Here a single bomb killed five men, wounded nine, and killed no less than fifty valuable horses, besides injuring about twenty more. A bomb or big shell in crowded horse-lines was always one of the ugliest sights of many very ugly that the war had to display.

On the night of September the 15th the 109th Brigade took over the front, now slightly extended on the right toward Ploegsteert. There was constant patrol activity in the days that followed, but no further ground was to be gained by those methods. The enemy was maintaining himself very stoutly and his line bristled with machine-guns. It was evident that only a great "full-dress" assault would retake the Messines Ridge.

The tide of victory meanwhile had continued to flow strongly on other fronts. On the 12th of September the Third Army had crashed through the Hindenburg trenches at Havrincourt. Three days later the Balkan offensive, so long awaited that men had come to doubt its possibility, had been launched, and attended with overwhelming success. Within a few days Bulgaria was prostrate and Turkey out of the war. It would have been poetical justice had it fallen to the lot of the 36th Division to have a hand in the second capture of the Messines Ridge, as the 62nd Division had taken Havrincourt for the second time. If that were denied it, it was only because it had a task even more important to perform, a task the successful prosecution of which would render to the enemy the famous ridge of no avail. As a necessary complement to the great convergent thrusts of British, French, and American armies further south, a powerful offensive, mainly Anglo-Belgian, but in which a French force also took part, had been planned in Flanders, from Voormezeele northwards. It was to be under the supreme command of His Majesty the King of the Belgians, so that co-ordination between the three nationalities should be assured. For this the 36th Division was required. For the third time in its career, but in circumstances vastly different to the two first, it was directed upon Ypres. For the new battle some training had been obtained by the 107th and 108th Brigades during the days that the 109th held the line.

The movements were carried out with greatest secrecy. All marches took place after dark, on the nights of September the 21st and 22nd. The 107th moved thus to Wormhoudt, north of Cassel, the 109th Brigade to Eecke, east of that town, and the 108th to Houtquerque. The Divisional Artillery moved straight to the neighbourhood of Ypres. The Infantry of the Division was not to take part in the first day's attack, and, for the preliminary barrage, the 153rd Brigade R.F.A. was to be attached to the 9th Division, the 173rd Brigade to the 29th Division, on its right, the troops of which were in line slightly over a mile east of the famous ruined town.

After a few days of rest and training, the concentration took place on the nights of the 26th and 27th. By the morning of the 28th, the date of the attack, the three Brigades were in camps between Poperinghe and Vlamertinghe. Headquarters were at Vogeltje Château, near the better-known Lovie Château, in the woodlands west of Poperinghe. The Division was again in General Jacob's II. Corps, under which it had served in April, May, and June. It was in Corps Reserve, its mission being to hold itself in readiness for a move forward to assist in the exploitation of any success gained by the first-line Divisions.

The late operations had been heartening. Despite, however, their difficulty and costliness, they represented, at least till the final stages, no more than hard and steady pressure upon a rearguard. No great number of prisoners could be taken in such fighting, while the casualties to be inflicted upon the enemy were comparatively small. The Division had not yet had a hand in one of the great offensives. All ranks knew that the attack about to open ranked in that category, and that resistance of far more serious quality was to be expected. For that they were prepared. It is no exaggeration to say that they looked forward to the coming struggle, just because they believed it would be the last. Officers who came back from England the day after the opening of the attack, when the news that from Ypres to the sea the whole line was advancing had been flashed abroad, describe the returning leave-boat as being so full of cheerful faces that it might have been taken for one homeward bound. Some were less ambitious than others. In one officer's diary is expressed the opinion that the Passchendaele Ridge, if captured, would serve as a good "jumping-off" ground for an offensive the following spring! But for the most part, men, beholding victory upon victory, had come to believe that the war could be ended this year. For that speed was essential, else winter would come to the aid of the enemy and give him time to collect himself. That reasoning could be grasped by all, and acted upon all as an added spur to endeavour in the days that followed.

## CHAPTER XIV

### THE ADVANCE TO FINAL VICTORY (I):
### SEPTEMBER 28TH TO OCTOBER 17TH, 1918

THE attack of the II. Corps was to be carried out with the 29th Division on the right and the 9th on the left. The left flank of the latter Division lay on the Zonnebeke Road at Mill Cott. On its left was the 8th Belgian Division. The Belgians did not desire to attack without preliminary bombardment, and for three hours before Zero their artillery shelled the German positions and battery areas. The artillery on the II. Corps front fired for five minutes only before Zero, which was at 5-30 a.m. on the 28th of September. The preliminary attack was to be carried out under a creeping barrage, with a large proportion of smoke-shell. In density this was far less than the "creepers" of 1917, there being a gun to upwards of fifty yards. The German defences, however, owing to the drain caused by reverses elsewhere, were no longer manned in the strength of those days, nor was the resistance likely to be of a quality so high. The task, however, was formidable enough, the ground being only less difficult than during the Battles of Ypres, 1917.

The attack, launched in heavy rain, was a complete success. The German infantry was left in the lurch by its artillery, and, save at isolated points, made no serious resistance. The attacking troops, Belgians and British, went

## ATTACK OF SEPTEMBER 28TH 263

forward with the greatest dash and determination. The Belgian infantry, which had not been involved in the great reverses of the British and French, was by this time of excellent quality, its ranks filled by young men of good physique. Neither wire nor shell-pocked waste could check the assault. The Frezenberg Ridge, that had resisted so many attacks of old, was in the hands of the 9th Division a little more than an hour after the beginning of the advance. By night the 29th Division had Gheluvelt, with its heroic memories of the 2nd Worcesters' charge on the 31st of October, 1914, and was astride the Menin Road a mile east of it. The Belgians had Zonnebeke, and were in touch with the 9th Division on the Broodseinde Ridge. But it was the 9th which had most accomplished. Passing its third Brigade through in early afternoon, it had seized the village of Becelaere. At its greatest point the day's advance exceeded six thousand yards. Verily were times changed in these regions.

By an early hour it had been apparent that affairs were marching swiftly, and at eleven in the morning the II. Corps ordered the 36th Division to move forward, with its Infantry Brigades in echelon. The 109th was ordered to entrain first, and was carried by light railway to Potijze, where it detrained at 3 p.m. It then received orders to march to the neighbourhood of the Bellewaarde Lake. The 108th Brigade was moved east of Ypres at noon; the 107th to Potijze later in the afternoon. So fast had been the advance that the 107th Brigade's first orders were to move no further than Vlamertinghe, but on arrival the men were told to keep their places in the trucks, which bore them forward another three miles before dusk. Headquarters of the Division were established in the old dug-outs of the Ypres Ramparts at 2 p.m.

The plan for the 29th of September was that one Brigade of the 36th—the 109th—was to come into line between the 29th and 9th Divisions. The 109th Brigade was to be supported by the 153rd Brigade R.F.A., hitherto under the orders of the 9th Division, if its batteries could be got into action in time. As a matter of fact, owing to the shocking state of the roads, they were not able to fire a shot till the next day. The 109th Brigade was to pass through the 27th Brigade in Becelaere, the latter Brigade then following in rear of the assaulting Brigade of its own Division. The objective of the 109th was Terhand, but, if this were easily attained, the intention was to exploit the success. It was attacking with the 2nd Inniskillings on the right, the 9th on the left, and the 1st in support. A dawn assault would have been desirable, but, owing to the difficulty the 109th Brigade experienced in advancing by night across broken country on roads so damaged and thronged, it was postponed till 9-30 a.m. The Brigade's difficulties were increased by heavy bombing of the approaches to the line by enemy aircraft during the hours of darkness.

The rain continued all night, accompanied by great cold, and in this blasted area there was no shelter for the troops. By a stroke of fortune, however, the weather improved in the morning, the sun appearing just about the hour of Zero. The advance was at first very rapid. If the 109th had no artillery support, it had small opposition from that arm. Its difficulties were caused by machine-guns, singly or in nests of from two to five, cleverly disposed in depth behind hedges or in buildings. For hedges there were now, and, though the ground had been heavily shelled, it was no longer the sea of mud and shell-holes of the old Salient battle-ground.

These German machine-guns were attacked with greatest *élan*. Often the leading infantry put them out of action by rifle-fire before the Lewis guns, a serious burden on such ground, could be brought into action against them. Still, there is no reason to doubt that the rate of advance could have been swifter had artillery support been available. The left battalion, the 9th Inniskillings, aided by the magnificent rush of the 9th Division to north of it, found matters considerably easier than did the 2nd Inniskillings on the right. From two o'clock onwards the latter was held up by machine-gun fire from Terhand, while the former pressed forward

## ADVANCE OF SEPTEMBER 29TH

north of the village. Terhand fell at last at a quarter to four. By this time the 9th Inniskillings was on the southern outskirts of Dadizeele, which was captured by the 9th Division a few minutes later. Then, at six o'clock, the 9th Inniskillings forced its way into Vijfwegen, a road-side hamlet a mile south of Dadizeele.

The day's advance had been once more remarkable, but much more so on the left of the II. Corps than on its right flank. The 9th Division, from Becelaere to Dadizeele, had gained well-nigh three miles of ground. From Vijfwegen, however, the line ran almost west—that is to say, it faced south—to Terhand, and thence to south of Becelaere, where the 29th Division had been held up.

At 4 a.m. the 108th Brigade had moved off in support to the 109th, being upon the high ground west of Becelaere by 7 p.m. It was ordered to move forward again, pass through the 109th at dawn, and advance with as objective the great Menin-Roulers highway from Kezelberg northward. The 29th Division, meanwhile, was to make a great effort to force its way up into line on the right. "D" Company of the Machine-Gun Battalion was attached to the 108th Brigade, together with its own Stokes Mortar Battery.

The position to be attacked had few artificial defences—the German wired line defending Menin and Roulers was just west of Dadizeele and Vijfwegen, and had already been pierced—but it was naturally strong. The embankment of the huge main road formed good protection to the enemy. But the key to the position was a hillock half-way between the road and Vijfwegen—Hill 41. Sixty feet above the surrounding country, crowned with several farms and their outbuildings, which had been strengthened with concrete, it was at once invaluable to the enemy and an excellent defensive position in fighting of this nature, when very little artillery was available to shake its machine-gun detachments prior to the infantry assault. With plenty, even of field artillery, it would not have been a very formidable obstacle, while a concentration of heavy artillery would have blown the defenders off its crest. But the big guns were still far behind.

At 7-30 a.m. the 108th Brigade passed through the troops of the 109th. The 9th Irish Fusiliers was on the right, the 12th Rifles on the left, and the 1st Irish Fusiliers in reserve, eight hundred yards behind the leading battalions. Each had one section of machine-guns and one Stokes mortar attached. The advance encountered considerable machine-gun fire from Hill 41 and the Menin-Roulers Road. Despite this, north of the hill it went forward in splendid fashion. The men of the 12th Rifles fought their way through the Zuidhoek Copse, and reached the Menin-Roulers Road by 10-30 a.m. Touch being gained here with the 9th Division, the 12th Rifles, according to previous agreement, took over from its troops as far north as Klephoek Cross Roads. On the right the 9th Irish Fusiliers reached the Gheluwe-Vijfwegen Road, and pressed on south of the latter village and past the southern flank of Hill 41. But upon the hill itself the German machine-gunners resisted all attacks. On the right of the 9th Irish Fusiliers the 29th Division made great strides, despite machine-guns distributed in depth all along its front. Though it did not take Gheluwe, and was unable to do so all day, its left flank reached the Gheluwe-Vijfwegen Road in touch with the 108th Brigade.

At last the 9th Irish Fusiliers also reached the Menin-Roulers Road, at Kezelberg, and attempted to work up it and obtain touch with its comrades of the 12th Rifles, a thousand yards further north, thus surrounding Hill 41. One strongly held farm-house, with twelve prisoners, was taken at 12-30, but thereafter fire from the hill prevented any move northward.

The capture of Hill 41 evidently required a serious effort. General Coffin arranged with the 9th Division that its 50th Brigade R.F.A. should support an attack with a barrage of smoke and high explosive. Behind this one company of the 12th Rifles was to advance at 4 p.m.

The Riflemen, in face of heavy fire, went forward most

gallantly. The German resistance was equally determined. For every hedge there was a battle, the bayonet being frequently used. Thirty-one prisoners were taken, and about the same number of dead Germans counted after the attack. The crest, however, could not be reached, a line being established just short of it. But the strength of the German defence had been under-estimated. The story of Mœuvres was repeated with regard to this battalion. Before reinforcements could move up a heavy German bombardment came as prelude to a counter-attack, estimated at three hundred strong. Atop the hill it was held by the fire of Lewis guns, but, with their superiority of numbers, the Germans pushed round on either flank, rendering the position untenable. At six o'clock the company was compelled to fall back. Its casualties had not been heavy considering the fierce nature of the fighting.

The 107th Brigade had reached the line of Becelaere by the morning, and had been ordered to push up a battalion on the right of the 108th Brigade in the afternoon. The 2nd Rifles had attempted to advance upon Klythoek, on the Menin-Roulers Road, but had been held up by heavy machine-gun fire. Another attempt to advance was planned for the morning of October the 1st. This time there was more effective artillery support, two batteries of 6-inch howitzers being able to shell Hill 41 at long range. To attack the hill, two companies of the reserve battalion, the 1st Rifles, were brought up. The 12th Rifles was to co-operate on the left, and the 2nd Rifles of the 107th Brigade on the right. The 9th Division was to endeavour to cross the Menin-Roulers Road and capture Ledeghem, on the Menin-Roulers Railway. The new attack was launched at 6-15 a.m. in heavy mist. On the right the leading companies of the 2nd Rifles lost direction. The commanding officer, Lieut.-Colonel Bridcott, was killed while attempting to reorganize them. On the left also the attack failed. On Hill 41, however, the companies of the 1st Irish Fusiliers, fighting their way desperately forward in face of heavy resistance, reached Twigg Farm, just short of the crest, and captured that place with twenty-two prisoners. Further they were unable to go in face of the machine-gun fire. The fire from the eastern slope of the hill was also causing serious trouble to the troops of the 9th Division, now approaching the Menin-Roulers Railway. After capturing Ledeghem the Lowland Brigade made an attempt to turn Hill 41 from the north, to aid the 36th Division, but was beaten off in turn by the irrepressible machine-guns.

One more attempt finally to clear the obstinate hill was made that day by the 1st Inniskilling Fusiliers of the 109th Brigade, swinging in from the north. It was unsuccessful in its object, but it achieved another not less important. The Germans were about to launch a heavy counter-attack on the exposed right flank of the 9th Division, when this diversion checked them. The affair is thus reported in the *History of the 9th (Scottish) Division*:

"Lieut.-Colonel Smyth saw the Germans collecting troops for a great counter-stroke, and the K.O.S.B. were bracing themselves for a desperate resistance at Manhattan Farm, when the timely arrival of the 1st Inniskilling Fusiliers, who made a most heroic attack on Hill 41 from the north, scared the enemy and turned his efforts solely to defence. Though the Inniskillings failed to capture the hill, their plucky effort probably saved the K.O.S.B., and so great was the admiration of the latter and the troops of the Ninth Division who witnessed the attack, that the G.O.C. at their request wrote at once to the Thirty-sixth Division expressing the admiration and thanks of the officers and men of the Ninth."

Local counter-attacks did come against Twigg Farm, to be beaten off with loss by the company of the 1st Irish Fusiliers which held it. That night the 109th Brigade relieved the 108th.

The action of this day and of those following cannot be understood without a brief survey of the general situation. The British advance of the first two days, at its greatest point, from east of Ypres to the Menin-Roulers Road, had been eight miles. The Germans had been broken and

## REVIEW OF SITUATION

thrown into confusion. But the very rapidity of the Allied advance, over such roads as those which crossed the welter of the old Ypres Salient, had created new difficulties. It was hard enough, as has been related, to bring guns forward. But that was by no means the main difficulty, even where the artillery was concerned. Batteries in an advance go forward only. The limbers which feed them, the lorries which feed the limbers from the train, must go forward and backward. Therein lay the real trouble. The roads were choked. The only tolerable among them, because, bad though they were, the remains of the old *pavé* held them together, were the Menin and Zonnebeke Roads. Upon each was a solid mass of transport, which often for hours at a time remained immobile. A few days after the events already recorded, wagons of the 107th Brigade took thirty-six hours to proceed from Potijze Château to Terhand. Captain Walker thus describes the Zonnebeke Road on the night of the 30th of September :

"I had never previously realized the number and variety of vehicles which move in support of three Divisions; indeed, I think this road fed only the 9th and 36th Divisions.* There were limbers by scores with rations; there were G.S. wagons with forage for the battalion transports forward; there were R.E. wagons, mess-carts, guns and ammunition; there were lorries stuck in shell-holes in the road, and the cause of most of the trouble. On every odd bit of ground bordering the road were French cavalrymen. The surface and the language were equally bad, and there was mud everywhere. I had to wind my way through these troubles for several miles. During my journey there was practically no movement of the traffic. It had taken 'C' Company's transport fourteen hours to do the six miles from Ypres to the Ridge, and the Company bivouacked on the road for a night. A Gotha flew down that road at midnight, dropping bombs at regular intervals. I'm glad I missed that. There must have been many casualties, for that road was a mass of animals and men. Why

* This supposition is correct. The 29th Division used the Menin Road.

only one Gotha was out that night beats me. 'D' Company, which was supposed to be with the advancing infantry, was held up with everybody else. Major Wood, the O.C., was panic-stricken, having the General's orders to be in action at a stated time and place, and, putting eight guns on pack mules, set off across the desolation. I believe about four guns did eventually come into action, but a couple of mules got into shell-holes from which they could not be extricated, and had to be despatched."

On the one hand, then, the Germans, now driven back to the fringe of civilized and unbroken country, with roads and railways behind them, were enabled to make some hasty attempts at reorganization; on the other, the Allies, having overrun their supplies, were yet under the necessity of keeping up steady pressure, to prevent the enemy from improving and settling down upon those positions. Doubtless the enemy had expected to be driven back and eventually to form up upon the line of the Lys, but he had been driven back much more quickly than he had anticipated, and was now anxious lest his troops should fall back piecemeal upon the river, and its line be prematurely forced, as the British line of the Somme had been forced in March. He was therefore bringing up fresh troops, and, above all, artillery, with the support of which a complete change had appeared in the fighting quality of his infantry. The next fortnight was to be marked by a constant see-saw, by desperate, if minor, stroke and counter-stroke. Little more ground was to be won by the Allies till they had mastered the difficulties behind them, pushed forward adequate artillery and ammunition for a new "full-dress" attack to provide the initial momentum for a great new advance.

On October the 2nd, the day after its relief of the 108th Brigade, the 109th experienced the strength of the enemy's artillery and his determination. At 5 p.m. a heavy barrage of artillery of all calibres fell upon the front line, upon Dadizeele, and all approaches. Half an hour later the German infantry advanced to the attack. The force of the barrage had caused a withdrawal from some forward positions. These the enemy penetrated, but was quickly driven out with the bayonet. By night the line was completely restored.

It was during this attack that Captain G. J. Bruce, D.S.O., M.C., Brigade Major, 109th Brigade, making his way forward through the barrage to ascertain the position, was killed. Captain Bruce was one of the Division's original officers, and his total service with it now amounted to over four years, except for a few months in 1917, when he had been Brigade Major of the 47th Infantry Brigade, 16th Division. His quickness and cleverness, and his wonderful eye for country, which filled many a good professional soldier with envy, made him a very fine example of the "civilian" staff officer. His personal bravery was quite proverbial among all ranks of the Division. He was one of those rare and fortunate men who do not seem to require a mental effort, a summoning of resolution, to face great danger. He walked into it as naturally and as unconcernedly as he walked into his office. By all who knew him well George Bruce will long be remembered as a sagacious soldier and a fine spirit.

The next three days passed without further attempt at progress on the front of the 36th Division. All along the line, indeed, the advance was held up, and preparations were in train for an important new attack. For this it was necessary that the troops should have some preliminary rest. On the night of the 4th the 108th Brigade again relieved the 109th, while the 107th was relieved by troops of the 35th Division. On the 7th the 109th Brigade moved back across the devastation to a camp between Ypres and Poperinghe, where baths and clean clothes could be provided, and training for the new battle carried out. The 107th Brigade had not such good fortune, as it was retired as far only as Polygon Wood, and accommodated in canvas trench shelters.

Meanwhile artillery had moved up in force. By October the 7th there was in position covering the 36th Division's frontage its own Divisional Artillery, the 113th Army

Brigade, and three batteries of the 4th French Cavalry Division. Medium trench mortars, including the 6-inch Stokes, had also been brought forward in face of extraordinary difficulties. The enemy's artillery was very active, and the shelling in its intensity now recalled the days of the big battles of trench warfare.

On October the 11th, after an intense artillery preparation, in which the trench mortars took part, two platoons of the 9th Irish Fusiliers captured Goldflake Farm, with fourteen prisoners and three light machine-guns. This very strong "pill-box," on the southern slope of Hill 41, had defied all previous attempts. It did not on this occasion remain long in our hands. At evening, after a tremendous bombardment, the enemy launched an attack on the hill. Not only was Goldflake Farm retaken, but from Twigg and Mansard Farms, on the crest, our men were driven out. An immediate counter-attack caused Twigg Farm to change hands for the third time. Next morning before it was light a patrol got back Mansard Farm, with another prisoner and another machine-gun. That was the last of the local fighting. All things were now prepared for attack upon a very different scale.

The 35th Division, it has been recorded, had come into line on the right of the 36th. At the same time the 29th, its old right-hand neighbour, had been moved up to its left flank, from Klephoek northward, and now separated it from the 9th Division. The Second Army and the Belgians were now to attack with the objective of the Lys. This operation, if successful, would almost certainly cause the enemy to evacuate the great industrial cities of Lille, Roubaix, and Tourcoing.

The first general objective of the II. Corps was the Courtrai-Ingelmunster Railway. Upon this the 36th Division was directed, from the Lys on the right to the northern skirts of the town of Heule. It had also upon its front two other small towns, Moorseele and Gulleghem. The three were in a straight line from west to east; Moorseele being about two and a half miles from the present position,

## ATTACK OF OCTOBER 14TH

Gulleghem four and a half, and Heule six. The attack was to be carried out by the 107th Brigade on the right, and the 109th on the left. To the former was attached the 121st, and to the latter the 150th Field Company, while each had a company of the Machine-Gun Battalion. A section of each Field Company was in readiness to bridge the Heulebeek if necessary. The Divisional Reserve consisted of the 108th Brigade, the 36th Machine-Gun Battalion (less two companies), the 16th Rifles (Pioneers), the 122nd Field Company, two platoons of VIII. Corps Cyclists, and a company of the 104th Machine-Gun Battalion. Each Brigade was to attack with one battalion in line, one in support, and one in reserve. The Division's frontage was about a thousand yards, though on the objective of the Courtrai-Ingelmunster Railway it grew to fifteen hundred.

With the artillery now at the disposal of the Division, and the considerable heavy artillery at that of the II. Corps, the barrage was to be something like the barrage of old days. There was, in fact, one field gun or howitzer to a little more than twenty yards. There was to be no preliminary bombardment. The barrage was to come down two hundred yards in front of the forming-up line of the infantry three minutes before Zero, and to begin to creep forward at that hour. It was to move at a rate that would have seemed incredible a year ago, one hundred yards in two minutes, with a pause of fifteen minutes every fifteen hundred yards. East of Moorseele the field artillery barrage was to halt from Zero plus 115 minutes to Zero plus 132 minutes, then to cease. Upon this line the infantry was to remain an hour, to allow the support battalions to pass through the leaders, and batteries of field artillery to move up west of the town and aid the next advance.

At two o'clock on the morning of October the 14th the attacking troops were formed up east of the Vijfwegen-Zuidhoek Road, in trenches hastily dug by the Pioneers and 122nd Field Company. At the same hour the 108th Brigade began a quiet withdrawal, leaving its outposts on Hill 41 in position. The batteries of the field artillery were in

T

position close up to the front line. Even then their final barrage east of Moorseele would be at almost extreme range for the 18-pounders.

At 5-32, on a morning most fortunately fine, but foggy, the thunder of the barrage broke out all along the line. Three minutes later it began to move forward, followed by the infantry. The mist made the keeping of direction difficult, and the attackers eventually fell behind the barrage. It had served its purpose, however, in keeping down fire from the German front-line "pill-boxes," which had been the cause of so much trouble in the last fortnight. Behind it the infantrymen swept in with the bayonet, and the struggle that had so long endured was ended in a few fierce moments.

East of the Menin-Roulers Railway the enemy had ample opportunity to stop the advance, had he been the grim-fighting German of old. But this he certainly was not, though the 1st Bavarian Reserve Division, opposed to the 36th, was one of his best. By eight o'clock the 15th Rifles, the leading battalion of the 107th Brigade, were upon the outskirts of Moorseele. Their neighbours, the 1st Inniskillings, were slightly ahead, having reached the Rolleghem-Cappelle Road north of the village. Here they were held up by machine-gun fire from the town, till the latter was captured by the 15th Rifles. Then a line was swiftly consolidated east of Moorseele, while the support battalions, the 1st Rifles on the right and 2nd Inniskillings on the left, made ready to pass through, and the batteries were rushed forward into action close to the western outskirts of the town. This operation was splendidly accomplished. The first action of Major R. R. Sharp, D.S.O., M.C., commanding A/173, on reaching Moorseele, now being heavily bombarded, was to ascend the church steeple. From there he saw a German 77-mm. battery doing great damage. Fire opened by his battery, under his observation, killed the detachment and horses of this battery and blew up its ammunition, dumped beside the guns. The latter were captured in the subsequent advance.

All had gone excellently so far. Casualties had been light, and strong positions had been taken with surprising ease. Prisoners numbered over a hundred and fifty, while ten field guns and five horses had also been taken. As for light machine-guns, with which the whole German front had bristled, they were now tossed in heaps, too large to be counted for the time being. It was a fine achievement to have accomplished between half-past five and ten o'clock. But it was the beginning only of the day's work.

At 10-35 the advance was resumed, in weather still misty. Once more all went well. There had been no trouble with the Heulebeek, the bridges across which had not been destroyed by the enemy. For over a mile the two battalions went forward almost unchecked, driving in or capturing the machine-gun groups that disputed their passage. Then, a thousand yards west of Gulleghem, came resistance more severe. The machine-gun fire had greatly increased, and the town was defended by three lines of wire. Attempts were made to outflank the town from north and south. They were partially successful, some of the wire being negotiated, but not all. By midnight a line three hundred yards west of Gulleghem was being consolidated, and arrangements were in train for an attack at nine the following day with a fresh barrage. On the right the troops of the 36th Division were in touch with those of the 35th Division; on the left with those of the 29th, held up in front of the village of Salines. To the north the attack had been equally successful, and the whole line ran almost due north and south, the Belgians, who had fought magnificently, having their heads slightly in front. It had been a splendid day's work; for the Allies one of the great days of the war. With casualties comparatively light, they had driven back the enemy four miles upon a wide front, capturing ten thousand prisoners and over a hundred guns.

The barrage for the 15th, in view of the events of the preceding day, was slowed down slightly, to a hundred yards in three minutes. East of Gulleghem there was to be a halt of three-quarters of an hour, to allow the third battalion of each Brigade to pass through and advance upon Heule.

With the first onrush resistance was swept aside. Twenty minutes after Zero the 1st Rifles was across the Gulleghem-Wevelghem Road. A few minutes later the 2nd Inniskillings had the whole of Gulleghem in its area, save a few "pockets" of machine-guns which could be cleared at leisure. On the left the 87th Brigade took Salines about the same time. The 1st Rifles, destined to pass through its sister battalion on the front of the 107th Brigade, did not move up quite swiftly enough, and, as a consequence, lost the barrage. The 9th Inniskillings, on the left, with the advantage of a good main road in its area, pushed ahead north of the Heule-beek. By two o'clock its troops were through Heule, and upon the objective of the Courtrai-Ingelmunster Railway, east of the town. It had advanced a mile and a half in two and a half hours.

The 1st Rifles, meanwhile, without artillery support, had been brought to a halt by machine-gun fire from farms and hedges. A new barrage was arranged, to commence at 4 p.m. Under its cover the 1st Rifles quickly overran the enemy machine-guns. By 7 p.m. the battalion was on the railway embankment, in touch with the 9th Inniskillings. On the left the 29th Division had likewise reached the railway, while further north the 9th Division and the Belgians, who had made one of the greatest advances of a day in face of opposition, were miles east of it, in possession of Cuerne and Bavichove. The left flank of the 35th Division, on the other hand, was a thousand yards in rear of the right of the 107th Brigade.

The original intention had been to pass the troops of the 108th Brigade, the head of which was on Moorseele at the time the morning's attack was launched, through those of the other Brigades that afternoon, to advance upon the Lys at Courtrai. The slight delay above recorded caused a change in this arrangement. The 108th Brigade was now ordered to pass through at dawn on the 16th, and establish itself upon the Lys. During the night the 107th Brigade was ordered to send out a patrol to discover whether the Germans were going to make a stand west of the great canalized river.

By a curious coincidence there happened to be in the 2nd Rifles an officer, Lieutenant F. Adams, who was a native of the city of Courtrai. He was naturally chosen to make the reconnaissance, but his intimate knowledge of Courtrai may not have been altogether an advantage, for he made an investigation so thorough that he was not back till the following morning, when the barrage for the advance of the 108th Brigade had commenced. He had discovered that the Germans had evacuated all the quarter of the city north-west of the river, and blown up the five bridges which spanned the latter. When this news, and also the information that the troops of the 29th Division were on the Lys, north of the city, was received, the barrage was instantly stopped and the 12th Rifles, with no other protection than that of advanced and flank guards, marched down the road from Heule into Courtrai.

There were scenes of great enthusiasm among the citizens, who came forth into the streets from their cellars to greet the troops. But the Germans were not far off. As the first British troops appeared on the quays of the Lys, here eighty feet wide, heavy machine-gun fire burst out all along the opposite bank. Anything more difficult than to force a crossing, in the heart of a city full of friendly civilians, to whom and to whose property it was desired to do as little damage as might be, against German troops of the old mettle, could not well be imagined. But the Germans opposite were not of the old mettle, and General Vaughan decided to attempt to throw a bridge across in broad daylight. The 122nd Field Company with its pontoons had moved forward in readiness.

At 2 p.m. a smoke-screen was put down. Five minutes later, under its cover, the first boat-load was across. The men leapt ashore exultingly and drove the Germans from the bank. They had had scarce a casualty. Another boat-load followed, and in an incredibly short time the bridge was practicable for infantry. But the German artillery soon had its range. The men of the 122nd Field Company, who displayed the greatest gallantry, suffered heavy loss, and eventually the bridge was destroyed. The party on the other shore, however, held its ground without difficulty. The machine-gunners of "C" Company, attached to the Brigade, distinguished themselves particularly in this day's operations.

The obvious course now was to await darkness, throw another bridge across, clear the city of Germans, and be ready to advance eastward at peep of day. But news arrived meanwhile which altered these plans. The Allies were not going to batter Courtrai. They were going to force the Lys to northward, swing half-right, and drive down upon the Scheldt, or Escaut, as this portion of the river is called by French-speaking people, thus turning all the great industrial towns. As a fact, the evacuation of Lille, the westernmost, was proceeding at this very moment. The 36th Division was required for the new thrust, and was to be relieved at once by the 123rd Brigade of the 41st Division.

In these circumstances, as the bridgehead—without a bridge—was useless to the relieving Brigade, the bridgehead party was quietly and skilfully withdrawn at dusk and ferried across, together with six captured Germans. The relief was complete by eight o'clock, and the 108th Brigade marched back through new-won Heule and Gulleghem, to the village of Drei Masten, north of the latter town. The other Brigades had begun to move back earlier in the afternoon.

If the troops had been cheerful before, they were jubilant now. They knew themselves infinitely better men than the enemy, who, still supported by huge masses of artillery and by machine-gun fire which General Jacob later described as "the heaviest ever experienced in this war," never awaited their onslaught long. It was evident to all now that the war would be over by Christmas. A little longer and the German Army would be beaten to its knees.

The worst danger, the greatest obstacle to the launching of the death-thrust, was now, in fact, behind, not in front. It lay in those terrible roads of the devastated area far behind, with which the troops, now upon the untouched soil of the richest agricultural land in Europe, might feel they had no connection, but across which every mouthful of food they ate and every bullet they fired had to come. The strain upon the mechanism of the lorries was tremendous, and they were constantly breaking down. The strain upon their drivers was no less, and at this period they were less easy to replace than their wagons. The loss of horses, too, from bombing, in the Artillery and the Supply Services, had been very serious and could not be replaced at the moment. To add to the difficulties of communication, rations had to be brought up for the Belgian civilians, many of whom had been left stripped bare and in danger of starvation by the Germans, who took horses, carts, cattle, fowls, and all stores they could lay hand upon, in their retreat. In the hardest work they were ever called on to perform, the A.S.C., both mechanical and horsed services, scored a triumph. The success they achieved was due in part to good organization and industry. But it was due, above all, to the grit and determination of the junior officers and drivers in the performance of their tasks. The lorry-driver, who stuck for fifteen hours at his wheel amid the ruts and turmoil of the Menin Road, as many of them did, with bombs crashing down at night; the section of the Divisional Train bringing up its wagons through valleys wreathed and stinking with gas, these men in truth deserved well of the infantrymen facing the bullets further forward, and were in truth their companions-in-arms.

## CHAPTER XV

### THE ADVANCE TO FINAL VICTORY (II):
### OCTOBER 18TH TO NOVEMBER 11TH, 1918

IN the forcing of the Lys the 36th Division was to have the honour of the "left of the line," a real honour, because in an attack only a good Division was employed on the flank of an Allied Army. The reputation of the 9th Division, which had hitherto occupied that position, is too high to stand in need of glorification. But the 36th Division was not only to move on the flank of the British Army; it was to be its left flank-guard across the Lys, which was to be crossed by it first of any British Division, and considerably before its Allies on the left.

On the afternoon of the 18th of October General Coffin's headquarters were established in Lendelede, a town of upwards of four thousand inhabitants. Here the Germans had left behind perhaps the most valuable gift they could at this juncture have bestowed—excellent baths, where three hundred men could be bathed within an hour. Accommodation generally was now very good in a country so thickly populated, but there were still some unpleasant surprises. One such was the discovery by one unit, that in an excellent stable, recommended to it by a civilian, there was in each of ten stalls a dead horse, killed a week earlier by a single burst of Belgian shrapnel. That evening the relief of the 3rd Belgian Division, along the left bank

## PLAN FOR FORCING THE LYS

of the Lys, from Bavichove to the point of junction between the river and the Canal de Roulers à la Lys, was carried out by the 109th Brigade. Heavy bombing of the roads by enemy aeroplanes made it an affair of great difficulty. A French Division, the 164th, was coming in on the left of the 36th, but there was no prospect of its being ready to cross till the night of the 20th. As every moment was of importance, the 36th Division had orders to effect a passage more than twenty-four hours earlier.

General Coffin's scheme was in itself a scathing commentary upon the decadence of German moral. It was one which would not have been contemplated in the heroic age of the German infantry. In those days an isolated battalion, pushed across to form a bridgehead, would have been flung back into the river almost before it had had time to draw breath. But times had changed, and methods changed with them. Extreme boldness now paid as it had never paid in the previous course of the war. With adequate artillery support great risks could be taken, for the German machine-gunners frequently left their positions under heavy shell-fire. Moreover, there were no more "pill-boxes."

The Germans, it must be explained, appeared to be holding the opposite bank of the Lys in some strength. At several points they had put up wire fences to defend it. Opposite Oyghem, near the 36th Division's left flank, was one very large moated farm, round which they had dug a trench. The plan was that one battalion of the 109th Brigade should be ferried across at dusk on the 19th, should push forward to the main Courtrai-Ghent Road, from east of Beveren to Dries, on a front of a thousand yards. That accomplished, a second battalion was to cross, to form flank from the Oyghem-Desselghem Road to the left of the leading battalion. Two machine-gun companies were allotted to the operation, "B" to fire a barrage, "C" with its sections attached to the battalions of the 109th Brigade. The original intention had been for the 121st and 150th Field Companies to effect crossings for the infantry opposite both Oyghem and Beveren. A daring daylight reconnaissance of the river-bank by Lieutenant W. Brunyate, of the latter company, caused the Oyghem crossing to be abandoned, and the construction of a bridge at that point postponed till the first part of the programme was complete. The bank here was very steep, was heavily wired, and commanded by machine-guns. The farm of which mention has been made would have been in itself a formidable obstacle. Three bridging wagons with full bridging equipment had been brought up the previous night and hidden in farm buildings beside the river bank, north-west of Beveren, by the 121st Field Company. The pontoons of the 150th Field Company were hidden slightly further north.

At dusk two pontoons were launched, and at 7-25 p.m. the passage of the 9th Inniskillings began. Two trips were actually made before the enemy fired a shot; then machine-gun fire burst out, followed a little later by that of artillery. Nevertheless, by 8 p.m. the whole battalion and its attached section of machine-guns* were across, with one casualty only. Hastily in the darkness the battalion formed up. Then the British barrage dropped, and it began its advance over open country. The night was cloud-veiled, but the full moon was of great assistance to subsequent operations. Capturing such machine-gun detachments as did not fly, the 9th Inniskillings worked its way steadily forward, and crossed the Beveren-Dries Road, four hundred yards short of its objective, the main road from Courtrai to Ghent. Almost immediately afterwards, however, it was held up by heavy machine-gun fire. It had not accomplished quite all that had been hoped, but it had done enough. The still more complicated task of bringing across a second battalion to guard the left flank remained.

Directly the 9th was over, the 121st Field Company set about throwing across a "half-pontoon" bridge. It was found, however, that the river was here actually over a hundred feet wide, considerably more than was anticipated from

* *i.e.*, three guns. By this time none of the Machine-Gun Companies had men enough to man more than twelve guns.

the information in our possession, and that two pontoons in halves would not reach across. Since pontoons were infinitely precious—some having been sunk at Courtrai—as many as possible being required for a subsequent heavy bridge, an attempt was made to assemble a trestle-bridge instead. But under the very heavy shell-fire now falling upon the river this had to be abandoned for want of time, and eventually a pontoon was borrowed from the 150th Field Company to complete the bridge. It was ready at ten o'clock, just as the leading platoon of the 1st Inniskillings appeared on the bank. The battalion had four hours for its crossing and assembly on the further bank.

On the left flank of the attack were four villages, Desselghem, Spriete, Straete, and Dries. Of these the first was considerable, the others tiny hamlets which were really part of it.* Desselghem and Spriete were to be attacked by the two leading companies; Straete and Dries by the supporting companies, which were to pass through them. The operation of bringing the battalion across, forming it up and attacking north-eastward, at right angles to the line of attack of the 9th Inniskillings, of supporting the new attack by barrage fire, would have been considered of the greatest difficulty in the mimic warfare of manœuvres, and would almost certainly have been characterized as impossible by the umpires. In this case the whole programme, owing to good staff work, intelligent local leadership, and the dash of the private soldier, was carried through without a hitch. Spriete and Desselghem were cleared; then the supporting companies went through. Their task was a sterner one, since the Germans had had time to make some preparation for resistance. Straete was captured after fierce close fighting, the Inniskillings frequently using the bayonet. On the right the other company reached the outskirts of Dries, but was unable to make further headway, and there consolidated its position. Here again, though not quite all was

* This country is, in reality, one vast garden city. Groups of a dozen houses have their names. It has not been found possible to show them all on the small-scale map illustrating this chapter.

won, elbow-room sufficient had been gained. Eighty prisoners had been taken, and passed back over the pontoon bridge.

It was now the turn of the 107th Brigade. The sappers passed a busy and disturbed night. The shelling of the

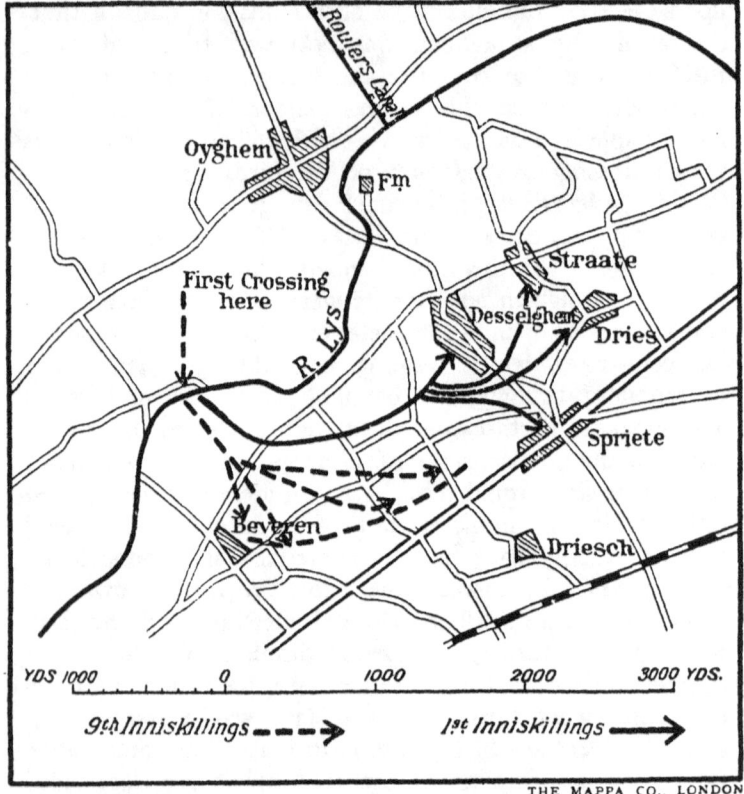

Lys continued, and there was a direct hit on the bridge, a pontoon being damaged and a length of the superstructure destroyed. By desperately hard work all repairs were completed for the leading battalion of the 107th Brigade, the 15th Rifles, to cross at 2 a.m. This battalion, followed by the 1st, moved forward, the former forming up west of the

Courtrai-Ghent Road, in relief of the 9th Inniskillings, which withdrew through its ranks. Troops of the 9th Division had crossed about midnight, but, as may easily be imagined, it was not without considerable difficulty that touch was obtained with them. This, however, was at last accomplished, but the line at the point of junction was perilously close to the river, owing to the fact that German machine-gunners still held out in Beveren.

At 6 a.m. on the 20th the new attack began. Beveren was quickly taken, with some aid from the Scots Fusiliers of the 9th Division. Machine-gun fire was very heavy, and the 15th Rifles had considerable casualties. The commanding officer, Lieut.-Colonel B. Y. Jones, D.S.O., was killed. But the advance continued at a great pace. The main Courtrai-Ghent-Antwerp Railway was crossed before eight o'clock. An hour later the line was astride the road from Deerlyck—already in the hands of the 9th Division—to Waereghem. A mill on that road gave considerable trouble, but was eventually taken by a platoon of the 1st Rifles. Further progress for the time being was found impossible. The advance had reached a point two and a half miles from the Lys, and could no longer be supported by artillery fire. At 12-30 p.m. the 1st Inniskillings made another attempt to clear Dries, and reached the centre of the hamlet. Resistance was now quite determined, and it was decided to await the crossing of the French before attempting any move on the left flank. About two hundred prisoners had been captured in the day's operations.

The Engineers had continued their good work. By evening a pontoon bridge for first-line transport had been thrown across by the 150th Field Company. The 121st had completed a good permanent foot-bridge, and, returning to the abandoned trestle, for which all materials had been collected locally, had finished that also. At night the 108th Brigade and a French regiment on the left made the crossing. Artillery, however, could not cross yet awhile. The 108th Brigade was to relieve the 109th, and the advance was to be continued for another twenty-four hours without it.

The advance of the 21st was timed for 7-30 a.m. It was to be carried out by the 1st Rifles of the 107th Brigade, and the 1st Irish Fusiliers of the 108th. It was, however, important to be rid of the hornet's nest in Dries upon the flank, and this village was cleared by a company of the 12th Rifles before the attack began. Without artillery this attack was of the greatest difficulty. There were no hedges, and it was the custom in this part of the country to lop the lower branches off the trees. Consequently, the attacking force was constantly exposed to long-range machine-gun fire. Moreover, the 133rd French Regiment, since it had to fight its way from the river bank, was always in rear. In all the circumstances the advance of the day, which found the right of the 107th Brigade at Knock, north of Vichte, and the left of the 108th at Spitael, on the Ghent Railway, was highly creditable to the troops concerned. The advance of the 107th Brigade, with the 9th Division on its right, was to be resumed on the morrow, but it was decided that the 108th Brigade should not move till the French had come up into line.

By the morning of the 22nd the Lys was crossed by bridge after bridge in the area of the 36th Division; there being, besides numerous foot-bridges, three medium bridges for first-line transport, and a trestle which was subsequently used by French motor-lorries. On the night of the 21st the four batteries of the 153rd Brigade R.F.A. crossed the river, to fire a barrage in support of the 107th Brigade next day. On the right, upwards of half the distance between the parallel rivers, the Lys and the Escaut, had now been covered. From the Gaverbeek onwards the advance was now faced by rising ground, which culminated in a general ridge before the drop down, over some two miles, to the valley of the latter river. The various little crests of this chain afforded excellent positions to the enemy, and it was evident that, if so disposed, he could make a very effective stand before falling back across the Escaut. The first of them had to be attacked on this morning. It was taken by the 2nd Rifles. The barrage, small though it would have been reckoned in old days, and as it was in comparison with the German barrage which had to be faced, nevertheless made a wonderful difference to the attack. The little rise, about a mile north-east of Vichte and topped by a windmill, was carried. But there followed the most resolute counter-attack experienced for a long time by the 36th Division. It was made by a Prussian Assault Battalion, and succeeded in driving our men off the crest and back for almost eight hundred yards. Colonel Becher, commanding the 2nd Rifles, organized a new attack by two companies, which, going forward with the greatest gallantry, once more drove the Germans off the crest and re-established the position. The left flank swung sharply back, the junction with the 108th Brigade being on the Deerlyck-Waereghem Road. On the left of the 108th Brigade the French, after heavy fighting, were established in Spitael.

On the 23rd, as the enemy appeared to be withdrawing, the advance was continued all along the line behind a screen of scouts. A squadron of French dragoons, attached to the Division, made a spirited dash for the Escaut crossing at Berchen, but came under heavy machine-gun fire from the second line of hills, which it was evident the enemy held in force. He had, in fact, withdrawn a mile or so during the previous night. On the extreme left a company of the 1st Irish Fusiliers, entering Heirweg, was vigorously counter-attacked and driven out with the loss of several prisoners. Eventually a liaison post was established by British and French at the station, just west of the hamlet. On the right the 1st Rifles had captured Vossenhoek and Hutteghem. The advance had been well maintained. The men of the 107th Brigade were now, however, weary, and the battalions very weak. It was decided to relieve the Brigade that night by the 109th. This was carried out without event.

The following day was given to reorganization. Two batteries of the 173rd Brigade had crossed the river on the 22nd, the remainder were now brought over in readiness to support an attack upon the ridge. This took place at 9 a.m. on the 25th. The 109th Brigade on the right had two battalions, the 1st and 2nd Inniskillings, in line; the 108th one only, the 12th Rifles. The advance was covered by a barrage moving at the rate of a hundred yards in three minutes. On the right not much progress was made, in face of heavy machine-gun fire. Loss of direction, due to fog and the smoke-screen of the enemy barrage, caused considerable difficulty. Eventually a line east of Hutsbosch was consolidated. On the left the 12th Rifles made an advance of half a mile, in face of the most determined opposition encountered since the fighting at Hill 41. Every house was held, and the Germans fought their machine-guns desperately. No less than ten were counted in ten separate houses at the day's end. The advance would have been greater had the French supported it on the left, but their line had not moved beyond Heirweg. The work of the 12th Rifles on this day was probably the best performed by that battalion, amid much good work accomplished since the beginning of offensive operations. Repeatedly the men had charged in upon houses defended by machine-guns, and bayoneted the detachments.

The 9th Division had captured the twin crests of Ingoyghem and Ooteghem, and it was determined that the 109th Brigade should, the same afternoon, assault that of Kleineberg, to their north-east, which would have brought the right of the Division, its left drawn back through circumstances beyond its control, into the van of the advance. A new barrage, starting at 5 p.m., was hastily planned and admirably carried out. Unfortunately, however, orders did not reach the battalions soon enough, and, at the appointed hour, three companies only, two of the 1st Inniskillings and one of the 2nd, went forward to the attack. And it must be remembered that companies were now never more than fifty strong. The crest was actually reached, but the advance had been on a frontage so narrow that it was impossible to maintain the position. A farm-house at the foot of the slope was, however, held and consolidated.

The 26th was a day of calm, broken when night fell by tremendous shelling, above all with gas, which seemed almost to have superseded high explosive and shrapnel in the enemy's armoury. Nor was a further advance contemplated on the 27th, owing to the complete exhaustion of the troops. A wounded prisoner had, however, reported that it was the enemy's intention to withdraw at once to the Escaut, and our outposts were on the *qui vive* for signs of such a movement. About 2 p.m. that afternoon they were rewarded. Small bodies of the enemy were seen retiring from the Kleineberg Ridge. Instantly patrols of the 109th Brigade were pushed forward and occupied it. And so this last goal of the 36th Division, after three years' campaigning, was reached without a shot fired. The 108th Brigade, in attempting to follow suit, met with a certain resistance, but the 9th Irish Fusiliers had the railway "halt" west of Anseghem before dusk. Attempts were made to push onward to the river, but it was found that the Germans still held Bergstraat with machine-guns, and no further progress could be made. It was quite evident that they were not going to fall back on the Escaut till forced to do so. Their policy, directed with great skill—for never did the work of their divisional and regimental commanders shine more brightly than in these days—was to give up what could not be held, and no more, thus husbanding till the last the declining moral of their infantrymen, and delaying the advance as long as might be. A resistance more rigid, with the German soldier in his present temper, would inevitably have led to a break through, somewhere or other, and a consequent rout.

The bolt of the 36th Division was now shot. Weary flesh was at last proclaiming itself master over spirit unwearied. The only thing that had kept the men so long on their legs in this winter warfare was the excellence of the accommodation behind the line. Such a campaign in devastated country would have been unthinkable. Even as it was, they had been subjected to great hardship and exposure, while the constant gas shelling had had some effect on many hundreds who had not left the ranks. The casualties since the beginning of offensive operations numbered over three thousand. Of these, six-sevenths were wounded, and a very large proportion, most fortunately, suffering from light wounds from machine-gun bullets, or a temporarily disabling whiff of gas. But not more than a tenth of these casualties, or of a certain sick wastage, had been replaced by reinforcements. As a consequence battalions in action had seldom more than two hundred or two hundred and fifty bayonets. Other arms had suffered in less, but still in high proportion, while the loss of transport animals was becoming serious. All preparations were made for a renewal of the attack, but on the afternoon of the 27th cane a wire from the X. Corps to the effect that the Division would be relieved by the 34th, and would come under its orders the following day, being withdrawn for rest and reorganization. Soon after dusk on the 27th the 101st Brigade of the 34th Division relieved the two weak Brigades of the 36th in the line, which began their march back to the area about Courtrai. Though little they knew it, their part in the war was finished.

The Artillery and Medium Trench Mortar Batteries had further work to perform, when the 34th Division, having pushed up to the banks of the Escaut, forced its crossing in the first week of November. The 107th, 108th, and 109th Light Trench Mortar Batteries were also lent to the 34th Division on that occasion. The distinction of having fired the last shot of any unit of the 36th Division is claimed by both artillerymen and Stokes gunners of the 108th Light Trench Mortar Battery, in action after the other two had expended all their ammunition. Let both divide the crown. No other unit would begrudge it to either.

In the late operations the 36th Division had inscribed, on these its final pages, one of the brightest chapters of its career. It had been a period marked by a brilliant co-operation of every arm, combatant and non-combatant. Amid many great achievements, perhaps the most satisfactory of all had been that of the Engineers. For once their work, always so hard, but generally so obscure and thankless, had stood out in the foreground. Upon it had hinged the whole attack across the Lys. They had carried out, with supreme skill, devotion, and success, what is perhaps the sapper's first task in warfare, of which he is popularly supposed to dream, that of putting the infantry across a great river, to be launched to victory from the further bank. General Jacob's message, a few days before the Division was finally withdrawn, is the best testimonial to what the troops and their leaders had accomplished. It ran as follows :

" Major-General C. COFFIN, V.C., D.S.O.,
     Commanding 36th Division.

" The 36th (Ulster) Division has been fighting continuously since the 28th September in the operations in Flanders. The spirit, dash, and initiative shown by all ranks have been splendid, and beyond all praise. The leadership displayed by yourself and your Brigade and other Commanders could not have been bettered. The conditions under which the men have had to fight have been, and are still, very trying, but nothing seems to stop your gallant Division.

" I have also been much struck with the good staff work of the Division, and it is very creditable to all concerned.

" Will you kindly express to the Commanders, Staffs, and all ranks of the Division my heartiest congratulations and thanks for their work.

" When the history is written of what the Division has done in Flanders during the past month, it will prove to be a record of magnificent fighting and wonderful progress; for, during this period, an advance has been made of about twenty-five miles over the worst of country, and under the heaviest machine-gun fire ever experienced in this war. This advance has entailed constant fighting, but the 36th Division has overcome every obstacle, and has proved itself one of the best fighting Divisions in the Army, well commanded and well staffed.

" My best wishes to you all.
         " C. N. JACOB, Lieutenant-General,
              Commanding II. Corps."

On November the 2nd, Divisional Headquarters and the 107th Brigade moved to Mouscron, practically a suburb of Tourcoing, but on the other side of the frontier, in Belgium. Training and reorganization were carried out. Ranks filled up, and the troops, in splendid billets, speedily threw off their fatigue. Another turn in the line was still expected. But that was not required. If the 36th Division was not actually "in at the death," it had afterwards the satisfaction of knowing that the war was really won when it left the firing-line. The very day after, October the 28th, the German *communiqué* was signed by the "Chief of the General Staff of the Field Army"—Hindenburg—instead of the "First Quarter-Master General"—Ludendorff. The meaning of that was instantly grasped. Ludendorff, the great gambler, whose final throws had brought him so near success, had resigned. A day later, and it was announced that Austria had thrown up the sponge. On the 7th of November the German *parlementaires* passed through the French lines at Guise, on their way to interview Marshal Foch. Then came the news of the Armistice.

It was celebrated by the troops in France without that wild hilarity, wild almost to hysteria, that greeted it in London. Perhaps the man who had been trudging forward, week by week, facing the machine-guns, if in front, sniffing for gas, and, by night, listening anxiously for the purr of the Gotha, if in rear, hardly realized that it was all over. The men were, none the less, intensely happy. Everywhere they were *fêted* and acclaimed by the civilians whom they had freed from four long years of bondage. Best of all, after years of discomfort and exposure, they slept softly, undisturbed by the crash of bombs.

And so, as Lord Fisher afterwards put it, "at the eleventh hour of the eleventh day of the eleventh month," the war came to its end.

This History contains few of those Special Orders of the Day which, long after the events that gave them birth, are inclined to appear heavy, and sometimes fail to accord with present sentiment. That of General Jacob has been

## SPECIAL ORDER OF MARSHAL FOCH

quoted because it was under his fine leadership that the men of the 36th Division marched to final victory. It would not be fitting to conclude this chapter without recalling that issued at the end of hostilities to all the Allied Armies by the Marshal in supreme command, who inherits from his teacher, the greatest soldier his country and the modern world ever produced, the gift of making a few words majestic and ever-memorable. Amidst our present discontents some of the glory of these words of Marshal Foch may appear tarnished, but, like the words of Napoleon to his troops in Egypt, they will endure, when immediate sorrows and disappointments are forgotten, perhaps when the very causes for which men laid down their lives by millions have become obscure.

" Officiers, sous-officiers, soldats des Armées Alliées.

" Après avoir résolument arrêté l'ennemi, vous l'avez, pendant des mois, avec une foi et une énergie inlassables, attaqué sans répit.

" Vous avez gagné la plus grande bataille de l'Histoire et sauvé la cause la plus sacrée : la Liberté du Monde.

" Soyez fiers !

" D'une gloire immortelle vous avez paré vos drapeaux.

" La Postérité vous garde sa reconnaissance.

"Le Maréchal de France,
Commandant en Chef les Armées Alliées,
F. FOCH."

## CHAPTER XVI

### THE END: NOVEMBER 1918 TO JUNE 1919

BUT little remains to be told. The war was over, and men were eager to be home. There was a certain disappointment that the Division was not to form part of the British garrison on the Rhine. As a fact, one Division only of the New Armies was chosen for this duty. It was the 9th, with which, since April, in days of reverse and days of victory, the 36th had been in comradeship as close as any two Divisions can have known in the course of the war. None begrudged to it this seal upon its splendid record. And, apart from a momentary regret at missing the sight of that apotheosis of victory so long awaited, officers and men speedily recognised that their lot, during the remaining days of their incorporation, was fallen in fairer ground. The end of the 36th Division's existence, amid a friendly and a grateful populace, was far happier than it would have been amid the restrictions and comically correct civilities of Cologne and the Bridgehead.

Soon after the Armistice the 36th Division settled down for the winter astride the Franco-Belgian frontier. Headquarters, the 107th and 108th Infantry Brigades, the 121st and 122nd Field Companies R.E., and the 16th Rifles (Pioneers) were one side, at Mouscron. The Artillery, in Tourcoing, the 109th Brigade and 150th Field Company, at Roncq, were the other. The Pioneers had the hardest work, being employed on railway reconstruction and upon the Escaut bridges. Some military training, mainly ceremonial, was carried out. But chief energies were devoted to recreation and to the education scheme, which attempted to provide for the young soldiers some preparation for the civil life to which they would shortly be returning. The idea was a worthy one, and was organized with skill and enthusiasm, yet it is to be doubted whether a large proportion had much benefit of it. By the time it was really in full swing, demobilization was at the same stage. The majority of the men attended but a few classes before they returned, and can have acquired but a smattering of the subjects they were pursuing. December was the most successful month, when there were recorded 54,203 attendances at the various classes. On the lighter side there were competitions in Rugby and Association football, cross-country running, boxing, and rifle-shooting. Christmas, the fifth since the Division's formation, its fourth since crossing the Channel, was happily celebrated. The Divisional Canteen had on this occasion its greatest triumph. The position was difficult. Behind lay the area of the Ypres battlefields; around, the country had been practically denuded of foodstuffs by the Germans. The Canteen Officer had, in the first place, made arrangements with a farmer near Dunkirk to attend markets in that region, buy up poultry, and feed them on her farm till it was time to kill them for Christmas. Had a British officer done the buying, the prices would have been prohibitive. It was soon found that the good *fermière's* estate would not hold all the birds required, and a further order was placed with the *Halles* in Paris, through a Dunkirk merchant. Pigs were also bought, to be killed on the appointed day. But difficulties grew with demands. Lorries broke down in the swamps about Ypres. The Canteen Officer began to wonder whether his head upon a charger would not be the chief dish of the occasion. On Christmas Eve the Paris consignment arrived at Dunkirk, but it was in the middle of a line of trucks which could not be disentangled, and would not have been for days. Finally, after some shunting, a lorry was got alongside. When the lorry arrived at Mouscron it was found to contain also a large case of eggs, a luxury unknown for months, a special order for some unit in Dunkirk. Naturally it was then impossible to send it back. Every man in the Division had plentiful fare, while, adds the Canteen Officer modestly, "no other division in the district got anything better than bully beef." The present writer can bear witness that the turkeys ordered for divisions on the Rhine arrived in many cases long after Christmas, and frequently had to be buried forthwith by special parties.

In the combatant ranks, alas! there were few who had spent the first Christmas with the Division.

The following day there was the great ball given by the ladies of Ghent to the British Army, which was attended by fifty officers of the 36th Division. At the end of January, H.R.H. the Prince of Wales, on his return from Germany, paid the Division a visit of two days. This visit was informal and marked by no parades, but the Prince, despite very bad weather, visited a number of units, and had long conversations with officers and men on their experiences.

January was also the month when the flood of demobilization rose to its height. In its course over four thousand officers and men were sent home. In the following month came orders for one battalion to be sent to Germany for service. The 12th Royal Irish Rifles was chosen, and made up to strength from volunteers of the 1st, 2nd, and 15th battalions of that regiment. On March the 2nd it entrained at Mouscron, where the whole Division, less the Artillery, was now concentrated, and proceeded to join the 2nd (now the Light) Division on the Rhine. Soon afterwards the *cadres* of the regular battalions began to move home. On March the 12th the Field Marshal Commanding-in-Chief paid a farewell visit to the Division. When he laid down those duties that he had so splendidly and courageously performed, it was indeed clear that the era of the Great War was at an end. A few days later General Coffin, under whose vigorous leadership the 36th Division had achieved its final triumphs, left it to command a Brigade in the British Army of the Rhine. Divisional Headquarters were reduced to *cadre*, the new commander being Brigadier-General P. Leveson-Gower.

The last words were not written till June. Then the *cadres* of the remaining service battalions proceeded to the Base, and Headquarters formally closed. In January the 36th Division had practically ceased to exist. Now, six months later, its name departed from official registers.

Its History would not be complete without some reference to the Ulster Divisional Fund. This Fund owed its inception to General Nugent's forethought. The 36th Division was certainly the only one to look forward to the period after the war as early as 1915. Before quitting the Division in 1918, General Nugent executed a Trust Deed in favour of Lord Dunleath and Sir Robert Kennedy, establishing a Trust for the benefit of officers and men of the Division, their wives, widows, children, orphans, or dependants. Roughly speaking, a sum of £18,750 has been administered by the Administration Committee, to whom the Trustees delegated the management of the Fund. Of this over £14,000 was derived from divisional undertakings, including the canteens, the concert party, the cinema, etc., and over £2,000 from dividends and interest. It must be remembered that the sums derived from divisional undertakings represent a proportion only of their actual profits. Large sums were expended in France, on sports outfits, on Christmas fare, on free buffets at horse shows and other entertainments, and on the still more important buffets for "walking wounded" during the progress of a battle. The Fund was opened to applications for relief in February 1919. It has now been practically all distributed in grants to relieve and assist men of the Division, and has been without doubt of very great value. The total number of grants made exceeds two thousand five hundred.

The record of the 36th Division is high and honourable. The names of the actions in which it fought, given

298   HISTORY OF 36TH (ULSTER) DIVISION

according to the official report of the "Battles Nomenclature Committee," are as follows:

- 1916  The Battle of Albert, July.
- 1917  The Battle of Messines, June;
    The Battle of Langemarck, August;
    The Battle of Cambrai, November.
- 1918  The Battle of St. Quentin, with Actions for Somme Crossings, 21st–25th March;
    The Battle of Rosières, 26th–27th March;
    The Battle of Messines, 10th–11th April (108th Brigade and one Company 36th Machine-Gun Battalion only);
    The Battle of Bailleul, 13th–15th April (108th Brigade and one Company 36th Machine-Gun Battalion only);
    The Advance in Flanders, 18th August–6th September;
    The Battle of Ypres, 28th September – 2nd October;
    The Battle of Courtrai, 14th–19th October, with Action of Ooteghem, 25th October.

These names are given because, unfamiliar as they may sound to many of the men who fought in the actions, they are their official titles. It will be seen that from the first time the Division fought a big battle there is one considerable gap only, between the Battle of Albert, 1916, and the Battle of Messines, 1917. That gap is partly to be explained, no doubt, by the fact that the Division, after its great losses on the Somme, was never really up to strength till the spring of 1917. The cause of that, again, is not far to seek. The stream of recruits from the voluntary system was drying up by 1916 all over the country, and from the Military Service Act of that year Ireland was excepted. The people of Ulster had certainly no cause for

## CHARACTERISTICS OF 36TH DIVISION 299

shame with regard to its response during the voluntary period. Belfast claims to stand second on the roll of British cities for numbers of recruits in proportion to population, up to the imposition of universal service. But, after Messines, a large number of English reinforcements arrived, while, in late 1917 and 1918, as has been recorded, five regular battalions of Ulster regiments joined the Division. Of the offensive battles, it was engaged in two defeats, but in one of these it was completely victorious upon its own front, being compelled to withdraw because of failure elsewhere. The 36th Division, then, failed once only in attack, in the Battle of Langemarck. And, on that day, in the circumstances wherein the troops found themselves, it may be doubted whether success was within mortal compass. In defensive fighting it proved itself equally devoted, possessed above all of a hidden spring of fortitude which enabled it, as we say of a gallant horse, to "come again" when apparently at its last breath from exhaustion.

In bright days and dark there can be no doubt but that much of its success sprang from the mutual confidence and affection which existed between all arms. If we can employ a word so inhuman as machine to describe a corporation of men that was intensely alive, that had a soul of its own, we may say that it was a machine that worked smoothly because it was weak in none of its parts. And we must not forget, as men are prone to forget, that, if some parts bore a weight heavier than others, each was of equal importance in the working of the machine. This record has been mainly concerned with the fighting arms and, of these, to by far the greatest extent with the infantry. For that no apology is made. It is as just as it is inevitable. It is not only upon the infantry that all hinges; it is mainly by a record of the infantry's movements that the story of battles is told. Not alone the other fighting arms, Artillery, Engineers, Signals, Pioneers, Machine-Gunners, but Medical and Supply Services also were animated by the same high spirit of devotion. Of the two last comparatively little has been said, and perhaps least of all of the Supply

Services. That is a compliment rather than the reverse. Happy, says Montesquieu, is the people whose annals are humdrum. The saying may be applied to Supply Services in war. The Royal Army Service Corps of the 36th Division has few remarkable dates or occurrences in its record, but that record is one long chain of which the alternating links are steady work, forethought, and resource. The other service of supply, the Ordnance, was always at a peculiarly high standard, the Division being most fortunate in possessing a very efficient D.A.D.O.S. in Captain Mackenzie, over a long period. Staff Officers might come and might go, but "Dados" went on for ever.

There may be required some explanation of why, in this narrative, the series of victories in 1918 is compressed in detail by comparison with such actions as Messines and Cambrai. One reason is that the records of the latter are far more complete. Another is that final victory was won not only by the men who went forward so gallantly to achieve it, but by all their silent comrades whose graves lay behind them, who had fought a far more bitter battle.

These took the blows of the enemy upon their breasts, but, ere they fell, the blows delivered by their arms had enfeebled him, so that those who came after could strike home. Like Mr. Valiant-for-truth, they might have proclaimed with their last breath: "My sword I give to him that shall succeed me in my pilgrimage, and my courage and skill to him that can get it. My marks and scars I carry with me." For them, as for him, we may humbly believe that, when they passed over, all the trumpets sounded on the other side.

The 36th (Ulster) Division is but a memory to-day. This book, of the imperfections of which as he writes its concluding lines the author is but too acutely aware, represents in some sort an official tribute, an attempt to put into words the silent tribute borne by many thousands of hearts. That tribute is paid not alone to victors in the flesh, but to those other victors who had put it off before they themselves knew what part they had in victory. When we commemorate that great corporation of men which was the 36th (Ulster) Division, our minds should embrace the whole company of dead and living, for they are of one brotherhood.

The worth of that brotherhood it is hoped these chapters have not wholly failed to commemorate. But the power of better pens than that of this writer were inadequate to express, to those who have not looked upon a battle of modern war, to the younger generation, which we pray may not see one, what strength there must be in the fibres of the will if they are not to snap beneath its strain. Leadership, training, discipline, the pride which springs from the individual's association with and amalgamation in a great combatant formation, have their part in the toughening of those human cords. Of themselves they do not suffice. To engender that which was brought forth in the exploits of the Ulster Division, they must mate with a racial spirit possessing already in amplitude the seeds of endurance and of valour.

THE END

# APPENDICES

# APPENDIX I

# ORDER OF BATTLE OF THE 36TH (ULSTER) DIVISION*

GENERAL OFFICER COMMANDING.

    Major-General C. H. Powell, C.B. Till Sept. 1915.
    Major-General O. S. Nugent, C.B., D.S.O. Till 6th May, 1918.
    Major-General C. Coffin, V.C., C.B., D.S.O.

ROYAL ARTILLERY.

  C.R.A.

    (Brigadier-General R. J. Elkington, commanding 1st/1st London Divisional Artillery, attached. Till 12th December, 1915.)
    Brigadier-General H. J. Brock, C.B., C.M.G., D.S.O. Till 23rd September, 1918.
    Brigadier-General C. St. L. Hawkes, D.S.O.

  BRIGADES.

    (1/1st, 1/2nd, 1/3rd, 1/4th London Brigades, attached. Till 12th December, 1915.)

*Changes in command or formation subsequent to the Armistice are not noticed.

BRIGADES *(contd.)*

### 153rd Brigade R.F.A.

A, B, C, D Batteries (18-pounder).

Reorganized 22nd May, 1916, into three 4-gun 18-pounder and one 4-gun 4.5 howitzer batteries. (D to 154th Brigade. C/154 joined, becoming D/153.)

Reorganized 14th September, 1916, into three 6-gun 18-pounder and one 4-gun 4.5 howitzer batteries. (A broken up, one section to B, one section to C. A/154 and one section C/154 joined, becoming A/153.)

D made up to 6-gun battery 13th January, 1917. (One section from D/172.)

### 154th Brigade R.F.A.

A, B, C, D Batteries (howitzer).

A transferred to 46th Division 28th February, 1916.

Reorganized 22nd May, 1916, into three 4-gun 18-pounder batteries. (B to 173rd Brigade. D/173 joined, becoming B/154. C to 153rd Brigade. D/153 joined, becoming C/154. D to 172nd Brigade. D/172 joined, becoming A/154.)

Broken up 14th September, 1916. (A and one section of C to 153rd Brigade. B and one section of C to 173rd Brigade.)

### 172nd Brigade R.F.A.

A, B, C, D Batteries (18-pounder).

Reorganized 22nd May, 1916, into three 4-gun 18-pounder and one 4-gun 4.5 howitzer batteries. (D to 154th Brigade. D/154 joined, becoming D/172.)

Reorganized 14th September, 1916, into two 6-gun 18-pounder and one 4-gun 4.5 howitzer batteries. (C broken up and divided between A and B.)

D/529 howitzer from England joined 7th October, 1916, becoming C/172.

One section of D to 153rd Brigade and one to 173rd Brigade, 13th January, 1917.

Brigade became 113th Army Brigade R.F.A., 22nd February, 1917. (A to 77th Brigade.)

## ORDER OF BATTLE

BRIGADES (contd.)

173rd Brigade R.F.A.

A, B, C, D Batteries (18-pounder).
Reorganized 22nd May, 1916, into three 4-gun 18-pounder and one 4-gun 4.5 howitzer batteries. (D to 154th Brigade. B/154 joined, becoming D/173.)
Reorganized 14th September, 1916, into three 6-gun 18-pounder and one 4-gun 4.5 howitzer. (B broken up and divided between A and C. B/154 and one section C/154 joined, becoming B/173.) D made up to 6-gun battery 13th January, 1917. (One section from D/172.)

Divisional Ammunition Column. (Until May 1916 there had been four Brigade Ammunition Columns.)

### ROYAL ENGINEERS.

121st Field Company, R.E.
122nd Field Company, R.E.
150th Field Company, R.E.

### INFANTRY BRIGADES.

107TH INFANTRY BRIGADE.

COMMANDERS.

Brigadier-General Couchman, C.B. Till 20th October, 1915.
Brigadier-General W. M. Withycombe, C.M.G., D.S.O. Till 7th March, 1917.
Brigadier-General F. J. M. Rowley, D.S.O. Till 2nd June, 1917.
Brigadier-General W. M. Withycombe, C.M.G., D.S.O. Till 30th April, 1918.
Brigadier-General E. I. de S. Thorpe, C.M.G., D.S.O. Till 13th September, 1918.
Brigadier-General H. J. Brock, C.B., C.M.G., D.S.O.

BATTALIONS.

8th Battalion Royal Irish Rifles.

Amalgamated with 9th Battalion Royal Irish Rifles, 29th August, 1917, as 8th/9th Battalion Royal Irish Rifles.

9th Battalion Royal Irish Rifles.

Amalgamated with 8th Battalion Royal Irish Rifles, 29th August, 1917, as 8th/9th Battalion Royal Irish Rifles.

8th/9th Battalion Royal Irish Rifles.
Disbanded 7th February, 1918.

10th Battalion Royal Irish Rifles.
Disbanded 20th February, 1918.

15th Battalion Royal Irish Rifles.

1st Battalion Royal Irish Fusiliers.
Joined from 4th Division 2nd August, 1917.
To 108th Brigade 8th February, 1918.

1st Battalion Royal Irish Rifles.
Joined from 8th Division 7th February, 1918.

2nd Battalion Royal Irish Rifles.
Joined from 108th Brigade 8th February, 1918.

This Brigade was attached to 4th Division from 6th November, 1915, to 7th February, 1916, being replaced during that period by the 12th Infantry Brigade.

108TH INFANTRY BRIGADE.

COMMANDERS.

Brigadier-General C. Hacket Pain, C.B. Till 4th December, 1916.
Brigadier-General C. R. J. Griffith, C.B., C.M.G., D.S.O. Till 21st May, 1918.
Brigadier-General E. Vaughan, C.M.G., D.S.O.

## ORDER OF BATTLE

BATTALIONS.

11th Battalion Royal Irish Rifles.

Amalgamated with 13th Battalion Royal Irish Rifles, 14th November, 1917, as 11th/13th Battalion Royal Irish Rifles.

12th Battalion Royal Irish Rifles.

13th Battalion Royal Irish Rifles.

Amalgamated with 11th Battalion Royal Irish Rifles, 14th November, 1917, as 11th/13th Battalion Royal Irish Rifles.

11th/13th Battalion Royal Irish Rifles.

Disbanded 10th February, 1918.

9th Battalion Royal Irish Fusiliers.

Absorbed dismounted squadrons of North Irish Horse, September 1917, becoming 9th (N.I.H.) Battalion Royal Irish Fusiliers.

2nd Battalion Royal Irish Rifles.

Joined from 25th Division 14th November, 1917. To 107th Brigade 8th February, 1918.

1st Battalion Royal Irish Fusiliers.

Joined from 107th Brigade 8th February, 1918.

109TH INFANTRY BRIGADE.

COMMANDERS.

Brigadier-General T. E. Hickman, C.B., D.S.O. Till 27th May, 1916.

Brigadier-General R. J. Shuter, D.S.O. Till 13th January, 1917.

Brigadier-General A. St. Q. Ricardo, C.M.G., C.B.E., D.S.O. Till 12th December, 1917.

Brigadier-General W. F. Hessey, D.S.O. Till 18th April, 1918.

Brigadier-General E. Vaughan, C.M.G., D.S.O. Till 21st May, 1918.

Brigadier-General W. F. Hessey, D.S.O.

BATTALIONS.

9th Battalion Royal Inniskilling Fusiliers.

10th Battalion Royal Inniskilling Fusiliers.
Disbanded 19th February, 1918.

11th Battalion Royal Inniskilling Fusiliers.
Disbanded 8th February, 1918.

14th Battalion Royal Irish Rifles.
Disbanded 21st February, 1918.

1st Battalion Royal Inniskilling Fusiliers.
Joined from 29th Division 19th February, 1918.

2nd Battalion Royal Inniskilling Fusiliers.
Joined from 32nd Division 4th February, 1918.

PIONEER BATTALION.

16th Battalion Royal Irish Rifles.

DIVISIONAL TROOPS.

Service Squadron, 6th Inniskilling Dragoons.
Left Division. 1st June, 1916; to X. Corps Cavalry.
36th Divisional Signal Company.
Divisional Cyclist Company. Broken up 31st May, 1916; half to X. Corps Cyclist Battalion, half to 15th Royal Irish Rifles.

R.A.M.C.

108th Field Ambulance.
109th Field Ambulance.
110th Field Ambulance.

Divisional Train, R.A.S.C.
Divisional Supply Column.
48th Mobile Veterinary Section.

## ORDER OF BATTLE

MACHINE-GUN CORPS.

107th Brigade Machine-Gun Company.
Formed January 1916.

108th Brigade Machine-Gun Company.
Formed January 1916.

109th Brigade Machine-Gun Company.
Formed January 1916.

266th Machine-Gun Company.
Joined from England 18th January, 1918.

36th Battalion Machine-Gun Corps formed from these four Companies 1st March, 1918.

As no similar official list is available, the compilation of the following entailed considerable research, knowledge, and patience. Before printing, copies of the list were submitted to representatives of units for corrections and additions.

[Officers and other ranks (except in the case of those awarded the Victoria Cross) have opposite their names their regiments or corps only ; not the numbers of battalions or other units. It was impossible to insert these numbers in every case, and so it was thought best to do so in none. In the case of the infantry, many officers and other ranks served in several battalions of the same regiment at different periods.

Officers of the Regular Army, Territorial Army, or Special Reserve, who served on staffs of formations of the Division, are entered under their regiments. Those who commanded infantry brigades are entered as " Cmndg. —— Brigade," without the names of their regiments. Those who served with infantry battalions are entered under the regiments to which those battalions belonged : for example, Lieut.-Col. C. F. Meares, an officer of the Royal Irish Fusiliers, who commanded the 16th Royal Irish Rifles (Pioneers), is entered under the latter regiment.

All names beginning with " M'," a form very frequent in the North of Ireland, are included under " Mc," as it was in this form they generally appeared in " Part II. Orders " in the field, and subsequently in the *London Gazette*.]

# APPENDIX II

## A List of
## HONOURS AND AWARDS
### Gained by Officers and Other Ranks while serving with the 36th (Ulster) Division
### 1914–1918

### VICTORIA CROSS

Captain ERIC NORMAN FRANKLAND BELL, 9th Batt. Royal Inniskilling Fusiliers.

      For most conspicuous bravery at Thiepval, on 1st July, 1916. He was in command of a trench mortar battery, and advanced with the infantry to the attack. When our front line was hung up by enfilading machine-gun fire, Captain Bell crept forward and shot the machine-gunner. Later, on no less than three occasions, when our bombing parties, which were clearing the enemy's trenches, were unable to advance, he went forward alone and threw trench mortar bombs among the enemy. When he had no more bombs available; he stood on the parapet, under intense fire, and used a rifle with great coolness and effect on the enemy advancing to counter-attack. Finally he was killed rallying and reorganizing infantry parties which had lost their officers. All this was outside the scope of his normal duties with his battery. He gave his life in his supreme devotion to duty.

## VICTORIA CROSS (contd.)

Lieutenant GEOFFREY ST. GEORGE SHILLINGTON CATHER, 9th Batt. Royal Irish Fusiliers.

For most conspicuous bravery near Hamel, France, on 1st July, 1916. From 7 p.m. till midnight he searched " No Man's Land," and brought in three wounded men. Next morning, at 8 a.m., he continued his search, brought in another wounded man, and gave water to others, arranging for their rescue later. Finally, at 10-30 a.m., he took out water to another man, and was proceeding further on when he was himself killed. All this was carried out in full view of the enemy, and under direct machine-gun fire and intermittent artillery fire. He set a splendid example of courage and self-sacrifice.

Second-Lieutenant JAMES SAMUEL EMERSON, 9th Batt. Royal Inniskilling Fusiliers.

For repeated acts of most conspicuous bravery north of La Vacquerie, on 6th December, 1917. He led the company in an attack, and cleared four hundred yards of trench. Though wounded, when the enemy attacked in superior numbers, he sprang out of the trench with eight men and met the attack in the open, killing many and taking six prisoners. For three hours after this, all other officers having been casualties, he remained with his company, refusing to go to the dressing station, and repeatedly repelled bombing attacks. Later, when the enemy again attacked in superior numbers, he led his men to repel the attack, and was mortally wounded. His heroism, when worn out and exhausted from loss of blood, inspired his men to hold out, though almost surrounded, till reinforcements arrived and dislodged the enemy.

Private NORMAN HARVEY, 1st Batt. Royal Inniskilling Fusiliers.

For most conspicuous bravery and devotion to duty near Ingoyghem, on the 25th October, 1918, when his battalion was held up and suffered many casualties from enemy machine-guns. On his own initiative he rushed forward and engaged the enemy single-handed, disposing of twenty enemy and capturing two guns. Later, when his company was checked by another enemy strongpoint, he again rushed forward alone and put the enemy to flight. Subsequently, after dark, he voluntarily carried out, single-handed, an important reconnaissance, and gained valuable information. Private Harvey throughout the day displayed the greatest valour, and his several actions enabled the line to advance, saved many casualties, and inspired all.

# HONOURS AND AWARDS

## VICTORIA CROSS (*contd.*)

Second-Lieutenant CECIL LEONARD KNOX, R.E.

For most conspicuous bravery and devotion to duty. Twelve bridges were entrusted to this officer for demolition, and all of them were successfully destroyed. In the case of one steel-girder bridge, the destruction of which he personally supervised, the time-fuse failed to act. Without hesitation, Second-Lieutenant Knox ran to the bridge, under heavy machine-gun and rifle fire, and, when the enemy were actually upon the bridge, he tore away the time-fuse and lit the instantaneous-fuse, to do which he had to get under the bridge. This was an act of the highest devotion to duty, entailing the gravest risks, which, as a practical civil engineer, he fully realized.

Private WILLIAM FREDERICK M'FADZEAN, 14th Batt. Royal Irish Rifles.

For most conspicuous bravery near Thiepval Wood, on 1st July, 1916. While in a concentration trench and opening a box of bombs for distribution prior to an attack, the box slipped down into the trench, which was crowded with men, and two of the safety-pins fell out. Private M'Fadzean, instantly realizing the danger to his comrades, with heroic courage threw himself on the top of the bombs. The bombs exploded, blowing him to pieces, but only one other man was injured. He well knew his danger, being himself a bomber, but without a moment's hesitation he gave his life for his comrades.

Lance-Corporal ERNEST SEAMAN, 2nd Batt. Royal Inniskilling Fusiliers.

For most conspicuous bravery and devotion to duty. When the right flank of his company was held up by a nest of enemy machine-guns, he, with great courage and initiative, rushed forward under heavy fire with his Lewis gun, and engaged the position single-handed, capturing two machine-guns and twelve prisoners, and killing one officer and two men. Later in the day he again rushed another enemy machine-gun position, capturing the gun under heavy fire. He was killed immediately after. His courage and dash were beyond all praise, and it was entirely due to the very gallant conduct of Lance-Corporal Seaman that his company was enabled to rush forward to its objective and capture many prisoners.

## VICTORIA CROSS (*contd.*)

Private ROBERT QUIGG, 12th Batt. Royal Irish Rifles.

For most conspicuous bravery at Hamel, France, on 1st July, 1916. He advanced to the assault with his platoon three times. Early next morning, hearing a rumour that his platoon officer was lying out wounded, he went out seven times to look for him, under heavy shell and machine-gun fire, each time bringing back a wounded man. The last man he dragged in on a waterproof sheet from within a few yards of the enemy's wire. He was seven hours engaged in this most gallant work, and finally was so exhausted that he had to give it up.

Second-Lieutenant EDMUND DE WIND, 15th Batt. Royal Irish Rifles.

For most conspicuous bravery and self-sacrifice on 21st March, 1918, at the Racecourse Redoubt, near Grugies. For seven hours he held this important post, and, though twice wounded and practically single-handed, he maintained his position till another section could be got to his help. On two occasions, with two N.C.O.'s only, he got out on top, under heavy machine-gun and rifle fire, and cleared the enemy out of the trench, killing many. He continued to repel attack after attack until he was mortally wounded and collapsed. His valour, self-sacrifice, and example were of the highest order.

# HONOURS AND AWARDS

## COMPANION OF THE MOST HONOURABLE ORDER OF THE BATH

Brock, Brig.-Gen. H. J.,
*C.M.G., D.S.O.* . . Cmndg. R.A.
Coffin, Maj.-Gen. C.,
*V.C., D.S.O.* . Cmndg. 36th Div.

Griffith, Brig.-Gen. C. R. J.,
*C.M.G.,D.S.O.*, Cmndg. 108th Bde.
Nugent, Maj.-Gen. O. S. W.,
*D.S.O.* . . . . . Cmndg. 36th Div.

## COMPANION OF THE ORDER OF ST. MICHAEL AND ST. GEORGE

Brock, Brig.-Gen. H. J.,
*C.B., D.S.O.* . . . Cmndg. R.A.
Cole-Hamilton, Lt.-Col. C. G.,
*D.S.O.* . . . . . . . R. Ir. Rif.
Comyn, Lt.-Col. L. J., *D.S.O.*,
Conn. Rangers.
Greig, Lt.-Col. F. J. . . R.A.M.C.
Goodwin, Lt.-Col. W. R., *D.S.O.*,
R. Ir. Rif.
Hawkes, Brig.-Gen. C. St. L. G.,
*D.S.O.* . . . . . . Cmndg. R.A.
Hunt, Lt.-Col. J. P., *D.S.O.*,
*D.C.M.* . . . . . . R. Ir. Rif.
Knott, Lt.-Col. J. E., *D.S.O.*,
R. Innis. Fus.
Oliphant, Lt.-Col. P. E. K. Blair,
*D.S.O.* . . . . . . . R. Ir. Rif.

Pakenham, Col. H. A. . R. Ir. Rif.
Place, Lt.-Col. C. O., *D.S.O.* . R.E.
Potter, Lt.-Col. C. F., *D.S.O.* R.A.
Ricardo, Brig.-Gen. A. St. Q.,
*D.S.O.* . . . Cmndg. 10th Bde.
Roch, Col. R. S., *D.S.O.* R.A.M.C.
Savage, Col. W. H. . . R. Ir. Rif.
Simpson, Lt.-Col. H. C., *D.S.O.* R.A.
Smythe, Lt.-Col. R. C., *D.S.O.*,
R. Innis. Fus.
Thompson, Lt.-Col. A. G.,
*D.S.O.* . . . . . . Indian Army.
Thompson, Lt.-Col. R. G. . . R.A.
Thorpe, Brig.-Gen. E. I. de S.,
*D.S.O.* . . . . Cmndg. 107th Bde.
Vaughan, Brig.-Gen. E., *D.S.O.*,
Cmndg. 108th Bde.

## THIRD BAR TO DISTINGUISHED SERVICE ORDER

Knox, Lt.-Col. R. S. . . . . . . . . . . . . . . . . . R. Innis. Fus.

## SECOND BAR TO DISTINGUISHED SERVICE ORDER

Knox, Lt.-Col. R. S. . . . . . . . . . . . . . . . . . R. Innis Fus.

## BAR TO DISTINGUISHED SERVICE ORDER

Cole-Hamilton, Lt.-Col. C. G.,
*C.M.G.* . . . . . R. Ir. Rif.
Crawford, Lt.-Col. E. W. R. Innis. Fus.
Dent, Lt.-Col. J. R. C., *M.C.*,
R. Innis. Fus.
Goodwin, Lt.-Col. W. R.,
*C.M.G.* . . . . . . R. Ir. Rif.
Hunt, Lt.-Col. J. P.,
*C.M.G., D.C.M.* . . R. Ir. Rif.

Hessey, Brig.-Gen. W. F.,
Cmndg. 109th Bde.
Jones, Lt.-Col. B. J. . . R. Ir. Rif.
Knox, Lt.-Col. R. S., R. Innis. Fus.
McCarthy-O'Leary, Lt.-Col.
H. W. D. . . . . . R. Ir. Rif.
Peacocke, Lt.-Col. W. J.,
R. Innis. Fus.

## DISTINGUISHED SERVICE ORDER

Allen, Lt.-Col. Sir W. J., R. Ir. Rif.
Blacker, Lt.-Col. S. W.   R. Ir. Fus.
Bowen, Lt.-Col. F. O.  . R. Ir. Rif.
Brock, Brig.-Gen. H. J.,
  *C.B.*, *C.M.G.* . . . Cmndg. R.A.
Bruce, Maj. G. J., *M.C.*, Genl. List.
Burnand, Lt.-Col. N. G.  R. Ir. Rif.
Clements, Maj. S. U. L. . R. Ir. Fus.
Clendinning, Maj. H.  . R. Ir. Rif.
Comyn, Lt.-Col. L. J., *C.M.G.*,
           Conn. Rangers.
Crawford, Lt.-Col. E. W.,
           R. Innis. Fus.
Crozier, Brig.-Gen. F. P.,
  *C.B.*, *C.M.G.* . . . . R. Ir. Rif.
Dent, Lt.-Col. J. R. C., *M.C.*,
           R. Innis. Fus.
Despard, Capt. C. B., *M.C.*,
           R. Ir. Fus.
Dunbar, Lt.-Col. B. H. V., R.A.M.C.
Edwards, Maj. G. R. O.  . R.F.A.
Elwes, Lt.-Col. H. C., *M.V.O.*,
           R. Ir. Rif.
Farnham, Lt.-Col. A. K., Lord,
           R. Innis. Fus.
Forde, Lt.-Col. G. M., *M.C.*,
           R. Innis. Fus.
Franklyn, Maj. G. E.W.,*M.C.*, R.A.
Gallagher, Lt. H. . . R. Innis. Fus.
Gooch, Maj. H., *M.C.*, . . . R.E.
Goodwin, Lt.-Col. W. R., *C.M.G.*,
           R. Ir. Rif.
Gordon, Lt.-Col. F. L. . R. Ir. Rif.
Grant-Suttie, Maj. H. F., *M.C.* R.A.
Green, Lt.-Col. S. H., *M.C.*,
           West Yorks. Regt.
Hardie, Lt.-Col. C. C. A. . . R.E.
Hawkes, Brig.-Gen. C. St. L. G.,
  *C.M.G.* . . . . . Cmndg. R.A.
Hunt, Lt.-Col. J. P., *C.M.G.*,
  *D.C.M.* . . . . . . R. Ir. Rif.
Huskisson, Maj. G., *M.C.* . .R.F.A.
Ivey, Maj. T. H. . . . R. Ir. Rif.
Jones, Lt.-Col. B. J. . . R. Ir. Rif.
Knott, Lt.-Col. J. E., *C.M.G.*,
           R. Innis. Fus.
Knox, Lt.-Col. R. S.  R. Innis. Fus.
Lowe, Lt.-Col. T. A., *M.C.*, R.Ir.Fus.

McCallum, Maj. J. D. M., R. Ir. Rif.
McCarthy-O'Leary, Lt.-Col.
  H. W. D. . . . . . R. Ir. Rif.
McKee, Maj. J. . . . . R. Ir. Rif.
Mackenzie, Lt.-Col. R. H., *M.C.*,
           Cmndg. R.E.
Macrory, Lt.-Col. F. S. N.,
           R. Innis. Fus.
Magill, Lt.-Col. R. . . . R.A.M.C.
Maxwell, Lt.-Col. R. D. P.,
           R. Ir. Rif.
May, Maj. E. R. H. . . R. Ir. Rif.
Meares, Lt.-Col. C. F. . R. Ir. Rif.
Montgomery, Maj. W. A., R. Ir. Rif.
Muriel, Maj. J. C. . R. Innis. Fus.
Nicholls, Maj. W. . . . . .R.F.A.
Oliphant, Lt.-Col. P. E. K. Blair,
  *C.M.G.* . . . . . . R. Ir. Rif.
Peacocke, Lt.-Col. W. J.,
           R. Innis. Fus.
Potter, Lt.-Col. C. F., *C.M.G.*, R.A.
Pratt, Lt.-Col. A. C.  R. Innis. Fus.
Rivis, Lt.-Col. T. C. L. . . R.A.S.C.
Roch, Lt.-Col. R. S., *C.M.G.*,
           R.A.M.C.
Rogers, Maj. V. B., *M.C.*, Genl. List.
Rowley, Brig.-Gen. F. G. M.,
           Cmndg. 107th Bde.
Scott, Maj. C. A. R. . . . .R.F.A.
Scott, Capt. W., *M.C.* . R. Ir. Fus.
Sharp, Capt. R. R., *M.C.* . .R.F.A.
Simpson, Lt.-Col. H. C., *C.M.G.*,
           R.A.
Smyth, Maj. W., *M.C.* . . . R.E.
Smythe, Lt.-Col. R. C., *C.M.G.*,
           R. Ir. Fus.
Stewart, Capt. J. H., *M.C.*,
           R. Ir. Rif.
Stidston, Lt.-Col. C. A. . R.A.M.C.
Stranack, Maj. C. E. . . . . R.A.
Sugden, Capt. J. E. . . R. Ir. Rif.
Thompson, Maj. G. . . R. Ir. Rif.
Vivian, Lt.-Col. the Hon. O. R.,
  *M.V.O.* . . . . . . R. Ir. Rif.
Withycombe, Brig.-Gen. W. M.,
  *C.B.*, *C.M.G.* Cmndg. 107th Bde.
Woods, Lt.-Col. P. J. . R. Ir. Rif.
Young, Maj. T. F., *M.C.* . . R.E.

## SECOND BAR TO MILITARY CROSS

Fullerton, Capt. A. . . R.A.M.C.
Law, Capt. R. O. H. . R. Ir. Rif.
Lyness, Capt. W. J. . . R. Ir. Rif.
Paton, Rev. J. G.,Army Chap. Dept.

# HONOURS AND AWARDS 319

## BAR TO MILITARY CROSS

Adams, 2/Lt. T. J. . . R. Innis. Fus.
Apperson, Capt. G. J. . R. Ir. Rif.
Bruce, Maj. G. J., *D.S.O.* Genl. List.
Charlton, Lt. J. W. . R. Innis. Fus.
Condon, Capt. J. E. S. . R. Ir. Rif.
Crawford, 2/Lt. C. O. . R. Ir. Rif.
Crosbie, Capt. T. E. C. . R. Ir. Fus.
Cuming, Lt. A. E. McM. R. Ir. Fus.
Darling, 2/Lt. J. . . . R. Ir. Fus.
Deakin, Lt. G. . . . . . . R.E.
Dobbyn, Lt. A. L. . . . R. Ir. Fus.
Dodd, Lt. F. . . . . . . . R.E.
Duffin, Maj. J. T. . . . Genl. List.
Duncan, Capt. L. S. . . R. Ir. Rif.
Forde, Lt.-Col. G. M., *D.S.O.*,
    R. Innis. Fus.
Fullerton, Capt. A. . . R.A.M.C.
Gavin, Capt. N. J. H. . R.A.M.C.
Gibson, Lt. M. H. . . . R. Ir. Rif.
Godson, Capt. E. A. . . R. Ir. Fus.
Halahan, Rev. F. J.
    Army Chap. Dept.
Harding, Capt. C. H. . . R. Ir. Rif.
Higgins, Lt. R. L. . R. Innis. Fus.
Holmes, 2/Lt. C. . . . R. Ir. Rif.
Huskisson, Maj. G., *D.S.O.* . R.F.A.
Kane, Capt. R. C. R. . . R. Ir. Rif.
Kitchen, Lt. H. M. . . . . M.G.C.
Knight, Capt. W. M., R. Innis. Fus.
Knox, 2/Lt. R. K. . . . R. Ir. Rif.
Knox, Capt. T. K. . . . . R.E.
Lacey, Lt. and Q.M. J. C. de,
    R. Innis. Fus.
Law, Capt. R. O. H. . . R. Ir. Rif.
Lendrum, Capt. A. C. R. Innis. Fus.
Logan, 2/Lt. S. . . . . R. Ir. Fus.
Lyness, Capt. W. J. . . R. Ir. Rif.
Lynch, Capt. V. J. . . R. Ir. Fus.
McDowell, Capt. W. J. . R. Ir. Rif.
Marshall, Capt. E. L., R. Innis. Fus.
May, Lt. T. W. . . R. Innis. Fus.
Miller, Capt. P. M. . . . R. Ir. Rif.
Morris, Rev, W. F.
    Army Chap. Dept.
Murphy, Capt. J. J., *D.C.M.*,
    R. Ir. Fus.
Ormandy, Lt. H. . . . . . R.E.
Paton, Rev. J. G.,
    Army Chap. Dept.
Patton, Capt. E. . . . R. Ir. Rif.
Patton, Capt. J. H. A. . R. Ir. Rif.
Purdy, 2/Lt. W. H. R. Innis. Fus.
Rawlins, 2/Lt. S. B. . . . . R.F.A.
Reddy, 2/Lt. J. J. . . . R. Ir. Rif.
Rose, Maj. R. de R. . . R. Ir. Rif.
Russell, Maj. W. . . . R.A.M.C.
Smyth, Maj. W., *D.S.O.* . . R.E.
Steele, 2/Lt. C. H. . . . R. Ir. Fus.
Tooley, Capt. F. S. . . R. Ir. Rif.
Watts, Capt. R. . . . . . R.A.S.C.

## THE MILITARY CROSS

Abraham, 2/Lt. R., *M.M.*
    R. Innis. Fus.
Achilles, Lt. H. M. . . . . R.F.A.
Adams, 2/Lt. F. . . . . R. Ir. Rif.
Adams, 2/Lt. J. . . . . R.A.M.C.
Adams, 2/Lt. Thos. R. Innis. Fus.
Adams, 2/Lt. T. J. . R. Innis. Fus.
Allen, Capt. S. . . . . Genl. List.
Allkins, Lt. A. W. . . . . . M.G.C.
Anderson, Capt. A. M. . R. Ir. Rif.
Angle, 2/Lt. A. A. . . . . . M.G.C.
Apperson, Capt. G. J. . R. Ir. Rif.
Armstrong, C.S.M. W. . R. Ir. Rif.
Bally, Rev. H. S. Army Chap. Dept.
Barbour, R.Q.M.S. J. . R. Ir. Fus.
Barker, 2/Lt. J. . . . . . M.G.C.
Barrett, Capt. E. R., R. Innis. Fus.
Barrington-Foote, Capt. R. C.,
    R.F.A.
Barrowman, 2/Lt. R. S.,
    R. Innis. Fus.
Battershill, Lt. E. F. . . R. Ir. Rif.
Bayly, Capt. L. M. . . R. Ir. Rif.
Beavis, Capt. M. J. . . . R.F.A.
Beckett, 2/Lt. C. G. . . . M.G.C.
Bell, Capt. W. R. . . . R. Ir. Rif.
Belt, Capt. C. B. . . . R. Ir. Rif.
Bennett, 2/Lt. J. T. M. R. Innis. Fus.
Bennett, Lt. T. M. . . R. Ir. Rif.
Beveridge, Capt. G. . . . .R.F.A.
Blair, Capt. R. G. . . . R.A.M.C.
Bleakley, R.S.M. G. R. Innis. Fus.
Boomer, Lt. W. C. . . R. Ir. Rif.
Boulton, Lt. L. G. . . . . M.G.C.
Bowerbank, Lt. W. . . . M.G.C.
Boyce, Capt. T. W. R. Innis. Fus.
Boyle, Lt. R. M. . R. Innis. Fus.
Brabazon, 2/Lt. R. E. F.
    R. Innis. Fus.
Briggs, Lt. and Q.M. A.,
    R. Innis. Fus.
Broadbent, Maj. E. R., 8th Hussars.

## HISTORY OF 36TH (ULSTER) DIVISION

### THE MILITARY CROSS (contd.)

Broome, Capt. F. N. . . . . .R.F.A.
Brown, Lt. T. . . . R. Innis. Fus.
Browne, 2/Lt. J. . . . R. Ir. Rif.
Browne, Capt. M. H. . . . Genl. List.
Brunyate, Lt. W. M. W. . . R.E.
Bruce, Maj. G. J., *D.S.O.* Genl. List.
Bryson, 2/Lt. J. . . . . R. Ir. Fus.
Buchan, Capt. T. O. M.
                   The Queen's.
Buckley, 2/Lt. H. A. .R. Innis. Fus.
Bullock, C.S.M. S. . .R. Innis. Fus.
Burdge, 2/Lt. G. C. .R. Innis. Fus.
Burrows, 2/Lt. H. C. . . R. Ir. Fus.
Burrows, Capt. O. V. . R.A.M.C.
Caiger-Watson, 2/Lt. G., R. Ir. Fus.
Callingham, Lt. G. S. . . . .R.F.A.
Campbell, Lt. R. T. . . R. Ir. Rif.
Campbell, Major, S. B. B., R.A.M.C.
Carfrae, Maj. C. T. . . . . R.F.A.
Carse, 2/Lt. D. A., *M.M.* . .R.F.A.
Caskey, 2/Lt. J. A. .R. Innis. Fus.
Castle, Maj. C. M. . . . R. Ir. Rif.
Chalmers, Lt. J. L. . . R. Ir. Fus.
Chambers, Lt. R. A. .R. Innis. Fus.
Charlton, Lt. J. W. .R. Innis. Fus.
Chase, Capt. C. D. . . . R. Ir. Rif.
Clarke, Capt. J. S. . . . R.A.M.C.
Clotworthy, Capt. N. . R. Ir. Rif.
Clough, 2/Lt. L. G. . . . .M.G.C.
Coffman, Lt. M. B.,
        U.S.A. att. R. Ir. Rif.
Collings, Lt. A. . . . . R. Ir. Rif.
Conder, Capt. A. F. R. . R.A.M.C.
Condon, Capt. J. E. S. . R. Ir. Rif.
Corner, Lt. J. W. . . . R. Ir. Rif.
Corkey, Capt. I. W. . . R. Ir. Rif.
Cousland, Capt. K. H. . . .R.F.A.
Cowan, Maj. W. McC. C. . .R.F.A.
Cowser, Capt. R. J. . . . R.A.S.C.
Cox, Lt. T. W. . . .R. Innis. Fus.
Craig, Capt. H. D. C. . . . . H.L.I.
Crawford, 2/Lt. C. O. . R. Ir. Rif.
Crosbie, Capt. T. E. C. . R. Ir. Rif.
Crosbie, Capt. W. E. . R.A.M.C.
Cullen, 2/Lt. J. . . . . R. Ir. Fus.
Cullen, Capt. P. J. . . . R. Ir. Rif.
Cuming, Lt. A. E. McM. R. Ir. Fus.
Curley, Lt. J. . . . . .R. Innis. Fus.
Cuthbert, Lt. J. . . . . . .R.F.A.
Dalgleish, C.S.M. R. . . R. Ir. Rif.
Darling, 2/Lt. J. . . . R. Ir. Fus.
Davidson, Capt. D. N. F.
                R. Innis. Fus.
Davis, 2/Lt. J. E. . .R. Innis. Fus.

Dawson, 2/Lt. N. C. . . R. Ir. Rif.
Deakin, Lt. G. . . . . . . R.E.
Dean, Capt. H. S. . . . R. Ir. Fus.
Deans, Lt. S. . . . . . R. Ir. Rif.
Delacour-Bles, Lt. J. M. . .M.G.C.
Delahey, 2/Lt. W. A. . . . R.E.
Despard, Capt. C. B., *D.S.O.*,
                R. Ir. Fus.
Devitt, 2/Lt. G. W. . . . .R.F.A.
Dickson, 2/Lt. A. McC. . R. Ir. Rif.
Dobbyn, Lt. A. L. . . . R. Ir. Fus.
Dodd, Lt. T. . . . . . . . R.E.
Dolan, 2/Lt. J. J. . . . R. Ir. Rif.
Donnelly, Maj. F. . . . . . R.E.
Donohoe, Rev. F., Army Chap. Dept.
Douglas, Capt. J. C. . . R. Ir. Rif.
Drean, 2/Lt. R. S. . .R. Innis. Fus.
Duffin, Maj. J. T. . . . Genl. List.
Duncan, Lt. L. S., *D.S.O.*, R. Ir. Rif.
Dundee, 2/Lt. A. . . . R. Ir. Rif.
Dundee, Capt. C. . . . R.A.M.C.
Dunlop, Capt. J. L. . . R.A.M.C.
Dunworth, Capt. P. J., R. Innis. Fus.
Eaton, 2/Lt. R. O. . . . R. Ir. Fus.
Ellis, Capt. S. G. . . . . .R.F.A.
Ellis, Capt. W. . . . . R. Ir. Rif.
Ellwood, S.S.M. A. . . R.A.M.C.
Emerson, Maj. H. . . . R.A.M.C.
Fagan, 2/Lt. J. J. A. . . . . R.E.
Falkiner, 2/Lt. F. E. R. . R. Ir. Rif.
Falle, Capt. T. de C. . . R. Ir. Fus.
Fanning, 2/Lt. R. J. .R. Innis. Fus.
Ferguson, Capt. A. . . R. Ir. Fus.
Ferrier, Capt. A. . . . . . R.E.
Findlay, Capt. J. . . . R. Ir. Rif.
Finney, 2/Lt. J. . . .R. Innis. Fus.
Fitzgerald, Capt. J. G. E. . .M.G.C.
Flood, Capt. R. S. . . . R. Ir. Fus.
Ford, 2/Lt. R. E. . . . . .R.F.A.
Forde, Lt.-Col. G. M., *D.S.O.*,
               R. Innis. Fus.
Fox, Capt. L. W. . . . . .R.F.A.
Fox, Lt. S. . . . . . . . .M.G.C.
Fullerton, Capt. A. . . R.A.M.C.
Furness, Capt. W. S., R. Innis. Fus.
Furniss, Lt. J. E. . . . R. Ir. Rif.
Gale, Maj. H. D. . . . . .R.F.A.
Gavin, Capt. M. J. H. . R.A.M.C.
Gibson, Rev. A., Army Chap. Dept.
Gibson, 2/Lt. A. J. E. . R. Ir. Rif.
Gibson, Lt. M. H. . . . R. Ir. Rif.
Gilmore, 2/Lt. A. W. F., R. Ir. Rif.
Gimson, Lt. A. F. . . . . .R.F.A.
Given, Capt. T F. . . . R. Ir. Fus.

# HONOURS AND AWARDS

## THE MILITARY CROSS (contd.)

Glegg, Capt. J. D. . . . R. Dub. Fus.
Glendinning, 2/Lt. J. H., R. Ir. Rif.
Godson, Capt. E. A. . . R. Ir. Fus.
Gooch, Maj. H., *D.S.O.* . . . R.E.
Gordon, Capt. H. C. . R. Innis. Fus.
Grant, 2/Lt. F. M. . . . . R.F.A.
Green, Lt.-Col. S. H., *D.S.O.*,
                West Yorks. Regt.
Greenaway, 2/Lt. W. J., R. Ir. Fus.
Griffiths, Lt. T. E.
              U.S.A. att. R. Ir. Fus.
Grove-White, Capt. I. A., R. Ir. Rif.
Guinness, Maj. H. R. G. . R.F.A.
Hackett, Capt. L. A. H., R. Ir. Rif.
Haigh, Lt. J. W. . . . R. Ir. Rif.
Haire, Capt. A. L. . . R. Innis. Fus.
Halahan, Rev. F. J.
              Army Chap. Dept.
Hall, Capt. A. H. . . . R. Ir. Rif.
Hamilton, 2/Lt. R. . . . R.F.A.
Hanson, Capt. R. S. . . R. Ir. Rif.
Harbord, Capt. S. G. . . . . R.A.
Harcourt, 2/Lt. W. L. . R. Ir. Rif.
Harding, Capt. C. H. . . R. Ir. Rif.
Harland, S.M. T. . . . R.A.M.C.
Harpur, 2/Lt. H. de la M.,R. Ir. Rif.
Harrison, 2/Lt. J. D., *M.M.*,
                      R. Ir. Rif.
Haslett, 2/Lt. J. . . . R. Ir. Rif.
Haslett, 2/Lt. T. F. . . R. Ir. Rif.
Haughey, 2/Lt. H. . . R. Ir. Fus.
Henahan, Capt. M. . . R. Ir. Fus.
Henderson, 2/Lt. G. Y., R. Ir. Rif.
Hewitt, 2/Lt. J. O. N., R. Innis. Fus.
Higgins, Lt. R. L. . . R. Innis. Fus.
Hill, C.S.M. C. . . . . R. Ir. Rif.
Hill, Capt. F. J. . . . R. Ir. Rif.
Hine, Lt. E. E. . . . . R. Ir. Rif.
Hogg, Lt. W. F. . . . R. Ir. Rif.
Holland, 2/Lt. E. J. F. . R. Ir. Rif.
Holmes, 2/Lt. C. . . . R. Ir. Rif.
Horner, Maj. A. L. . . . R.A.V.C.
Houston, 2/Lt. T. . . . R. Ir. Fus.
Howard, Capt. A. W., R. Innis. Fus.
Hunter, Lt. W. F. . . . R. Ir. Rif.
Huskisson, Maj. G., *D.S.O.*,
Hutchison, Rev. W. H.,
              Army Chap. Dept.
Idiens, 2/Lt. S. . . . . . M.G.C.
Ireland, Capt. J. . . . R. Ir. Rif.
Irvine, Capt. G. M. F., R. Innis. Fus.
Irwin, 2/Lt. R. B. W., R. Innis. Fus.
Jackson, Lt. A. M. . . . . . R.E.
Jackson, 2/Lt. C. . . . R. Ir. Rif.

Johnston, Capt. E. . . R. Ir. Rif.
Johnston, 2/Lt. J. A., R. Innis. Fus.
Johnston, Lt.-Col. J. G., R.A.M.C.
Kane, Capt. R. C. R. . . . R. Ir. Rif.
Kelleher, 2/Lt. P. St. J. H.,
                      R. Ir. Rif.
Kelly, C.S.M. J. H. . . R. Ir. Rif.
Kemp, Capt. A. F., *D.C.M.*,
                      R. Ir. Rif.
Kennedy, Capt. E. N. . . . R.F.A.
Kennedy, Lt. J. F. . . . . R.F.A.
Kennedy, R.Q.M.S. J. W.,
                    R. Innis. Fus.
Kennedy, Lt. R. N. . . R. Ir. Rif.
Kenworthy, 2/Lt. C. H. H.,
                    R. Innis. Fus.
King, 2/Lt. J. . . . R. Innis. Fus.
Kitchen, Lt. H. N. . . . M.G.C.
Knight, Capt. W. M., R. Innis. Fus.
Knox, Lt. J. . . . . . R. Ir. Rif.
Knox, 2/Lt. R. K. . . . R. Ir. Rif.
Knox, Capt. T. K. . . . . . R.E.
Knox, Capt. W. H., R. Innis. Fus.
Lacey, Lt. and Q.M. J. C. de,
                  R. Innis. Fus.
Lamont, 2/Lt. F. . . . R. Ir. Rif.
Lancaster, 2/Lt. E. J., R. Innis. Fus.
Lavelle, 2/Lt. M. . R. Innis. Fus.
Lavery, Lt. D. . . . . R. Ir. Rif.
Law, Capt. R. O. H. . . R. Ir. Rif.
Leahy, 2/Lt. T. C. . . R. Ir. Fus.
Ledlie, Lt. J. C. St. J. . R. Ir. Rif.
Lendrum, Capt. A. C., R. Innis. Fus.
Lennon, 2/Lt. J., *D.C.M.*, *M.M.*,
                    R. Ir. Fus.
Lepper, Maj. E. F. . . . R. Ir. Rif.
Leslie, Maj. C. G., 3rd Dragoon Gds.
Lewis, Maj. P. B. . . . R. Ir. Rif.
Lindsay, Capt. G. E. . . R.A.M.C.
Linton, 2/Lt. W. T. . . R. Ir. Rif.
Logan, 2/Lt. S. . . . . R. Ir. Fus.
Lodge, 2/Lt. J. E. H., R. Innis. Fus.
Loveys, Lt. J. . . . . . R.F.A.
Lowry, C.S.M. J. A. . . R. Ir. Rif.
Luce, Capt. A. A. . . . R. Ir. Rif.
Lyle, Capt. S. J. . . . . R. Ir. Rif.
Lynch, Capt. V. J. . . R. Ir. Fus.
Lyness, Capt. W. J. . . R. Ir. Rif.
McCaw, Capt. J. . R. Innis. Fus.
McClelland, Capt. E. W.
                  R. Innis. Fus.
McClinton, Capt. A. N. . R. Ir. Rif.
McConnell, 2/Lt. R. B.
                  R. Innis. Fus.

## HISTORY OF 36TH (ULSTER) DIVISION

### THE MILITARY CROSS (contd.)

McCorkindale, 2/Lt. J. C. . R.F.A.
McCrea, 2/Lt. T. . . .R. Innis. Fus.
McCullough, 2/Lt. W. J., R. Ir. Rif.
McDowell, Capt. W. J. . R. Ir. Rif.
McFerran, 2/Lt. M. A. . R. Ir. Rif.
McGranahan, 2/Lt. J. W.,R. Ir. Rif.
Macgregor, 2/Lt. R. P. . R. Ir. Rif.
McHugh, 2/Lt. D. . . . R. Ir. Rif.
McIntosh, 2/Lt. H. . . R. Ir. Rif.
McKeen, 2/Lt. J. . . R. Innis. Fus.
MeKenna, 2/Lt. J. . . . R. Ir. Rif.
Mackenzie, Capt. C. A. . R.A.O.C.
Mackeown, Capt. R. F. . Genl. List.
McKinley, 2/Lt. R. W.,
        R. Innis. Fus.
McKinstry, Lt. J. . . . R. Ir. Rif.
McKnight, 2/Lt. T. . R. Innis. Fus.
McMaster, Capt. C. . . R. Ir. Rif.
McMechan, 2/Lt. J. .R. Innis. Fus.
Macpherson, 2/Lt. W. A. S.,
        R. Ir. Rif.
Maguire, Capt. T. . R. Innis. Fus.
Malone, 2/Lt. J. T. . . R. Ir. Rif.
Malone, Capt. W. A. . . R. Ir. Rif.
Malone, Lt. W. R. . . R. Ir. Rif.
Manning, Rev. C. C.,
       Army Chap. Dept.
Marriott-Watson, 2/Lt. R. R.,
        R. Ir. Rif.
Marshall, Capt. E. L., R. Innis. Fus.
Martin, Capt. H. . . . . R.F.A.
Maxwell, Capt. J. . . R. Ir. Rif.
May, Lt. T. W. . . R. Innis. Fus.
Meagher, 2/Lt. L. J. . . R. Ir. Rif.
Mearns, C.S.M. J. W. . R. Ir. Rif.
Menaul, Capt. W. J. . . Genl. List.
Miller, Capt. P. M. . . R. Ir. Rif.
Milliken, Lt. J. . . . . R. Ir. Rif.
Mills, Capt. F. . . . . M.G.C.
Milne, Capt. C. W. .R. Innis. Fus.
Mitchell, 2/Lt. H. D. . . R. Ir. Rif.
Mitchell, 2/Lt. J. . R. Innis. Fus.
Mitchell, 2/Lt. J. E. M. . R. Ir. Rif.
Moffatt, C.S.M. W. . . R. Ir. Rif.
Montgomery, Lt. F. P. . R.A.M.C.
Monteflore, Capt.T.H.Sebag, R.F.A.
Moon, Capt. W. J. K., R. Innis. Fus.
Moore, Capt. K. M. . . Genl. List.
Moore, Lt. M. E. J. . . R. Ir. Rif.
Moore, Capt. W. . R. Innis. Fus.
Moore, 2/Lt. W. . . . R. Ir. Rif.
Moreland, 2/Lt. J. A. . R. Ir. Rif.
Morgan, Lt. H. S.,
     U.S.A. att. R.A.M.C.

Morris, Rev. W. F.,
      Army Chap. Dept.
Morrison, Capt. T. D., R. Innis. Fus.
Morrow, 2/Lt. H. G. . . R. Ir. Rif.
Moyles, 2/Lt. D. A. . . R. Ir. Rif.
Mulholland, Maj. J. A. . R. Ir. Rif.
Mulholland, Maj. P. D. . . M.G.C.
Muller, Lt.-Col. J. . . . . M.G.C.
Munn, 2/Lt. N. B. . . . R. Ir. Rif.
Munn, Capt. R. B. S. . . . M.G.C.
Murphy, Capt. J. J., *D.C.M.*,
        R. Ir. Fus.
Murray, Capt. P. S. . . R. Ir. Rif.
Myles, Capt. J. S. . R. Innis. Fus.
Nathan, Lt. R. P. . . . R.F.A.
Nelson, 2/Lt. W. . R. Innis. Fus.
Newton, Capt. and Q.M. J.,
        R. Ir. Rif.
Nicholl, Capt. J. D. . . R. Ir. Rif.
O'Brien, Capt. J. D. . . R. Ir. Rif.
Odbert, 2/Lt. W. H. . . R. Ir. Rif.
Oliver, 2/Lt. D. E. . . . . R.F.A.
Ormandy, Lt. H. . . . . R.E.
Ozzard, 2/Lt. H. T. . . R. Ir. Fus.
Painting, Lt. A. A. . . . M.G.C.
Parcell, 2/Lt. H. G. . . . R.F.A.
Partridge, 2/Lt. J. H. . R. Ir. Fus.
Paton, Rev. J. G.,Army Chap. Dept.
Pattern, Capt. E. . . . R. Ir. Rif.
Patton, Capt. J. H. A. . R. Ir. Rif.
Patterson, 2/Lt. A., R. Innis. Fus.
Patterson, 2/Lt. W. H.,
        R. Innis. Fus.
Pearson, Capt. W. . . . R. Ir. Rif.
Picken, Capt. S. E. . . . R.A.M.C.
Pierce, Lt. I. . . . R. Innis. Fus.
Potts, 2/Lt. G. . . . . . R.E.
Poynter, 2/Lt. E. W. . . R.F.A.
Price, Capt. F. A. . . . . R.F.A.
Price, 2/Lt. W. . . R. Innis. Fus.
Purce, Capt. G. R. B. . R.A.M.C.
Purdy, 2/Lt. W. H. .R. Innis. Fus.
Rabone, Capt. E. L. . . Genl. List.
Rawlins, 2/Lt. S. B. . . . R.F.A.
Reddy, 2/Lt. J. J. . . R. Ir. Rif.
Renwick, Capt. R. . . . R. Ir. Rif.
Reynolds, 2/Lt. E. W. . R. Ir. Fus.
Richards, Lt. M. J. . . . R.F.A.
Richardson, Capt. A. W. C.,
      Bedford Regt.
Robinson, Lt. G. . . . R. Ir. Fus.
Robson, Capt. R. I. . . R. Ir. Rif.
Rogers, Maj. V. B., *D.S.O.*
        Genl. List.

# HONOURS AND AWARDS

## THE MILITARY CROSS (contd.)

Rogers, Lt. W. . . . . R. Ir. Rif.
Roland, 2/Lt. R. F. . R. Innis. Fus.
Rose, Maj. R. de R. . . R. Ir. Rif.
Rothwell, 2/Lt. T. . R. Innis. Fus.
Rounsefell, 2/Lt. E. de W.,
    R. Ir. Rif.
Russell, Maj.W. . . . R.A.M.C.
Rutter, 2/Lt. F. J. . . . R. Ir. Rif.

Saunderson, Lt. W. R. . R. Ir. Rif.
Saunderson, Lt. W. R. . R. Ir. Fus.
Schweder, Lt. R. P. . . . R.F.A.
Scott, Lt. D. H. . . . Div. Cyclists.
Scott, Lt. R. C. . . . . R. Ir. Rif.
Scott, Capt. W., *D.S.O.*.. R. Ir. Fus.
Sharp, 2/Lt. R. . . . . . . R.F.A.
Sharp, Capt. R. R., *D.S.O.* R.F.A.
Shawe, 2/Lt. H. R. . R. Innis. Fus.
Shearer, 2/Lt. T. H. . . . R.F.A.
Sheat, 2/Lt. E. I. . R. Innis. Fus.
Sheehan, Lt. H. J. . . . R. Ir. Rif.
Shepperd, Capt. H. F. . R. Ir. Rif.
Shields, 2/Lt. J. H. . . . . R.E.
Shiner, Lt. E. E. J. . . . R.F.A.
Simpson, Capt. J. H. . . R. Ir. Rif.
Slater, Lt. C. H. . . . . R. Ir. Rif.
Smith, Lt. C. M. . . R. Innis. Fus.
Smith, Lt. J. I. . . . . R. Ir. Fus.
Smith, Capt. P. B. . . . . R.F.A.
Smyth, Maj. E. F. . . R. Ir. Rif.
Smyth, Maj. W., *D.S.O.* . . R.E.
Solomon, Capt. R. B. . . R.F.A.
Somers, Capt. W. . . . R. Ir. Rif.
Somerset, 2/Lt. I. . . . R. Ir. Rif.
Sowerby, Capt. E. S. . . R.A.M.C.
Sparkes, Capt. W. . . . R. Ir. Fus.
Spence, Rev. A., Army Chap. Dept.
Spence, Capt. J. G. . . R.A.M.C.
Spender, Lt.-Col. W. B., *D.S.O.*,
    R. of O.
Sprott, Lt. —. . . . . R. Ir. Rif.
Stapylton-Smith, Lt. J. B. . R.E.
Steel, Capt. W. C. . . . . R.F.A.
Steele, 2/Lt. C. H. . . . R. Ir. Fus.
Stephenson, Lt. T. B. . R. Ir. Rif.
Stevens, C.S.M. R. S. . R. Ir. Rif.
Stevenson, 2/Lt. L. W. H.,
    R. Innis. Fus.
Stewart, Capt. J. E. . . . . R.E.
Stewart, Capt. J. H., *D.S.O.*,
    R. Ir. Rif.
Stewart, 2/Lt. J. N. G. . R. Ir. Rif.
Stokes, 2/Lt. A. O. . . R. Ir. Rif.
Strong, 2/Lt. C. A. . . R. Innis. Fus.

Stronge, Capt. C. N. L.,
    R. Innis. Fus.
Stuart, Capt. W. G. B. . R. Ir. Rif.
Sweeny, 2/Lt. T. C. . R. Innis. Fus.
Tait, Maj. M. W. . . . . M.G.C.
Talbot, 2/Lt. R. M. . R. Innis. Fus.
Tayler, Capt. H. . . . R. Ir. Rif.
Taylor, Lt. J. . . . . R. Innis. Fus.
Teele, Capt. W. B. . . R. Ir. Rif.
Telford, Capt. E. A. . . R. Ir. Rif.
Thomas, Lt. J. G. S. . . . M.G.C.
Thomas, 2/Lt. S. G. . . R. Ir. Rif.
Thompson, 2/Lt. R. L. . R. Ir. Rif.
Thorne, 2/Lt. C. E. . . . . R.E.
Thornely, Capt. F. B. . R. Ir. Rif.
Thornton, Capt. A. P. . R. Ir. Rif.
Thornton, R.Q.M.S. S. W.,R. Ir. Rif.
Tiptaft, 2/Lt. C. P. . . R. Ir. Rif.
Todd, 2/Lt. A. E. . . . R. Ir. Rif.
Tooley, Capt. F. S. . . R. Ir. Rif.
Trousdale, Capt. E. H. . . R.A.S.C.
Turpin, Lt. D. O. . . . R. Ir. Rif.
Turner, R.S.M. C. H. . R. Ir. Fus.
Turner, I.t. E. G. L. . . R. Ir. Fus.
Tyner, 2/Lt. J. B. . R. Innis. Fus.
Unsworth, 2/Lt. V. . . R. Ir. Rif.
Vesey, Lt. T. W. . . . R. Ir. Fus.
Vigers, Lt.-Col. T. W. . . . R.E.
Waddell, Capt. C. D. . . R. Ir. Rif.
Waldren, R.S.M. T. H.,
    R. Innis. Fus.
Walkington, Lt. D. B. . R. Ir. Rif.
Watson, Capt. J. . . . . R.A.S.C.
Watt, Lt. G. R. . . . . . R.F.A.
Watts, Capt. R. . . . . . R.A.S.C.
Wheatley, Capt. E. A. . . . R.E.
Whelan, C.S.M. R. S. . R. Ir. Rif.
Whinyate, Capt. R. . . . R.F.A.
White, C.S.M. A. . R. Innis. Fus.
White, Lt. T. J. . . . . R. Ir. Rif.
Willcox, Lt. J. T. A. . . R. Ir. Rif.
Williams, 2/Lt. J. H. . . . R.F.A.
Williams, Capt. R. D. . R. Ir. Rif.
Wilson, 2/Lt. G. W. . . . R.F.A.
Wilson, Lt. J. . . . . . . M.G.C.
Wilton, Capt. J. M. E.,R. Innis. Fus.
Wintle, Lt. A. L. C. . R. Innis. Fus.
Wood, Lt. C. C. . . . . R. Ir. Rif.
Wright, 2/Lt. J. McH. . R. Ir. Rif.
Wright, Rev. J. J.,
    Army Chap. Dept.
Young, 2/Lt. J. B. . . . . R. Ir. Fus.
Young, 2/Lt. R. . . . . R. Ir. Rif.
Young, Maj. T. F., *D.S.O.* . R.E.

# 324 HISTORY OF 36TH (ULSTER) DIVISION

## BAR TO DISTINGUISHED CONDUCT MEDAL

Fisher, L/Cpl. J. . . . . M.G.C.
Gilmour, Pte. J. P. . . . M.G.C.

McIlveen, C.Q.M.S. W.  R. Ir. Rif.

## DISTINGUISHED CONDUCT MEDAL

Adams, C.S.M. R. . . R. Innis. Fus.
Alcorn, Pte. J. . . . R. Innis. Fus.
Armour, L/Cpl. J. . . . R. Ir. Rif.
Armstrong, L/Cpl. R. . R. Ir. Fus.
Anderson, Sgt. J. I. . R. Innis. Fus.
Baines, C.S.M. J. . . . R. Ir. Rif.
Bamford, L/Sgt. R. . . R. Ir. Fus.
Barker, Sgt. W. . . R. Innis. Fus.
Barr, C.S.M. R. . . . . R. Ir. Rif.
Barr, Sgt. W. J. . . . R. Ir. Rif.
Bell, Cpl. H. . . . . . R. Ir. Rif.
Belshaw, C.S.M. G. . R. Innis. Fus.
Blake, Cpl. E. . . . R. Innis. Fus.
Blake, Rfm. T. C. . . R. Ir. Rif.
Bloom, L/Cpl. J. . . . . R.E.
Boal, L/Cpl. W. J. . R. Innis. Fus.
Bow, Rfm. D. . . . . R. Ir. Rif.
Bowes, Cpl. J. H. . R. Innis. Fus.
Boyd, Sgt. R. J. . . . R. Innis. Fus.
Bradley, Sgt. J., *M.M.*,
                              R. Innis. Fus.
Brooker, Pte. E. F. . R. Innis. Fus.
Burke, L/Cpl. J. . . R. Innis. Fus.
Cahill, L/Cpl. J. . . . . R. Ir. Fus.
Capstick, Sgt. M. . . . . M.G.C.
Carpenter, C.S.M. W. . . M.G.C.
Carton, L/Cpl. J. . . . R. Ir. Rif.
Carvell, Sgt. S. . . . . R. Ir. Fus.
Chambers, Cpl. J. . . . R. Ir. Rif.
Chapman, C.S.M. J. E.,
                              R. Innis. Fus.
Clarke, Sgt. J. . . . R. Innis. Fus.
Clarke, Cpl. R., *M.M.*, R. Innis. Fus.
Conn, C.S.M. J. . . . R. Innis. Fus.
Cook, R.S.M. H. C. . . . R.F.A.
Corish, Sgt. P. . . . . . R. Ir. Fus.
Creese, C.Q.M.S. M. G. . . M.G.C.
Croft, C.S.M. J. . . . . R. Ir. Rif.
Cromie, Sgt. J. . . . . R. Ir. Rif.
Cumming, R.Q.M.S. S. . R. Ir. Rif.
Cunningham, Sgt. J. . . R. Ir. Rif.
Curry, L/Cpl. W. . . . R. Ir. Rif.
Dalrymple, L/Cpl. J. A.,
                              R. Innis. Fus.
Darling, B.Q.M.S. F. . . . R.F.A.
Darrach, Pte. J. . . R. Innis. Fus.
Davidson, Sgt. W. . . R. Ir. Rif.
Deane, Sgt. J. . . . . R. Ir. Rif.

Dickson, Sgt. J., *M.M.*,
                             R. Innis. Fus.
Dillon, Rfm. J. . . . . R. Ir. Rif.
Doherty, Sgt. J. . . . . R. Ir. Rif.
Downey, Sgt. J. . . . . R. Ir. Fus.
Dudgeon, Sgt. E. C., *M.M.* . R.E.
Duke, Rfm. W. . . . . R. Ir. Rif.
Eaton, Sgt. J., *M.M.* . R. Ir. Rif.
Edwardes, Sgt. O. J. . . . R.E.
Emmett, C.S.M. W. R. . . R.F.A.
Fisher, L/Cpl. J. . . . . M.G.C.
Fleming, Cpl. T. . . . R. Ir. Rif.
Forrest, Pte. E. T. . R. Innis. Fus.
France, Sgt. M. S. . . . . M.G.C.
Fryer, Sgt. T. . . . . . M.G.C.
Getgood, Cpl. S. . . . . R. Ir. Rif.
Gilmour, Pte. J. P. . . . M.G.C.
Hamilton, Sgt. J. . . . R. Ir. Rif.
Hamilton, C. S. M. R., R. Innis. Fus.
Harbinson, Sgt. J., *M.M.*, R. Ir. Rif.
Higgins, Rfm. T. . . . R. Ir. Rif.
Harrison, C.Q.M.S. S., *M.M.*,
                               R. Ir. Rif.
Haslett, Cpl. L., *M.M.*,
                             R. Innis. Fus.
Herdman, Cpl. R. . . . R. Ir. Rif.
Higgins, Sgt. H., *M.M.*, R. Ir. Rif.
Higgins, Rfm. T. . . . R. Ir. Rif.
Holmes, Sgt. A. E. . . . R. Ir. Rif.
Homersham, Sgt. F., *M.M.*,
                              R. Ir. Fus.
Hughes, Sgt. J., *M.M.* . R. Ir. Fus.
Hume, Sgt. J., *M.M.* . . M.G.C.
Humphreys, Cpl. W. . . . M.G.C.
Hunter, Sgt. J. A., *M.M.*,
                             R. Innis. Fus.
Hutchinson, Pte. J. . R. Innis. Fus.
Hynds, Pte. W. . . . R. Innis. Fus.
Irwin, Pte. R. . . . R. Innis. Fus.
Jackson, Cpl. A. H., *M.M.* . R.E.
Jackson, Sgt. J. E. . . . . R.E.
Jamieson, S.S.M. J. . . . M.G.C.
Jones, Sgt. C. . . . . R. Ir. Fus.
Jones, Rfm. W. J. . . R. Ir. Rif.
Kearney, Sgt. J. . . . R. Ir. Rif.
Kelly, Sgt. A. . . . . . R. Ir. Rif.
Kelly, Sgt. S. . . . . R. Innis. Fus.
Kennedy, Sgt. E. . . . . R.F.A.

# HONOURS AND AWARDS

## DISTINGUISHED CONDUCT MEDAL (contd.)

Kent, Sgt. E. . . . . . . R.F.A.
Kirkpatrick, Rfm. J. . R. Ir. Rif.
Kirkwood, L/Cpl. N. . . . R. Ir. Rif.
Laird, C.S.M. W. A. . R. Innis. Fus.
Lake, Sapper E. . . . . . R.E.
Lazard, Adjt. (Interpreter) A. A., French Army.
Lamb, Sgt. H. T. . . . . R.F.A.
Leach, Sgt. A. . . . . R. Ir. Rif.
Leighton, L/Cpl. R. H. P.,
    R. Innis. Fus.
Leslie, Pte. J. . . . . . . M.G.C.
Littlechild, Sgt. W. E. . . R.F.A.
Lockhart, Sgt. J. . . . R. Ir. Fus.
Longworth, Pte. W. . R. Innis. Fus.
Lowry, Sgt. G. E. . . R. Innis. Fus.
Lowry, Cpl. S., *M.M.* . . . R.E.
Lucas, C.S.M. R., *M.M.*, R. Ir. Fus.
Lyttle, Sgt. . . . . . R.A.M.C.
McBirnay, Sgt. T. . . . R. Ir. Rif.
McBride, Cpl. R. J. . . R. Ir. Fus.
McCabe, Pte. P. . . . . R. Ir. Rif.
McCarrol, Pte. E. . . . R. Ir. Rif.
McCaughey, Cpl. A. . . . R. Ir. Rif.
McCauley, Sgt. P. J. . . . R. Ir. Rif.
McClay, Sgt. T. . . . R. Innis. Fus.
McClean, C.S.M. W. J. . R. Ir. Fus.
McCormick, Sgt. B. . R. Innis. Fus.
McCready, Sgt. J. . . . R. Ir. Fus.
McCullough, R.S.M. J., *M.M.*,
    R. Ir. Fus.
McCullough, Sgt. R. . . R. Ir. Rif.
McGaley, Sgt. A. . . R. Innis. Fus.
McIlveen, C.Q.M.S. W. R. Ir. Rif.
McIlwraith, Cpl., *M.M.* . . R.E.
McInnes, Sgt. S. . . . . . R.E.
Mackey, C.S.M. J. J. . . R. Ir. Rif.
McKimm, Pte. G. . . R. Innis. Fus.
Mackintosh, C.S.M. J. L. . . R.E.
McMillan, Sgt. J. . . . R. Ir. Rif.
McNabney, Sgt. J., *M.M.* . R.E.
McPeake, Cpl. A. . . . R. Ir. Rif.
McQuiston, L/Cpl. T. . . R. Ir. Rif.
McWhirter, Rfm. J. . . R. Ir. Rif.
Magill, Sgt. T. . . . . R. Ir. Rif.
Magookins, C.S.M. W. D.,R. Ir. Rif.
Mallock, Pte. A. . . . R. Innis. Fus.
Mathers, C.S.M. J. . . . R. Ir. Rif.
Miller, R.S.M. D. . . . R. Ir. Rif.
Miller, Rfm. J. . . . . R. Ir. Rif.
Milligan, C.S.M. T. . . R. Ir. Rif.
Murray, C.S.M. J. . . . R. Ir. Rif.
Neale, Pte. T. . . . R. Innis. Fus.
Neely, Sgt. H. . . . . R. Ir. Rif.

Neill, Sapper J. . . . . . R.E.
Neill, Sgt. W. . . . . R. Ir. Fus.
Neilly, Cpl. W. . . . . . R.E.
Nesbitt, Sgt. A., *M.M.*,
    R. Innis. Fus.
Newman, C.S.M. M., *M.M.*,
    R. Innis. Fus.
Nicholls, Cpl. P. . . . . . R.E.
Palmer, L/Cpl. J. . . R. Innis. Fus.
Pameter, Sgt. . . . . . R. Ir. Fus.
Patterson, Sgt. J. . . . R. Ir. Rif.
Patterson, C.S.M. J. J.,
    R. Innis. Fus.
Pikeman, C.S.M. J. A., *M.M.*,
    R. Ir. Rif.
Pitt, Rfm. C. F. . . . . R. Ir. Rif.
Platt, Rfm. R. . . . . . R. Ir. Rif.
Potter, L/Cpl. J. . R. Innis. Fus.
Quee, Sgt. H. F. . . . R. Ir. Rif.
Quinn, Cpl. W. F., *M.M.*, R.A.M.C.
Redding, B.S.M. W. L. . R.F.A.
Reilly, L/Cpl. J. . . R. Innis. Fus.
Robinson, C.Q.M.S. J. . R. Ir. Fus.
Roe, Sgt. C. W., *M.M.*,
    R. Innis. Fus.
Roe, Cpl. H. . . . . . R. Ir. Fus.
Rose, C.S.M. T. de . . . M.G.C.
Rudling, Sgt. P. C. . . . R.F.A.
Scott, Cpl. R. . . . . . . R.E.
Scott, C.Q.M.S. T. . . . R. Ir. Rif.
Scott, L/Cpl. W. . R. Innis. Fus.
Selby, C.Q.M.S. H. . . R. Ir. Fus.
Shain, Bdr. J. . . . . . R.F.A.
Sharp, Bdr. T. . . . . . R.F.A.
Sherman, Sgt. S. J. . . . R.F.A.
Smith, Rfm. R. . . . . R. Ir. Rif.
Smyth, Sgt. H. . . . R. Innis. Fus.
Smyth, Sgt. R., *M.M.*, R. Innis. Fus.
Snodden, R.S.M. J. . R. Innis. Fus.
Somers, C.Q.M.S. R. G., R. Ir. Rif.
Stacey, Farr.-Sgt. H., *M.M.*, R.F.A.
Stead, Sgt. T. . . . . . R. Ir. Rif.
Stevens, Sgt. W. H. . . . R.F.A.
Shrimpton, Sgt. E. D. . . R.F.A.
Stubbings, Sgt. J. W., *M.M.*, M.G.C.
Symons, Pte. W. . . . R. Ir. Fus.
Taggart, C.S.M. C. B. . R. Ir. Rif.
Tait, L/Cpl. A. . . . . R. Ir. Rif.
Thompson, Rfm. R. . . R. Ir. Rif.
Turton, Cpl. F. . . . . . M.G.C.
Vennard, C.S.M. T. . . R. Ir. Fus.
Verner, Sgt. J. A. . . . R. Ir. Rif.
Walker, L/Cpl. C. H. . . R. Ir. Rif.
Waring, C.S.M. S. . . . . M.G.C.

# HISTORY OF 36TH (ULSTER) DIVISION

## DISTINGUISHED CONDUCT MEDAL (contd.)

Werner, Cpl. A. . . . . . R.F.A.
White, Sgt. R. . . . . . R.F.A.
Wilson, L/Cpl. R. C. . . R. Ir. Rif.
Woods, C.Q.M.S. J. . R. Innis. Fus.
Wright, Sapper B. R. . . . R.E.

Wyer, Sgt. A. . . . . . R. Innis. Fus.
Yardley, L/Cpl. W., *M.M.*
                                 R. Ir. Rif.
Yeates, L/Cpl. W., *M.M.*, R. Ir. Rif.
Young, Sgt. H. . . . . . R. Ir. Fus.

## BAR TO MILITARY MEDAL

Adams, Sgt. J. . . . . . R. Ir. Fus.
Angus, L/Cpl. J. . . . . . R.E.
Ashford, Sgt. T. . . . R. Ir. Fus.
Baker, Sgt. J. . . . . . . R.G.A.
Barton, Cpl. H. . . . . R. Ir. Fus.
Baxter, Driver A. . . . . R.F.A.
Blair, Cpl. J. . . . . . R. Innis. Fus.
Buck, Cpl. J. . . . . . . R.F.A.
Campbell, Rfm. J. . . . R. Ir. Rif.
Carolan, Cpl. A. . . . . R. Ir. Rif.
Carson, L/Cpl. R. J. . . R. Ir. Rif.
Cooke, L/Cpl. W. H. . R. Innis. Fus.
Crisp, Sgt. G. H. . . . . . R.E.
Eden, L/Cpl. R. . . . . R. Ir. Fus.
Gibson, L/Cpl. W. J. . R.A.M.C.
Gillespie, S/Sgt. R. S. . R.A.M.C.
Gillmann, Rfm. W. C., *D.C.M.*,
                                 R. Ir. Rif.
Gowdy, II. Cpl. W. J. . . . R.E.
Greaney, Rfm. B. J. . . R. Ir. Rif.
Hamilton, Sgt. W. D., R. Innis. Fus.
Harborne, Pte. G. . . R. Innis. Fus.
Harrison, C.Q.M.S. S., *D.C.M.*,
                                 R. Ir. Rif.
Higgins, Sgt. H., *D.C.M.*, R. Ir. Rif.
Hirst, Bdr. J. W. . . . . . R.F.A.
Homersham, Sgt. F., *D.C.M.*,
                                 R. Ir. Fus.
Houston, C.S.M. J. . . R. Ir. Rif.
Irwin, Sgt. H. E. . . . . . R.F.A.
Jackson, Cpl. A. H., *D.C.M.*, R.E.
Johnston, L/Cpl. S. J. . R. Ir. Rif.
Kane, Pte. R. . . . . R. Innis. Fus.

Laird, Sgt. W. . . . R. Innis. Fus.
Lindberg, Pte. R. . . . . R. Ir. Fus.
Long, Cpl. W. E. . . R. Innis. Fus.
Loughlin, Pte. D. . . R. Innis. Fus.
McCall, L/Cpl. R. . . . R. Ir. Fus.
McDowell, Pte. A. . . R. Innis. Fus.
McIlveen, Sgt. J. . . . R. Ir. Rif.
McIntyre, Sapper J. . . . . R.E.
McLaughlin, L/Cpl. M. . R. Ir. Fus.
McNabney, Sgt. J., *D.C.M.* . R.E.
McNeill, Sgt. R. . . . R. Innis. Fus.
Mager, Sgt. H. C. . . . . R.F.A.
Matier, Sgt. T. . . . . R. Ir. Rif.
Montgomery, Sgt. R., R. Innis. Fus.
Nicholson, Sgt. A. . . . . . R.E.
Owens, Sgt. P. . . . . R. Ir. Rif.
Owens, Sgt. T. . . . . . M.G.C.
Packer, Pte. W. L. . . R. Ir. Fus.
Patterson, Rfm. R. B. . R. Ir. Rif.
Pikeman, C.S.M. J. A., *D.C.M.*,
                                 R. Ir. Rif.
Ringland, Sgt. J. . . R. Innis. Fus.
Roberts, Rfm. S. . . . R. Ir. Rif.
Savage, Pte. J. . . . . R.A.M.C.
Scullion, Rfm. J. . . . R. Ir. Rif.
Smith, Pte. T. . . . . . R. Ir. Fus.
Soames, Cpl. C. . . . . . . R.E.
Taylor, Sgt. J. . . . R. Innis. Fus.
Thompson, Bdr. J. . . . R.F.A.
Wakem, Sgt. A. . . . . . R.F.A.
Walker, L/Cpl. S. . . R. Innis. Fus.
Wallen, C.S.M. H. . . R. Innis. Fus.
Wilson, Rfm. W. S. . . R. Ir. Rif.

## MILITARY MEDAL

Abraham, Pte. R. . . R. Innis. Fus.
Accleton, Cpl. A. . . . . . R.F.A.
Adams, L/Cpl. J. . . . . . M.G.C.
Adams, Sgt. J. . . . . . R. Ir. Fus.
Adams, Rfm. R. . . . . R. Ir. Rif.
Adamson, Pte. W. . . R. Ir. Fus.
Agnew, Rfm. G. . . . . R. Ir. Rif.
Ahern, Cpl. J. . . . . . . R.F.A.

Aicken, Pte. J. . . . . . M.G.C.
Ainsworth, L/Cpl. A., R. Innis. Fus.
Alexander, Rfm. N. . . R. Ir. Rif.
Alexander, Rfm. W. . . R. Ir. Rif.
Alicoat, Sgt. P. E. . . . R. Ir. Rif.
Allen, Rfm. T. J. . . . . R. Ir. Rif.
Anderson, Pte. E. . . . R. Ir. Rif.
Anderson, L/Cpl. H. . . R. Ir. Rif.

# HONOURS AND AWARDS

## MILITARY MEDAL (contd.)

| | |
|---|---|
| Anderson, Pte. J. . . . R. Ir. Fus. | Bell, Cpl. J. . . . . . R. Ir. Rif. |
| Anderson, Sgt. J. I., D.C.M., R. Innis. Fus. | Bell, L/Cpl. J. . . . R. Innis. Fus. |
| Anderson, Pte. W. . R. Innis. Fus. | Bell, Sapper R. . . . . . . R.E. |
| Andrews, Pte. A. S. . . R. Ir. Rif. | Bell, Rfm. S. . . . . . R. Ir. Rif. |
| Andrews, Pte. J. . . . R.A.M.C. | Bennett, Pte. J. . . . R. Innis. Fus. |
| Angus, L/Cpl. J. . . . . . R.E. | Bertie, Cpl. E. . . . R. Innis. Fus. |
| Anstey, Pte. J. . . . R. Innis. Fus. | Bill, Rfm. J. M. . . . R. Ir. Rif. |
| Appleby, Pte. E. . . . . M.G.C. | Bingham, Sgt. J. . . . . R.F.A. |
| Appleyard, Pte. T. V . . M.G.C. | Bingham, Rfm. W. J. . R. Ir. Rif. |
| Arkless, L/Cpl. B. . . R. Innis. Fus. | Birbeck, Rfm. T. . . . R. Ir. Rif. |
| Armour, L/Cpl. D. . . R. Innis. Fus. | Birkby, Pte. L. . . . . R.A.M.C. |
| Armour, L/Cpl. J. . . . R. Ir. Rif. | Birkmyre, L/Cpl. H. . . R. Ir. Rif. |
| Armour, L/Cpl. T. E. . R. Ir. Rif. | Black, Cpl. W. J. . . . R. Ir. Rif. |
| Armson, Rfm. P. . . . R. Ir. Rif. | Blackburn, Pte. T. . R. Innis. Fus. |
| Armstrong, Sgt. J. L. . R. Ir. Rif. | Blacker, Rfm. J. . . . R. Ir. Rif. |
| Armstrong, Sgt. R. . R. Innis. Fus. | Blackmore, Cpl. H. . . R. Ir. Rif. |
| Arnold, Sgt. F. . . . . R. Ir. Rif. | Blackwell, Pte. T. . . R. Innis. Fus. |
| Arthur, Pte. W. . . . . R.A.M.C. | Blair, Cpl. J. . . . . R. Innis. Fus. |
| Ashe, Rfm. E. . . . . R. Ir. Rif. | Blair, Rfm. S. . . . . R. Ir. Rif. |
| Ashford, Sgt. T. . . . . R. Ir. Fus. | Blake, Cpl. E. . . . R. Innis. Fus. |
| Atkins, Cpl. B. . . . . R. Ir. Fus. | Blakey, Sapper J. . . . . . R.E. |
| Auld, L/Cpl. A. . . . . R. Ir. Rif. | Blakley, Sgt. D. H. . R. Innis. Fus. |
| Averell, Pte. R. . . . . R. Ir. Fus. | Blunden, Sgt. A. . . . . R.F.A. |
| Bacon, Gnr. E. . . . . . R.G.A. | Bonner, Pte. R. . . . R. Innis. Fus. |
| Bailey, Pte. J. . . . . R. Ir. Rif. | Bonner, Bdr. S. . . . . . R.F.A. |
| Bailie, Pte. H. . . . . R.A.M.C. | Booth, Sapper R. . . . . . R.E. |
| Baillie, Sgt. W. . . . . R. Ir. Rif. | Boreland, Sgt. C. . . . R. Ir. Rif. |
| Baines, Sgt. T. . . . . R. Ir. Rif. | Boreland, L/Cpl. E. . . R. Ir. Rif. |
| Baker, Sgt. J. . . . . . . R.G.A. | Bowden, Pte. W. S. . . R. Ir. Rif. |
| Ball, Pioneer G. . . . . . . R.E. | Bowman, Bdr. W. B. . . R.F.A. |
| Ballam, Bdr. G. J. . . . . R.F.A. | Boxall, Pte. W. R. . . R.A.M.C. |
| Ballantine, Rfm. L. . . R. Ir. Rif. | Boyce, Sgt. T. . . . . R. Ir. Rif. |
| Banford, Rfm. W. F. . R. Ir. Rif. | Boyd, Cpl. B. . . . . R. Ir. Rif. |
| Bankhead, L/Cpl. W. J., R. Ir. Rif. | Boyd, Pte. C. . . . R. Innis. Fus. |
| Banks, Rfm. A. . . . . R. Ir. Rif. | Boyd, Rfm. J. . . . . R. Ir. Rif. |
| Barclay, Sapper W. . . . R.E. | Boyd, Sgt. J. B. . . . R. Ir. Rif. |
| Barnes, Cpl. E. . . . . R. Ir. Rif. | Boyd, Rfm. W. J. . . . R. Ir. Rif. |
| Barnhill, Cpl. D. . . R. Innis. Fus. | Boyle, Rfm. J. . . . . R. Ir. Rif. |
| Barr, Pte. T. E. . . . . R.A.M.C. | Bradbury, Pte. W. . R. Innis. Fus. |
| Barton, Cpl. H. . . . . R. Ir. Fus. | Bradley, Cpl. G. . . . . M.G.C. |
| Bastable, Pte. W. G., R. Innis. Fus. | Bradley, L/Cpl. J. . . R. Innis. Fus. |
| Bate, Rfm. W. R. . . . R. Ir. Rif. | Bradley, Sgt. J., D.C.M., R. Innis. Fus. |
| Baxter, Driver A. . . . . R.F.A. | Brady, Cpl. R. . . . R. Innis. Fus. |
| Baxter, Rfm. G. . . . . R. Ir. Rif. | Brangan, Sgt. J. . . R. Innis. Fus. |
| Baxter, Rfm. J. . . . . R. Ir. Rif. | Breen, Cpl. R. . . . . R. Ir. Rif. |
| Baxter, L/Cpl. S. . . . R. Ir. Rif. | Breeze, Rfm. W. J. . . R. Ir. Rif. |
| Baxter, L/Cpl. W. . . . R. Ir. Rif. | Brennan, Rfm. W. J. . R. Ir. Rif. |
| Bayes, Gnr. W. J. . . . . R.F.A. | Bright, Driver A. . . . . R.F.A. |
| Beattie, L/Cpl. R. . . . R. Ir. Rif. | Brind, L/Cpl. A. . . . R. Ir. Rif. |
| Beattie, Sgt. V. . . . . R. Ir. Rif. | Broadhead, Bdr. W. . . . R.F.A. |
| Beatty, Pte. J. R. . . R. Innis. Fus. | Broadhurst, Pioneer G. . . R.E. |
| Bell, C.S.M. H. . . . . R. Ir. Rif. | Broadhurst, Driver J. T. . . R.F.A. |
| Bell, S.S.M. H. C. . . . R.A.M.C. | Brown, Rfm. A. . . . R. Ir. Rif. |

## MILITARY MEDAL (contd.)

Brown, Rfm. D. . . . R. Ir. Rif.
Brown, Rfm. J. . . . R. Ir. Rif.
Brown, Rfm. T. . . . R. Ir. Rif.
Brown, Pte. T. A. . . R. Innis. Fus.
Brown, Rfm. W. . . . R. Ir. Rif.
Brown, Sgt. W. . . . R. Ir. Rif.
Bruce, Rfm. E. . . . . R. Ir. Rif.
Bryden, Pte. H. . . . R. Innis. Fus.
Buchanan, Pte. J. M.,
    R. Innis. Fus.
Buck, L/Cpl. A. . . . R. Ir. Fus.
Buck, Cpl. J. . . . . . R.F.A.
Buckley, Pte. R. . . . R. Ir. Fus.
Buick, L/Cpl. J. . . . R. Ir. Rif.
Bullick, Sgt. W. P. . . R. Ir. Rif.
Bunting, Sgt. S. . . . R. Ir. Rif.
Burke, Pte. J. . . . . R. Ir. Fus.
Burton, Sgt. A. T. . . R.A.M.C.
Butler, Sgt. W. . . . R.A.M.C.
Butterfield, Bdr. A. . . R.F.A.
Byrne, L/Cpl. E. O. . . R. Ir. Rif.
Cadoo, L/Cpl. G. . . R. Innis. Fus.
Cairns, Sgt. T. . . . R. Innis. Fus.
Cairns, L/Cpl. W. . . . R. Ir. Rif.
Camp, Cpl. F. . . . . . R.F.A.
Campbell, Sgt. A. . . R. Innis. Fus.
Campbell, Sgt. J. . . . R. Ir. Rif.
Campbell, Driver J. . . . . R.E.
Campbell, Rfm. J. (4434), R. Ir. Rif.
Campbell, Rfm. J. (15/12230),
    R. Ir. Rif.
Campbell, Driver W. . . . . R.E.
Canning, Bdr. J. . . . . R.F.A.
Canty, Gnr. C. E. . . . . R.F.A.
Capon, Cpl. H. E. . . . R. Ir. Rif.
Carlisle, Sgt. D. . . . . R. Ir. Rif.
Carlisle, Rfm. D. . . . R. Ir. Rif.
Carolan, Cpl. H. . . . . R. Ir. Rif.
Carson, Rfm. A. . . . R. Ir. Rif.
Carson, L/Cpl. R. J. . . R. Ir. Rif.
Carson, Pte. W. . . . R. Innis. Fus.
Carvell, Bdr. R. . . . . R.F.A.
Cathcart, Rfm. W. . . R. Ir. Rif.
Caughey, Cpl. J. . . . R. Ir. Rif.
Cavan, Rfm. J. . . . . R. Ir. Rif.
Cavins, Sgt. A. . . . . R. Ir. Rif.
Chambers, Pte. J. . . . R. Ir. Fus.
Chambers, Rfm. W. G. . . R. Ir. Rif.
Cherry, Pte. H. . . . R. Ir. Fus.
Child, Pte. W. . . . . M.G.C.
Christie, L/Cpl. W. . . R. Ir. Rif.
Christopher, L/Cpl. O. J. . . R.E.
Clark, L/Cpl. T. . . . R. Innis. Fus.
Clarke, L/Cpl. A. G. H. . . R. Ir. Fus.

Clarke, L/Cpl. D. . . . R. Ir. Fus.
Clarke, Sgt. J. (5164) . R. Ir. Rif.
Clarke, Sgt. J. (17444) . R. Ir. Rif.
Clarke, Cpl. J. . . . R. Innis. Fus.
Clarke, Pte. J. . . . . R. Ir. Fus.
Clarke, Cpl. R., $D.C.M.$,
    R. Innis. Fus.
Clarke, L/Cpl. S. J. . . R.A.M.C.
Clarke, Cpl. W. . . . . . R.E.
Clements, Gnr. E. . . . . R.F.A.
Clements, Sgt. G. . . . . R.G.A.
Clements, Cpl. T. . . . R. Ir. Fus.
Cleverley, L/Cpl. C. . . R. Ir. Rif.
Clintin, Sgt. H. . . . . R.F.A.
Clinton, Pte. H. . . . R. Innis. Fus.
Codling, Sgt. H. W. . . . R.F.A.
Cole, Sgt. E. F. . . . . R. Ir. Rif.
Collins, Sgt. J. A. . . R. Innis. Fus.
Collop, L/Cpl. H. . . . R. Ir. Rif.
Colville, Pte. J. . . . . M.G.C.
Connolly, Rfm. H. . . . R. Ir. Rif.
Connor, Pte. A. (18111),
    R. Innis. Fus.
Connor, Pte. A. (40639),
    R. Innis. Fus.
Conway, Rfm. J. . . . R. Ir. Rif.
Cook, Rfm. H. . . . . R. Ir. Rif.
Cook, Pte. W. . . . . R.A.M.C.
Cook, Rfm. W. A. . . . R. Ir. Rif.
Cook, Pte. W. T. . . R. Innis. Fus.
Cooke, Pte. A. . . . R. Innis. Fus.
Cooke, L/Cpl. R. . . . R. Innis. Fus.
Cooke, Sgt. R. J. . . R. Innis. Fus.
Cooke, L/Cpl. W. H. . . R. Innis. Fus.
Cooper, Gnr. E. . . . . . R.F.A.
Cooper, Pte. J. . . . . R.A.M.C.
Cooper, Cpl. T. . . . R. Innis. Fus.
Corbett, Bdr. C. W. . . . R.F.A.
Cornish, Rfm. F. . . . R. Ir. Rif.
Coulter, Pte. J. . . . . R. Ir. Fus.
Coulter, Sapper W. R. . . . R.E.
Courtney, Sgt. W. . . . R. Ir. Rif.
Cousins, Sgt. W. B. . . R. Ir. Rif.
Craig, Cpl. G. . . . . . R. Ir. Fus.
Craig, L/Cpl. R. . . . . R.A.M.C.
Craig, Cpl. S. . . . . . R. Ir. Rif.
Cranston, L/Cpl. G. . . . M.G.C.
Craven, L/Cpl. J. . . . R. Ir. Fus.
Craven, L/Cpl. R. H. . . R.A.M.C.
Crawford, Sgt. S. . . R. Innis. Fus.
Cremins, Pte. P. . . . R. Ir. Fus.
Crichton, Sgt. D. . . . R. Ir. Fus.
Crichton, II. Cpl. H. . . . . R.E.
Crisp, Sgt. G. H. . . . . . R.E.

## HONOURS AND AWARDS

### MILITARY MEDAL (contd.)

Crisp, Sgt. J. J. . . . . . . R.E.
Croad, Gnr. A. J. . . . . R.F.A.
Crone, Rfm. J. . . . . R. Ir. Rif.
Croome, Pte. W. . . R. Innis. Fus.
Cropley, Bdr. W. J. . . . R.F.A.
Cross, L/Cpl. S. . . . . R. Ir. Rif.
Crothers, L/Cpl. T. . . R. Ir. Rif.
Crowe, L/Cpl. E. . . . R. Ir. Rif.
Culbert, Pte. S. . . . R. Innis. Fus.
Cullen, Sgt. A. . . . . R. Ir. Rif.
Cullen, L/Sgt. J. . . R. Innis. Fus.
Cullinane, Pte. T. . . R. Innis. Fus.
Cully, Pte. J. . . . . . R. Ir. Fus.
Cumberland, Cpl. J. . . R. Ir. Rif.
Cummins, Pioneer W. . . . R.E.
Cunning, L/Cpl. T. . . . R. Ir. Rif.
Curtis, Rfm. E. . . . . R. Ir. Rif.
Dale, Sgt. J. H. . . . . R. Ir. Rif.
Dalzelle, Rfm. S. . . . R. Ir. Rif.
Davey, Sgt. W. . . . . . R.F.A.
Davidson, Rfm. J. C. . R. Ir. Rif.
Davies, Driver H. C. . . . R.F.A.
Davies, Sapper M. . . . . . R.E.
Davis, L/Cpl. J. D. . R. Innis. Fus.
Davis, Sgt. T. . . . . R. Ir. Rif.
Davis, L/Cpl. W. F. . . R. Ir. Rif.
Dawson, Driver J. H. . . R.F.A.
Dean, Gnr. S. . . . . . . R.F.A.
Decker, Pte. J. . . Div. Emp. Coy.
Degnan, Pte. J. . . . R. Innis. Fus.
Dempster, Rfm. A. C. . R. Ir. Rif.
Dempster, Cpl. T. J. . . R.A.M.C.
Dick, Sgt. G. . . . . R. Innis. Fus.
Dick, L/Cpl. I. . . . . R. Ir. Fus.
Dickens, Rfm. G. . . . R. Ir. Rif.
Dickens, Sgt. H. . . . . . R.F.A.
Dickson, Driver G. . . . R.F.A.
Dickson, Sgt. J., *D.C.M.*,
Diver, Pte. P. . . . . R. Innis. Fus.
Diver, L/Cpl. T. . . . . R. Ir. Rif.
Dixon, Sgt. J. . . . . R. Innis. Fus.
Dobbin, Rfm. R. . . . R. Ir. Rif.
Dodwell, L/Cpl. T. . R. Innis. Fus.
Doggart, L/Cpl. H. . . R. Ir. Rif.
Doherty, L/Cpl. H. B. . R. Ir. Rif.
Donaghy, Pte. D. . . . R. Innis. Fus.
Donald, Sgt. J. . . . R. Innis. Fus.
Donald, Cpl. S. . . . R. Innis. Fus.
Donaldson, Sgt. Jas., *D.C.M.*,
 R. Ir. Fus.
Donnell, Pte. S. . . . R. Innis. Fus.
Donnelly, S/Sgt. A. . . R.A.M.C.
Donnelly, Pte. J. J. . R. Innis. Fus.
Donohue, Pte. J. . . . R. Ir. Fus.

Donolly, Pte. E. . . . R.A.M.C.
Doonan, L/Cpl. F. J. . R. Innis. Fus.
Doran, Pte. P. . . . R. Innis. Fus.
Douthert, L/Cpl. J. . R. Innis. Fus.
Downes, Pte. A. . . . R. Innis. Fus.
Driss, Driver H. . . . . . R.F.A.
Dudgeon, Sgt. E. C., *D.C.M.*, R.E.
Duffy, Sgt. W. . . . . R. Ir. Rif.
Duggan, Pte. J. . . . R. Innis. Fus.
Dunn, Rfm. D. . . . . R. Ir. Rif.
Dunn, Cpl. W. . . . . R. Ir. Rif.
Eames, L/Cpl. W. . . R. Innis. Fus.
Eaton, Sgt. J., *D.C.M.* . R. Ir. Rif.
Eccles, L/Cpl. J. . . . R. Ir. Rif.
Eden, L/Cpl. R. . . . . R. Ir. Fus.
Edgar, Sgt. A. . . . . R. Rif. Ir.
Edgar, L/Cpl. J. . . . R. Ir. Rif.
Edwards, Pte. F. . . R. Innis. Fus.
Edwards, Cpl. J. R. . R. Innis. Fus.
Elliff, Cpl. A. . . . . . . R.F.A.
Elliott, Pte. A. . . . . . R.A.S.C.
Elliott, Pte. J. . . . . R. Ir. Fus.
Elliott, L/Cpl. W. . . R. Innis. Fus.
Ervine, Q.M.S. A. G. . . R. Ir. Rif.
Essery, Sgt. A. . . . . . . R.F.A.
Evans, Bdr. C. C. . . . . . R.F.A.
Evans, Sgt. E. . . . . . . R.F.A.
Evans, Sgt. G. . . R. Innis. Fus.
Everett, Cpl. S. . . . . . R.F.A.
Ewart, Rfm. J. . . . . R. Ir. Rif.
Ewing, Sgt. J. A. . . . R. Ir. Rif.
Fallon, Sgt. M. . . . . R. Ir. Fus.
Farnon, Pte. D. . . . . R.A.M.C.
Farquhar, Rfm. J. D. . R. Ir. Rif.
Farr, Pte. R. . . . . R. Innis. Fus.
Farrell, Pte. T. . . R. Innis. Fus.
Fawkes, Cpl. F. . . R. Innis. Fus.
Fawson, Sgt. A. L. . . R. Ir. Rif.
Feeley, Pte. J. H. . . . R.A.M.C.
Fegan, Cpl. J. . . . . R. Ir. Fus.
Felstead, Bdr. F. . . . . . R.F.A.
Ferguson, Rfm. C. . . . R. Ir. Rif.
Ferguson, Gnr. D. . . . . . R.F.A.
Ferguson, Rfm. H. . . . R. Ir. Rif.
Ferguson, L/Cpl. J. . . R. Ir. Rif.
Ferguson, Sgt. R. . . . R. Ir. Fus.
Ferguson, Pte. R. J. . . R. Ir. Fus.
Fergusson, Pte. W. K.,
 R. Innis. Fus.
Fern, L/Cpl. H. . . . R. Innis. Fus.
Ferris, L/Cpl. S. . . . . R. Ir. Rif.
Fillis, Pte. W. . . . R. Innis. Fus.
Finch, Pte. R. . . . . R.A.M.C.
Finlay, L/Cpl. J. . . . R. Ir. Rif.

## MILITARY MEDAL (contd.)

Finlay, Rfm. S. . . . . R. Ir. Rif.
Finlay, Pte. T. . . . R. Innis. Fus.
Finlay, Sgt. W. . . . . R. Ir. Rif.
Fisher, Sgt. D. J. . . . R. Ir. Rif.
Fitt, Pte. P. A. . . . . R. Ir. Fus.
Fitzgerald, Pte. H. . . R.A.M.C.
Fitz-Simon, Cpl. J. . . R. Ir. Rif.
Fitzsimons, Sgt. J. . . R. Ir. Rif.
Flanagan, Pte. H. . . . R. Ir. Fus.
Fleming, Sgt. H. . . . R. Ir. Rif.
Fleming, Cpl. W. . . R. Innis. Fus.
Flexon, Pte. J. . . . . R.A.M.C.
Forbes, Pte. A. . . . R. Innis. Fus.
Forster, Rfm. J. L. . . R. Ir. Rif.
Forsythe, L/Cpl. D. J. . R. Ir. Rif.
Forsythe, Sgt. S. . . R. Innis. Fus.
Foster, Cpl. F. . . . . R. Ir. Fus.
Fowler, Pte. A. . . . . . M.G.C.
Fowler, Bdr. J. . . . . . R.F.A.
Franklin, Pte. A. . . R. Innis. Fus.
Fry, Cpl. W. L. . . . . . . R.E.
Gageby, Sapper W. . . . . R.E.
Gallagher, L/Cpl. J. . R. Innis. Fus.
Galway, Rfm. W. J. . . R. Ir. Rif.
Gamble, Rfm. J. M. . . R. Ir. Rif.
Gardiner, Rfm. R. H. . . R. Ir. Rif.
Gardiner, Sgt. W. . . R. Innis. Fus.
Garland, Bdr. P. A. . . . R.F.A.
Garvin, Pte. G. . . . R. Innis. Fus.
Gascoyne, Rfm. A. . . R. Ir. Rif.
Gayner, L/Cpl. J. J. . . R. Ir. Rif.
George, Pte. W. . . . . R.A.M.C.
Getgood, Sgt. T. . . . R. Ir. Rif.
Gibson, Cpl. E. G. . . R. Ir. Rif.
Gibson, Sgt. J. . . . . R. Ir. Rif.
Gibson, II. Cpl. J. . . . . R.E.
Gibson, Pioneer, W. . . . R.E.
Gibson, L/Cpl. W. J. . R.A.M.C.
Gilchrist, Sgt. R. . . . R. Ir. Rif.
Gildea, Sgt. J. . . . . . . R.E.
Gillanders, Pte. R. . . R. Ir. Fus.
Gillespie, S/Sgt. R. S. . R.A.M.C.
Gilliland, Driver W. . . . . R.E.
Gillmann, Rfm. W. C., *D.C.M.*,
 R. Ir. Rif.
Gilmour, L/Cpl. H. . . R. Ir. Rif.
Gilmour, Sgt. I. . . . . R. Ir. Rif.
Girvan, L/Cpl. D. . . . R. Ir. Rif.
Girvan, Sgt. S. . . . . R. Ir. Rif.
Glasson, Fitter A. J. . . . R.F.A.
Glidie, II. Cpl. G. . . . . R.E.
Glover, L/Cpl. W. . . . R. Ir. Rif.
Godfrey, Pte. E. . . R. Innis. Fus.
Goldstone, Rfm. L. . . R. Ir. Rif.

Gooch, Sgt. W. H. . R. Innis. Fus.
Goodwin, Rfm. R. G. . . R. Ir. Rif.
Goody, Driver A. . . . . R.F.A.
Gordon, Cpl. W. V. . . R.A.M.C.
Gowdy, Col.-Sgt. J. . . R. Ir. Rif.
Gowdy, Sapper J. . . . . . R.E.
Gowdy, L/Cpl. R. . . . R. Ir. Rif.
Gowdy, II. Cpl. W. J. . . . R.E.
Gowing, Cpl. E. . . . . . . R.E.
Graham, L/Cpl. J. . . . R. Ir. Fus.
Graham, Rfm. J. . . . R. Ir. Rif.
Graham, L/Cpl. J. R., R. Innis. Fus.
Graham, B.S.M. R. D. . . R.F.A.
Grainger, Sgt. R. . . . . . R.E.
Grange, Sgt. R. . . . . . R.F.A.
Gray, L/Cpl. J. . . . R. Innis. Fus.
Gray, Rfm. J. . . . . R. Ir. Rif.
Gray, Sgt. P. . . . . R. Innis. Fus.
Gray, L/Cpl. R. J. . . . R. Ir. Rif.
Gray, Rfm. W. . . . . R. Ir. Rif.
Greanery, Rfm. B. J. . . R. Ir. Rif.
Greaves, Sgt. J. . . . R. Innis. Fus.
Green, Driver F. . . . . . R.F.A.
Green, Cpl. R. . . . . R. Innis. Fus.
Greene, C.S.M. J. . . . R. Ir. Rif.
Greenfield, Pte. K. S. . R.A.M.C.
Greenwood, Cpl. J. E. . R.A.M.C.
Greenwood, Cpl. T. . . R. Ir. Rif.
Greer, Sgt, J. . . . . . . M.G.C.
Gregory, Gnr. A. . . . . R.F.A.
Gregory, L/Cpl. H. . R. Innis. Fus.
Griffiths, Pte. D. . . R. Innis. Fus.
Grigg, L/Cpl. W., *D.C.M.*,R. Ir. Fus.
Groom, Rfm. W. . . . R. Ir. Rif.
Guest, Fitter D. R. . . . R.F.A.
Hadaway, Sgt. W. . . R. Ir. Rif.
Hagan, Bdr. J. . . . . . R.F.A.
Haire, L/Cpl. S. . . . R. Innis. Fus.
Hall, Pte. A. . . . . R. Innis. Fus.
Hall, Rfm. J. . . . . . R. Ir. Rif.
Hall, Sgt. R. . . . . . R.A.M.C.
Hallett, Rfm. W. . . . R. Ir. Rif.
Hamill, Cpl. T. J. . . . . . R.E.
Hamilton, Pte. J. . . . R. Ir. Fus.
Hamilton. II. Cpl. J. C. . . R.E.
Hamilton, L/Cpl. J. J. . . . R.E.
Hamilton, Rfm. N. . . R. Ir. Rif.
Hamilton, Sgt. R. . . R. Innis. Fus.
Hamilton, Sgt. W. D., R. Innis. Fus.
Hands, Bdr. McD. H. . . R.F.A.
Hanna, C.S.M. J. . . R. Innis. Fus.
Hanson, Cpl. J. H. . . . R. Ir. Rif.
Harbinson, Sgt. J., *D.C.M.*,
 R. Ir. Rif.

# HONOURS AND AWARDS

## MILITARY MEDAL (contd.)

|  |  |
|---|---|
| Harbinson, Pte. R. | R. Innis. Fus. |
| Harbinson, Pte. G. | R. Innis. Fus. |
| Hardy, Rfm. J. | R. Ir. Rif. |
| Harkness, Sgt. R. | R. Innis. Fus. |
| Harper, Sgt. M. T. | R. Ir. Rif. |
| Harris, B.S.M. H. | R. Innis. Fus. |
| Harris, C.Q.M.S. H. F. B., | R. Ir. Rif. |
| Harris, Gnr. J. R. | R.F.A. |
| Harrison, Pte. J. B. | R. Ir. Fus. |
| Harrison, Cpl. J. D. | R. Ir. Rif. |
| Harrison, C.Q.M.S. S., *D.C.M.*, | R. Ir. Rif. |
| Harrison, Rfm. T. J. | R. Ir. Rif. |
| Harte, Pte. J. | R. Innis. Fus. |
| Harvey, Sgt. J. | R. Ir. Rif. |
| Harvey, L/Cpl. W. | R. Ir. Rif. |
| Haslett, Cpl. L., *D.C.M.*, | R. Innis. Fus. |
| Hassan, L/Cpl. M. | R. Innis. Fus. |
| Hassard, Pte. A. | R. Innis. Fus. |
| Hatton, Gnr. G. W. | R.F.A. |
| Hawkins, Sgt. W. | R. Ir. Rif. |
| Hayes, Gnr. J. | R.F.A. |
| Hayes, Sapper W. | R.E. |
| Hayes, Gnr. W. J. | R.F.A. |
| Heaney, Pte. J. | R. Ir. Fus. |
| Heavans, Pte. W. | R. Innis. Fus. |
| Helps, Pte. A. S. | R. Ir. Rif. |
| Henderson, Rfm. W. | R. Ir. Rif. |
| Henry, Sgt. J. A. | R. Ir. Fus. |
| Henry, Rfm. W. | R. Ir. Rif. |
| Herald, Sgt. P. | R. Innis. Fus. |
| Herd, Bdr. A. | R.F.A. |
| Herron, Sgt. W. | R.E. |
| Hetherington, Sgt. H., | R. Innis. Fus. |
| Heywood, Sgt. W. | R.F.A. |
| Higgins, Sgt. H. | R. Ir. Rif. |
| Higgins, Driver W. G. | R.E. |
| Highman, Cpl. A. J. | R. Ir. Rif. |
| Hildersley, L/Cpl. A. | R. Ir. Rif. |
| Hill, L/Cpl. W. G. E. | R. Ir. Rif. |
| Hill, Bdr. W. H. | R.F.A. |
| Hirst, L/Cpl. E. T. | R. Ir. Rif. |
| Hirst, Bdr. J. W. | R.F.A. |
| Hislop, Sgt. S. | R. Innis. Fus. |
| Hoare, Pte. W. | R. Ir. Fus. |
| Hodgen, L/Cpl. J. | R. Ir. Rif. |
| Hodges, Rfm. H. | R. Ir. Rif. |
| Hogg, L/Cpl. G. | R. Innis. Fus. |
| Hogg, Rfm. S. | R. Ir. Rif. |
| Holland, Sgt. J. | R.F.A. |
| Holmes, Sgt. J. | R.E. |
| Holmes, Pte. J. G. | R.A.M.C. |
| Homersham, Sgt. F., *D.C.M.*, | R. Ir. Fus. |
| Hope, L/Cpl. J. R. | R. Ir. Rif. |
| Hopper, Cpl. J. | R. Innis. Fus. |
| Hornby, Cpl. H. | R.F.A. |
| Hoskins, Sgt. W. | R.F.A. |
| House, Rfm. W. | R. Ir. Rif. |
| Houston, C.S.M. J. | R. Ir. Rif. |
| Hoy, Rfm. W. | R. Ir. Rif. |
| Hudson, Rfm. R. G. | R. Ir. Rif. |
| Hughes, Rfm. C. | R. Ir. Rif. |
| Hughes, Sgt. J., *D.C.M.*, | R. Ir. Fus. |
| Hughes, Pte. J. F. | R. Innis. Fus. |
| Hughes, Sgt. W. | R. Ir. Rif. |
| Hugheston, Rfm. P. | R. Ir. Rif. |
| Hull, Pte. A. E. | R. Ir. Rif. |
| Hull, Sapper H. | R.E. |
| Hume, Sgt. J., *D.C.M.* | M.G.C. |
| Humphrey, Cpl. W. | R. Ir. Rif. |
| Humphreys, Sgt. R. | R. Ir. Rif. |
| Humpherys, Rfm. W. | R. Ir. Rif. |
| Hunt, Driver A. | R.F.A. |
| Hunt, Bdr. H. E. | R.F.A. |
| Hunt, Pte. J. | R.A.M.C. |
| Hunter, Cpl. B. | R. Innis. Fus. |
| Hunter, Sgt. J. | R. Ir. Rif. |
| Hunter, Pte. J. | R. Innis. Fus. |
| Hunter, Sgt. J. A., *D.C.M.*, | R. Innis. Fus. |
| Hunter, Sgt. S. J. | R. Innis. Fus. |
| Hutcheon, Cpl. A. | R.F.A. |
| Hutchinson, Pte. J. | R. Innis. Fus. |
| Hutchinson, Rfm. S. | R. Ir. Rif. |
| Ingham, Pte. R. | R. Ir. Fus. |
| Inkster, Pte. J. | R. Innis. Fus. |
| Ireland, Rfm. E. | R. Ir. Rif. |
| Irvine, Sgt. J. | R. Innis. Fus. |
| Irwin, Sgt. F. | R. Innis. Fus. |
| Irwin, L/Cpl. G. | R. Ir. Rif. |
| Irwin, Sgt. H. E. | R.F.A. |
| Irwin, Sgt. R. | R. Innis. Fus. |
| Irwin, Pte. R. | R. Innis. Fus. |
| Jack, Sgt. W. | R.F.A. |
| Jackson, Cpl. A. H., *D.C.M.*, | R.E. |
| Jackson, L/Cpl. E. | R. Ir. Rif. |
| Jackson, Sgt. J. | R. Innis. Fus. |
| Jackson, L/Cpl. R. | R. Ir. Rif. |
| Jackson, Sgt. V. | R.E. |
| James, Rfm. F. C. | R. Ir. Rif. |
| James, Rfm. F. L. | R. Ir. Rif. |
| James, Sapper J. | R.E. |
| Jeacock, L/Cpl. E. E. | R. Ir. Rif. |
| Jeffcott, Sgt. L. J. | R. Ir. Rif. |
| Jefferies, Gnr. J. | R.F.A. |

## MILITARY MEDAL (contd.)

|  |  |
|---|---|
| Jeffrey, Pte. R. | R. Innis. Fus. |
| Jeffries, Pte. A. | M.G.C. |
| Jeffries, II. Cpl. H. | R.E. |
| Jelley, Rfm. W. J. | R. Ir. Rif. |
| Jennings, L/Cpl. F. | R. Ir. Fus. |
| Johnston, L/Cpl. A. | R. Ir. Rif. |
| Johnston, L/Cpl. F. | R. Innis. Fus. |
| Johnston, Sgt. G. | R. Innis. Fus. |
| Johnston, Sgt. G. | R. Ir. Rif. |
| Johnston, L/Cpl. G. M. | R. Ir. Rif. |
| Johnston, Sgt. R. | R. Ir Rif. |
| Johnston, Cpl. S. | R. Innis. Fus. |
| Johnston, L/Cpl. S. J. | R. Ir. Rif. |
| Johnston, Pte. W. | R. Innis. Fus. |
| Johnston, Sgt. W. J. | R. Ir. Rif. |
| Johnstone, Sgt. R. | R. Ir. Fus. |
| Jones, Cpl. D. | R. Innis. Fus. |
| Jones, Pte. F. | R. Innis. Fus. |
| Jones, Rfm. J. | R. Ir. Rif. |
| Jones, Rfm. R. | R. Ir. Rif. |
| Jordan, Rfm. B. | R. Ir. Rif. |
| Joyce, L/Cpl. N. | R. Innis. Fus. |
| Kane, Pte. R. | R. Innis. Fus. |
| Kealy, L/Cpl. S. | R. Innis. Fus. |
| Kearns, L/Cpl. J. | R. Ir. Fus. |
| Keeling, L/Cpl. G. | R. Ir. Rif. |
| Keir, Cpl. A. M. | R.E. |
| Keith, L/Cpl. A. | R. Ir. Rif. |
| Kelly, Rfm. D. | R. Ir. Rif. |
| Kelly, Bdr. D. E. | R.F.A. |
| Kelly, Pte. H. | R. Ir. Fus. |
| Kelly, Rfm. J. | R. Ir. Rif. |
| Kelly, Pte. P. | R. Ir. Fus. |
| Kelly, Sgt. W. | R. Ir. Fus. |
| Kelly, Pte. W. | R. Innis. Fus. |
| Kelso, Sgt. F. | R. Ir. Rif. |
| Kemp, C.Q.M.S. H. | R. Innis. Fus. |
| Kennedy, Pte. A. | R.A.M.C. |
| Kennedy, Pte. J. | R. Ir. Fus. |
| Kennedy, Rfm. J. | R. Ir. Rif. |
| Kennedy, Driver W. | R.A.S.C. |
| Kenny, Sgt. W. H. | R. Innis. Fus. |
| Kerr, Sgt. T. | R. Ir. Rif. |
| Keys, Pte. T. | R. Innis. Fus. |
| Kidd, Rfm. E. | R. Ir. Rif. |
| Kidd, Sapper H. | R.E. |
| King, Sgt. A. | R.F.A. |
| King, Cpl. G. | R.E. |
| King, Rfm. R. | R. Ir. Rif. |
| King, Sgt. R. H. | R.E. |
| Kinghorn, Cpl. W. N. | R. Ir. Rif. |
| Kirby, C.S.M. L. | R. Innis. Fus. |
| Kirkpatrick, Cpl. J. | R. Ir. Rif. |
| Knaggs, Cpl. W. | R. Ir. Fus. |
| Knight, Rfm. T. | R. Ir. Rif. |
| Knox, L/Cpl. W. G. | R. Innis. Fus. |
| Kyle, Cpl. R. | R. Ir. Rif. |
| Laird, Sgt. W. | R. Innis. Fus. |
| Lally, Sgt. J. | R. Innis. Fus. |
| Lambert, Sgt. W. | R. Ir. Fus. |
| Lanigan, Sgt. J. | R. Ir. Rif. |
| Larmour, Rfm. A. | R. Ir. Rif. |
| Laverty, Sgt. S. | R. Ir. Rif. |
| Lavery, L/Cpl. W. | R. Innis. Fus. |
| Lawrence, Sgt. C. | R. Ir. Rif. |
| Leathern, Cpl. J. | R. Ir. Rif. |
| Letwine, Pte. L. | R. Ir. Fus. |
| Lecky, Pte. W. | R. Innis. Fus. |
| Letters, Pte. R. | R. Ir. Rif. |
| Lewins, Sgt. T. | R. Innis. Fus. |
| Lindberg, Pte. R. | R. Ir. Rif. |
| Lindsay, Pte. J. | M.G.C. |
| Lindsay, Cpl. J. | R. Ir. Rif. |
| Lindsay, Rfm. W. | R. Ir. Rif. |
| Little, Pte. W. | R. Innis. Fus. |
| Littlebury, Pte. W. | R. Ir. Fus. |
| Lloyd, Cpl. R. W. | R. Innis. Fus. |
| Lochray, Pte. D. | R.A.M.C. |
| Long, Sgt. J. | R.E. |
| Long, Sgt. J. E. | R. Ir. Fus. |
| Long, Cpl. W. E. | R. Innis. Fus. |
| Longhurst, L/Cpl. J. F. | R. Ir. Rif. |
| Longhurst, Sgt. O. | R. Innis. Fus. |
| Longstaff, L/Cpl. J. W. | R. Innis. Fus. |
| Lough, L/Cpl. F. | R. Ir. Rif. |
| Loughlin, Pte. D. | R. Innis. Fus. |
| Lowden, Rfm. W. | R. Ir. Rif. |
| Lowe, Sgt. J. | R.A.M.C. |
| Lowens, Rfm. J. E. | R. Ir. Rif. |
| Lowry, Rfm. G. | R. Ir. Rif. |
| Lowry, Cpl. S., D.C.M. | R.E. |
| Lowther, L/Cpl. M. | R. Innis. Fus. |
| Lucas, C.S.M. R., D.C.M. | R. Ir. Fus. |
| Lucas, Rfm. R. | R. Ir. Rif. |
| Lumsden, Pte. J. | R. Innis. Fus. |
| Lunny, Pte. J. | R. Innis. Fus. |
| Lusty, L/Cpl. R. | R. Innis. Fus. |
| Lyle, Sgt J. | R. Ir. Rif. |
| Lynn, Pte. W. J. | R. Ir. Fus. |
| Lytle, L/Cp¹. D. | R. Innis. Fus. |
| M'Alpine, Sapper C. | R.E. |
| McAtamney, Pte. W. | R. Innis. Fus. |
| McAteer, Rfm. J. | R. Ir. Fus. |
| Macauley, Sapper R. | R.E. |
| McBratney, Rfm. W. | R. Ir. Rif. |
| McCall, L/Cpl. W. | R. Ir. Fus. |

# HONOURS AND AWARDS

## MILITARY MEDAL (contd.)

| | |
|---|---|
| McCallum, Pte. W. . R. Innis. Fus. | McFeeters, Cpl. G. . . . . . R.E. |
| McCann, Cpl. F. . . . . R.A.M.C. | McFerran, Sgt. J. . . . R. Ir. Rif. |
| McCann, Bdr. P. . . . . R.F.A. | McGahey, L/Cpl. R. . R. Innis. Fus. |
| McCarley, Pte. W. . . R. Ir. Fus. | McGarrel, Rfm. W. . . R. Ir. Rif. |
| McCarthy, Rfm. T. . . R. Ir. Rif. | McGee, Pte. P. . . . R. Innis. Fus. |
| McCartney, Pte. H. . R. Innis. Fus. | McGirr, Pte. J. . . . R. Innis. Fus. |
| McCaskell, Cpl. A. . . R. Innis. Fus. | McGonagle, L/Cpl. S., R. Innis. Fus. |
| McCaughan, L/Cpl. G. L., R. Ir. Rif. | McGookin, II. Cpl. D. . . . R.E. |
| McChesney, Rfm. S. . . R. Ir. Rif. | McGough, Sgt. J. G. . . R. Ir. Rif. |
| McClatchey, Rfm. T. . R. Ir. Rif. | McGovern, Cpl. A. . . R. Innis. Fus. |
| McClay, Cpl. T. . . . R. Innis. Fus. | McGowan, Cpl. A. . . . R. Ir. Rif. |
| McClay, Cpl. W. . . R. Innis. Fus. | McGowan, Pte. A. . . R. Innis. Fus. |
| McClean, Cpl. D. . . . R. Ir. Rif. | McGrann, Rfm. D. . . R. Ir. Rif. |
| McClean, Sapper E. . . . . R.E. | MacGrath, Sgt. J. . . . . . R.E. |
| McClean, II. Cpl. G. H. . . . R.E. | McGready, Pte. D. . . R. Innis. Fus. |
| McClelland, Pte. G. . . R. Ir. Fus. | McGreghan, Rfm. H. . R. Ir. Rif. |
| McClelland, Pte. T. A. . R. Ir. Fus. | McGuinness, Pte. J. . R. Innis. Fus. |
| McClements, Cpl. A. . . R. Ir. Rif. | McIlroy, L/Cpl. T. . . R. Innis. Fus. |
| McClintock, Sgt. R. J., R. Innis. Fus. | McIlveen, Sgt. J. . . . R. Ir. Rif. |
| McClintock, L/Cpl. S. . R. Ir. Rif. | McIlveen, Rfm. J. . . . R. Ir. Rif. |
| McClintock, L/Cpl. T., R. Innis. Fus. | McIlwaine, L/Cpl. J. . R. Innis. Fus. |
| McClune, Sgt. J. . . . R. Ir. Rif. | McIlwaine, L/Cpl. S. . R. Innis. Fus. |
| McCluney, Pte. H. . . R. Ir. Fus. | McIlwaine, L/Cpl. S. . . R. Ir. Rif. |
| McClung, L/Cpl. R. . . R. Ir. Rif. | McIlwrath, Cpl. H. . . R. Ir. Rif. |
| McConky, Sgt. C. . . . R. Ir. Rif. | McIlwrath, Cpl. S., *D.C.M.* . R.E. |
| McConnell, L/Cpl. G. . R. Ir. Rif. | McIntosh, Gnr. T. . . . . R.F.A. |
| McConnell, Sapper G. . . . R.E. | McIntyre, Sgt. D. J. . R. Innis. Fus. |
| McConnell, Cpl. H. . . R. Ir. Rif. | McIntyre, L/Cpl. J. . R. Innis. Fus. |
| McConnell, Pte. J. . . R. Innis. Fus. | McIntyre, Sapper J. . . . . R.E. |
| McConnell, Rfm. R. J. . R. Ir. Rif. | McKane, Sapper A. . . . . R.E. |
| McConnell, L/Cpl. S. . . R. Ir. Rif. | McKay, L/Cpl. A. . . . R. Ir. Rif. |
| McCormack, Sgt. J. . . . R.F.A. | McKay, Sgt. R. . . . . R.A.M.C. |
| McCormick, Pte. R. J. . R. Ir. Fus. | McKay, Pte. W. . . . R.A.M.C. |
| McCormick, Pte. W. . . R.A.M.C. | McKee, Sapper J. . . . . . R.E. |
| McCormick, L/Cpl. W. J., R. Ir. Rif. | McKee, Rfm. J. (11/6658) R. Ir. Rif. |
| McCoubrey, L/Cpl. S. . R. Ir. Rif. | McKee, Rfm. J. (15436), R. Ir. Rif. |
| McCoy, Pte. W. J. . . R.A.M.C. | McKee, L/Cpl. R. . . . R. Ir. Rif. |
| McCrea, L/Cpl. W. . . R. Ir. Rif. | McKeaver, Sgt. S. . . . R. Ir. Rif. |
| McCrum, Rfm. J. . . . R. Ir. Rif. | McKeown, Cpl. G. . . R. Innis. Fus. |
| McCullough, R.S.M. J. . R. Ir. Fus. | McKeown, Cpl. J. . . . R. Ir. Rif. |
| McCullough, L/Cpl. J. F., R. Ir. Fus. | McKeown, Cpl. W. . R. Innis. Fus. |
| McCullough, Rfm. W. . R. Ir. Rif. | Mackintosh, L/Cpl. J. . R. Ir. Fus. |
| McDermott, Pte. J. . R. Innis. Fus. | McKnight, Rfm. H. . . R. Ir. Rif. |
| McDermott, Cpl. W. J. . R. Ir. Rif. | McKnight, Gnr. S. . . . . R.F.A. |
| McDonald, Pte. J. . . . R. Ir. Rif. | McKnight, L/Cpl. W. J., R. Ir. Rif. |
| McDonald, Rfm. J. . . R. Ir. Rif. | McKnight, L/Cpl. W. T. . . R.E. |
| McDonald, Pte. T. . . R. Innis. Fus. | McLaren, L/Cpl. J. . . . . R.E. |
| McDowell, Pte. A. . . R. Innis. Fus. | McLarty, Rfm. F. . . . R. Ir. Rif. |
| McDowell, Sgt. J. . . . R. Ir. Rif. | McLaughlin, Rfm. J. . . R. Ir. Rif. |
| McEbury, Pte. J. T. . R. Innis. Fus. | McLaughlin, L/Cpl. M. . R. Ir. Fus. |
| McElroy, Pte. J. . . . R. Innis. Fus. | McLaughlin, Rfm. J. . . R. Ir. Rif. |
| McFaddon, L/Cpl. D. . . . R.E. | McMartin, Rfm. V. . . R. Ir. Rif. |
| McFall, Sgt. T. . . . . R. Ir. Rif. | McMillen, Rfm. W. . . R. Ir. Rif. |
| McFarland, Sapper A. . . . R.E. | McMullan, L/Cpl. A. . R. Innis. Fus. |

## MILITARY MEDAL (contd.)

McMullan, Rfm. D. . . R. Ir. Rif.
McNabney, Sgt. J., *D.C.M.* . . R.E.
McNally, C.S.M. W. .R. Innis. Fus.
McNamee, Pte. J. F. . R. Innis. Fus.
McNeill, Sgt. R. . . . R. Innis. Fus.
McNerlin, Cpl. W. J. H.,
                        R. Innis. Fus.
McNutt, L/Cpl. J. . . R. Innis. Fus.
McPhail, Cpl. J. . . . . . . R.E.
McVicker, Cpl. J. W. . . . R.E.
McWhirter, Rfm. J. . . R. Ir. Rif.
Magee, Rfm. R. . . . . R. Ir. Rif.
Magee, Sgt. W. . . . . R. Ir. Rif.
Magee, Pte. W. G. . .R. Innis. Fus.
Mager, Sgt. H. C. . . . . R.F.A.
Magill, Pte. M. . . . R. Innis. Fus.
Magill, Sgt. W. A. . . . R. Ir. Rif.
Maginnis, C.S.M. A. . R. Ir. Rif.
Magowan, Sgt. J. . . . R. Ir. Rif.
Magowan, Driver R. . . R.A.S.C.
Magowan, Pte. W. . .R. Innis. Fus.
Mahaffy, Rfm. A. . . . R. Ir. Rif.
Makinson, Cpl. A. . . R. Ir. Fus.
Maltby, Cpl. H. . . . . . R.F.A.
Manderson, Sgt. E. A. . R. Ir. Rif.
Mann, L/Cpl. A. . . . . R. Ir. Rif.
Mannis, Sgt. G. . . . . . R. Ir. Rif.
Markin, Rfm. A. W. . . R. Ir. Rif.
Marks, Sgt. M. H. . . . . R.F.A.
Marsden, Pte. P. . . . . . M.G.C.
Marshall, Rfm. A. . . . R. Ir. Rif.
Marshall, Pte. J. W. . R. Ir. Fus.
Marshall, Sapper R. . . . . R.E.
Martin, Sapper L. R. . . . R.E.
Maskery, Sgt. I. M. . . . R.F.A.
Matier, Sgt. T. . . . . R. Ir. Rif.
Matthews, Pte. A. . .R. Innis. Fus.
Matthews, L/Cpl. T. . . R. Ir. Rif.
Maude, Rfm. E. E. . . . R. Ir. Rif.
Maxwell, Rfm. B. . . . R. Ir. Rif.
Maxwell, Rfm. J. . . . R. Ir. Rif.
May, L/Cpl. N. . . . . R. Ir. Rif.
Maybury, L/Cpl. D. .R. Innis. Fus.
Mayes, Gnr. W. . . . . . R.F.A.
Meaney, Cpl. T. . . . . R. Ir. Rif.
Meeke, Pte. J. . . . R. Innis. Fus.
Megaghy, Pte. R. . .R. Innis. Fus.
Meharg, Rfm. R. . . . R. Ir. Rif.
Mellon, Rfm. R. . . . . R. Ir. Rif.
Mendon, Pte. J. . . .R. Innis. Fus.
Merritt, Gnr. J. . . . . . R.F.A.
Millar, L/Cpl. A. . . . R. Ir. Rif.
Millar, Cpl. G. . . . . R.A.M.C.
Millen, Pte. W. . . .R. Innis. Fus.

Miller, Pte. G. F. . . . R. Ir. Fus.
Miller, Rfm. J. (40060) . R. Ir. Rif.
Miller, Rfm. J. (9/778) . R. Ir. Rif.
Mills, Sgt. E. P. . . . .R. Innis. Fus.
Mills, Sgt. L. . . . . . . R. Ir. Rif.
Milne, Sgt. E. . . . . . R. Ir. Rif.
Milner, Sapper W. . . . . R.E.
Minford, Rfm. A. . . . R. Ir. Rif.
Minnis, Sgt. D. . . . . R. Ir. Rif.
Minnis, Sgt. W. . . . . . . R.E.
Minter, Rfm. F. G. . . R. Ir. Rif.
Mitchell, Pte. D. . .R. Innis. Fus.
Mitchell, Sgt. G. . . . R. Ir. Rif.
Mitchell, Sgt. J. . . .R. Innis. Fus.
Mitchell, Pte. J. E. . . R.A.M.C.
Mitchell, Pte. R. . .R. Innis. Fus.
Mitchell, Sapper W. . . . R.E.
Mitchell, Sgt. W. J. . . R. Ir. Fus.
Mitchen, Rfm. C. . . . R. Ir. Rif.
Mitcheson, Sgt. J. . . . . R.E.
Moag, L/Cpl. D. . . . R. Ir. Rif.
Moffatt, S/Sgt. D. . . . R.A.M.C.
Moffatt, C.S.M. W., *M.C.*, R. Ir. Rif.
Monger, Pte. F. J. . .R. Innis. Fus.
Montgomery, Sgt. G. . . R. Ir. Rif.
Montgomery, L/Cpl. J. . R. Ir. Rif.
Montgomery, Pte. J. .R. Innis. Fus.
Montgomery, Sgt. R. . R. Innis. Fus.
Moore, Rfm. A. . . . . R. Ir. Rif.
Moore, L/Cpl. B. . .R. Innis. Fus.
Moore, Cpl. E. . . . . R. Ir. Rif.
Moore, Cpl. H. . . . . . . R.E.
Moore, L/Cpl. J. . . . . . R.E.
Moore, Sapper J. . . . . . R.E.
Moore, Pte. L. . . .R. Innis. Fus.
Moore, Sgt. R. . . . . R. Ir. Rif.
Moran, Pte. J. . . . . R. Ir. Fus.
Morgan, Sgt. W. H. . . R. Ir. Rif.
Moorhead, Sgt. W. . . R. Ir. Fus.
Morrison, Rfm. J. . . . R. Ir. Rif.
Morrison, Pte. J. . . . R. Ir. Fus.
Morrow, L/Cpl. J. . . . R. Ir. Rif.
Morrow, Pte. J. . . . . . M.G.C.
Morton, Sgt. J. . . . . R.A.M.C.
Morton, Pte. J. . . . . R. Ir. Fus.
Morton, Cpl. T. . . . . R. Ir. Rif.
Morton, Pte. T. . . . . R. Ir. Fus.
Morton, Sgt. W. . . . R. Ir. Rif.
Muir, L/Cpl. W. . . .R. Innis. Fus.
Mulholland, Sgt. G. . . R. Ir. Fus.
Munro, L/Cpl. G. . . . . M.G.C.
Murkin, Rfm. O. J. . . R. Ir. Rif.
Murray, Rfm. A. . . . R. Ir. Rif.
Murray, Sgt. R. . . .R. Innis. Fus.

## HONOURS AND AWARDS

### MILITARY MEDAL (contd.)

| | |
|---|---|
| Murtagh, Pte. M. | R. Ir. Fus. |
| Mycock, Pte. F. | R. Innis. Fus. |
| Myers, Pte. C. | R. Ir. Fus. |
| Nash, Pte. E. M. | R. Ir. Fus. |
| Nash, Bdr. J. | R.F.A. |
| Neeson, Pte. J. | R. Ir. Fus. |
| Neill, L/Cpl. A. | R. Ir. Rif. |
| Neill, Pte. R. | R. Innis. Fus. |
| Neill, Pte. S. | R.A.M.C. |
| Nelson, L/Cpl. A. E. | R. Ir. Rif. |
| Nelson, Rfm. N. S. | R. Ir. Rif. |
| Nelson, Rfm. T. A. | R. Ir. Rif. |
| Nesbit, Sgt. G. | R. Ir. Fus. |
| Nesbitt, Sgt. A., *D.C.M.*, | R. Innis. Fus. |
| Nevins, Cpl. M. J. | R. Ir. Rif. |
| Newman, C.Q.M.S. G., | R. Innis. Fus. |
| Newton, II. Cpl. A. E. | R.E. |
| Nichol, Cpl. W. | R. Innis. Fus. |
| Nicholson, Sgt. A. | R.E. |
| Nightingale, Cpl. G. | R.F.A. |
| Noble, Pte. J. | R. Innis. Fus. |
| Noone, L/Cpl. E. | R. Ir. Rif. |
| Norris, Pte. R. | R. Ir. Fus. |
| Nutt, L/Cpl. J. | R. Ir. Rif. |
| O'Brien, Rfm. J. | R. Ir. Rif. |
| O'Hanlon, L/Cpl. J. | R. Ir. Rif. |
| O'Hara, Sgt. J. | R. Innis. Fus. |
| Oliver, Rfm. H. | R. Ir. Rif. |
| O'Neill, Pte. E. | R. Innis. Fus. |
| Onion, Pte. H. | R. Innis. Fus. |
| Orbinson, L/Cpl. J. A. | R. Ir. Rif. |
| Orgill, Pte. F. | R. Innis. Fus. |
| Orgles, L/Cpl. J. E. | R. Ir. Rif. |
| Owens, Sapper A. | R.E. |
| Owens, L/Cpl. A. E. | R.E. |
| Owens, Sgt. P. | R. Ir. Rif. |
| Owens, L/Cpl. P. | R. Innis. Fus. |
| Owens, Sgt. T. | M.G.C. |
| Ownsworth, Cpl. A. | R.F.A. |
| Pacey, Sgt. L. | R.F.A. |
| Packer, Pte. W. L. | R. Ir. Fus. |
| Padley, Pioneer E. M. | R.E. |
| Painter, Gnr. S. F. | R.F.A. |
| Pallister, Rfm. H. T. | R. Ir. Rif. |
| Palmer, Sgt. E. | R.A.M.C. |
| Palmer, Bdr. S. R. H. | R.F.A. |
| Palmer, Sgt. W. H. | R. Ir. Rif. |
| Parke, Pte. H. | R. Ir. Fus. |
| Parke, Sgt. J. | R. Innis. Fus. |
| Parker, Rfm. S. | R. Ir. Rif. |
| Parker, Driver V. G. | R.F.A. |
| Parkhill, Sapper J. | R.E. |
| Parks, Rfm. S. | R. Ir. Rif. |
| Patchett, Rfm. H. | R. Ir. Rif. |
| Patterson, Rfm. J. | R. Ir. Rif. |
| Patterson, Pte. R. | R.A.M.C. |
| Patterson, Rfm. R. | R. Ir. Rif. |
| Patterson, Rfm. R. B. | R. Ir. Rif. |
| Patterson, Rfm. T. | R. Ir. Rif. |
| Patton, Rfm. W. R. | R. Ir. Rif. |
| Paul, Pte. J. | R. Ir. Fus. |
| Payne, Pte. C. | R. Innis. Fus. |
| Payne, Bdr. C. O. | R.F.A. |
| Paysden, Rfm. G. | R. Ir. Rif. |
| Peake, Cpl. W. J. | R. Ir. Rif. |
| Pearce, Sapper A. | R.E. |
| Pearson, Pte. F. | R. Innis. Fus. |
| Peers, Pte. A. | R. Ir. Rif. |
| Peet, Pte. F. J. | M.G.C. |
| Pelan, Sapper M. | R.E. |
| Peters, Sgt. H. C. | M.G.C. |
| Phear, Sgt. H. W. | R.F.A. |
| Phillips, Pte. E. | R. Innis. Fus. |
| Phillips, Sapper R. C. | R.E. |
| Phoenix, II. Cpl. H. | R.E. |
| Pickis, Gnr. S. | R.F.A. |
| Pikeman, C.S.M. S. A., *D.C.M.*, | R. Ir. Rif. |
| Pinion, Driver J. | R.F.A. |
| Pitt, Cpl. R. B. | R.F.A. |
| Platt, Sgt. W. | R.F.A. |
| Plumley, Cpl. R. | R. Innis. Fus. |
| Pollock, Cpl. J. | R. Innis. Fus. |
| Pollock, L/Cpl. J. | R. Ir. Rif. |
| Pollock, Sgt. R. | R. Innis. Fus. |
| Powell, Bdr. H. | R.F.A. |
| Preston, Rfm. A. | R. Ir. Rif. |
| Price, Rfm. F. J. | R. Ir. Rif. |
| Prince, Sgt. J. E. | R.F.A. |
| Proctor, Rfm. R. | R. Ir. Rif. |
| Prole, Pte. R. | R.A.M.C. |
| Pue, L/Cpl. A. | R. Ir. Rif. |
| Pulford, Sgt. A. | R.E. |
| Pulford, Sgt. H. | R.E. |
| Pulham, Gnr. W. F. | R.F.A. |
| Purdy, Sgt. W. | M.G.C. |
| Pye, Pte. E. | R. Ir. Fus. |
| Quail, Rfm. W. | R. Ir. Rif. |
| Quigley, Rfm. H. | R. Ir. Rif. |
| Quinn, Cpl. W. F. | R.A.M.C. |
| Radcliffe, Pte. J. W. | R. Innis. Fus. |
| Rainbird, II. Cpl. H. H. | R.E. |
| Ramsay, Pte. R. | R. Innis. Fus. |
| Ramsay, Rfm. W. J. | R. Ir. Rif. |
| Ranscombe, Sgt. W. | R.F.A. |
| Ratcliffe, L/Cpl. L. | R. Innis. Fus. |
| Rattray, Bdr. A. | R.F.A. |

## MILITARY MEDAL (contd.)

|  |  |
|---|---|
| Ray, Rfm. A. W. | R. Ir. Rif. |
| Reed, Rfm. A. C. | R. Ir. Rif. |
| Reid, Sgt. E. | R. Ir. Rif. |
| Reid, Pte. H. | R.A.M.C. |
| Reid, Sgt. P. H. | R. Ir. Rif. |
| Reid, Rfm. S. | R. Ir. Rif. |
| Remington, Gnr. R. | R.F.A. |
| Rennick, L/Cpl. H. | R. Innis. Fus. |
| Reynolds, Rfm. J. | R. Ir. Rif. |
| Richardson. Pte. A. | R. Innis. Fus. |
| Rickwood, Rfm. E. | R. Ir. Rif. |
| Riddle, L/Cpl. J. | R. Innis. Fus. |
| Riley, Rfm. J. | R. Ir. Rif. |
| Ringland, Sgt. J. | R. Innis. Fus. |
| Roberts, Rfm. S. | R. Ir. Rif. |
| Robertson, Sgt. F. | R. Ir. Rif. |
| Robertson, Cpl. R. | R.E. |
| Robinson, Cpl. C. | R. Ir. Fus. |
| Robinson, Cpl. E. | R. Ir. Fus. |
| Robinson, Pte. P. F. G. | M.G.C. |
| Robson, Sgt. W. | R.E. |
| Robson, Cpl. W. | R. Innis. Fus. |
| Roe, Sgt. C., *D.C.M.* | R. Ir. Fus. |
| Roffey, Gnr. S. | R.F.A. |
| Rogers, Sgt. | M.G.C. |
| Rogers, Pte. A. | M.G.C. |
| Rogers, Pte. F. C. | R. Ir. Fus. |
| Rogers, Pte. J. | R. Ir. Fus. |
| Ronan, Rfm. P. | R. Ir. Rif. |
| Ross, Rfm. C. F. | R. Ir. Rif. |
| Ross, Sgt. F. | R. Ir. Rif. |
| Roulston, Sgt. R. | R. Innis. Fus. |
| Roulstone, Sgt. J. | R. Innis. Fus. |
| Rowney, Cpl. J. | R.E. |
| Rush, Rfm. J. | R. Ir. Rif. |
| Russell, L/Cpl. J. | R. Innis. Fus. |
| Russell, Pte. J. | R. Innis. Fus. |
| Russell, Cpl. R. | R. Ir. Fus. |
| Russell, C.S.M. W. J., *M.S.M.*, | R.E. |
| Russell, Sgt. W. J. | R. Ir. Rif. |
| Russell, Sgt. W. L. | R. Ir. Rif. |
| Rutherford, Cpl. J. | R. Innis. Fus. |
| Rutledge, L/Cpl. W. | R. Innis. Fus. |
| Ryan, L/Cpl. F. | R. Ir. Fus. |
| Sallinger, L/Cpl. M. | R. Ir. Rif. |
| Salmon, Sgt. G. W. | R.A.V.C. |
| Sands, Pte. J. | R. Innis. Fus. |
| Savage, Cpl. E. | R. Ir. Rif. |
| Savage, Pte. J. | R.A.M.C. |
| Savage, Rfm. W. | R. Ir. Rif. |
| Savage, Bdr. W. J. | R.F.A. |
| Scheffers, Sapper W. H. | R.E. |
| Scott, L/Cpl. E. | R. Ir. Rif. |
| Scott, L/Cpl. R. | R. Ir. Rif. |
| Scott, Sgt. T. | R. Ir. Fus. |
| Scott, Rfm. W. | R. Ir. Rif. |
| Scullion, Rfm. J. | R. Ir. Rif. |
| Service, Cpl. D. | R. Ir. Fus. |
| Shanks, Pte. C. | R. Ir. Fus. |
| Shanks, L/Cpl. W. | R. Innis. Fus. |
| Sharman, Pte. J. | R.A.M.C. |
| Sharp, L/Cpl. J. | R. Ir. Fus. |
| Shavin, Cpl. J. | R.F.A. |
| Shaw, Rfm. C. | R. Ir. Rif. |
| Shaw, Pte. G. T. | R. Innis. Fus. |
| Sheers, Sgt. J. | R. Innis. Fus. |
| Shields, L/Cpl. F. | R. Innis. Fus. |
| Shields, L/Cpl. J. | R. Ir. Rif. |
| Shields, Sgt. S. | R. Ir. Rif. |
| Shields, Pte. W. | R. Innis. Fus. |
| Shimmins, Gnr. J. E. | R.F.A. |
| Siebert, Rfm. W. | R. Ir. Rif. |
| Simms, Rfm. J. | R. Ir. Rif. |
| Simpson, L/Cpl. H. | R. Innis. Fus. |
| Sinclair, Sgt. A. | R. Ir. Rif. |
| Sinclair, Cpl. A | R. Innis. Fus. |
| Sloan, Rfm. J. | R. Ir. Rif. |
| Sloane, Rfm. T. J. | R. Ir. Rif. |
| Smallwood, L/Cpl. J. | R. Ir. Fus. |
| Smith, Sgt. A. | R. Ir. Rif. |
| Smith, Pte. A. | R. Innis. Fus. |
| Smith, Pte. A. S. | R. Innis. Fus. |
| Smith, Sgt. E. H. | R.F.A. |
| Smith, Cpl. G. | R. Ir. Rif. |
| Smith, Pte. G. | R. Innis. Fus. |
| Smith, Pte. G. H. | R. Ir. Fus. |
| Smith, Sgt. H. | R. Ir. Rif. |
| Smith, Gnr. H. | R.F.A. |
| Smith, L/Cpl. J. H. | R. Ir. Rif. |
| Smith, Pte. S. | R. Innis. Fus. |
| Smith, Pte. T. | R. Ir. Fus. |
| Smyth, Rfm. A. | R. Ir. Rif. |
| Smyth, Sgt. R., *D.C.M.*, | R. Innis. Fus. |
| Smyth, Rfm. W. | R. Ir. Rif. |
| Soames, Cpl. C. | R.E. |
| Spencer, Driver J. E. | R.F.A. |
| Spencer, Pte. R. A. | R.A.S.C. |
| Spencer, Cpl. T. | M.G.C. |
| Stacey, Farrier/Sgt. H. | R.F.A. |
| Stanley, L/Cpl. J. A. W., | R. Ir. Rif. |
| Stebbings, Cpl. W. | R.F.A. |
| Steel, Sgt. J. | R. Ir. Rif. |
| Steele, Pte. G. | R. Ir. Fus. |
| Steele, L/Cpl. W. S. | R. Ir. Rif. |
| Stevenson, Rfm. A. | R. Ir. Rif. |
| Stevenson, Pte. J. | R. Ir. Fus. |
| Stevenson, Rfm. J. | R. Ir. Rif. |

# HONOURS AND AWARDS

## MILITARY MEDAL (contd.)

Stevenson, L/Cpl. S. . . R. Ir. Rif.
Stevenson, C.S.M. W. . R. Ir. Fus.
Stevenson, Rfm. W. . . R. Ir. Rif.
Stewart, Rfm. H. . . . R. Ir. Rif.
Stewart, Rfm. T. . . . R. Ir. Rif.
Stewart, C.S.M. W. . R. Innis. Fus.
Stewart, Sapper W. . . . . R.E.
Stewart, Rfm. W. . . . R. Ir. Rif.
Stitt, Cpl. S. . . . . R. Innis. Fus.
Storey, Cpl. T. . . . . R. Ir. Rif.
Streatfield, Rfm. W. . . R. Ir. Rif.
Strickland, Pte. R. A. S. , R.A.M.C.
Stringer, Pte. F. W. . R. Innis. Fus.
Stubbings, Sgt. J. W., *D.C.M.*,
                                    M.G.C.
Summerscales, Sgt. V. R., R. Ir. Rif.
Sumner, Pte. J. . . . R. Innis. Fus.
Swan, Pte. S. W. . . . . M.G.C.
Swan, L/Cpl. W. .. . . M.M.P.
Sweeney, Pioneer E. . . . . R.E.
Sweeney, L/Cpl. J. . . . R. Ir. Fus.
Sweeny, Pte. J. . . . R. Innis. Fus.
Sweet, II. Cpl. W. S. . . . R.E.
Tannahill, Cpl. H. . . . R. Ir. Rif.
Taplin, Cpl. W. . . . . R. Ir. Rif.
Tarbett, Sgt. R. . . . . R.A.M.C.
Tarring, Gnr. F. W. . . . R.F.A.
Tasker, Pte. C. . . . . R. Ir. Fus.
Taylor, Pte. A. . . . R. Innis. Fus.
Taylor, L/Cpl. A. P. . . R. Ir. Rif.
Taylor, Rfm. G. D. . . R. Ir. Rif.
Taylor, Sgt. J. . . . R. Innis. Fus.
Templeton, Pte. W. . . R.A.M.C.
Thompson, Sgt. A. . . . . R.E.
Thompson, Gnr. A. . . . R.F.A.
Thompson, Pte. C. . . R. Innis. Fus.
Thompson, Pte. C. A. . R. Ir. Fus.
Thompson, Bdr. J. . . . R.F.A.
Thompson, Rfm. J. . . R. Ir. Rif.
Thompson, Sgt. O. . . R. Innis. Fus.
Thompson, Pte. S. . . R.A.M.C.
Tisseman, Pte. J. . . R. Innis. Fus.
Titchener, Sgt. J. H. . . . R.F.A.
Toomey, Pte. J. . . . R. Ir. Fus.
Topping, Cpl. A. . . . R. Ir. Rif.
Townsley, L/Cpl. D. . . . . R.E.
Tozer, Sgt. W. . . . . R.A.S.C.
Trickey, Rfm. A. G. . . R. Ir. Rif.
Tucker, Rfm. O. . . . R. Ir. Rif.
Tulip, Pte. O. . . . . R. Innis. Fus.
Turkington, Sgt. A. . . R. Ir. Fus.
Turkington, Rfm. J. . . R. Ir. Rif.
Turner, C.Q.M.S. J. . . R. Ir. Rif.
Turner, Sgt. J. (18845) . R. Ir. Rif.

Turner, Sgt. J. (12159) . R. Ir. Rif.
Turner, Sgt. W. A. . . . R.F.A.
Turney, Pte. E. . . . . R.A.M.C.
Tweedie, Sgt. R. . . . R. Ir. Rif.
Tymble, Sgt. W. T. . . . . R.E.
Tyther, Rfm. T. W. . . R. Ir. Rif.
Upton, Pte. W. . . . R. Innis. Fus.
Usher, C.Q.M.S. F. H. . . . R.E.
Venard, Sgt. A. . . . . R. Ir. Fus.
Verity, Rfm. H. . . . . R. Ir. Rif.
Vogan, Sgt. R. . . . . R. Ir. Fus.
Vickers, Pte. R. . . . . . R.A.S.C.
Vickers, Rfm. W. P. . . R. Ir. Rif.
Wakem, Sgt. A. . . . . . R.F.A.
Walker, L/Cpl. C. H. . R. Ir. Rif.
Walker, Rfm. E. McK. . R. Ir. Rif.
Walker, Pte. G. . . . . R. Ir. Fus.
Walker, L/Cpl. S. . R. Innis. Fus.
Walker, Pte. T. . . . . R.A.M.C.
Walker, Rfm. W. (9266), R. Ir. Rif.
Walker, Rfm. W. (19276), R. Ir. Rif.
Walker, L/Cpl. W. H. . . M.G.C.
Walkingshaw, Rfm. J. . R. Ir. Rif.
Wallace, Pte. G. . . . R. Innis. Fus.
Wallen, C.S.M. H. . . R. Innis. Fus.
Walmsley, Bdr. S. . . . . R.F.A.
Walsh, Cpl. J. H. . . . . . R.E.
Ward, Cpl. E. . . . . . R.A.S.C.
Ward, L/Cpl. T. . . . R. Innis. Fus.
Ward, Sapper T. . . . . . R.E.
Wardley, Driver E. . . . . R.E.
Ware, Pte. F. S. . . . R. Ir. Fus.
Warnock, Rfm. J. . . . R Ir. Rif.
Warren, Sgt. J. . . . R. Innis. Fus.
Wasson, Pte. S. . . . . R. Ir. Fus.
Waterhouse. Pte. J. . R. Innis. Fus.
Watson, Cpl. T. . . . . . M.G.C.
Watt, Pte. T. . . . . R. Innis. Fus.
Watters, Rfm. R. . . . R. Ir. Rif.
Weatherup, Cpl. W. . . R. Ir. Rif.
Wegg, Rfm. G. . . . . R Ir. Rif.
Weir, L/Cpl. J. . . . . R. Ir. Rif.
Weir, Pte. W. H. . . R. Innis. Fus.
Welch, L/Cpl. C. E. . . . M.M.P.
Welsh, Pioneer P. H. . . . . R.E.
West, L/Cpl. J. . . . . R. Ir. Rif.
Westwood, Rfm. P. . . R. Ir. Rif.
Whelan, II. Cpl. J. . . . . R.E.
Whelan, Sgt. R. . . . . R. Ir. Rif.
White, C.S.M. A., *M.C.*,
                             R. Innis. Fus.
White, Gnr. F. . . . . . R.F.A.
White, L/Cpl. J. . . . . R. Ir. Rif.
Whiteside, L/Cpl. S. . . R. Ir. Fus.

# 338 HISTORY OF 36TH (ULSTER) DIVISION

## MILITARY MEDAL (contd.)

Whitla, Rfm. J. . . . . R. Ir. Rif.
Wilkinson, Gnr. A. R. . . R.F.A.
Will, Pte. M. G. . . . . . M.G.C.
Willacy, L/Cpl. J. . . R. Innis. Fus.
Williams, Pte. H. . . . R. Ir. Fus.
Williamson, C.S.M. G. . R. Ir. Fus.
Williamson, Cpl. H. G. . R. Ir. Fus.
Williamson, Cpl. J. . . R.A.M.C.
Williamson, L/Cpl. J., R. Innis. Fus.
Williamson, Pte. T. J., R. Innis. Fus.
Williamson, Sgt. W. J. . . R.F.A.
Willott, Rfm. J. . . . . R. Ir. Rif.
Wilmot, Sgt. J. . . . R. Innis. Fus.
Wilson, Rfm. A. . . . . R. Ir. Rif.
Wilson, Pte. C. . . . R. Innis. Fus.
Wilson, Gnr. F. . . . . . R.F.A.
Wilson, Sgt. G. . . . . . . R.E.
Wilson, Rfm. H. . . . R. Ir. Rif.
Wilson, Rfm. J. . . . . R. Ir. Rif.
Wilson, Rfm. J. J. . . . R. Ir. Rif.
Wilson. Cpl. J. M. . . . . . R.E.
Wilson, Sgt. T. . . . . R.A.M.C.

Wilson, Driver T. . . . . R.F.A.
Wilson, Cpl. W. J. . . . . . R.E.
Wilson, Rfm. W. S. . . R. Ir. Rif.
Woodruff, Rfm. W. . . R. Ir. Rif.
Woods, Cpl. W. H. . . R. Ir. Rif.
Woodside, Rfm. W. . . R. Ir. Rif.
Woodward, Rfm. G. . . R. Ir. Rif.
Workman, Driver J. H. . R.A.S.C.
Workman, Rfm. W. . . R. Ir. Rif.
Wray, Pte. C. . . . . R. Innis. Fus.
Wright, Pte. A. . . . R. Innis. Fus.
Wright, Rfm. A. . . . R. Ir. Rif.
Wright, Pte. W. . . . . R. Ir. Fus.
Wrigley, Driver O. . . . R.F.A.
Wynne, Pte. R. . . . R. Innis. Fus.
Yardley, Cpl. W., *D.C.M.*, R. Ir. Rif.
Yeaman, L/Cpl. W. J. . R. Ir. Rif.
Yeates, L/Cpl. W., *D.C.M.*,
R. Ir. Rif.
Yendall, Cpl. W. . . . R. Ir. Rif.
Young, Rfm. S. . . . . R. Ir. Rif.
Young, Cpl. T. . . . . R. Ir. Rif.

## MERITORIOUS SERVICE MEDAL

Alexander, Sgt. J. . . . R. Ir. Rif.
Anderson, Farrier/Sgt. C. . R.F.A.
Anderson, Cpl. H. . . . R. Ir. Rif.
Anderson, S/Sgt. J. . . R.A.S.C.
Armstrong, Sgt. R. . R. Innis. Fus.
Armstrong, Pte. W. . R. Innis. Fus.
Ballantine, Sgt. R. . . . . . R.E.
Barham, Driver A. I. E. . R.F.A.
Benfield, B.S.M. H. C. . . R.F.A.
Best, Rfm. F. V. . . . R. Ir. Rif.
Blewitt, Cpl. J. . . . . . R.A.S.C.
Boost, Sgt. T. W. . . . . R.F.A.
Bowers, S.M. H. C. . . . R.F.A.
Bowra, Sgt. H. . . . . . R.F.A.
Brennen, Condr. V. T. . R.A.O.C.
Brew, L/Cpl. J. . . . . . M.G.C.
Brown, Sgt. G. . . . . R.A.M.C.
Bunting, Sgt. W. J. . . R.A.M.C.
Burney, Sgt. T. . . . . R. Ir. Rif.
Byers, Cpl. S. . . . . R. Innis. Fus.
Callaway, C.Q.M.S. F. . R. Ir. Fus.
Campbell, C.S.M. J. . . . R.A.S.C.
Campbell, Pte. S. E. . . R.A.M.C.
Carmichael, C.Q.M.S. R. D.,
R. Ir. Rif.
Clancy, Q.M.S. P. J. . . R. Ir. Fus.
Clarke, Sgt. W. H. . . R. Ir. Rif.
Cormican, Sgt. J. . . . . R.A.S.C.

Corr, Sgt. M. . . . . . R. Ir. Rif.
Corrigan, R.Q.M.S. L. C., R. Ir. Rif.
Cumming, R.Q.M.S. S., *D.C.M.*,
R. Ir. Rif.
Currall, S.S.M. T. . . . . M.M.P.
Davies, Cpl. E. . . . . R. Ir. Rif.
Dennison, Q.M.S. W. J., R.A.M.C.
Donnelly, Sgt. J. . . . R. Ir. Fus.
Dool, Rfm. W. . . . . R. Ir. Rif.
Duggan, C.S.M. J. G., R. Innis. Fus.
Elphick, R.S.M. R. J. . R. Ir. Rif.
Ervine, Q.M.S. A. G.,*M.M.*,
R. Ir. Rif.
Ferguson, C.S.M. L. . . . . R.E.
Field, Cpl. A. . . . . . R. Ir. Rif.
Fleming, Sgt. H. . . . R. Ir. Rif.
Fleming, C.S.M. J. . . R. Innis. Fus.
Fooks, Sgt. J. . . . . . R.A.M.C.
France, Sgt. M. S., *D.C.M.*, M.G.C.
Freeman, Sub-Condr. N. A.,
R.A.O.C.
Gallaugher, Sgt. W. . R. Innis. Fus.
Gowdy, Col.-Sgt. J., *M.M.*,
R. Ir. Rif.
Griff, Sgt. H. E. . . . R. Innis. Fus.
Guinn, Rfm. R. . . . . R. Ir. Rif.
Hanna, C.S.M. T. . . R. Innis. Fus.
Harkness, Sgt. R. . . R. Innis. Fus.

# HONOURS AND AWARDS

## MERITORIOUS SERVICE MEDAL (contd.)

Harmon, C.Q.M.S. S., R. Innis. Fus.
Harvey, Sgt. T. G. . . . R.A.S.C.
Hastings, L/Cpl. M. .R. Innis. Fus.
Haydock, S.Q.M.S. J. . . R.A.S.C.
Hayes, Driver A. . . . . R.F.A.
Hazley, Sgt. J. H. . . R. Innis. Fus.
Highman, Sgt. A. J. . . R. Ir. Rif.
Holmes, Sgt. J. . . . . R. Ir. Rif.
Hosie, S/Sgt. J. D. R. . . R.A.S.C.
Hughes, B.Q.M.S. E. F. B., R.F.A.
Hunt, Bdr. A. H. . . . . R.F.A.
Irwin, Sapper S. . . . . . R.E.
James, S/Sgt. C. F. . . . R.A.V.C.
Jamison, Pioneer Sgt. J., R. Ir. Rif.
Jamison, R.S.M. W. . . R. Ir. Rif.
Jardin, S.Q.M.S. A. . . . R.A.S.C.
Keith, Sgt. J. . . . . . R. Ir. Fus.
Kelly, C.Q.M.S. C. D. . R. Ir. Rif.
Kennedy, Sgt. J. . . . . R.A.S.C.
Kerr, Sgt. G. . . . . . R.A.M.C.
King, Sgt. P. W. . . . . R.A.S.C.
Laird, C.S.M. W. A. . R. Innis. Fus.
Lambert, S/Sgt. W. H. . . R.A.S.C.
Lapsley, Cpl. S. . . . R. Innis. Fus.
Larmour, C.Q.M.S. E. M. . R.E.
Leonard, Cpl. J. B. . . R. Ir. Rif.
Lester, S.Q.M.S. H. C. . R.A.S.C.
Letson, C.Q.M.S. H. . . R. Ir. Rif.
Lloyd, Pte. E. E. . . R. Innis. Fus.
McClure, Sgt. D. . . . . R.A.S.C.
McComb, Cpl. R. Employment Coy.
McConville, C.Q.M.S. T., R. Ir. Fus.
McCormick, Driver H. . . . R.E.
McCoy, Sgt. J. . . . . . M.G.C.
McCurdy, Sgt. R. . . . R.A.M.C.
McFerran, Sgt. J. . . . R. Ir. Rif.
McGuigan, Cpl. A. C. . . R. Ir. Rif.
McGuinness, Pte. E. . . Div. H.Q.
McLaren, R.Q.M.S. A. L. V.,
    R. Innis. Fus.
McNeil S. M. A. C. . . . R.A.S.C.
McWilliams, Rfm. D. . . R. Ir. Rif.
Maddock, Sapper R. D. . . R.E.
Martin, L/Cpl. W. J. . . R. Ir. Rif.
Meneilly, Rfm. H. . . . R. Ir. Rif.
Mitchell, Q.M.S. J. A. . . . R.E.
Moore, Col.-Sgt. W. A. . R. Ir. Rif.

Morrison, Sgt. F. . . . R.A.M.C.
Morrow, Rfm. S. . . . R. Ir. Rif.
Neary, Sgt. L. . . . R. Innis. Fus.
Nelson, Sgt. S. . . . . R. Ir. Rif.
Ness, Sgt. R. . . . . . R. Ir. Rif.
O'Rawe, Rfm. J. . . . R. Ir. Rif.
Owens, Pte. W. . . . R. Innis. Fus.
Pasley, Rfm. W. O. . . R. Ir. Rif.
Pate, C.S.M. J. . . . . . . R.E.
Pedlow, Sgt. S. J. . . . R. Ir. Rif.
Powers, Sgt. R. B. . . . R. Ir. Rif.
Pyper, Cpl. R. . . . . . . R.E.
Rands, S.S.M. R. . . . . R.A.S.C.
Rigby, Pte. H. . . . . . R.A.S.C.
Robinson, Cpl. C., *M.M.*, R. Ir. Fus.
Rogers, Pte. J. . . . . . M.G.C.
Russell, C.S.M. W. J., *M.M.*, R.E.
Salters, Sub-Condr. J. . . R.A.O.C.
Sheldrake, Sgt. H. T. . . . M.M.P.
Sherar, C.Q.M.S. H. N. . . R.A.S.C.
Sherwood, Q.M.S. T.,
    107th Bde. H.Q.
Sills, L/Cpl. A. K. . . . R.A.O.C.
Silvey, C.S.M. R. . . . R. Ir. Rif.
Smyth, Rfm. D. . . . . . R. Ir. Rif.
Spencer, L/Cpl. T. . . . . M.M.P.
Stafford, R.Q.M.S. T. H., R. Ir. Rif.
Stewart, Sgt. J. . . . . R. Ir. Rif.
Stewart, Sgt. P. . . . . . M.G.C.
Sullivan, Sgt. W. . . . R. Ir. Fus.
Swain, S.Q.M.S. J. . . . R.F.A.
Swann, Sgt. R. . . . . R. Ir. Rif.
Taylor, C.Q.M.S. W. . R. Ir. Rif.
Thompson, Sgt. A. E. . R. Ir. Rif.
Thompson, L/Cpl. H. J. . . R.E.
Thompson, Sgt. J. . . . . R.E.
Thompson, Cpl. T. J. . . R.A.M.C.
Turner, Sgt. A. . . . . . R.F.A.
Turner, C.Q.M.S. J., *M.M.*,
    R. Ir. Rif.
Turner, Sgt. W. J. . . . R.A.M.C.
Tynan, R.S.M. F. . . . R. Ir. Fus.
Walmsley, Bdr. S. . . . . R.F.A.
Waring, C.Q.M.S. T. . . R. Ir. Rif.
Warry, Sgt. E. . . . . . R.E.
White, Sgt. J. C. . . . R. Ir. Rif.
Williams, S.M. G. . . . . M.M.P.

## HISTORY OF 36TH (ULSTER) DIVISION

### FOREIGN HONOURS

#### FRENCH LEGION D'HONNEUR

Allen, Lt.-Col. Sir W. J., *D.S.O.*, R. Ir. Rif.
Blacker, Lt.-Col. S. W., *D.S.O.*, R. Ir. Fus.
Craig, Maj. C. C. . . . . R. Ir. Rif.
Haslett, Maj. H. R. . . R. Ir. Rif.
Magill, Lt.-Col. R., *D.S.O.*, R.A.M.C.
Mirrless, Maj. W. H. B. . R.F.A.
Pakenham, Col. H. A., *C.M.G.*, R. Ir. Rif.
Vaughan, Brig.-Gen. E., *D.S.O.*, Cmndg. 108th Bde.

#### FRENCH MEDAILLE MILITAIRE

Baker, Bdr. E. . . . . . R.F.A.
Glass, Sgt. R. W. . . . R. Ir. Rif.
Graham, C.S.M. H. F., R. Innis. Fus.
Higgins, Rfm. T., *D.C.M.*, R. Ir. Rif.
Hughes, Pte. S. A. . . . . M.G.C.
Johnson, R.S.M. H., R. Innis. Fus.
Laird, Sgt. W., *M.M.*, R. Innis. Fus.
McBride, Sgt. R. J., *D.C.M.*, R. Ir. Rif.
McCarrol, Rfm. . . . . . R. Ir. Rif.
McIlveen, Sgt. J., *M.M.*, R. Ir. Rif.
McMillan, Sgt. J. . . . R. Ir. Rif.
Moore, Sgt. W. J. . . . R. Ir. Rif.
Potter, L/Cpl. J. . . R. Innis. Fus.
Tynan, R.S.M. F. . . . R. Ir. Fus.
Wilkinson, C.S.M. S. . R. Ir. Rif.
Wilson, L/Cpl. R. C., *D.C.M.*, R. Ir. Rif.
Wright, Sapper B. R., *D.C.M.*, R.E.

#### FRENCH CROIX DE GUERRE

Allen, Capt. S., *M.C.* . Genl. List.
Anderson, Lt. A. M. . . R. Ir. Rif.
Atkinson, L/Cpl. F. . . . M.G.C.
Beezley, Lt. F. W. . . . M.G.C.
Bell, Sgt. A. S. . . . . R.A.M.C.
Bell, Lt. H. C. . . . . . R.A.S.C.
Benson, Lt. T. R. . . . . . R.E.
Breeze, Sgt. J. . . . . R. Ir. Rif.
Brock, Brig.-Gen. H. J., *C.B.*, *C.M.G.*, *D.S.O.* . . Cmndg. R.A.
Brown, Bdr. C. . . . . . R.F.A.
Brown, Capt. W. A. Weber, R.A.S.C.
Bunting, Capt. T. E., *D.C.M.*, R. Ir. Fus.
Campbell, Sgt. J. . . . R. Ir. Fus.
Charlton, Capt. J. W., *M.C.*, R. Innis. Fus.
Christie, Maj. A. W. S. . R.A.M.C.
Corrigan, R.Q.M.S. L. S., R. Ir. Rif.
Crawford, Lt.-Col. S W., *D.S.O.*, R. Innis. Fus.
Crompton, 2/Lt. J. J. . R.A.M.C.
Davidson, Capt. D. N. F., *M.C.*, R. Innis. Fus.
Deane, Sgt. J., *D.C.M.* . R. Ir. Rif.
Dent, Lt.-Col. J. R. C., *D.S.O.*, *M.C.* . . . R. Innis. Fus.
Dixon, Lt. H. R. . . . . . R.E.
Doig, Lt. G. F. . . . . R. Ir. Rif.
Ferguson, Cpl. F. . . . R. Ir. Rif.
Findlay, Sgt. H. . . . . M.G.C.
Ford, 2/Lt. F. J. . . . . . R.E.
Goodall, S/Sgt. L. D. . . R.A.M.C.
Goodwin, Lt.-Col. W. R., *C.M.G.*, *D.S.O.* . . . R. Ir. Rif.
Goyder, Capt. G. B. . . Genl. List.
Green, Pte. R. . . R. Innis. Fus.
Green, Lt.-Col. S. H., *D.S.O.*, *M.C.* . West Yorks. Regt.
Griffiths, Gnr. F. K., *D.C.M.*, R.F.A.
Grove-White, Capt. I. A., R. Ir. Rif.
Hatfull, Lt. and Q.M. L. E., R.Ir.Rif.
Hawkes, Brig.-Gen. C. St. L. G., *D.S.O.* . . . . . Cmndg. R.A.
Hessey, Brig.-Gen. W. F., *D.S.O.*, Cmndg. 109th Bde.
Hewitt, 2/Lt. J. O'N., R. Innis. Fus.
Hill, Cpl. W. . . . . . . R.F.A.
Hodgson, Maj. G. C. S., *M.C.*, W. Somerset Yeo.
Hooks, Sgt. J. . . . . . R. Ir. Rif.
Hoskiss, Sgt. W. . . . . R.F.A.
Howard, Maj. A. W. . R. Innis. Fus.
Hutchinson, Pte. J. . R. Innis. Fus.
Jamison, R.S.M. W. . . R. Ir. Rif.
Kerr, Capt. C. H. . . . R. Ir. Fus.

# HONOURS AND AWARDS

## FRENCH CROIX DE GUERRE (contd.)

Kirby, C.S.M. L. . . R. Innis. Fus.
Knox, Lt.-Col. R. S., *D.S.O.*,
 R. Innis. Fus.
Leach, Sgt. A. . . . . R. Ir. Rif.
Loughlin, Cpl. D., *M.M.*,
 R. Innis. Fus.
Lyness, Capt. W. J., *M.C.*, R. Ir. Rif.
McAtamney, Rfm. D. . R. Ir. Rif.
McCabe, Rfm. P. . . . R. Ir. Rif.
McCallum, Maj. J. D. M., *D.S.O.*,
 R. Ir. Rif.
McCaw, Capt. J., *M.C.*,
 R. Innis. Fus.
McClurg, Sgt. R. . . . R. Ir. Rif.
McDowell, Capt. S. S. . R. Ir. Rif.
McFaull, C.Q.M.S., W . R. Ir. Rif.
MacKenzie, Lt.-Col. R. H.,
 *D.S.O., M.C.* . . . . . . R.E.
McKnight, C.Q.M.S. H. K.,
 R. Innis. Fus.
Magill, C.S.M. D. R. . . R. Ir. Fus.
Meares, Lt.-Col. C. F., *D.S.O.*,
 R. Ir. Rif.
Moffatt, R.S.M. H. . R. Innis. Fus.
Montgomery, Sgt. W. . . M.G.C.
Montserrat, Capt. W. R. . R.F.A.
Moran, Pte. J. . . . R. Innis. Fus.
Morrison, Capt. T. D., *M.C.*,
 R. Innis. Fus.
Mulholland, Maj. J. A., *M.C.*,
 R. Ir. Rif.
Murphy, Sgt. W. . . . M.G.C.
O'Grady, Lt.-Col. D. de C., R.A.M.C.
O'Hanlon, L/Cpl. J. . . R. Ir. Fus.
Parnell, Lt. and Q.M. W., R.A M.C.
Patterson, Cpl. H. J. . . . R.F.A.
Peacocke, Lt.-Col. W. J., *D.S.O.*,
 R. Innis. Fus.
Pemberton, Gnr. L. J. . . R.F.A.

Quinn, Sgt. W. J. . . . . . R.E.
Quinn, Sgt. W. J. . . . . M.G.C.
Rattray, Lt. N. A. . . . R. Ir. Fus.
Rickards, Maj. G. A., *M.C.*, R.F.A.
Robinson, Maj. H. C. . . . R.A.S.C.
Roch, Col. H. S., *D.S.O.*, R.A.M.C.
Rogers, Maj. V. B., *D.S.O., M.C.*
Rose, C.S.M. T. de, *D.C.M.*, M.G.C.
Ross, Maj. R. O., *M.C.* . . . N.I.H.
Rule, 2/Lt. C. . . . . . R. Ir. Rif.
Scott, B.S.M. W. . . . . R.F.A.
Sharp, Maj. R. R., *D.S.O., M.C.*,
 R.F.A.
Simpson, Lt.-Col. H. C.,
 *C.M.G., D.S.O.* . . . . . R.A.
Skimmin, Sapper A. . . . . R.E.
Solomon, Capt. R. B., *M.C.*, R.F.A.
Stevenson, L/Cpl. J. . . R. Ir. Rif.
Sturgeon, Sgt. J. . . . . . R.E.
Swan, Capt. W. N. . . R. Ir. Rif.
Tamplin, Maj. R. F. A., *D.S.O.*,
 R. Ir. Fus.
Tate, Lt. T. M. . . . . R. Ir. Rif.
Taylor, Sgt. F. . . . . . R.F.A.
Thompson, Lt.-Col. A. G., *D.S.O.*,
 Indian Army.
Thompson, Maj. G., *D.S.O.*,
 R. Ir. Rif.
Thompson, Rfm. R. . . R. Ir. Rif.
Vaughan, 2/Lt. C. H. . R. Innis. Fus.
Walker, Sgt. F. W. . . . . R.F.A.
Wallace, Capt. A. . . . R. Ir. Rif.
Watts, Capt. R., *M.C.* . . R. Ir. Rif.
Wightman, S.S.M. B. . R.A.M.C.
Wilkins, Capt. C. F.,
 *D.S.O., M.C.* . . . . . R. Ir. Rif.
Williamson, Rfm. A. E., R. Ir. Rif.
Wood, Cpl. G. H. . . . . R.F.A.
Wylie, Sapper G. . . . . . R.E.

## FRENCH MEDAILLE D'HONNEUR

Ward, R.S.M. W. . . . . . . . . . . . . . . R. Ir. Rif.

## FRENCH ORDRE DE MERITE AGRICOLE

O'Neill, Maj. the Rt. Hon. H., M.P. . . . . . . . . . . . R. Ir. Rif.

## BELGIAN ORDRE DE LEOPOLD

Becher, Lt.-Col. C.M.L., *D.S.O.*,
 R. Ir. Rif.
Boyd, Sgt. R. J. . . . R. Innis. Fus.
Duncan, Capt. L. S., *M.C.*, R. Ir. Rif.

Gordon, Capt. H.C., *M.C.*, R. In. Fus.
McKee, Maj. J., *D.S.O.*, R. Ir. Rif.
O'Neill, Sgt. J. . . . R. Innis. Fus.
Williams, C.S.M. G. A. . R. Ir. Fus.

## BELGIAN ORDRE DE LA COURONNE

Bell, Lt. and Q.M. D. F., R. Innis. Fus.
Coffin, Maj.-Gen. C., *V.C.*, *C.B.*, *D.S.O.* . . . . Cmndg. 36th Div.
McNeill, Lt. W. N. . . R. Ir. Rif.
McCarthy-O'Leary, Lt.-Col. H. W. D., *D.S.O.* . . R. Ir. Rif.
Wilson, Lt. and Q.M. G. W., R. Ir. Fus.

## BELGIAN DECORATION MILITAIRE

Baxter, Rfm. H. . . . R. Ir. Rif.
Connolly, Pte. B. . . . R. Ir. Fus.
Forrest, Pte. E. M., *D.C.M.*, R. Innis. Fus.
Grattan, Rfm. J. . . . R. Ir. Rif.
Meredith, Sgt. J. . . . R. Ir. Rif.
Millichamp, Sgt. H. . . R.F.A.
Morton, Pte. T. . . . . R. Ir. Fus.
Pepper, Cpl. J. . . . . M.G.C.
Quinn, Cpl. W. F., *D.C.M.*, *M.M.*, R.A.M.C.
Robson, Sgt. W., *M.M.* . . R.E.
Rowan, Sgt. P. . . . R. Innis. Fus.
Simons, Pte. W. . . . . R. Ir. Rif.
Stewart, Pte. T. . . . . R. Ir. Fus.
Sullivan, Gnr. C. . . . . R.F.A.
Wheatley, Pte. H. S. . R. Innis. Fus.

## BELGIAN CROIX DE GUERRE

Aitken, Cpl. J. A. . . . R. Ir. Rif.
Askew, Sglr. E. . . . . . R.F.A.
Barrett, Sgt. J. . . . . R. Ir. Rif.
Bateman, Sgt. P. R. . . . R.A.S.C.
Beckerson, Rev. W. F., Army Chap. Dept.
Bell, C.S.M. H., *M.M.* . R. Ir. Rif.
Birney, Sgt. T. . . . . R. Ir. Rif.
Blake, Lt. H. E. . . . . . . R.E.
Bowers, Sgt. R. B. . . . R. Ir. Rif.
Brock, Brig.-Gen. H. J., *C.B.*, *C.M.G.*, *D.S.O.* . . Cmndg. R.A.
Buddy, Gnr. H. . . . . . R.F.A.
Burrows, S/Sgt. F. R. . R.A.M.C.
Carolan, L/Cpl. J. . . R. Innis. Fus.
Carson, L/Cpl. A. . . . R. Ir. Rif.
Carton, L/Cpl. J., *D.C.M.* R. Ir. Rif.
Cassidy, L/Cpl. H. . . R. Innis. Fus.
Chambers, Cpl. A. . . R. Innis. Fus.
Cleary, L/Cpl. G. . . . R. Ir. Rif.
Craig, L/Cpl. T. . . . . R. Ir. Rif.
Creese, C.Q.M.S. R. G., *D.C.M.*, M.G.C.
Dawson, Lt. D. M. . . . R. Ir. Rif.
Dick, L/Cpl. I., *M.M.* . R. Ir. Fus.
Donnan, Sgt. C. . . . . R. Ir. Rif.
Donohue, Rev. F., *M.C.*, Army Chap. Dept.
Doogan, C.S.M. M. J., 107th Bde. H.Q.
Douglas, L/Cpl. G. . . . R. Ir. Rif.
Duncan, Capt. L. S., *M.C.*, R. Ir. Rif.
Dunne, C.Q.M.S. J. . . R. Ir. Rif.
Edmonds, Bdr. G. . . . . R.F.A.
Edwards, Cpl. C. . . . R. Ir. Fus.
Edwards, Capt. and Q.M. G., R. Ir. Rif.
Ellis, Maj. S. G. . . . . . R.F.A.
Evans, Lt. T. H., *M.C.*, Genl. List.
Farquhar, II. Cpl. C. . . . . R.E.
Fitzgerald, Capt. C. W. B., R. Innis. Fus.
Fox, Capt. L. W., *M.C.* . R.F.A.
Franklyn, Maj. G. E. W., *M.C.* . . . . . . . . . R.F.A.
French, B.S.M. J. . . . . R.F.A.
Galbraith, Sgt. W. H. . R. Ir. Rif.
Garner, Maj. C. W. . . R. Ir. Rif.
Glegg, Capt. J. D., *M.C.*, R. Dub. Fus.
Glenn, Pte. D. . . . R. Innis. Fus.
Godfrey, C.S.M. S. . R. Innis. Fus.
Godson, Capt. E. A., *M.C.*, R. Ir. Fus.
Gordon, Cpl. C. . . . . R. Ir. Rif.
Graham, Sgt. J. . . . . . M.G.C.
Graham, 2/Lt. W. G. . R. Ir. Fus.
Green, Lt.-Col. S. H., *D.S.O.*, *M.C.*, West Yorks. Regt.
Greenwood, Cpl. A. . . R. Ir. Rif.
Haigh, Lt. J. H., *M.C.* . R. Ir. Rif.
Harbinson, Sgt. J., *D.C.M.*, *M.M.* . . . R. Ir. Rif.
Harris, C.S.M. W. J. . . R. Ir. Rif.
Harrison, Sgt. J. W. . . . . . R.E.

# HONOURS AND AWARDS

## BELGIAN CROIX DE GUERRE (contd.)

Hawkins, Lt. A. G. J. . . Int. Corps.
Hazelton, Bdr. F. . . . . . R.F.A.
Healas, B.S.M. H. . . . . R.F.A.
Herdman, Cpl. R., *D.C.M.*,
    R. Ir. Rif.
Hill, Capt. F. J., *M.C.* . R. Ir. Rif.
Hindmarsh, Sgt. M. . . . R.A.V.C.
Howarth, II. Cpl. A. . . . . R.E.
Hulse, Maj. A. . . . . . R. Ir. Fus.
Hunt, Rfm. A. . . . . . R. Ir. Rif.
Hutchings, R.S.M. W. . R. Ir. Rif.
Irvine, Rfm. J. . . . . . R. Ir. Rif.
Jardin, S.Q.M.S. A., *M.S.M.*,
    R.A.S.C.
Kane, Pte. R., *M.M.* . . R. Innis. Fus.
King, Cpl. R. H. . . . . . R.E.
Kirkpatrick, Sgt. J. . R. Innis. Fus.
Knaggs, L/Cpl. R. W. . R. Ir. Fus.
Laverty, Pte. W. J. . R. Innis. Fus.
Lawler, Sgt. E. . . . R. Innis. Fus.
Leckey, Sgt. H. . . . . . . R.E.
Leeper, Capt. J. C. . . . R. Ir. Rif.
Leslie, Maj. C. G., *M.C.*,
    3rd Dragoon Gds.
Leverett, Sgt.-Drmr. E., R. Ir. Fus.
Lindsay, Capt. G. E., *M.C.*,
    R.A.M.C.
Lockhart, Sgt. J. . . . R. Ir. Fus.
Lowe, Lt.-Col. T. A.,
  *D.S.O.*, *M.C.*. . . . R. Ir. Fus.
McBirney, Sgt. T., *D.C.M.*,
    R. Ir. Rif.
McCartney, Driver G. . . . R.E.
McCullough, Rfm. T. . R. Ir. Rif.
McCune, Sgt. A. . . . . R. Ir. Rif.
McDowell, Sgt. J. . . . R. Ir. Rif.
McDowell, Rfm. J. . . . R. Ir. Rif.
McIldowie, Capt. G. . . . . R.E.
McKane, Rfm. J. . . . R. Ir. Rif.
McKnight, C.Q.M.S. H. K.,
    R. Innis. Fus.
McLarty, L/Cpl. F., *M.M.*,
    R. Ir. Rif.
Macmillan, Maj. C. H. . . . R.E.
McMurray, Rfm. J. E. . R. Ir. Rif.
McNeill, II./Cpl. W. J. . . . R.E.
McSeveny, Sgt. S. . . . . M.G.C.
McVeigh, L/Cpl. W. . . R. Ir. Rif.
Magee, Capt. F. W. H. . . R.F.A.
Magee, Pte. W. G., *M.M.*,
    R. Innis. Fus.
Mansell, Sgt. W. A. . . R.A.M.C.
Menaul, Capt. W. J., *M.C.*,
    Genl. List.

Miller, Capt. J. C. . . . R.A.V.C.
Milne, Capt. C. W. . R. Innis. Fus.
Moore, Sgt. R. . . . . . . R.E.
Moorhouse, Maj. G. S. . . M.G.C.
Morgan, C.Q.M.S. V. . . . . R.E.
Muller, Lt.-Col. J., *M.C.* . M.G.C.
Murphy, Rev. W. G.
    Army Chap. Dept.
Neary, Sgt. L. . . . R. Innis. Fus.
Neville, Sgt. C. . . . . R. Ir. Rif.
Nightingale, Bdr. J. H. . . R.F.A.
O'Hara, Pte. P. . . . . R. Ir. Fus.
O'Hara, L/Cpl. W. . . R. Ir. Rif.
Ormerod, Cpl. J. E. . . . . R.E.
Perritt, Lt. and Q.M. W. E.,
    R.A.M.C.
Porterfield, Sgt. A. . R. Innis. Fus.
Purdon-Coote, Maj. C. R. . R.A.S.C.
Purdy, 2/Lt. W. H. . R. Innis. Fus.
Quigley, Rfm. M. . . . R. Ir. Rif.
Rands, S.S.M. R. . . . . R.A.S.C.
Riley, Lt.-Col. J. H. G. . . R.F.A.
Rivis, Lt.-Col. T. C. L., *D.S.O.*,
    R.A.S.C.
Robb, Capt. J. C. . . . R.A.M.C.
Rogers, Lt. W., *M.C.* . R. Ir. Rif.
Rosbotham, Sgt. S. . . R. Ir. Fus.
Savage, Sgt. T. . . . R. Innis. Fus.
Scott, C.Q.M.S. T. . . . R. Ir. Rif.
Searle, F.Q.M.S. S. . . . R.F.A.
Shaw, Sgt. J. C. . . . . R. Ir. Rif.
Sloane, Bdr. S. . . . . . R.F.A.
Small, Sgt. S. . . . . R. Ir. Rif.
Smyth, Maj. W., *D.S.O.*, *M.C.*, R.E.
Snodden, R.S.M. J., *D.C.M.*,
    R. Innis. Fus.
Sparks, Capt. W., *M.C.* R. Ir. Fus.
Sterling, Pte. J. . . . . R.A.M.C.
Stewart, Cpl. A. . . . . . R.F.A.
Stronge, Capt. C. N. L., *M.C.*,
    R. Innis. Fus.
Tait, Maj. M. W., *M.C.* . M.G.C.
Thompson, Lt.-Col. A. G.,
  *D.S.O.* . . . . . Indian Army.
Thompson, Sgt. J. . . R. Innis. Fus.
Thornely, Capt. F. B., *M.C.*,
    R. Ir. Rif.
Tweedie, Rfm. J. . . . R. Ir. Rif.
Underhill, Driver E. . . . R.F.A.
Vaughan, Brig.-Gen. E., *D.S.O.*,
    Cmndg. 108th Bde.
Walker, Capt. D. . . . . M.G.C.
Wallen, C.S.M. H., *M.M.*,
    R. Innis. Fus.

### BELGIAN CROIX DE GUERRE (contd.)

Watson, Rev. R., Army Chap. Dept.
Watt, L/Cpl. J. . . . . . . . R.E.
Watterson, Cpl. E. . R. Innis. Fus.
Weldon, Cpl. J. . . . . R. Ir. Rif.
Wilgar, Lt. W. J. . . . . M.G.C.
Wilson, Sgt. G. . . . . . . . R.E.
Wilson, S/Sgt. T. . . . R.A.M.C.
Woodward, R.Q.M.S. H.,
R. Innis. Fus.
Yardley, Cpl. W., *D.C.M.*, *M.M.*,
R. Ir. Rif.

### ITALIAN ORDER OF ST. MAURICE AND ST. LAZARUS

Nugent, Maj.-Gen. O. S. W., *C.B.*, *D.S.O.* . . . . . . . Cmndg. 36th Div.

### ITALIAN SILVER MEDAL FOR MILITARY VALOUR

Howe, Lt. W. . . . . . . . . . . . . . . . . . . . . . . . . R.E.

### ITALIAN BRONZE MEDAL FOR MILITARY VALOUR

Gillespie, S/Sgt. R. S., *M.M.*, R.A.M.C.
Henry, Rfm. W. . . . . R. Ir. Rif.
Lyttle, L/Cpl. D., *M.M.*, R.Innis.Fus.
McMullan, Rfm. H. . . R. Ir. Rif.
Petman, Rfm. W. B. . R. Ir. Rif.

### RUSSIAN CROSS OF ST. GEORGE

Fleming, Cpl. T., *D.C.M.* R. Ir. Rif.
Hunter, Sgt. J. A.,
*D.C.M.*, *M.M.*. . R. Innis. Fus.
Kennedy, Sgt. E., *D.C.M.* R.F.A.
Quigg, Rfm. R., *V.C.* . R. Ir. Rif.

### MONTENEGRIN ORDER OF ST. DANILO

Simpson, Lt.-Col. H. C.,
*C.M.G.*, *D.S.O.* . . . . . R.A.
Thornton, Capt. A. J. P. *M.C.*,
R. Ir. Rif.

Whilst every care has been taken in the compilation of the foregoing list, omissions and other errors are unavoidable.

# INDEX

# INDEX

Abbeville, 24-26.
Acheux, 29.
Achiet-le-Grand, 136.
    -le-Petit, 167, 170.
Acquin, 107.
Adams, Lieut. F., 277.
Aicken, Rfm., 96.
Aisne, battle of the, 15.
Aisne House, 116.
Aire, 63.
Albert, H.M. King of Belgians, 259.
Albert, 137.
    battle of, 298.
    -Arras Road, 48, 50.
    -Bapaume - Cambrai Road, 126, 127, 129, 139, 147, 148, 153-155, 157, 158.
Amiens, 22, 136, 221, 243.
    defences, 23.
    -Ham - St. Quentin Road, 181, 182, 229.
    -Roye Road, 250.
Ancre, River, 23, 29, 31, 35-37, 44-48, 51-56, 65, 91, 120.
Andechy, 221-224, 228, 229.
Anneux, 154-156.
    Chapel, 156.
Annois, 210, 211.
Anseghem, 289.
Anthoine, Gen., 110.
Anton's Farm, 65.
Antrim, Co., 7.
Ararat O.P., 200.
Argyll & S. Highlanders, 10th, 128.
Armagh, Co., 7.
Armentières, 234, 253.

Armies, First, 250.
    Second, 67, 68, 79, 84, 87, 122, 166, 243, 249, 272.
    Third, 26, 27, 160, 167, 187, 193, 259.
    Fourth, 43, 250.
    Fifth, 108, 110, 187, 202, 202, 209, 230.
    First French, 110, 228, 250.
    Sixth French, 43.
    Belgian, 245.
    Fourth German, 122.
    Eighteenth German, 191.
Armin, Gen. Sixt von, 102.
Army Corps, II., 114, 234, 240, 245, 260, 262, 263, 265, 272, 273.
    III., 146, 149, 150, 155, 170, 176, 186, 200, 202, 204.
    IV., 133, 137, 146, 149, 155, 163, 165-167, 169.
    V., 146, 157, 179.
    VII., 170.
    VIII., 44, 55.
    IX., 70, 75, 80, 83, 94, 97, 98, 104, 122, 240.
    X., 44, 47, 55, 290.
    XVII., 167.
    XVIII., 183, 185, 190, 191, 206, 221, 231.
    XIX., 108, 111.
    Australian, 243.
    II. Anzac, 85, 101.
    XVI. French, 246.
    Portuguese, 234.

Arquèves, 23.
Arras, 109, 167, 169.
Artemps, 202-204.
Artois, 108.
Arvillers, 227.
Asquith, Mr. H. H., 4 (foot-note).
Aubigny, 210, 213, 214.
Auchonvillers, 35.
Ault, 232.
Authuille, 39, 48, 61.
Auxi-le-Château, 63.
Aveluy Wood, 42, 48, 50, 51, 54, 58.
Avesne, 202.
Aviatik Farm, 114.
Avre, River, 219, 221, 226.
Avricourt, 218, 219.

Bacquencourt, 206.
Bailey, Pte., 205.
Bailleul, 65, 78, 79, 89, 103, 239, 236, 248, 251.
Ballycastle, 17.
Ballykinlar, 7, 11.
Bancourt, 170.
Bapaume, 35, 68, 125, 130, 167.
Barastre, 142, 167.
Battery Valley, 194.
Battle Zone, Artillery Group (at St. Quentin), 194.
Bavichove, 276, 281.
Bayenghem, 64.
Beaucamp, 126, 170.
Beaucourt, 44.
    Station, 44, 46, 53.
Beaulencourt, 167, 181.
Beaulieu-les-Fontaines, 211-213.
Beaumetz, 157, 166.
Beaumont-en-Beine, 212, 216.
Beaumont-Hamel, 28, 44.
Becelaere, 263-265, 267.
Becher, Lieut.-Col. C. M. L., 287.
Belfast, 6-8, 12, 13, 15, 17, 299.
Bell, Capt. E. N. F., 59.
Belle Eglise Farm, 38.
Bellewaarde Lake, 263.
Belt, Capt. C. B., 117.
Berchen, 287.
Bergstraat, 289.
Berguette, 63.
Berlancourt, 217, 218.
Bernard, Col. H. C., 55, 59.
Bernard, Lieut.-Col. J., 50.
Bernaville, 24, 62, 63.
Bertincourt, 135, 141, 170.
Bethancourt, 218.
Beveren, 281, 282, 285.

Bihucourt, 35.
Blacker, Lieut.-Col. S. W., 53.
Blaringhem, 63.
Blauwepoortbeek, 104.
Blood, Gen. Sir B., 8.
Boadicea Redoubt, 190, 201.
Boisdinghem, 64.
Border Camp, 242.
  House, 116, 118.
Bordon, 20, 26.
Bouchoir, 222.
Boulogne, 21, 22.
Bourlon, 156, 157, 160, 163-167, 179.
  Wood, 129, 145-147, 156, 161, 165, 166, 168, 171.
Boursies, 157.
Boyes, 181.
Boyle, Major J. C., 62.
Boyle, Lieut. J. K., 215, 216.
Boyle's Farm, 65.
Boyne, battle of the, 51.
Bramshott, 20.
Brandhoek, 112.
Breen, Pte., 74.
Bresle, River, 232.
Brew, Major J., 223.
Bridcott, Lieut.-Col., 267.
Brigades, 2nd Cav., 153, 156.
  6th Cav., 216.
  7th Cav., 216.
  Canadian Cav., 216.
  10th Inf., 27.
  11th Inf., 27, 29.
  12th Inf., 24, 25, 29.
  26th Inf. (Highland), 238.
  27th Inf. (Lowland), 130, 264, 268.
  32nd Inf., 100.
  34th Inf., 98.
  41st Inf., 200.
  60th Inf., 202, 204.
  61st Inf., 199, 202, 204, 205, 208, 210, 219.
  87th Inf., 276.
  88th Inf., 170, 171.
  101st Inf., 290.
  107th Inf., 7, 10, 13, 22-24, 27-29, 41, 45-47, 51, 54, 55, 58, 59, 63-65, 75, 79, 85, 90, 100, 104, 106, 111, 112, 114, 119, 126, 131, 133, 141, 142, 147, 154, 157, 163, 165, 166, 170, 175, 177, 182, 184, 185, 189, 192, 193, 198, 202, 205, 206, 212, 217, 220-222, 224, 225, 227,

## INDEX

Brigades, 107th Inf. (contd.)
228, 233, 242, 244, 245,
249, 253, 256-258, 260,
263, 267, 269, 271, 273,
276, 284, 286, 287, 292,
294.
108th Inf., 7, 10, 13, 15,
23, 25, 29, 41, 45, 46,
48, 54, 64, 65, 75, 85,
89, 100, 106, 112, 114,
117, 118, 126, 134, 141,
142, 147, 154, 157, 165,
166, 170, 171, 175, 177,
184, 185, 189, 193, 200,
202, 205, 209, 217, 219,
221, 222, 232, 234-236,
238, 240, 244, 245, 251,
253-256, 260, 263, 265,
268, 270, 271, 273, 276-
278, 285-288, 294.
109th Inf., 5, 7, 10, 15, 23,
25, 29, 35, 41, 42, 45,
46, 48, 58, 64, 65, 75,
85, 90, 93, 94, 100, 104,
106, 112, 114, 117, 118,
126, 128, 134, 135, 142,
147, 148, 151, 153, 155-
157, 165, 166, 170, 171,
175, 178, 182, 185, 189,
193, 205, 206, 217, 219-
222, 226, 228, 233, 243,
245, 249, 251, 252, 256,
259, 260, 263-266, 268,
270, 271, 273, 281, 285,
287, 289, 294.
121st Inf., 165.
123rd Inf., 278.
146th Inf., 56, 57.
147th Inf., 41.
148th Inf., 58, 59.
164th Inf., 111.
165th Inf., 111, 112.
166th Inf., 111, 112.
178th Inf., 236, 237.
182nd Inf., 171.
186th Inf., 152, 154.
189th Inf., 177.
South African Inf., 126, 234, 235.
1st/1st London R.F.A., 23.
14th Army R.F.A., 182.
17th R.F.A., 176.
50th Army, R.F.A., 266.
91st R.F.A., 212.
93rd R.F.A., 147.
108th Army, R.F.A., 115.
Brigades, 113th Army, R.F.A., 76, 271.
150th R.F.A., 115.
153rd R.F.A., 8, 10, 39, 76, 96, 97, 147, 155, 168, 190, 218, 260, 263, 286.
154th R.F.A., 8, 10, 39, 76.
172nd R.F.A., 8, 10, 39, 61, 76.
173rd R.F.A., 8, 10, 39, 76, 96, 97, 147, 155, 168, 198, 287.
280th R.F.A., 147.
Special (Gas Services), 49.
Brigade Supply Officer, 33.
British Empire League, 8.
Brock, Brig.-Gen. H. J., 10, 70, 80, 115, 176, 218, 221, 245, 258.
Brock's Benefit, 38, 44.
Broodseinde Ridge, 263.
Brouchy, 205, 206, 211-214.
Bruce, Capt. G. J., 211, 226, 271.
Bruges, 109.
Brunyate, Lieut. W., 282.
Brush, Lieut.-Col., 43.
Bryans, Capt. J. C., 215, 216.
Buchoire, 218.
Bullecourt, 127, 146.
Bull Ring, 74, 80.
Bus-les-Artois, 141.
Busseboom, 78.
Byng, Gen. Hon. Sir J., 145.

Calais, 245.
Cambrai, 43, 129, 139, 146, 156, 167, 179, 180, 183.
battle of, 139 et seq.; 186, 300.
Campbell, Lieut.-Col., 140.
Canal du Nord, 127, 128, 139, 145, 146-148, 152-154, 157-160, 163-165.
line, 157.
Canaples, 24.
Candas, 27.
-Acheux Railway, 37.
Cannectancourt, 229.
Canny-sur-Matz, 229.
Canopus Trench, 243.
Cantaing, 153, 156, 171.
Cantigny, 228.
Capricorn Keep, 118.
Carporetto, battle of, 143.
Carson, Sir E., 2-5, 19.
Cassel, 243, 249.
Casualty Clearing Station, 40th, 7.

Cather, Lieut. G., 59.
Cavalry Corps, the, 146.
    Regiment, IX. Corps, 98.
Cavan, Co., 7.
Cayeux, 26, 35.
Champagne, 186.
    French Offensive, 1917, 82, 109, 143.
Château-Thierry, 243, 250.
Clairfaye Farm, 41, 48.
Clandeboye, 7, 11.
Clements, Cpl. T., 74.
Clements, Lieut.-Col. S. U. L., 165.
Cochrane, Brig.-Gen. J. K., 202, 211, 213, 214, 219.
Cochrane, Rfm., 96.
Coffin, Maj.-Gen. C., 244, 252, 266, 280, 281, 291, 296.
Cole-Hamilton, Lieut.-Col. C. G., 201.
Collézy, 216.
Cologne, 294.
Comyn, Lieut.-Col. L., 136.
Conn, Cpl. J., 60.
Contay, 181.
Contescourt, 198, 200.
Conteville, 63.
Conway, Pte., 205.
Corbie, 181, 182.
Couchman, Brig.-Gen. G. H. H., 10, 24.
Couillet Wood, 150, 171, 175.
Coullemelle, 228.
Courcelles-le-Comte, 167, 170.
Courtrai, 276-278, 283, 290.
    -Ghent Road, 281, 282, 285.
    -Ghent Railway, 285, 286.
    -Ingelmunster Railway, 272, 273, 276.
Craig, Capt. C., 59.
Craig, Sir J., Bt., 3-6, 9.
Crawford, Lt.-Col. J., 205.
Crèvecœur, 146.
Crisolles, 217.
Croix de Poperinghe, 248.
Crown Prince, the German, 187.
Croydon, 8.
Crucifix (at Thiepval), 45, 46, 57, 60.
Cuerne, 276.
Cugny, 205, 210, 211, 214-216.
Cumming, Lieut. A. E., 198, 223.
Custom House (at Neuve Eglise), 254.
Cyclist Company, 36th Divisional, 7, 11, 35.
    Regiment, VIII. Corps, 273.

Dadizeele, 265, 270.
Dallon, 200.
Davenescourt, 227.
Daylight Corner, 83.
D.C.L.I., 7th, 204, 205, 211, 213, 214.
Débeney, Gen., 228.
Despard, Capt. C. B., 239.
De Broeken, 253.
Deconinck Farm, 104.
Deerlyck, 285, 287.
Demicourt, 126, 130, 140, 155, 168.
    -Flesquières Road, 147, 151, 152, 154, 162.
Dessart Wood, 171.
Desselghem, 281, 283.
Dickebusch, 78.
Diependaal Beek, 84.
Dieppe, 178.
Divisions, Guards', 166, 167, 169.
    1st, 233.
    2nd, 168, 296.
    4th, 16, 23, 24, 27-29, 133.
    6th, 171.
    8th, 184.
    9th, 123, 126, 128, 234, 235, 239, 243, 249-251, 262-269, 272, 276, 280, 285, 288, 294.
    10th, 5.
    11th, 84, 98, 100, 104.
    12th, 62.
    14th, 185, 189, 196, 199, 200, 202, 204, 207, 210, 212, 214, 216.
    16th, 84, 85, 94-96, 101, 114, 117, 134.
    19th, 84, 234-236.
    20th, 65, 199, 206, 217.
    25th, 84, 94, 96, 97, 134, 235-237.
    29th, 44, 169, 170, 184, 254-256, 260, 262, 263, 265, 266, 269 (footnote), 272, 275-277.
    30th, 185, 189, 198, 202, 209, 221, 222, 242, 258.
    31st, 36, 251, 254, 256, 257.
    32nd, 38, 44, 56, 80, 184.
    34th, 290.
    35th, 251, 271, 272, 275.
    36th (Ulster).
    origin of, 2.
    recruiting of, 6.
    training of, 11 *et seq.*; 23 *et seq.*; 41, 83, 107, 142, 245.

## INDEX

351

Divisions, 36th (Ulster)—*contd.*
  religious element in, 16.
  moves to England, 17.
  tributes to, by Lord Kitchener, 18 ; by C.-in-C., 240 ; by Gen. Jacob, 291.
  reviewed by the King, 21.
  arrival in France, 22.
  takes over line on Ancre, 29.
  prepares for Somme offensive, 37.
  raids by, 38, 41, 49, 72, 74, 80, 90, 131, 249.
  casualties of, 50, 59, 100, 119, 233, 240, 256, 290.
  attacks on the Ancre, 52 *et seq.*
  prisoners taken in battle, 59, 100, 156, 256, 257, 267, 272, 275, 284, 285.
  moves to Flanders, 63.
  mining on front of, 67.
  prepares for battle of Messines, 82.
  attacks at Messines, 92 *et seq.*
  enters line at Ypres, 111, 232.
  attacks at Ypres, 116 *et seq.*
  moves to Cambrai Area, 125.
  prepares for battle of Cambrai, 139 *et seq.*
  attacks at Cambrai, 151 *et seq.*
  relieved at Cambrai, 166.
  enters line on Welsh Ridge, 171.
  local offensives by, 172 *et seq.* ; 250 *et seq.*
  relieves French before St. Quentin, 182.
  reorganization of, 184.
  defensive preparations of, 190, 245.
  attacked by the enemy at St. Quentin, 194.
  its flank turned, 199.
  withdrawal to St. Quentin Canal, 202.
  withdrawal to Somme Canal, 204.
  relieved by French, 217, 227.

Divisions, 36th (Ulster)—*contd.*
  "fills the gap" on the Avre, 221 *et seq.*
  action of its artillery with French, 229.
  action of its 108th Brigade at Kemmel, 234 *et seq.*
  carries out withdrawals in Salient, 241 *et seq.*
  relief of, at Ypres, 245.
  relieves French at Bailleul, 246.
  presses retreating enemy, 253 *et seq.*
  concentrates for attack at Ypres, 260.
  enters line at Becelaere, 264.
  reaches Menin - Roulers Road, 266.
  attacks at Moorseele, 273.
  enters Courtrai, 277.
  moves to Lendelede, 280.
  forces line of the Lys, 282 *et seq.*
  occupies its last objective, Kleineberg, 289.
  settles down for winter, 1918, 294.
  its demobilization, 296 *et seq.*
  record of, 297 *et seq.*
  characteristics of, 299 *et seq.*
37th, 106.
38th, 29.
40th, 157, 160, 163-166.
41st, 65, 278.
47th, 167, 168.
48th, 23, 114, 118.
49th, 41, 44, 47, 56, 59, 62, 64.
51st, 139, 142, 147, 150, 153, 156-158, 163, 164, 166.
55th, 108, 110-112, 130, 243.
56th, 146, 153, 155, 157, 159, 163, 168.
59th, 167.
61st, 119, 180, 170, 171, 173, 185, 192, 198.
62nd, 140, 142, 147, 150, 153, 155-158, 160, 163, 166, 167, 259.
63rd (R.N.), 177, 178, 181.
1st Australian, 250.

Divisions, New Zealand, 79, 97.
    1st Cav., 153, 157.
    3rd Cav., 216.
    6th French, 182.
    9th French, 217, 218.
    41st French, 246.
    62nd French, 217, 218, 220, 221, 229.
    77th French, 229.
    164th French, 281.
    4th French Cav., 272.
    3rd Belgian, 280.
    4th Belgian, 242.
    8th Belgian, 262.
    12th Belgian, 245.
    Belgian Cav., 247.
    2nd German, 90.
    26th German, 25.
    20th Landwehr (German), 151.
    31st Landwehr (German), 242.
    1st Bavarian Res., 274.
Divisional Artillery,
    11th, 106.
    36th, 7, 8, 10, 19, 26, 29, 35, 39, 46, 60, 62, 64, 69, 74, 76, 80, 103, 106-108, 113, 115, 125, 130, 167, 176, 181, 182, 244, 245, 249, 257, 260, 271, 290, 294, 299.
    61st, 115.
Divisional Amm. Column, 36th, 8, 10, 39, 102, 244.
    Canteen, 136, 295.
    Head Q., 36th, 22, 24, 29, 51, 80, 86, 100, 104, 106, 112, 135, 137, 138, 155, 182, 206, 212, 232, 233, 246, 248, 249, 252, 260, 263, 292, 297.
    Supply Column, 36th, 33, 102, 212.
    Train, 36th, 11, 50, 112, 212, 259, 279.
Doignies, 155, 157, 166, 168.
Domart-en-Ponthieu, 24, 27.
Donegal, Co., 7.
Dorsetshire Regt., 1st, 39.
Douchy, 183.
Doullens-Arras Road, 177.
Douve, River, 65-67, 77, 253, 257.
Down, Co., 7.
Dranoutre, 78, 80, 89, 90, 253.
Drei Masten, 278.
Dries, 281-283, 285, 286.
Drocourt-Quéant Switch, 145, 146.

Drummond, Capt. C., 213.
Dunkirk, 100, 295, 296.
Dunleath, Lord, 297.
Dury, 182, 204.

Earl Farm, 93.
East Ham, 8.
Eaucourt, 205, 206, 208, 211, 213.
Eecke, 260.
Eley Arty. Group (March 1918), 206, 218, 221.
Ellis, Maj.-Gen., 145.
Elverdinghe, 113.
Emerson, Lieut. J. S., 173, 174.
Enfer Farm, 88.
    Wood, 93, 97, 99.
Englebelmer-Martinsart Road, 51.
Enniskillen, 15.
Entrenching Batts.,
    21st, 184, 205, 209, 222.
    22nd, 184.
    23rd, 184, 209.
Eperlecques, 64.
Epine de Dallon Redoubt, 198.
Erches, 219, 222-226.
Erskine Arty. Group (March 1918), 206, 217, 218.
Ervin, Pte., 74.
Escaut, River, 278, 286, 287, 289, 290, 295.
    Canal de l', 145, 146, 160, 179.
Esmery-Hallon, 212.
Esquelbecq, 64.
Essertaux, 228.
Essex Regt., 2nd, 35.
Essigny, 189, 191, 199.
Estaires, 105, 234.
Estouilly, 202.
Etricourt, 127.

Falkiner, Lieut. F. E. R., 95, 96.
Farnham, Lieut.-Col. Lord, 201.
Fay Farm, 200.
Fayolle, Gen., 43.
Fémy Wood, 131.
Fermanagh, Co., 7.
Field Ambulance,
    108th, 7, 11, 19, 48, 89.
    109th, 7, 11, 89.
    110th, 7, 11, 25, 48, 89.
Field Company,
    121st, 7, 10, 26, 62, 88, 97, 167, 203, 222, 224, 241, 273, 281, 282, 285, 294.

# INDEX 353

Field Company,
  122nd, 7, 10, 26, 37, 48, 62, 88, 99, 222, 241, 273, 277, 278, 294.
  150th, 10, 48, 62, 88, 97, 100, 108, 203, 241, 273, 282, 283, 285, 294.
Finner, 7, 11.
Fisher, Admiral Lord, 292.
Fitzgerald, Col., 18.
Flanders, 30, 40, 63, 77, 121, 133, 134, 137, 143, 186, 250, 259, 291.
Flavy-le-Martel, 210, 211.
  -le-Meldeux, 212.
Flesquières, 150, 152, 153, 155, 156, 179.
Flesselles, 32.
Flêtre, 79.
Fluquièrcs, 204.
Foch, Marshal, 144 (foot-note), 292, 293.
Fontainehouck, 248.
Fontaine-les-Clercs, 186, 200, 201, 203.
  -Notre-Dame, 156, 158, 163 164.
Forceville, 48, 61.
Fort Hill, 118.
Fosseux, 167.
Foucard Trench, 196.
Fox, Lieut. J. J., 258.
French Arty. (with 36th Div. July 1st, 1916), 42, 47, 56.
  Regt., 133rd, 286.
Fréniches, 206, 212, 218.
Fretoy-le-Château, 218.
Frévent, 63.
Frezenberg, 123, 263.
Furnell, Lieut.-Col. M., 223.

Gabion Farm, 257.
Gaffiken, Major G. H., 59.
Gallagher, Lieut. (later Capt.) H., 60, 101.
Gallipoli Copse, 114, 116.
Gamaches, 229, 232.
Gapaard, 104, 234.
Gauchy, 195.
Gaverbeek, 286.
Gavin, Capt. N. J., 120.
Geddes, Sir E., 77.
George the Fifth, H.M. King, 19, 21, 249.
Gheluvelt, 263.
Gheluwe, 266.

Ghent, 109, 296.
G.H.Q., 137, 138, 171, 187.
Gilmour, Rfm. J., 224, 225.
Givenchy, 234.
Godson, Lieut., 72.
Golancourt, 210, 211, 213, 214, 216.
Goldfish Château, 111.
Goldflake Farm, 272.
Gomiecourt, 167, 170.
Gonnelieu, 146, 169, 170.
Goodwin, Lieut.-Col. W. R., 159.
Gooseberry Farm, 255, 256.
Gough, Gen. Sir H., 108, 110, 187.
Gough, Brig.-Gen. J., 3.
Gouzeaucourt, 169.
Graincourt, 126, 153, 155, 157, 162, 171.
Grand Bois, 104.
Grandcourt, 57.
  -Thiepval Road, 45.
  -St. Pierre Divion Road, 46.
Grand Ravin, 127, 128, 154.
  Séraucourt, 189, 190, 203.
Grant Suttie, Major H. F., 258.
Gravenstafel Road, 115.
Green, Maj. (later Lieut.-Col.) S. H., 107, 136.
Green House, 115.
Greig, Col. F. J., 7, 18, 19.
Grévillers, 35.
Griffith, Brig.-Gen. C. R., 39, 46, 57, 100, 200, 222, 223, 234, 244, 245.
Grugies, 188.
  Valley, 188, 192, 195.
Guerbigny, 219, 221, 223, 224.
Gulleghem, 272, 273, 275, 276.
Guiscard, 209, 214, 217, 219.
Guise, 191, 292.
Guy Farm, 97.

Haagedoorne, 79, 249, 253.
Hacket Pain, Brig.-Gen. G., 10, 39.
Haig, F.M. Sir D., 3, 37, 143, 182, 183, 228, 240, 296.
Haigh, Lieut. J. W., 175.
Halahan, Rev. F. J., 119.
Ham, 183, 206, 209, 210.
Hamel, 29-31, 36, 48, 61.
Hangest-en-Santerre, 227.
Happencourt, 202, 204, 208.
Harington, Maj.-Gen. C. H., 122.
Harman, Maj.-Gen. A. E., 216.
Harponville, 41.
Havre, 21, 26.

Havrincourt, 126-129, 142, 145, 150, 154, 155, 259.
　　Wood, 127, 129, 131, 133, 139, 140-142, 147, 149, 170, 176.
Hawkes, Brig.-Gen. C. St. L., 258.
Hazebrouck, 63, 92, 234.
Heavy Arty., IV. Corps, 141, 165, 168.
Hédauville, 48.
Heirweg, 287, 288.
Hell Farm, 235.
Hermies, 126, 127, 129, 130, 134, 137, 140, 150, 155, 157, 162, 166.
Hessey, Brig.-Gen. W. F., 178, 213, 224, 245.
Heule, 272, 273, 276-278.
Heulebeek, 273, 275, 276.
Hickman, Brig.-Gen. T. E., 3-5, 9, 10, 39.
Highland Ridge, 171, 175.
Hill 35, 117.
Hill 41, 265-268, 272, 273.
Hill 63, 77, 235, 254, 255, 258.
Hill 90, 152.
Hill 94, 97.
Hindenburg, Marshal von, 292.
Hindenburg Line, 109, 126, 127, 129, 131, 145, 146, 149, 151, 153, 157-160, 163-165, 171-174, 178, 250, 259.
Hindu Cott, 115, 116.
Hobart Street, 159, 163.
Hoegenacker Ridge, 250, 251.
Holywood, 15.
Hospital Farm, 239.
Houtquerque, 260.
Hunter, Gen. Sir A., 21.
Hutier, Gen. O. von, 191.
Hutsbosch, 288.
Hutteghem, 287.
Hyde Park Corner, 78, 258.

Inchy-en-Artois, 147, 165.
Ingoyghem, 288.
Inniskilling Dragoons,
　　Service Squadron, 7, 11.
Inniskilling Fusiliers,
　　1st, 184, 200, 202, 204, 205, 220, 253, 264, 268, 274, 283, 285, 288.
　　2nd, 184, 201, 220, 253, 264, 274, 288.
　　5th, 5.
　　6th, 5.

Inniskilling Fusiliers (contd.)
　　9th, 5, 10, 17, 38, 45, 48, 49, 52, 57, 78, 85, 94, 95, 152, 156, 174, 175, 202, 204, 206, 210, 213, 214, 217, 264, 265, 276, 282, 283.
　　10th, 10, 15, 36, 37, 39, 45, 52, 75, 85, 94, 95, 118, 151, 152, 154, 156, 184.
　　11th, 11, 15, 42, 45, 53, 56, 74-76, 85, 93, 112, 118, 152, 154, 174, 178, 184.
　　12th, 11.
Irish Fusiliers,
　　1st, 27, 125, 131, 133, 142, 165, 184, 200, 235-237, 250, 254-256, 266-268, 286, 287.
　　9th, 10, 15, 46, 48, 53, 59, 72, 90, 112, 117, 132, 134, 157, 159, 160, 164, 177, 200, 212, 219, 235-237, 250, 255, 266, 272, 289.
　　10th, 11.
Irish Rifles,
　　1st, 184, 198, 200, 206, 208, 210, 211, 214, 216, 226, 267, 274, 276, 284·287, 296.
　　2nd, 134, 165, 175, 184, 198, 210, 211, 215, 220, 226, 249, 257, 267, 277, 286, 287, 296.
　　7th, 134.
　　8th, 10, 27, 28, 46, 56, 57, 60, 85, 134.
　　9th, 10, 29, 46, 56, 59, 74, 85, 93, 134.
　　8/9th, 134, 164, 184.
　　10th, 10, 46, 55, 75, 85, 94, 112, 131, 157, 158, 183, 184.
　　11th, 10, 25, 46, 48, 50, 57, 75, 85, 98, 131.
　　12th, 10, 41, 46, 53, 85, 98, 118, 128, 131, 157, 159, 160, 164, 195, 197, 235-237, 240, 254, 255, 266, 267, 277, 286, 287, 296.
　　13th, 10, 46, 49, 50, 54, 56, 90, 112, 117.
　　11/13th, 134, 184.
　　14th, 11, 25, 45, 53, 85, 92-94, 112, 115, 117, 142, 151, 156, 172.
　　15th, 10, 27, 42, 46, 51, 54, 56, 85, 94, 95, 112, 132, 157, 158, 164, 165, 195, 201, 220, 250, 258, 274, 284, 285, 296.

# INDEX

Irish Rifles (contd.)
  16th (Pioneers), 11, 23, 26, 37, 42, 56, 59, 62, 76, 78, 98, 106-108, 115, 125, 130, 134, 142, 154, 167, 171, 185, 199, 205, 212, 222, 245, 273, 294, 295, 299.
  17th, 18th, 19th, and 20th, 11.
Irles, 35.
Itancourt, 183, 191.

Jacob, Lieut.-Gen. C. W., 260, 278, 291, 292.
Jacob's Ladder, 30.
Jeanne d'Arc Redoubt, 190, 196, 201.
Jew's Hill, 116.
Johnston, Capt. R., 49.
Johnston, Capt. L. J., 195-197.
Jones, Lieut.-Col. B. Y., 285.
Juliet Farm, 242, 244.
Jump Point, 88, 94, 97.
Jussy, 205, 207, 210.

Kangaroo Alley, 154.
Kelly, Lieut.-Col. P. E., 236, 239.
Kemmel, 78, 234, 238.
  -Wytschaete Road, 65, 80, 104.
  Hill, 81, 84, 86, 90, 92, 100, 103, 105, 237, 239, 242, 243, 246, 253.
Kennedy, Sir R., 297.
Kezelberg, 265, 266.
Kidd, Rfm., 74.
King, Lieut.-Col. W. A. de C., 81.
King Edward's Horse, 153, 154.
King's Liverpool Regt., 12th, 204, 214.
Kingsway, 237.
Kipling, Mr. R., 3.
Kitchener, Lord, 3, 4, 6, 18, 19, 21.
Kleineberg, 288, 289.
Klephoek, 266, 267, 272
Knock, 286.
Knott, Lieut.-Col. J. E., 258.
Knox, Lieut. C. L., 203, 249.
Knox, Maj. (later Lieut.-Col.) R. S., 213.
Kortepyp, 64, 254.
K.O.Y.L.I., 4th, 58.
  5th, 58.
K.R.R.C., 7th, 210.
Kruisstraat Cabaret, 74, 88, 257.

La Clytte, 234, 238.
L'Alouette, 255.
Lancashire Dump, 50.
Lancashire Fusiliers, 2nd, 25.
La Neuville-en-Beine, 214.
Langemarck, battle of, 111 et seq.; 125, 299.
La Vacquerie, 169.
Lavesne, 202.
Leader, Lieut.-Col., 56.
Léalvillers, 41.
Lechelle, 142, 170.
L'Echelle St. Aurin, 221.
Ledeghem, 267, 268.
Ledlie, Lieut. J. C., 117.
Left Arty. Group (at St. Quentin), 194, 200.
Le Hamel, 189, 202, 203, 208.
Lejeune Trench, 196.
Lendelede, 280.
Le Pontchu Quarry, 196, 197.
Le Sars, 126.
Leveson-Gower, Brig.-Gen. P., 297.
Lewes, 8, 20.
Libermont, 221.
Liberty Hall, 11.
Lignières, 226.
Lille, 272, 278.
Lindenhoek, 83, 88, 99, 253.
Little Wood, 128, 135.
Lizerolles, 200.
Low, Major A., 212.
Lock 4 (on Canal du Nord), 157, 163.
Lock 5, 156, 158, 163, 164.
Lock 6, 152, 155, 156.
Locker-Lampson, Commander O., 5.
Locre, 90, 246.
Lombartzyde, 109.
London Territorial Arty., 1st/1st, 21, 26, 29.
Londonderry, Co., 7.
Loos, battle of, 24, 43.
Lucheux, 171, 181.
Ludendorff, Gen., 43, 109, 143, 187, 230, 243, 292.
Lumbres, 79.
Lumm Farm, 85, 88, 96, 97.
Lurgan, 7.
  Switch, 134.
Lys, River, 234, 270, 272, 276, 277, 278, 280, 284-286, 291.
  battle of, 234 et seq.; 242, 248.

McCalmont, Gen. Sir H., 17.
McCarthy-O'Leary, Lieut.-Col. H., 222, 226.

Machine-Gun Battalion,
  36th, 185, 199, 206, 212, 224, 234, 265, 273, 299.
  104th, 273.
Machine-Gun Company,
  32nd, 87.
  33rd, 87.
  107th, 58, 158.
  108th, 26, 87, 97.
  109th, 26, 39, 173.
  266th, 185.
Mackenzie, Capt. C. A., 300.
MacKenzie, Lieut.-Col. R. H., 258.
Macnaghten, Sir H., Bt., 60.
Macrory, Lieut.-Col. F. S. N., 52, 119.
Maedelstede Farm, 79.
Mailly-Maillet, 27, 35.
  —Serre Road, 27-29.
Malone Park, 17.
Malmaison, battle of, 82.
Manancourt, 136.
Mangin, Gen., 109 (foot-note), 229.
Manhattan Farm, 268.
Mansard Farm, 272.
Manufacture Farm, 199.
Marcoing, 153, 171, 172, 175.
Marne, battle of the, 15.
Martinsart, 35, 41, 48, 50, 59, 117.
  -Albert Road, 48.
  Wood, 49.
Mary Redan, 44.
Masnières, 145, 146, 160, 169, 179.
Maurois, M. André, 139.
Maxwell, Brig.-Gen. F. A., 130.
Maxwell, Major (later Lieut.-Col.) R. P., 50, 117, 119.
Menin, 265.
  Road (from Ypres), 130, 263, 269, 279.
  -Roulers Road, 265-268.
  -Roulers Railway, 267, 268, 274.
Merris, 104, 106, 250.
Merry Mauves, 137.
Mersey Camp, 112.
Mesnil, 30, 31, 35, 42.
  Ridge, 35, 38, 44, 58, 125.
Messines, 66, 67, 71, 86, 98, 100.
  battle of, 72, 82, *et seq.* ; 107, 109, 110, 115, 120-122, 125, 151, 155, 236, 298-300.
  -Wytschaete Ridge, 67, 79, 80, 83, 84, 86, 99, 101, 234, 236, 259.
  -Wytschaete Road, 84, 95, 235.
Meteren, 243, 248-250.
Metz-en-Couture, 140, 169, 176.
Mill Cott, 262.
Miller, Capt. P. K., 95, 220, 224, 226, 227.
Miller, Major, 158.
Miraumont, 125.
Mobile Veterinary Section,
  48th, 11.
Mœuvres, 127, 145, 147, 154, 157, 159, 160, 163, 164, 179, 267.
Monaghan, Co., 7.
Monmouthshire Regt., 2nd, 27.
Montalimont Farm, 214.
Mont des Cats, 243, 246.
Montdidier, 221, 228.
Mont d'Origny, 191.
Montesquieu, 300.
Mont Kokereele, 243, 253.
Mont Noir, 64, 65, 103, 243, 253.
Mont Rouge, 239, 243, 246.
Mont Vidaigne, 239, 243.
Moore, Lieut. M. E. Y., 215.
Moorseele, 272-274, 276.
Moreuil, 181.
Mouquet Switch, 56.
Mouscron, 292, 294, 296.
Mulholland, Major P. O., 173, 174.
Munster Fusiliers, 95.
Murray, Gen. Sir A., 14, 18, 19.
Napoleon, 144, 293.

Nesle, 182, 221.
Neuve Chapelle, battle of, 15.
Neuve Eglise, 236, 237, 251-256.
  -Lindenhoek Road, 90.
  -Warneton Road, 65.
Neuville, 135, 141.
  St. Amand, 188.
Newry, 7, 19.
Newtownards, 7, 11.
Nieppe, 254.
  Forest of, 240.
Nivelle, Gen., 109, 143.
Norbury, 8.
North Irish Horse, 132, 134.
Noyelles, 153-155, 171.
Noyon, 229.
Nugent, Maj.-Gen. O. S. W., 20, 21, 28, 37, 43, 55, 58, 63, 81, 92, 97, 104, 111, 112, 118, 119, 122, 123, 128, 130, 148, 171, 177, 180, 182, 198-200, 202, 204, 205, 213, 219, 222, 228, 229, 244, 245, 297.

# INDEX 357

Offoy, 209.
Oise, River, 188, 230.
Oisy-le-Verger, 145, 161.
Oliphant, Major (later Lieut.-Col.) P. B., 57, 233 (foot-note).
Ollézy, 182, 183, 202, 204, 206, 210, 211.
Omagh, 5, 6.
Oosttaverne, 84, 98, 99.
Ooteghem, 288.
Ordnance. 36th Div., 102, 300.
Orival Wood, 155, 156.
Ostend, 109.
Ouderdom, 78.
Outtersteene, 106.
Ovillers 62.
Oxelaere, 249.
Oyghem, 281, 282.

Paris, 243, 295.
Passchendaele, 109, 143, 144, 238, 240, 261.
Patton, Capt. E., 227.
Peacocke, Major (later Lieut.-Col.) J., 38, 57, 200.
Peckham Farm, 84, 88, 90, 94.
Peronne, 127, 188.
Pétain, Gen., 143.
Petite Douve Farm, 67, 75.
Piccadilly Trench, 65.
Picardy, 43.
Pick House, 88, 94, 235.
Pilkem, 110.
Pithon, 205, 206, 208.
Place, Lieut.-Col. C. O., 55, 88, 223, 233.
Plémont Hill, 229.
Ploegsteert, 78, 235, 259.
   -Messines Road, 67.
Plug Street Wood, 64, 78, 254.
Plumer, Gen. Sir H., 67, 82, 122, 242.
Plus Douve Farm, 77, 253.
Poelcappelle, 143, 233, 238, 240, 242
Poix, 229.
Polygon Wood, 271.
Pommern Castle, 111.
   Redoubt, 111.
Pond Farm, 115, 117, 118.
Pont Remy, 25.
Poperinghe, 108, 111, 245, 260, 271.
   -Ypres Road, 108.
Potijze, 263, 269.
Potter Arty. Group (March 1918), 206, 217, 218, 221.

Powell, Maj.-Gen. Sir C. H., 9, 13, 18, 20.
Pratt, Lieut.-Col. A. C., 119.
Proven, 245, 246.
Puchevillers, 181.
Pys, 35.

" Q " of 36th Division, 136.
Quarry Redoubt, 200.
   Wood, 163.
Queen Lane, 126.
Quesmy, 217, 218.
Quigg, Pte. R., 60.

Rabone, Capt. E. L., 217.
Racecourse Redoubt, 190, 195, 201.
Railway Wood, 130.
R.A.M.C. of 36th Div., 7, 11, 14, 19, 61, 119, 299.
Randalstown, 15.
R.A.S.C. of 36th Div., 7, 300.
Ravelsberg, 252, 253.
Rawlinson, Gen. Sir H., 43.
Recques, 64.
Redan, the, 28, 29.
Red Lodge, 64.
Redmond, Major W., 101.
R.E. Farm, 69, 70.
Rheims, 243.
Rhine, River, 294, 296, 297.
Ribécourt, 126, 128, 140, 150, 154.
Ricardo, Capt. (later Lieut.-Col. and Brig.-Gen.) A., 5, 38, 52, 94, 121, 130, 135, 142, 147-149, 178, 245.
Ricardo Redoubt, 204, 205.
Richthofen, Lieut. von (German airman), 105.
Rifle Brigade, 1st, 27.
Right Arty. Group (at St. Quentin), 193.
Robécourt, Canal de, 218.
Roberts, Earl, 2, 4.
Rocourt, 183.
Rocquigny, 167, 170.
Rolleghem-Cappelle, 274.
Rose, Major R., 215.
Rose Wood, 104.
Rossignol-Messines Road, 73.
Roubaix, 272.
Roulers, 109, 265.
   -Lys Canal, 281.
Round Trench, 163, 164.
Rouy, 218.
Roye, 220-222.

Roozebeek, 104.
Rubempré, 62.
Ruyalcourt, 127, 141.

Sains-lez-Marquion, 157.
St. Jans Cappel, 65, 100, 248, 252, 259.
St. Jean, 234.
St. Julien, 110, 111.
St. Omer, 63, 64, 107.
St. Pierre Divion, 46, 56.
St. Quentin, 182, 183, 191, 192, 197.
    -La Fère Road, 188, 195, 196.
    Canal, 189, 194, 202, 204, 205, 207, 210, 211, 230, 231.
St. Simon, 188, 202, 203, 207.
Saleux, 229.
Sanders, Cpl., 59.
Sanderson, Lieut., 56.
Sanitary Section, 76th, 11.
Scheldt, River, see Escaut.
Scherpenberg, 83, 239, 243, 246.
Schuler Farm, 114-116.
Schwaben Redoubt, 44, 45, 56-58.
Scotch Street, 168.
Scott Farm, 93, 94.
Seaford, 17, 19, 22.
Sensée, River, 127, 145, 146, 160, 179.
Sermaize, 217.
Serre, 35.
Sharman Crawford, Col. R. G., 11.
Sharp, Major R. R., 274.
Shuter, Brig.-Gen. R., 39, 45.
Siege Camp, 239.
Signal Company, 36th Divisional, 7, 11, 84, 107, 138, 155, 178, 299.
Simpson, Lieut.-Col. H. C., 147, 149, 168, 218.
Skip Point, 88, 93.
Smyth, Capt. (lajer Major) W., 213, 241.
Somerville, Lieut.-Col., 117, 119.
Somerset L.I., 7th, 204, 210, 211.
Somme, Dept. of the, 22, 25, 26, 66.
    River, 25, 26, 68, 71, 182, 186-188, 206, 270, 298.
    Canal de la, 127, 188, 204, 205, 207, 208, 210, 217, 230, 231.
    battle of the, 14, 41 *et seq.*; 72, 75, 89, 90, 110.
    Farm, 115-117.

Sommette-Eaucourt, 204, 205, 210, 211.
Sorel-le-Grand, 71.
Sourdon, 227, 228.
South Midland Farm, 254.
Spanbroek (or Spanbroekmolen), 68, 75, 79, 84, 87, 88, 90, 92, 99, 235.
Spender, Capt. W. B., 9.
Speyside, 54.
Sphinx Wood, 183, 189, 195.
Spitael, 286, 287.
Spree Farm, 115.
Spriete, 283.
Square Copse, 154.
Staenyzer Cabaret, 85, 97.
Stapylton-Smith, Lieut. J. B., 203.
Station Redoubt, 200.
Steenbecque, 63.
Steenebeek, Stream (on Messines Ridge), 67, 86, 93, 94, 99.
Steenebeek, Stream (at St. Julien), 240-242.
Steenwerck, 254.
Stinking Farm, 256.
Straete, 283.
Strazeele, 106.
Strohm, Lieut. E. C., 215.
Sunken Road, see Thiepval-Hamel Road.
Sydenham, 8.

Tadpole Copse, 159.
Tank Corps, 163.
Tardenois, battle of, 250.
Ten Elms Camp, 233.
Terdeghem, 246, 249.
Terguier, 188.
Terhand, 264, 265, 269.
Thiennes, 63.
Thiepval, 36, 51, 53-58, 62, 89.
    Wood, 35, 36, 38, 39, 44-46, 48, 50, 52, 54, 57, 59, 61.
    -Hamel Road, 38, 49, 51.
Thompson, Capt. T. Y., 215.
Thompson, Lieut.-Col. A. G., 233.
Thorpe, Brig.-Gen. E., 245, 258.
Tilques, 64.
Torreken Farm, 88.
Tourcoing, 272, 292, 294.
Trench Mortar Batteries of 36th Division,
    Heavy, 47, 69.
    Medium, 47, 50, 70, 272, 290.
    Light (Stokes), 47, 48, 52, 70, 87, 175.

# INDEX 359

Trench Mortar Batteries (*contd.*)
  107th Light, 24, 222, 290.
  108th Light, 265, 290.
  109th Light, 290.
Trescault, 129, 131, 139, 140, 146, 169.
Tudor, Maj.-Gen. H. H., 145.
Tugny, 202-204.
Tunnelling Company,
  171st, 68, 88.
  Australian, 77.
Twigg Farm, 267, 268, 272.
Tyrone, Co., 7.
  Regt. U.V.F., 5, 6.

Ugny-le-Gay, 214.
Ulster Camp, 80, 104.
  Volunteer Force, 2-6, 8, 12, 14, 21, 185.
Urvillers, 188, 189, 199.

Vallulart Wood, 141.
Varennes, 41.
Vaughan, Brig.-Gen. E., 245, 277.
Vaughan, Lieut. C. H., 172.
Vaux, 202.
Vélu Wood, 142.
Verdun, battle of, 35, 47, 167.
Verlaines, 209.
Vichte, 286, 287.
Vigers, Major T. W., 155.
Vijfwegen, 265, 273.
Villers-Bretonneux, 243.
Villers-Guislain, 169.
Villers-Plouich, 170-172.
Villers-Tournelle, 228.
Villeselve, 211, 214-217.
Vimy Ridge, 82, 149.
Vivian, Lieut.-Col. Hon. O., 209.
Vlamertinghe, 112, 113, 131, 260, 263.
Vogeltje Château, 260.
Voormezeele, 243, 259.
Vossenhoek, 287.
Voyennes, 188, 207.

Waereghem, 285, 287.
Wales, H.R.H. the Prince of, 296.
Walker, Capt. D., 173, 174, 224, 226, 227, 236, 256, 269.
Warsy, 219.
Watkins Williams, Major, 216.
Watou, 108.

Watson, Lieut. R. B. Marriott, 215.
Welsh Ridge, 169, 171, 172, 175, 176, 178.
Westhoek Ridge, 131.
Westhof Farm, 253.
Westoutre, 239.
Westroosabeke, 144.
West Yorks Regt., 1st/6th, 56.
Wevelghem, 276.
White Gates, 253, 255.
Wieltje, 111, 112, 119, 234, 240.
Wigan Copse, 131.
William Redan, 42.
Wilson, Gen. Sir H., 186.
Winnizeele, 119, 125.
Winter Trench, 258.
Wizernes, 107, 108.
Woods, Major P., 59.
Wormhoudt, 260.
Wright, Capt., 50.
Wulverghem, 66, 235-237, 253, 254, 257.
  -Messines Road, 65, 76, 235, 236, 254, 257.
  -Wytschaete Road, 69, 74, 79, 84.
Wytschaete, 85, 86, 88, 95, 98, 108, 235, 238.

York and Lancs Regt., 4th, 58.
Yorkshire Bank, 128, 129, 131, 132, 154.
York Town, surrender of, 230.
Young, Lieut. R., 224.
Ypres, 35, 67, 130, 176, 232-234, 242, 245, 248, 259, 261, 263, 268, 271, 295.
  Canal, 103-105, 241, 242.
  -Menin Road, see Menin Road.
  -Zonnebeke Road, 110, 262, 269.
  Salient, 78, 105, 106, 108, 110, 119, 125, 126, 130, 232, 240, 269.
  first battle of, 15, 66,
  second battle of, 15.
  third battle of, 108, 262.
Yser Canal, 109.
Ytres, 128, 135, 136, 141, 155, 167.

Zeebrugge, 109.
Zonnebeke, 263.
Zuidhoek Copse, 266.

www.ingramcontent.com/pod-product-compliance
Lightning Source LLC
Chambersburg PA
CBHW021828220426
43663CB00005B/164